# Stan Kenton

## This Is an Orchestra!

by Michael Sparke

Number 5: North Texas Lives of Musicians

University of North Texas Press
Denton, Texas

10  9  8  7  6  5  4  3  2  1

Permissions:
University of North Texas Press
1155 Union Circle #311336
Denton, TX  76203-5017

The paper used in this book meets the minimum requirements of the
American National Standard for Permanence of Paper for Printed Library
Materials, z39.48.1984. Binding materials have been chosen for durability.

Library of Congress Cataloging-in-Publication Data

Sparke, Michael.
  Stan Kenton : this is an orchestra! / by Michael Sparke.
     p. cm. — (North Texas lives of musicians ; no. 5)
  Includes bibliographical references and index.
  ISBN 978-1-57441-284-0 (cloth : alk. paper)
  1. Kenton, Stan. 2. Jazz musicians—United States—Biography.  I. Title. II.
Series: North Texas lives of musicians series ; no. 5.
  ML422.K35S63 2010
  784.4'8165092—dc22
  [B]

                                           2009053624

Stan Kenton: This Is an Orchestra! is Number 5 in the North Texas Lives of
Musicians Series

This book is dedicated with respect to Stan's three deceased devotees who had the greatest impact on my life, listed in the order of my first knowing them:

Jack Hartley (USA): 1923–2003

Pete Venudor (Holland): 1934–2007

Tony Cox (UK): 1933–2004

"THEY LOVED THE MUSIC"

# Contents

# List of Illustrations

# Preface

When I mentioned to a friend that I'd been commissioned to write a book about Stan Kenton, he groaned. "Not another book about Stan," he said, ignoring the fact that hard-core fans can never get enough about their favorite artist. But if I hadn't realized it before, it realerted me to the fact any new publication would need to be substantially different from those that had preceded it.

In fact, most earlier books have been discographies, and of the five narratives, four are wholly factual in content, with no personal opinions expressed by the author. The exception is *Straight Ahead* by Carol Easton, a professional writer who expressed some perceptive insights into the Kenton career, but who also collected the most flak from both musicians and fans alike for her pains.

So it was with some trepidation that I decided the time was right for a critical analysis of Kenton's music and his personal role in its creation. During Stan's life-time there were so many forces ranged against him that he needed and deserved the unequivocal support of those who valued his endeavors. But 30-plus years after his death, I believe it is time to step back and take stock, and place the music and the men who made it into perspective. And if that means incurring the wrath of those who to this day deify their idol, then so be it. For all his virtues, Kenton was human; he made mistakes, had strengths and weaknesses, self-doubts and over-confidence, and was buffeted by forces outside his control, just like the rest of us.

Naturally, the opinions expressed herein are my own, though almost always backed by musicians with personal experience who were there. And on controversial issues I try to give both viewpoints—just like the fans, different musicians often have very differing opinions about the same music. Though united by a common Sound, Kenton's music encompassed many varied styles, from the very commercial to the highly esoteric, and no one has the right to assume their own opinions are the "right" ones. But this is my book, and as Stan used to say to those who queried his repertoire, "If you don't like what I play, go form your own band!"

All the big band giants of the 20th century have their champions. Duke Ellington admirers naturally believe their hero was the best; Woody's fans think it was the Herman Herds. Stan Kenton devotees know their man was the greatest of them all, a colossus who literally changed the shape of popular music, and whose influence is still heard in film scores and big band backings well into the 21st century. The truth is that many bands played their role, and Glenn Miller is probably the best remembered big band leader of them all. But nothing will shake the Kenton-lovers' conviction, nor should it. We know we are right, because his is the music we enjoy the most. And if, as I think it does despite the honest appraisal, my own admiration and regard for Stan Kenton and his music shine forth throughout this book, I shall be more than happy.

*Michael Sparke, June 2009*

Readers might like to know that the discography, *Stan Kenton: The Studio Sessions*, by Michael Sparke and Pete Venudor, is still available. The complete Personnels, Recording Dates, Soloists, and Arrangers/ Composers provided for every title recorded by Kenton for Capitol and Creative World, as well as the lesser official labels, ideally complement the historical narrative of this book. *The Studio Sessions* is available for $30 plus $5 shipping from the publisher, Gerry Dexter, 213 Forest Street, Lake Geneva, WI 53147, or online at *gdex@wi.rr.com*. There will be no second printing.

# Acknowledgments

In addition to the three Kenton experts to whom this book is dedicated, I owe so much to so many, both living and deceased, that a complete list would be self-defeating. If your name is not specifically mentioned, I am still grateful!

Among non-musician friends, I would single out Tony Agostinelli for his unstinted support over a great many years, and who made available to me a majority of the emails posted to the Kentonia web-site. My gratitude also goes out to Arnie Chadwick, Edward Chaplin, Peter Hall, Steven Harris, Roy Holmes, Dave Kay, Bill Lichtenauer, John Loeffler, Gordon Plummer, Michel Ruppli, Jerry Schwartz, Randy Taylor, Terry Vosbein, and Gerard van der Wal.

It is from Stan himself, and so many of his musicians, that so much of the information in this book has originated, via letters, tapes, and personal interviews, many conducted during the Rendezvous in Britain conventions overseen by Murray Patterson between 1992 and 2000. Over 130 alumni responded in total, far too many to list here, but I would thank them all, especially those quoted within these pages. Some went out of their way to be helpful beyond the ordinary, including:

STAN KENTON, Audree (Coke) Kenton, Jim Amlotte, Al Anthony, Milt Bernhart, Eddie Bert, Dwight Carver, Joe Coccia, Bob Curnow, Bill Fritz, Phil Gilbert, Ken Hanna, Joel Kaye, Bill Mathieu, Don Reed, Clinton Roemer, Bill Russo, Tony Scodwell, Dick Shearer, Mike Suter, Mike Vax, and John Worster.

Plus all those who deserve special mention that I've neglected to name. I thank you all.

Special thanks to Peter Stent for his help in processing the photographs, and to Karen DeVinney, without whose patience and painstaking editing of my sometimes untidy manuscript, this book could never have been accomplished.

# Prelude

**Stella was the dominant voice** throughout Stanley's childhood, and indeed well into his adult life. She had married Floyd Kenton two months after conception, and some months later the couple moved from the family home in Colorado to temporary accommodation in Kansas. There could have been many reasons for the relocation, but the obvious incentive was to hide the then-unpardonable sin of having conceived before marriage. The baby was christened Stanley Newcomb (Stella's maiden name), his birth certificate quoting 120 South Fern Street, Wichita, Kansas, as the birth place, and December 15, 1911, as the date. Floyd's occupation was given as Butcher.

To complete the cover-up, when the family returned to Colorado, the boy's birthday was stated as February 19, 1912, a date Stanley believed to be true until well into adulthood. Audree Kenton comments: "Stanley's true birth date has always been a deep family secret. It's something we never let the public know; even when Stanley died, the small marker we put on his grave at the cemetery showed 1912 as the birthdate."[1]

Thomas Floyd Kenton was originally from Missouri, and said to be related to the frontiersman Simon Kenton. Though possessed of undeniable charm, Floyd was something of a dreamer, and failed to hold down any job for very long. Reports speak of him as a roofing worker and automobile mechanic. Stella Emily Kenton, straitlaced of Irish-Scottish descent, was 21 years old at Stanley's birth, and is shown on the certificate as Housewife. Later additions to the family provided Stanley with two sisters, Beulah (born 1914) and Erma Mae (1917). Both married in later life, and settled with their families in California.

Stanley always felt closer to his mother than to his dad. From Stella he inherited his spirit of determination to succeed, set of values, and attitude to life. From his father came Stanley's charisma, his sense of originality and adventure—and his sometime lack of business acumen. After several moves, in 1924 the family finally settled in Bell, a suburb of

Los Angeles, and the place Stanley would regard as his home-town. Now, at the age of 12, the boy began attending Bell High School.

Stella was a proficient pianist herself, but when she attempted to teach Stanley to play, he simply wasn't interested. It wasn't until he heard jazz being played that he became switched on to music, and with that fresh incentive, determined to master the piano himself, one of his early teachers being Frank Hurst, organist at a local theatre. When he was about 15, Stanley met pianist-arranger Ralph Yaw, who introduced him to the recordings of Earl Hines and Louis Armstrong, musicians who impressed him profoundly, and at 16 he started playing in public—at a hamburger joint for 50 cents a night plus tips! Stanley also sold his first arrangement, a waltz version of Drigo's "Serenade," for which he received seven dollars from an eight-piece band in Long Beach.

Such activities inevitably affected his school-work, especially when Stanley formed his own group, ingeniously named the Bell-Tones, although they rarely played in public. Nevertheless, in the summer of 1930 a tall, lean 18-year-old Stanley graduated from Bell, with a determination to make his way in the world by doing what he knew and enjoyed best: playing piano. But these were the Depression years in America; jobs were not easy to come by, and thus it was that during the next ten years, while Stanley served his apprenticeship, he was to play with virtually all types of bands and musicians, each in turn adding to his background, knowledge, and experience of the world of popular music.

Most of the bands Stanley played with are forgotten names today. His first big break came in 1933 when he was hired as pianist by Everett Hoagland. Kenton would later claim that he learned more from Hoagland's leadership than from anyone else: "I played with Everett for about a year and a half, and I know that many of the things I applied to my own bands in later years I can trace back to the schooling I received from Everett Hoagland."[2] Also in the band were Vido Musso and Bob Gioga, and it was while playing with Hoagland at Balboa that Stanley first met Violet Peters, a striking girl of strong personality, and Kenton's future wife. They married July 31, 1935, with daughter Leslie born six years later in 1941.

In April 1936 Gus Arnheim was reorganizing his band Benny Goodman-style, following Benny's success as the King of Swing, and Gus invited Stanley to take the piano chair. Arnheim's was a nationally recognized organization, and Stanley made his first recordings, including several short solos, when Gus recorded 14 big-band titles for Brunswick in the summer of 1937.

The more Kenton achieved, the more he realized how much he had to learn. Despite money being tight, when Arnheim disbanded, Stanley managed to study with a succession of classical teachers, the only kind available in 1937. Joseph Ricardi counted Jose Iturbi among his students, while John Crown was a concert pianist who became Head of Music at the University of California. For composition, Kenton turned to Charles Dalmores, a 70-year-old French horn virtuoso, who introduced Stanley to the music of Ravel, Stravinsky, and Bartok. None was perhaps the teacher the average jazzman might turn to for tuition, but then Kenton never was your average jazzman!

With the backing of promoter Al Jarvis, in 1938 Vido Musso formed a short-lived band with Stanley at the piano. Bassist was Howard Rumsey, who elaborates: "The Musso band that recorded for Keystone was really pretty good. It certainly was a workshop for Stan, because although he never wrote a note for the band, he was formulating ideas all the time he was in it. He was also on an extensive self-training program during this period—study, practice, listening: he even carried a silent key-board in the trunk of his car so he could practice anytime, anywhere. To me, Musso's band was the forerunner of the original Kenton orchestra. Utilizing spread-voicing with Bob Gioga's baritone saxophone at the bottom, it was definitely influenced by the Lunceford band, and as you know, after its failure Stan went on to form his original band and took some of us with him."

It didn't happen straight away. After the job with Musso folded, Stanley worked in the NBC House Band and in various Hollywood studios and clubs. As Stan told it: "In my years around Hollywood, I never really dreamed of organizing a band—I never thought of myself as a bandleader. I decided that I wanted to be something important around Hollywood, and I realized that if this was going to take place I had to be able to school myself to be an all-round piano player—a good utility pianist—someone who could play all sorts of music and all kinds of things, so that I could work myself into the studios and radio stations, and that's what I was pursuing. I felt if I could become an all-round pianist I would realize a good career in music."[3]

Kenton seemed well set to achieve this ambition in late 1939, when he accepted the post of pianist and Assistant Musical Director in Manny Strand's orchestra at the Earl Carroll Theatre Restaurant in Hollywood, where he was noticed by George Avakian: "In Los Angeles there wasn't much good music. There's one first-class musician, however, in Stan Kenton, who plays piano in the Hines-Sullivan tradition, but at present is forced to work in a rhumba outfit in a classy nitery."[4]

It was a position that afforded security and a good salary in a prestige night-spot, but which provided scant musical satisfaction. Stanley had ideas of his own he wanted to express, and the first Kenton band was really born out of necessity as much as intention. Having written a bunch of orchestrations that he felt were exciting and different, Stanley couldn't find anyone willing to play them. So he formed a spare-time rehearsal band of like-minded musician-friends who were willing to participate in workshop sessions for the sheer joy of playing a music they found challenging and stimulating. "Stan furnished refreshments," noted bassist Buddy Hayes, "but he had no money, and everyone enjoyed it so much, we didn't ask for money at that time."[5] Thus it was that Kenton found himself a leader almost by chance, though in effect propelled forward by events leading directly from his own musical creativity.

Kenton himself confessed, "You know, I had a wild idea in the beginning. My concept of leading a band was to get the guys together, write for them, rehearse them and play piano for the band, then get a front man to lead them. I figured I had no business meeting people, shaking hands—in fact, I was terrified. But I couldn't find a front man, so I had to resort to my own devices."[6]

Jack Ordean told me, "It's an interesting story, how we got five saxes together with a few arrangements and rhythm section, and went on to bigger things. I think it was 1940 when Stan called and asked if I'd be interested in getting a sax section together to rehearse some arrangements he had just written. That's when we started the Kenton band, with just saxes and rhythm. Later we added a trumpet, then a second trumpet and a trombone. We played a few dances around LA, added two more to make five brass, and Stan started to feature much more brass work. A dedicated, hard-working band, always up for it!"

By the summer of 1940 Kenton knew he wanted to lead his own band. He quit his job at Earl Carroll's, and tried to sell himself to the bookers, who weren't buying! Buddy Hayes again: "They said he was too far out. If he could get a Guy Lombardo-type band they could use him."[7] But Stanley was persistent, and fired with the enthusiasm of the young for something he believed in passionately. He realized he needed audition records to help sell the band, and cut acetates on several dates at Music City, a Hollywood record store part-owned by Glenn Wallichs, who was soon to become involved in the formation of Capitol Records. The place was an unofficial hang-out for musicians, songwriters, pluggers—anyone connected with the Hollywood music business.

Attached to the store was a small recording studio, recalled by Clinton Roemer as a "record your voice to send home to the folks" sort of place, and certainly barely large enough to seat the dozen men in the Kenton band. Saxist Bob Snell remembered: "I was on the November 1940 test session that included 'Etude For Saxophones.' Stan laughingly called it, 'Voyage of a Reed'!" Four of the more commercial titles were packaged in a presentation with announcements by Chet Huntley for Stanley to hawk around to the agents, and though they didn't result in any immediate bookings, they did help to convince people that Stanley was serious about becoming a bandleader, at a time when many others in the business were claiming a similar ambition but not doing anything constructive about it. (The Music City recording of "Etude for Saxophones" was issued on *The Kenton Era*, and several other titles are available on the Dynaflow and Tantara labels.)

As 1940 merged into 1941, the band rehearsed constantly, and did secure a few local bookings, notably at the Diana Ballroom in Los Angeles, where the teenagers stopped dancing to listen to the music. Kenton was heartened by this relative success, and threw himself ever more determinedly into improving his orchestra. Now all he needed was that all-important breakthrough into the big time . . .

# 1.

# Balboa Bandwagon

## (1941)

**Human nature being the way it is,** it's unlikely music was uppermost on the minds of most youngsters crowding the Californian beach-side resort of Balboa, some 30 miles south of Los Angeles. But for many, music came a close second to socializing, and word that summer of 1941 was that the band playing the Rendezvous Ballroom was HOT. It was also completely unknown. Whoever had heard of Stanley Kenton and his Orchestra?

Big names in the nation's dance-halls were the likes of Glenn Miller, Benny Goodman, Tommy Dorsey. They might play the Rendezvous for the odd one-nighter, but only the swankiest hotels, or the most prestigious theatres, could afford to book these bands on extended engagements. A struggling "territory" band would accept the lowest union scale the management could get away with paying.

Widely recognized as the premier dance spot of the locality, the Rendezvous had been totally rebuilt after a fire in 1935. Clinton Roemer (Kenton's chief copyist after the war) worked at the Rendezvous, and casts a fascinating insight into the mores of the period: "Of the many ballrooms along the coast, the Rendezvous without a doubt was the most popular as well as the most famous. The management was strict at enforcing the rules. Women could not wear slacks, and men were required to wear long-sleeved sweaters or jackets over their shirts. No shorts, tennis shoes or sandals were permitted. An unwritten 'whites only' policy existed. Although many styles of dancing were seen at the Rendezvous, jitterbug dancing was definitely not allowed, nor were spins where the couples separated."[1]

If the basic architecture was drab, the Rendezvous' position facing the Pacific was romantic, and the interior attractive in red and gray. In 1941, Audree Kenton danced to Stan's music with her future husband Jimmy Lyons, and recalls: "Balboa was noted for being a gathering-place for American youngsters during the summer vacations. It swung, literally, with thousands and thousands of college and high-school students, and the Rendezvous was the center of things. It really wasn't much in the way of a hall, it was a very plain, barn-like building on the ocean-front in Balboa, but the Rendezvous always had a certain glamor to it. There was a great, empty area downstairs with a marvellous inlaid wooden dance floor, an arched wooden ceiling, and a balcony around three sides. The acoustics weren't bad—bands liked to play there."[2]

Stanley Kenton certainly longed to. With just a handful of local one-nighters under his belt, Stan knew that to become established, his band needed the security of a summer residency. As he explained, "I had my eye on the Rendezvous Ballroom, because that was kind of the center of big band jazz in the area, and some other important people had gotten started there, and I felt like that was the place it could happen for us."[3] (Claude Thornhill for one had struggled until "making it" as house-band at Balboa in 1940.)

Strongest competition for the job came from Johnny Richards, but it was Kenton who won out. The announcement was made in Stanley's presence by Glenn Miller during a one-nighter to a packed house on May 29, and Kenton's summer residency began the following Friday night, June 6, 1941. Thereafter, Stan always regarded that date as the start of his professional career as a band-leader, and the Rendezvous as his "home."

Avoiding the popular but repetitive "One O'Clock Jump"/"In the Mood"-type swing riffs, Kenton instead fired the kids' enthusiasm with his punchy, hyped-up arrangements of tunes like "La Cumparsita" and "Arkansas Traveler," played with the relentless, staccato accents that set the band's style during the beginning years. Stan himself described the music as "very dramatic in content; all the introductions sounded like Paramount Pictures fanfares, and the endings like MGM closing the picture. They were full of choppy off-beats and experimental things that were actually very crude, but somehow, crude as everything was, there was enough heart in the band to attract attention."[4]

Stan was also well aware that a touch of humor never went amiss, as Bob Gioga recalled: "'St. James Infirmary' was the first of Stan's rare ventures as a vocalist. Earl Collier, one of the sharpest and most talented musicians in the band, detected a lull, and the dancers now crowded 'round the stand expecting something great, were not rewarded. It was more than Earl could stand, and he started yelling ad libs to Stan. The crowd loved it, and it became the comedy number for the band—always a must on the stage. Later on, everyone started getting in on the act; our drummer Marvin George took a leading role, and unfortunately I did a 'queer' bit near the end. Audiences lapped it up!"[5]

The teenagers of southern California discovered Kenton. They related to his music, and the crowd's enthusiasm was reflected in the band's spirit, and urged the men to greater heights. Stan gave his all, and demanded as much from every member of the band, who responded with the zeal of men working for a cause, rather than a pay-packet. The sincerity was evident and contagious, and the kids loved it, as Audree Kenton recalls: "The band was so entirely different from anything the kids were used to. It was a totally different sound, and very exciting. Stanley was a dynamic, dramatic conductor. When Stan got up there he waved his arms and all but fell off the stage, twice a night. The youngsters responded to this, and what he was giving them was not what they were used to. It was not swing, in the way that Goodman and Shaw were swing; it was something new, and there was a tremendous excitement generated. Part of it was Stanley himself, a lot of it was the music, much of which he had written, and it just knocked the kids out. They had come to dance, but would end up standing in front of the bandstand, hour after hour."[6]

The soloists became local heroes, feted and honored in the manner of today's pop celebrities, though from the start, Kenton's was a writer's band, and the often quite brief solos complemented the orchestrations, rather than the other way round. Like Stan himself, Jack Ordean (alto saxophone) had served his apprenticeship with the bands of Gus Arnheim and Vido Musso, and received a lot of favorable publicity, but Jack never achieved the anticipated national fame. By the time Ordean returned to music after war service, alto styles had moved on, and all eyes were on Bird and his disciples.

Chico Alvarez was a skilled, authoritative trumpet player who never took a poor solo, but rarely outstretched himself either. Apart from three years in the army, Chico stayed with Stan until 1951, yet in all those years never recorded an identifying solo feature. A 1948 chart by Pete Rugolo of "You're Mine You" reveals Alvarez skirting deftly around the melody, and he switched easily from swing to a more modern, bop-oriented style, yet post-Kenton he quit jazz altogether.

In retrospect, the personality who has best stood the test of time, and most often endows the music of 1941 with that extra pizazz, is the Coleman Hawkins-styled tenor of Red Dorris. Milt Bernhart got it right when he called Dorris, "Really the star of the first Kenton band, and a tremendous talent."[7] Red also sang, in the deep Herb Jeffries-Billy Eckstine vocal range that Kenton most admired, and his ballads provided an essential change of pace from the up-tempo flag-wavers, though few songs were from the current hit parade.

Vocalists were very important to a band, and most all dance bands carried at least one girl singer, often picked as much for her looks as her voice. Life on the road was especially hard for a girl, as she was expected to sit on the bandstand, immaculately coiffured and gowned for hour after hour each night looking glamorous and happy, for the odd song in the spotlight. None of Stan's early "canaries" (including Kay Gregory, Terry Harlyn, and Helen Huntley) made a lasting impression, as none got to record with the band. Indeed, as bassist Howard Rumsey remembered it, "Kay Gregory sat on that stand every night, and all she got to sing was 'Hawaiian War Chant.'"[8] Instead it was Dorris who sang on Stan's first Decca date ("This Love of Mine" on September 11, 1941), and Dorris again who recorded "Do Nothin' Till You Hear from Me" on the band's initial Capitol session two years later. Not until May 1944 and the forthright Anita O'Day (who wouldn't take a back seat for anybody), does a girl singer really "arrive" with the Stan Kenton Orchestra, with "And Her Tears Flowed Like Wine."

From the start, Kenton sensed that the key to success lay in individuality, in making his band different from anyone else's: "I wanted every arrangement to be a production in itself. Spirit and enthusiasm had to predominate at all times. I wanted to present swing in as elevated a manner as possible."[9] The jerky, Lunceford-influenced rhythm certainly set the band apart, but it was Stan's early writing for saxophones that would have the greatest long-term significance. (The '41 band carried only five brass—three trumpets and two trombones—whereas the sax section was complete with five men from day one.)

As early as 1940, Stan had written four studies, or etudes, for saxophones which came to form the foundation upon which the whole Kenton Sound was based. "Reed Rapture" remained in the book for years, but the most enduring of all proved to be the perennial "Opus in Pastels." Recognizably different, and almost classical in appeal, Kenton's conception carried his signature and remained his personal property. Many arrangers over the years attempted to copy Stan's saxophone styling; some came close, but none ever quite succeeded. Whatever alchemy Kenton possessed, the secret died with him.

Stan explained: "I'd have to say the conception of the Kenton saxophone section in the beginning days was my own, though I was influenced greatly by Benny Carter, who was one of the giants of jazz. We thought of Bob Gioga's baritone as being the bottom of the section, and we widened and spread the voices so that the sax section would stand by itself, and wouldn't have to be dependent on the rest of the band for any of its character. Jack Ordean, as talented a lead player as he was, didn't have a lot to do with the sound or the character of the section. Ordean naturally colored the section with his tone, but mostly the thing that was unique about the saxes was done through the writing. We wrote as though it was a complete unit on its own, by myself at the start, and then of course Ralph Yaw had a lot to do with it, and Joe Rizzo also had a hand."[10]

As the band's library expanded, Stan could no longer cope with all the writing, and had to bring in others to help. Ralph Yaw, though 13 years older than Kenton, was a musician-friend from Stanley's boyhood, and had previously arranged for Chick Webb and Cab Calloway. Yaw was highly enthused by Stan's new ideas, though the extent of Ralph's creative input into the establishment of the orchestra's style is hard to validate. Yaw himself commented: "The band I am working with is something quite special and different. Stanley Kenton is the leader and I am working with him. We do the arranging, and I think we have cooked up something new in style. A swell new treatment of saxes and a couple of other style tricks do it. The saxes are treated to my mind in the right way for the first time. It really scares me."[11] Ralph often refused compensation because he knew money was tight, and he enjoyed writing for a band with which he felt so much accord. Originals like "Balboa Bash," "Two Moods," and "Take Sixteen" are testimony to his skill.

Joe Rizzo had some classical training, and made himself known to Kenton during the Balboa engagement. "Joe was a young fellow who felt the same way musically as I did," Stan recalled. "Some of the things he wrote were even recorded on our first recording contract for the Decca people. Joe arranged 'This Love of Mine' and 'El Choclo,' and there were many things he had written which were a very important part of the beginning library."[12] Rizzo was later drafted into the army, but continued to write for the band while in service until 1944. In later years he settled for security, and became a permanent arranger on Lawrence Welk's TV show.

In the 1940s radio was the equivalent of today's TV, and bands filled a lot of air-time. Every leader's ambition was to have his own radio show, and such was Kenton's impact that when the Mutual Broadcasting System expressed an interest in airing the band nationally, the merchants of Balboa clubbed together to help pay for the installation of a line from the Rendezvous to the MBS radio station at Santa Ana. Starting July 5, 1941, MBS broadcast Kenton coast-to-coast for half an hour every Saturday afternoon. As Stan related: "We had a very important broadcast that was picked up on *Swing Show* each week, and it was kind of comical; we would let all the people in off the beach, even in their bare feet and bathing suits. They came in for nothing to hear us broadcast, because we wanted an audience there, so that listeners back east could hear us playing our music to a crowd and hear their reaction. And this was the thing that actually started calling attention nationally to what we were doing at the Rendezvous Ballroom."[13] (What "Old Bob," the janitor who lovingly cared for the carefully waxed ballroom floor, thought of the sand deposited all over his creation, is not recorded!)

Two of the best examples of authentic recordings from these Rendezvous broadcasts are included in the iconic Tantara four-CD set called *Revelations*. Both "Stardust" and "Sophisticated Lady" have a very different aura about them from any of the 1941 studio recordings, partly because of their length (both play for over four minutes), giving arranger Stanley time to stretch out. The band plays with a great deal of warmth, and the gorgeous saxophone section soli prove this innovative styling was already fully developed. "Stardust" has the added advantage of a featured Dorris tenor, one of the finest solos captured on disc by this under-rated sax-man.

As news of the Kenton band spread, musical and show business personalities as well as the youngsters came to hear the band at the Rendezvous, including Jimmie Lunceford (one of Stan's most enthusiastic boosters), *Down Beat* writer Dave Dexter, song-writer Johnny Mercer, and promoter Carlos Gastel. Among the regular Saturday night visitors was film star Errol Flynn, who used to sail in from San Pedro on his yacht, though Flynn's interest lay as much with the chicks as the music. He was often accompanied by a guy nobody took much notice of, by the name of Howard Hughes, even then a rather mysterious gentleman.

Already evident was a phenomenon that would haunt Stan throughout his career. Those who loved the Kenton music did so with an enthusiasm and intensity that belied their numbers, giving the impression that the band was more popular among the general public than was actually the case. Despite all the success stories, by no means every mid-week night at the Rendezvous was a rave-up. As Charles Emge wrote in *Down Beat*: "It would be an exaggeration to say the band has been a 'sensation.' It's too good to crash through in that manner."[14] And Stan himself reflected in 1969: "Today we talk about the large crowds that came to Balboa and all the excitement that was created, and honestly, I'm not sure business was all that good that summer. In fact I remember times that I actually worried about whether the owner of the ballroom was going to come out financially or not."[15]

Milt Bernhart explains as well as anyone, the anomaly that would remain Kenton's cross: "The first band was Lunceford-style, that was an idol of his. Even then Stan was reaching beyond his audience. Because even at Balboa, many of the kids didn't really come to listen. Most of the bands that played Balboa were Mickey Mouse bands: people just wanted to dance, and they didn't really care too much as long as you played songs they could dance to. But Kenton was one of the first that was going to teach them something. These people were going to walk out hearing something they hadn't heard before. I saw all of the top band-leaders, but none of them ever captured an audience and won them over like Stan."[16]

In retrospect, the summer of '41 was an age of glorious innocence. The trials of adolescence were about to begin.

# 2.

# Hollywood Highs and Big Apple Blues

(1941–1942)

Popular music, then as now, was part of show business, with the emphasis on business. To those running the jungle, musical creativity was only as commendable as the money it generated. These hardheaded business men would see Stan primarily in terms of dollar signs, as "Kenton" became a brand name to be marketed before the public like any other commodity in its particular field. Essential to every professional leader was a personal manager to watch over his interests. In 1941, Carlos Gastel was just starting his managerial career, and eager to sign new artists to join his principal client Sonny Dunham, whose band never made the big-time.

Gastel was not called the Happy Honduran without good reason. A man of gargantuan appetites, both for gourmet foods and life in general, Carlos lived in the fast lane, and was keen to have Kenton on his roster. Audree Kenton described Gastel as "One of the most colorful figures in show business—big, handsome, persuasive and flamboyant. Carlos was wild, an exciting man, and fun to be with."[1] But Gastel was also a brilliant entrepreneur with boundless energy, and as his career flourished he attracted many top stars into his fold, including Nat Cole, Peggy Lee, and Mel Torme.

In later years, Kenton liked to tell the story of how he and Gastel got together in a restaurant and hammered out an agreement written on a paper napkin, and Audree confirmed: "They never had a formal contract, it was always a hand-shake."[2] Throughout the Forties, Carlos worked tirelessly to further the Kenton career. Most of Gastel's moves were behind the scenes, and hence attracted little publicity, but it is widely acknowledged that Carlos has never received the recognition he deserves. Second only to Kenton himself, it was Gastel's business acumen that did much to push the band to the top. As Stan's publicist Noel Wedder phrased it: "Carlos Gastel was a true professional, a promotional genius who triumphantly moved the band from Southern Californian obscurity to a world-renowned attraction."[3]

Carlos moved swiftly. Within days, Stan was signed to a seven-year contract with GAC (General Amusement Corporation), one of America's most prestigious booking agencies, which took a special interest in promoting new bands. Top man was Tom Rockwell, who described Kenton as "the most promising band property to be uncovered since Artie Shaw."[4] Rockwell's first action was to complete a deal with Jack Kapp to record the band for Decca Records, one of the nation's foremost recording companies.

It was also the first big mistake. Of the "big three" (including Columbia and RCA Victor) Decca was the most conservative label, infamous for the signs "Where's the Melody?" prominently displayed in its recording studios. Jack Kapp could have had scant realization of the true nature of Kenton's music, and viewed the band simply as just another dance unit that might hit the high time and bring big bucks into the company's coffers. For his part, as a young bandleader still learning his trade, Kenton was in no position to assert his authority over the will of Decca's A&R man, who insisted on recording current "pops" on the band's first session (held in September in Decca's Hollywood studios). The sole exception was "Taboo," a popular number from the band's library.

Clinton Roemer attended the date and told me, "The mild ad-lib solos from this first Decca session were demanded by the producer, who wanted to hear more melody. This accounts for the rather tame Red Dorris solo on 'Adios.' What is on the record is nowhere near what Red played on the first couple of rehearsals. 'Adios' was already a fair-sized hit for Glenn Miller and was getting a lot of air-time, as was 'This Love of Mine' in Frank Sinatra's version for Tommy Dorsey. 'Nango' was a dance number from a current Fox movie musical. By the time the Kenton cover versions came out, I don't think they got too much exposure."[5] Reviews in 1941 were lukewarm; both *Down Beat* and *Metronome* referred to the "weak material," which was certainly not of Stanley's choosing.

Far more typical of the band's fare were the transcriptions recorded for C. P. MacGregor on 16-inch discs licensed only for radio play. Because of the band's association with Balboa, it was decided to create programs that would sound like the band playing live at the Rendezvous Ballroom, as Audree Kenton recalled, "We recorded dozens of titles for MacGregor. They were done in a very small studio, using the standard microphone set-up for those days. But engineer Victor Quan had great technical expertise, and had developed a system whereby everything sounded live when we recorded it, a sort of early echo chamber idea, so it really did sound like we were playing in a large hall. We also had Jimmy Lyons on hand, he wrote most of the narrative and introduced the titles, as he also did on the early MBS remotes from Balboa.

"To make a big crowd noise after each number we brought along all our friends and relatives to those sessions. Stanley's mother Stella came, also Beulah and Erma Mae (Stan's sisters) and all the band wives. And all the audience noise you hear on the early MacGregor transcriptions is not legitimate audience at all—it's us screaming, trying to make noise enough for hundreds of people. Directly a tune ended, the musicians would throw down their instruments and shout and applaud wildly. It was quite funny to watch, but there really was a great spirit in that band."[6]

The definitive CD release of all the MacGregor recordings is the chronological five-CD set on Naxos Jazz Legends. Around 60 titles from this period are played in excellent sound, affording a better opportunity to audition the 1941 band than many from much later periods. Some of the many highlights include Howard Rumsey's bass on "Concerto for Doghouse" (as "A Setting in Motion"), Chico Alvarez on "Balboa Bash," Stan's writing for "Harlem Folk Dance" and "Arkansas Traveler," the period charm of Red Dorris singing "Flamingo," and several versions of Stan's then untitled "Theme." The importance of the MacGregor recordings is best summed up by Kenton himself: "The transcriptions went east, to New York, and various places, and believe me, Victor Quan made us sound like I swear we never sounded. It was really because of those transcriptions that we were able to get started in music."[7]

Kenton had his feet firmly on the first rung of the ladder, but many bands achieved that far, only to promptly stumble and slip into oblivion. Stan had shown his abrasive and agitated stylings (at least as compared with the super-smooth swing of bands like Miller and Basie) excited the kids, but his appeal to more affluent, sophisticated dancers remained unproven. In any case, however big on the West Coast, no band could be said to have "arrived" in the national sense until it had been successful in the major cities across the country, in particular the Big Apple. New York could make or break an artist within the space of a single engagement. Thanks (no doubt) to the machinations of Carlos Gastel working on the GAC hierarchy, Stanley was booked into New York's Famous Door, a night club that featured jazz artists, for a four-week engagement commencing November 20. But fate decreed otherwise when an opportunity arose at the Hollywood Palladium.

Even today the name Hollywood Palladium has a certain panache attached to it. Still standing but long past its prime, in 1941 the Palladium was just one year old, a big-band mecca and the premier ballroom in all of LA. Audree Kenton explains: "The Palladium was all Hollywood. It had chandeliers, red velvet carpets, and it was a really ritzy place when it was new. They served liquor, and they served dinner—the food was terrible!—and soft drinks for the young people. It was a place for a young man to take his best girl, but it was going to cost him money. The Palladium was fancy, one of Hollywood's best, in an excellent location on Sunset Boulevard. It filled a need and was an immediate success the minute it opened, and did great business for 20 years."[8]

Only the top attractions played the Palladium, and manager Maurice Cohen made it a rule to book only well-established bands. Besides, Cohen had visited the Rendezvous during Stan's final week there, and had not found the music to his liking. He was no better impressed on his second Kenton audition at Glendale's Civic Auditorium on October 4. What did attract Cohen was the 3,600 attendance at Glendale, which had an average of 1,800. Shortly after this, Cohen found himself with a five-week gap in bookings, between the bands of Alvino Rey and Tommy Dorsey, following an unexpected cancellation. Already half-convinced of Kenton's pulling-power, Cohen was persuaded by Gastel and GAC's Ralph Wonders to give the orchestra its chance at the Palladium. The Famous Door's management was persuaded to postpone Stanley's appearance there to the New Year, and Kenton's November 25 opening at the Palladium was set.

After much deliberation, the billing was changed from Stanley to Stan, since all the kids used the less formal abbreviation anyway. Though he became universally "Stan" Kenton to his fans, close friends and family continued to address him by the preferred Stanley. "A Scorching New Discovery: Stan Kenton and His Sensational Orchestra" screeched the Palladium flyers, adding for good measure: "If There's a Spark of Rhythm In You, This Will Set You Ablaze." On opening night the Palladium reported some 3,200 customers, almost equalling the record high of 3,600 drawn by Jimmy Dorsey two months before.

Stan was a showman as well as a musician, as evidenced by his conducting (almost a gymnastic display in itself), and first night at the Palladium Stanley waited near the main entrance of the ballroom, while the band took their places. When they were all seated, Stan let go with a loud shout and ran across the floor, through the crowd which had already formed, and leapt onto the bandstand. As his feet touched the floor, he signalled the down-beat for the band's "Theme." The crowd loved it, and Billboard reported a "strong turnstile reading of 17,500 at the end of the first week," causing such headlines as "Stan Kenton's band scores sensational hit in first big week at Hollywood Palladium."

Undoubtedly many dancers turned out from curiosity to hear this new band they had read so much about. But the Palladium's patrons were generally older and more blasé than the Rendezvous' teenagers, and whether Stan's unorthodox stylings and absence of pop songs would have continued to draw the crowds in such numbers will never be known. In December '41 it was the Japanese who pulled the rug from under Kenton's feet. Attendances slumped during the dreadful uncertainty that followed the December 7 attack on Pearl Harbor. As America reeled into the holocaust of war, people remained tied to their radios while the networks maintained a 24-hour news service to up-date the latest reports on the war situation. Much of the late-night sustaining music between the news bulletins was aired from the Hollywood Palladium, the West Coast being America's last time-belt, and still open after night-spots on the East Coast had closed.

Despite the circumstances, it was a case of being in the right place at the right time, since during the emergency the networks pooled resources and aired the same programs coast-to-coast, and Kenton gained much valuable exposure from the extra nation-wide broadcasts. Count Basie would tell the story of how the Basie band was en route to a job in the middle of the night, when the Count had the bus stopped and invited his musicians to listen to one of Stan's Palladium broadcasts. "That," Basie told his bandsmen, "will be the next King!"[9]

Basie's prediction seemed on course, with the Famous Door booking beckoning and a bevy of recordings filmed for Soundies release on Panorams (visual juke-boxes). The best of these was "Reed Rapture," with seven saxes shown in V-formation (though Alvarez and fellow-trumpeter Earl Collier are there for visual effect only). Artistically filmed with clever use of silhouettes, the title is conducted by a very young, intense Stan Kenton, who also plays a short piano solo.

Then, early in 1942 the second big mistake took place, this time with far-reaching consequences, when the Famous Door was jilted for a second time, in favor of a New York opening at the Roseland Ballroom. Charles Emge was so right when he wrote in *Down Beat*: "The band is at the crucial point now. From here they go up or down. These boys believe in themselves and their music, but the real struggle is ahead. They've got to work, but they can't take the wrong spot."[10] Someone with the acumen of Carlos Gastel must have known that Roseland, home of hostesses and strict-tempo dancing (epitomized in song by Rodgers and

Hart's "Ten Cents a Dance") was never going to accommodate the jazz-happy Kenton crew.

Probably there were forces at work beyond Gastel's control; or at that point can it have seemed the Kenton outfit was so invincible nothing could stand in its way? Perhaps a clue lies in the fact that Roseland owner Lou Brecker had an interest in the Hollywood Palladium, where Stanley had recently played with such success. Certainly Brecker expected something similar at Roseland, for at Gastel's insistence it was stipulated in the contract that the band should play only music of Stan's choice, and that instead of the usual Mondays, the band should be off each Tuesday, by tradition "South American night," when the relief band would play instead.

"New York dancers will ACCLAIM the sensational music of America's next No. 1 HIT BAND," prophesied the Roseland flyers, indicating just how wide was the chasm between expectation and realization. In fact, from the very first night the Kenton band and the Roseland clientele failed to connect on any level. When Stan blasted out with "Arkansas Traveler" or "Harlem Folk Dance," the dancers stayed off the floor. And when the dancers didn't dance, the hostesses failed to earn, and complained to the management, who in turn bore down on Kenton. Very rapidly the situation reached crisis point.

Howard Rumsey recalled: "When we went to Roseland, there was a big sign outside reading 'Fred Astaire Says Stan Kenton Is Terrific!' I don't think Fred Astaire ever heard Stan Kenton! The band was hot, and it was like, 'We're from California, listen to us.' The dancers were saying, 'We're the best dancers in the world—watch us!' We never connected."[11]

After one week of a scheduled eight-week booking, Stan was fired. The band actually played for three weeks, the last two on notice. Dave Dexter's recall is compelling: "On Stan's opening night at Roseland you couldn't get in, the place was packed. Every music publisher in the East was there. Well, they all left after about an hour. They hated him, because he didn't have one 'plug' song. Stan didn't want any plug songs, he hated pop music. The dancers hated him too, because he didn't have any Latin rhythms. So when he was fired I was with him, standing on the curb in the snow, waiting for a cab, and trying to soothe his feelings. All Stan said was, 'And on top of this, the goddamn Japs lobbed some shells onto the beach in Santa Barbara. Let's get the hell out of here!'"[12]

Worse even than the job loss, was the blow to Kenton's confidence and prestige. "Highly overrated and oversold," quoted Down Beat.[13] Now Stan was forced to listen to his critics, and their advice on how to "improve" the band: Tone down the brass, play simpler arrangements, above all add pop songs to the repertoire. Stan may have been an idealist, but he was also a realist, and the fact was, in 1942 every big band was basically a dance unit that played its share of hit songs. Some, like Glenn Miller and Jimmy Dorsey, not only played the hits, their recordings *made* the hits. For every "Clarinet a la King," even a "jazz" band like Benny Goodman recorded three or four songs of the ilk of "Buckle Down Winsocki" and "If You Build a Better Mousetrap" (both from war-time movie musicals).

There would be a good case for arguing that even without the debacle that was Roseland, Stan would have been forced to change policy sooner or later. So Kenton took stock, and decided that a band with concessions was better than no band at all. As Stan phrased it: "I was really proud of the Balboa band. We played good music, and nobody will ever convince me that we didn't. It was different, walloping and getting better every day. Well, you know what happened in New York. We laid the biggest egg ever seen on Broadway. After that I got confused. I didn't know whether to please myself and the real fans by continuing to play good music, or whether I wouldn't do better by making compromises. And I went on like that for quite a while."[14]

Even in New York, not everything had been a disaster. Stan's second (and last) Decca session was a marked improvement over the first, because the band was allowed to play numbers from its own library. Highlights include a long (4:24) version of "St. James Infirmary," which had to be issued on Decca's 12-inch black label, and a spirited take on "El Choclo," with a beautifully formed Dorris tenor solo. In total, these Decca recordings are further convincing evidence that the groundwork for future conceptions was conceived by Stan himself. In the words of Pete Rugolo: "With the deep, low saxophones, the off-beat rhythm, and the high brass, you could tell it was Kenton from the start. The Kenton Sound was there on the very first records, it was very different from anybody else."[15]

With 15 weekly pay-packets to fill (Stan had added a third trombone in New York, and now Eve Knight came in as vocalist), Kenton couldn't afford to be without work, or his band would soon be raided by other leaders for eligible sidemen, and unheralded credit goes to Gastel and Rockwell that just two days after leaving Roseland, on February 28 Stan started his next job: a week's engagement that must have been set up while the band was working its notice in New York. In Stan's words: "We managed to survive through the goodness of a guy's heart that owned a couple of ballrooms in Boston." These were the Raymor-Playmor twin ballrooms, which advertised under the slogan: 2 Bands—2 Ballrooms—1

Admission. Billed as "The Glenn Miller of the West Coast" (!), Stan played in the Raymor room, "and our egos began to be kind of pumped up again, and we were reassured that we were going in the right direction, because we met a lot of enthusiasm in Boston, and we managed to hang on until we were due to open in April at the Meadowbrook."[16]

# 3.

# Hanging On

## (1942–1943)

New Jersey's Meadowbrook was one of America's more popular dance spots, so when the band was shunted out of there halfway through the engagement, Kenton knew the outlook was rough. He would have to play pop songs and accept whatever bookings GAC offered. Actually, a lot of the "pops" that entered the book, like "Skylark," "Serenade in Blue," "Don't Sit Under the Apple Tree," and "I Had the Craziest Dream" were considerably better than the second-rate schmaltz that Red Dorris had been featuring.

Stan's first theatre date (a combination of vaudeville and featured movie) actually brought him back to NYC in March 1942, but to Brooklyn rather than Manhattan, and at the somewhat less than illustrious Flatbush Theatre. Whatever, the audience sat and listened during the band spot, so in that respect it resembled a concert setting, and Kenton premiered a new work he had written in different tempos and symphonic style indicative of the direction Stan eventually wanted the band to take. Titled "Concerto to End All Concertos," the strong melody was one of Kenton's most enduring compositions, first recorded in 1946, and played regularly for a further decade. Stan explained, "I wrote 'Concerto' because I wanted people to hear a little of the trumpets and trombones, as well as the soloists. We used it as a showpiece, and made kind of a production out of it."[1]

The normal hazards of establishing a new band were now compounded by the war, which restricted travelling and meant constant changes in personnel as musicians fell victim to the draft. Others left of their own accord, including Howard Rumsey, the first of many Kenton bass players who would dissent with the drummer over time-keeping and who also regretted the loss of the "family feeling" that had inspired the original Balboa band. By the end of 1942 more than half the men who had played at Balboa were gone, as Stan recalled: "There was a constant flow of musicians coming and going all the time, and there was

21

always a scuffle to find musicians to replace those who had been drafted. I recall once a guitar player that I hired to take the place of a fellow who had been inducted, received his own induction papers before he'd even played a note with the band."[2]

Nor could Kenton afford to pay the high salaries the top guys could command. During the early Forties it was a real struggle to keep the band together at all, let alone make any money, and Stan (himself a married man with a baby to support) lived literally hand to mouth. Bob Gioga, in his role as Band Manager, proved a constant source of support to Kenton, both by his handling of everyday affairs in running the band, and maintaining morale when it was most needed. Bob would be the only member of the original Balboa outfit to survive without a break into the Fifties, finally surrendering his baritone chair in 1953.

Despite all the difficulties, Kenton strove continually to improve his band. Because he spent so little time himself at the piano, for most of 1942 Stan hired Ted Repay, the only full-time pianist other than Kenton ever to play in the band. But then Stan let him go because he missed the luxury of slipping into the piano seat himself whenever the mood arose. To compensate, Stan hired a fourth trumpet player to raise the level of the brass, and replaced Eve Knight with Dolly Mitchell—but still tended to rely on Red Dorris as his principal singer! But as always, it was the writers who brought new ideas into the band.

Ken Hanna (then just 21 years old) didn't have his own sound, but was adept at copying other people's. (Hanna's 1947 "Somnambulism" sounds more like Rugolo than Rugolo!) Ken studied the band's Decca recordings and learned what made Stanley tick before presenting himself to Kenton, who recalled: "Ken Hanna was the first guy I ever met, even before Rugolo, who had the same feeling as me. Ken came to a rehearsal and we hadn't played more than 16 bars when I realized he wrote exactly as I did, and I couldn't believe it."[3]

Stan hired Hanna to add to the band's pop library. Dorris vocals included "One Dozen Roses" and "I Left My Heart at the Stage Door Canteen." Then Ken was promptly drafted, and though he continued to mail in charts during his service days, he was no longer readily available to Stan at that time.

Enter Charlie Shirley, who moved to Kenton when Sam Donahue disbanded and joined the Navy with Artie Shaw in October 1942. Shirley recalled, "I jumped at the chance to write for the band, as Stan assured me he'd use anything I came up with in the way of experimental stuff, either pop or jazz. We brought in woodwinds and classic voicings on the ballads, and I feel I had some influence on the direction the band moved into after the war." Unfortunately, the first AFM recording ban was now in full swing, so only lo-fi broadcast recordings of songs like "Constantly" and "Moonlight Mood" remain.

Shirley was one of the literally hundreds of alumni who paid tribute to Stan personally: "That was a wild and woolly band, and we had many adventures, some of them quite funny, though they did tend to get a bit illicit from time to time. Never including Stan though. He was one of the straightest men I've ever met. Dedicated, clean, sober, and always concerned for his men and their welfare. His example inspired many of us to keep writing, even when it seemed that the 'squares' were taking over completely."[4]

As the war situation intensified, by the end of 1942 few of the guys in the band were the same as those who had left Hollywood on the big adventure east in January. Not only the players, but the band's style was also changing, with less emphasis on the jerky, staccato rhythms that had originally dominated. For most of December the band played a prestige engagement in the Panther Room of Chicago's Hotel Sherman, and during the preceding months Stan had learned a great deal of what was expected from a dance band in such a location to avoid being booted out after the first week. He tempered the jazz instrumentals like Shirley's "Steam Is on the Beam" and his own "Danger! Men Blasting" with plenty of pop songs from Red and Dolly, and earned the respect of both the public and critics in return:

> Samuel Lesner, *Chicago Daily News*, December 9, 1942: "Eddie Meyers on flute and Bob Gioga on English horn, with backgrounds by the band, provide a performance of 'mood music' entirely new in the popular field."

> *Chicago* paper, December 19, 1942: "Swing music in full bloom is blaringly mirrored in this comparatively young and large outfit. Kenton, youthful, aggressive salesman, is a suitable front for this powerhouse, which dishes out torrid rhythms with razor-edge precision."

> Bob Locke, *Chicago Sun*, December 6, 1942: "The music is massive and solid in structure, and is propelled by a wonderful, rhythmic beat. Many ideas have been borrowed from the successful Negro [*sic*] bands, enlarged and improved upon."

Buddy Childers was a fortnight shy of his seventeenth birthday when he first joined in January 1943. For the next ten years Buddy would be in and out of the band like a yo-yo, but mostly he was in, and rightly referred to as "The Boss of the Brass Section." Something of a "rough diamond," and possessed of all the brash abrasiveness of youth, Buddy did not endear himself to his peers, who responded by "making me the butt of every rotten joke and trick they could devise."[5] But Buddy survived his initiation, and in 1943 he had two things going for him: he was a good trumpet player, and at 17 he wasn't going to be inducted in a hurry.

As well as the high trumpets, Stan found great satisfaction in exploring the low sounds of the orchestra, illustrated right from the start by his exceptional writing for Bob Gioga's baritone sax. During 1943 another milestone took place when Bart Varsalona switched to bass trombone. According to Bart, "I had an idea. The band was playing a lot of heavy bottom, and I happened to see this bass trombone in the window of a music store in San Francisco. I went in and tried it out. It felt pretty comfortable and the price was right. I brought it on the job that night, and Kenton saw a difference immediately. He said, 'Great, keep it!'"[6] It's always dangerous to claim "a first," but use of a bass trombone in dance bands was certainly extremely rare at that time.

During the war, all show people gave freely of their time to entertain the armed forces with special live performances and recordings. Perhaps the largest dedicated organization, and certainly the one with the most bountiful legacy, was AFRS (Armed Forces Radio Service), which recorded both their own programs and preserved many radio broadcasts on 16-inch transcriptions that were sent regularly for rebroadcasting around the globe. Dance bands were the mainstay of series like *One Night Stand* and *Spotlight Bands,* and many Kenton programs have survived thanks to the work of AFRS (which being a non-commercial organization was granted immunity from the recording ban). Stan only narrowly escaped the draft himself because of his age and marital status, making him that much keener to help the war effort through entertainment, especially for those in uniform.

Most legendary of all the war-time morale-boosters was Bob Hope, who seemed the embodiment of all things American, yet was actually born in Britain. Hope's weekly NBC Tuesday night radio show, sponsored by Pepsodent and usually broadcast from a Service camp, with regulars Frances Langford, Barbara Jo Allen as Vera Vague, and Jerry Colonna, was a hot favorite among service personnel and civilians alike.

The music spot on the show was held by Skinnay Ennis, but became vacant when Skinnay received his army-call. The Kenton band filled in for a single show, and so impressed Hope with its disciplined, no-nonsense approach, that he determined Kenton should become his new house-band. And what Hope wanted, Hope usually got! In fact, everyone was delighted, except for Stan Kenton. The Bob Hope show (at that time literally called *The Pepsodent Show Starring Bob Hope*) played corn, and was far divorced from Stan's musical ideals. In the event, Kenton had little choice but to accede, since to refuse would have meant offending all-powerful GAC, who could punish him in a hundred different ways, in particular with indifferent bookings that could well drive the band into insolvency. As it was, being on call for the weekly broadcasts the band was unable to leave the LA area, except as part of the Hope entourage, but between shows could play only one-nighters within 100 miles of LA because of contractual commitments to the Hollywood Palladium that Stan had signed in 1941. Overall, it may be assumed Kenton was not best pleased with his lot.

At least the one-year contract with Hope ensured financial security. After two years of hard slog, a coterie of fans had been built up among jazz enthusiasts, but the band had acquired none of the trappings that guaranteed national acceptance: there had been no hit records, no regular radio show, no songs had become identified with the band in the public's mind, no singers had acquired popular significance. "At least I ought to get some laughs on the Hope Show," reasoned Kenton. "You don't get many of those out on the road." [7]

The Hope shows started September 21, 1943, and one of Stan's first actions was to add a fifth trumpet to the section (albeit for only four months at this time). What was more contentious was his choice of Karl George, because Karl was black, and during the war years studio bands were strictly segregated, something Kenton would have known full well. Stan himself had no prejudices, and Karl George was an excellent player, which will have been Kenton's first consideration. But the critical timing chosen by Stan to hire his first black musician, some four weeks into the Hope season, was a challenge to the status quo to say the least.

Hope's reaction would be crucial, and it was reported that when Bob first noticed George among the trumpets, he simply observed to Kenton, "I see you have a new guy in the band," but made no other comment, or (to his credit) raised any objection. It was simply accepted, despite press reports pointing out the unusual situation: "George turned down offers from Count Basie and Cab Calloway in favor of the Kenton offer. He is the first Negro [*sic*] to regularly play a commercial radio show with a white band on the West Coast."[8] Kenton was always a pioneer, and Karl stayed for nearly a year and a half as a featured player, including a "Harlem Folk Dance" solo on Stan's upcoming first Capitol record date.

In October 1943 Capitol and Decca succumbed to the Union's demands for increased session payments, and resumed recording. (Columbia and RCA held out for another full year!) Capitol President Glenn Wallichs assured Kenton his band and the fledgling record company would grow together, and Stan never regretted his decision to sign up. Somehow Capitol, with its slogan "First with the Hits from Hollywood," managed to combine commercialism with good music, and from the start supported Stan all the way.

It may have been Red Dorris' vocal on "Do Nothin' Till You Hear from Me" that made Billboard's Top 20, but the influential titles from Capitol Session No. 8, recorded November 19, 1943, were the two Kenton compositions "Eager Beaver" and the untitled "Theme." Stan had expanded his band's signature into a full-length, symphonic-style composition. Many voices have spoken of a similarity with a melody from Ravel's "Daphnis and Chloe," though Stan always denied any connection, and certainly the Kenton orchestration was entirely original. There was a lot of speculation about a suitable title, Stan wanting to label it "Production on Theme," but as he related, "Capitol finally decided that if your slogan is to be 'Artistry in Rhythm,' let's call it by that name, and of course it's stuck ever since."[9]

More importantly, "Artistry in Rhythm" contains the clearest evidence yet that the Kenton Sound was Stan's personal creation, including the high trumpets and the distinctive, choral trombone ensemble that became a Kenton trademark. Others, like Ray Wetzel and Kai Winding, might perfect those techniques in the future, but the foundations are already laid, and in retrospect are Stan's greatest legacy to his own orchestra.

Stan didn't give too much thought to the rather simple little riff he'd constructed during 1942 that he called "Eager Beaver," until it started catching on a year later. George Simon writing in the July 1943 *Metronome* mis-titled it "Roger Beaver," but was enthusiastic, calling it "An original that spotted some moving riffs and exceptionally interesting key changes," and as it developed into a Kenton "standard" Stan belatedly realized its potential: "I was trying to write something for my band that would be like 'In the Mood' for Glenn Miller, or 'Woodchopper's Ball' for Woody Herman. What I wanted was a commercial hit, a trademark, and fortunately it worked."[10]

If the recordings from this date of "Eager Beaver" and Frank Comstock's reworking of "Harlem Folk Dance" are compared with each other, a huge difference is immediately apparent: a difference that set Kenton apart from other bands, that delighted the fans, and that would soon infuriate the critics. Both arrangements "swing," insofar as there is regular pulsation and a steady beat. But "Harlem" has a more conventional, more "foottapping" swing. The rhythm on "Beaver" is far less relaxed, less loose. It is heavily accentuated, and plays with a relentlessly persistent, almost mechanical urgency. Stan's style, his sound, the way he wrote, made it almost impossible to "swing" in a light, airy manner. Kenton's music was heavy, masculine, solid, even on a simple riff like "Eager Beaver."

Since 99% of musicians and critics regarded "swing" as the essential component of good jazz, this immediately placed Stan on a collision course with his colleagues and jazz scribes. Fortunately, the fans were less intolerant. Large numbers would flock to his defense, and thrill to his music. It might be outside the jazz mainstream, but Stan was big enough to create his own musical river—and swim successfully in it for almost four adventurous decades.

# 4.

# Dance Band Days

## (1944–1945)

In theory, Kenton's reception into millions of homes every week, via America's most popular radio show, should have brought him international success. In reality, no one tuned into the Hope show to listen to the music. To most listeners, the house band was an anonymous unit, reduced to playing musical cues and accompanying the very "legit" voice of Frances Langford and the guest stars from the movie world who clamored to be on the show to bask in the reflected glory and the high audience ratings.

It was probably impossible to be around Hope so much without a little of the starshine rubbing off. For the first time, Kenton had close encounters with real stardom on a daily basis, and he must have wished for some of the enthusiasm and devotion that radiated towards Hope from the Service audiences to be deflected upon himself, to be a top star in his own right, rather than an aspiring bandleader just about holding his own in a highly competitive market. And if that meant reaching a wider audience than the kids who relished his "hep" music, perhaps that wouldn't be too great a price to pay. In Buddy Childers' words, "When I joined in January 1943 it was the last of the 'Balboa' band. It changed into something that didn't have that much personality for about three years, including the 'clarinets' band of 1944–45."[1]

That reference to clarinets came about when Red Dorris was inducted into the army in April 1944, a triple blow to Kenton who lost a tenor star, singer, and friend all at the same time. Dorris indeed had briefly led the band when Kenton was stricken with appendicitis earlier in the year. As replacement singer, Kenton brought in Gene Howard, whose appealing but disconcertingly bland voice lacked any individuality or uniqueness of its own.

"I was familiar with Stan's music and liked it," said Howard, "though it had been compared with everything from a machine-gun to a freight train. I explained I wasn't very adept on the saxophone (never having played one), but could write my own arrangements. Those were rough days for Stan—for all of us. It was early 1944, the war was at its peak, we were making very little money, and the problems of transportation and accommodations made it almost unbearable, but Stan was a constant inspiration which, together with his great sense of humor, kept us going."[2]

It was then that Stan came up with the idea to back Howard's ballads with a five-man clarinet section, presumably reckoning that if one clarinet could do it for Miller, a whole section would be five times better. It wasn't! For one thing, not all the sax men were equally skilled on the clarinet, so they were often out of tune, but even when they did blend, the sound was weak and unattractive. Kenton persevered with the concept for some two years, sharing the writing with Howard, before dropping the clarinets almost overnight in 1945.

Personnel changes required two new tenor-men at the same time in April 1944. For professional experience Stan hired Dave Matthews, and to limit expenses a youngster named Stan Getz. (Another future saxophone star, Art Pepper, had previously played briefly in the band before induction, and had played his first recorded solo on "Harlem Folk Dance" at the band's initial Capitol session in 1943.) Matthews quickly became bored with the band's increasingly commercial style, and when he quit in June, Getz moved into the solo chair, "And played Dave's solos better than Dave played them, note for note," recalled fellow-saxist Chet Ball. "Getz' style was varied at this time, as he could emulate most any tenor stylist of that period, but mostly his playing reminded me of Lester Young." One of Getz' features was Phil Moore's swinging "Sergeants' Mess" and another was Joe Rizzo's "Russian Lullaby." Getz was given semi-star status and gained valuable experience with Kenton, but left after a year, in April 1945, because Kenton told Getz he preferred the Hawkins/Matthews style of tenor playing, and regarded the Lester Young "cool" stylings that Getz was intent on developing as "too simple."

Matthews is featured on Joe Rizzo's arrangement of "Ol' Man River," from *The Kenton Era*. Rizzo makes no attempt to play down, even emphasizes the choppy nature of the tune, but continually drives forward at an exhilarating pace, with clever incorporation of thematic strands within the melody. The sense of swing comes from the various sections of the orchestra, rather than the heavily accented bass and drums, which operate almost as a separate section of the band, rather than an integrated unit providing the rhythmic pulse. Five short, well-spaced solos add variety, the first probably Matthews but conceivably Getz, a very fine statement from John Carroll's open trumpet, then definitely Matthews, a spot for Stan's piano, and a final comment from Eddie Meyers' alto sax. This one number shows beyond question how far the band has progressed as a professional, well-drilled instrument, based on the principles Rizzo had helped formulate at Balboa.

Lacking a clear direction from any single hired arranger, the band still looked to Kenton to set a lead, and Kenton was unsure. While he personally liked the Rizzo-type music, it was the schmaltz that the public preferred, and which he actually found easier to write. So Stan concentrated on Gene Howard's ballads, with songs like "Our Waltz" and "Together" especially anodyne examples of the genre. Things moved forward when Dolly Mitchell followed Red Dorris (with whom she had formed a romantic attachment) out of the band, to join Kay Kyser.

Stan was left without the essential adornment of a girl singer, and was encouraged by Carlos Gastel to take on Anita O'Day. Anita had made a name for herself with Gene Krupa, but was finding apathetic public response as a single, and manager Gastel persuaded her she needed more big-band experience. Kenton indeed had a spot open, but as Milt Bernhart put it: "Everybody knew that Anita was problems, on the hoof. If you brought her, you got somebody who was outspoken, who would complain about everything. And with Anita on Stan's band, the first thing was the drummer. Stan thought he was fine, but Anita called him a 'tub-thumper.' She wanted a swinger, and found the black drummer Jesse Price playing in a club and brought him to meet Stan."[3]

Musically, Anita and Stan were poles apart: she wanted above all to swing, and Kenton didn't. It was not the easiest of unions, but Stan probably came out best. For the first time the band featured a jazz voice, as opposed to a dance-band singer, and Anita brought him a hit record with her very first recording. Actually "And Her Tears Flowed Like Wine," a catchy tune by Charles Lawrence with lyrics by Joe Greene, complete with hand-clapping and band vocal, and orchestrated by Hope's resident arranger Buddy Baker, was her only hit with Stan, and she stayed nearly ten months. Nevertheless, Anita was a big attraction, as Stan recalled: "Anita had had a couple of hit records with Gene Krupa, so having her come with the Kenton band, which was pretty young in those days, was a big feather in our cap."[4]

"Tears" peaked at No. 4 in Billboard's Top 20, and for the first time other artists (including Ella Fitzgerald) were making cover versions of a Stan Kenton recording. Capitol's backing "How Many Hearts Have You Broken" came in at No. 9, but as Gene Howard wryly observed, that was mainly because it was on the back of "Tears." Then Jesse Price promptly quit to join Count Basie. Replacements no doubt weren't to

Anita's liking, but by then she'd found something else to focus on, like having "real jazz-man" Dave Matthews write her arrangements. ("In a Little Spanish Town" was a favorite.)

There was no suggestion from anyone when the Hope season ended that Stan should return for a second stint. The band was now established in its own right and on a sounder financial footing. Nevertheless, the new-found freedom brought about no sudden change of style. Stan continued his search for hits that would place Kenton platters on every juke-box in the land. Common sense, instinct, call it what you will, Stan was aware that the band had to be fully solvent, and acquire a strong power-base of dedicated fans, before he could push musical boundaries. Too many bands tried too hard, too fast, to last, the Boyd Raeburn orchestra being a prime example.

As lead saxist Al Anthony tells it, "And then came Gene Roland! Gene was in and out of the band like a yo-yo—he liked a good time. I won't go into details, but I do know this—Gene was a brilliant cat! No doubt about it. Of course, Stan knew all about Roland's life-style— that was Gene's choice—but Stan also knew this guy had no limitations. Gene liked to write swinging charts, Woody Herman was his favorite band, and Kenton wanted Gene to write his way, and so there were conflicts. But if you listen closely to Gene's charts you'll hear swing take place along with what Stan wanted. Try 'Two Moose in a Caboose.' The guys really liked Gene's writing—never knew what was going to happen. Talent, why this guy had so much he didn't really know what he could do—and don't forget, he also played trumpet, valve trombone and mellophonium at different times in the band. So now you know—then came Gene Roland!"[5]

Every musician's reminiscence is naturally related to his own experience in the band. In retrospect, as Anthony hints, Gene Roland's talent as musician and writer was equalled only by his unreliability and his inability to stick in one place for any length of time: personality defects which Kenton might overlook because he needed Roland's talents (Gene was the only arranger ever to feature in all four decades of Stan's career), but which at the same time would prevent Roland from ever acquiring quite the same status as the most famous Kenton stars. There's often a sense of frustration when musicians talk about Roland, of promise unfulfilled, of potential never quite realized.

While they were with Bob Hope the band had been spared some of the difficulties of war-time America, because Hope was working with servicemen for the War Department and hence received priority treatment. Now Stan experienced the full force of the shortages caused by emergency conditions. Because of gasoline shortages, the band often had to travel by trains, which were always packed to capacity. On one occasion Bob Gioga worked himself to the front of the line by shouting, "Make way for the recruits!" Despite Bob's inspirations, they often had to ride perhaps eight or twelve hours without a seat. The joys of the wartime road!

By the fall of 1944 Stan had raised the brass to its almost-full complement of four trombones and five trumpets, and hired Boots Mussulli as jazz alto player. So-called because he could plumb the lower reaches of his instrument, Boots was a full-toned, skillful soloist in the Benny Carter tradition who would play an increasingly important role in the band over the next few years. Mussulli is one of the giants of the "Artistry" orchestra now taking shape.

One of the drawbacks of a hit record was that fans expected the band to play that song at least once every performance, and when a vocal was involved the strain and monotony were exacerbated, until the singer came to detest the very song that had caused the success. Anita O'Day had never been really comfortable in the Kenton organization, which she found too stuffy and rigid for her free-wheeling life-style, and in February 1945 she quit, her departure being described in the media as "abrupt," or as one writer put it, "Anita jumped the band in one of her outbursts."[6] It must be said, O'Day recalled the circumstances quite differently, but Kenton confirmed the press reports: "We were in the middle of a job in St. Louis, and all of a sudden Anita comes up to me and says, 'I've had it!' And I said, 'You've had what?' She says, 'I'm leaving!' I said, 'You're leaving right now?' She says, 'Right now!' So I said, 'So long,' and she walked off the bandstand."[7]

Anita had been a popular personality, and her unprofessional departure left a gaping hole in the band's line-up. This time Gastel had no successor in the wings, and as Gene Howard recalled: "It seemed we never would find a suitable replacement. Every week a new girl would try out, but none of them seemed to have it. It wasn't until we opened at the Oriental Theatre in Chicago in the spring of 1945 that the first real prospect came along."[8]

Shirley Luster's biggest break thus far had been a short-lived tenancy with Boyd Raeburn, terminated when she was laid low with scarlet fever. Her career was making little progress when she heard Kenton was looking for a new singer, and presented him with some test recordings she had made. "Stan listened to my records and hired me," Shirley recalled. "I joined the orchestra on March 22, 1945, in Chicago—I can't remember my own birthday, but I'll never forget that date."

Stan made it clear she was hired only on a trial basis, and at first her songs were from Anita's book, in the absence of any fresh orchestrations, quite a modest beginning for the singer Milt Bernhart would describe as "The Queen of the Kenton Bandstand." In Stan's words: "I became interested in having Shirley sing with the band, and the big project was, how can we name her, because the name Shirley Luster sounded something like a hair-shampoo, and I didn't think it at all befitting. She agreed to change her name, and of course at that time she became June Christy."[9]

Audree Kenton comments: "June never had the command that Anita O'Day had. What June did was what Stanley told her to do: he created June."[10] Christy, young, inexperienced, and facing an uncertain future, was certainly more malleable than the forthright O'Day, and was unlikely to demand a change of drummer, or pontificate on how the band should swing. But neither did Kenton exercise a Svengali-like influence over the way she performed, and in fact June told George Simon: "Stan always inspired me, but he never told me how to sing."[11] At the same time, June's own style was far from fully developed in 1945, and she was replacing a particular sound to which the fans had become accustomed; so if Christy's main influence was O'Day, Stan wasn't likely to discourage her. As Gene Roland told Stan Woolley: "When June arrived she was more or less an O'Day impersonator. She had Anita's style, and even looked a little like her. At first she did Anita's material, and then Stan developed a style for her and we gradually got away from the O'Day thing."[12]

The Kenton band produced many stars over the years, but none bigger or brighter than June Christy, who was forever identified with the orchestra, especially as Pete Rugolo arranged many of her solo albums for Capitol Records. At first Kenton limited her repertoire to up-tempo tunes, labelling her with the slogan "The Little Girl that Sings with a Beat," but it soon became clear that she was equally suited to sing ballads when her iconic interpretation of "Willow Weep for Me" became a classic. Christy had no musical training, and was unable to read music. She sang by instinct and natural ability. If she was unaware of her technical limitations, her critics soon made her cognizant of them, complaining of faulty intonation, of an imperfect vibrato, and that she often sang flat. Sometimes it was true, and in classical music such defects would be damning. But jazz has its own set of rules, or rather non-rules, in which self-expression and individuality are more important than perfect technique. In jazz, if it sounds right, it is right, and Christy sounded just right to the thousands of fans who recognized in the character of her voice an extra quality, a husky timbre, and a highly personal way of phrasing and bending notes which far transcended any technical deficiency.

Stan was soon persuaded he had found the voice he was seeking, and personally vetoed any music lessons for Christy, which he was afraid would destroy her originality. Together, June's vocals and Stan's band enhanced each other, providing a perfect match, and one of the finest-ever combinations of jazz voice and orchestra. Kenton expressed it well when he said, "June brings something new to swing—not just rhythm, but real character."[13] And Conte Candoli once and for all put paid to those snide comments: "People talk about June's intonation, but I think that made her. That was her style. She would sing something a little flat, and raise it up, or lower it down, and that was her uniqueness. It didn't matter if it was flat, not at all."

June told me she was "scared stiff" when she first opened with the band, but if so it certainly didn't show on May 4, 1945, when Stan led his troops into Chicago's Universal Studios to record the first song specifically arranged for Christy by Gene Roland. "Tampico" is a novelty number with a catchy rhythm and snappy lyrics specially rewritten for Kenton. In time, Christy would come to dislike "Tampico" as much as O'Day hated "Tears Flowed Like Wine," but even June would admit how much she owed the song. She sings with such unassailable authority and enthusiasm that "June Christy" was firmly established as a "name" vocalist on the strength of her first-ever waxing, something which, she said, restored her confidence in her own abilities at a time when she most needed such assurance. "Tampico" was the magic record that cemented June's career, and stayed 13 weeks in the charts, reaching No. 4 in Billboard's Top 20.

Once Stan was satisfied they had the best possible rendition of "Tampico" in the can, the band settled down to record a composition Kenton called "Southern Scandal," so-termed because it was based on "Tara's Theme" from the movie *Gone With the Wind*, which involved an infamous relationship and was set in America's deep south. Even more than "Eager Beaver," "Scandal" was the creation that defined Kenton as an influential force in modern jazz. It swings, but is far too inflexible and structured to be a suitable vehicle for future improvisation. Indeed, Kenton's writing was generally too rigid to be so adapted; that honor fell in the Forties to Ray Wetzel's "Intermission Riff," in the Fifties to Roland's "Jump for Joe," and finally to Willie Maiden's "Little Minor Booze."

Kenton saw swing as one aspect of jazz, but not the all-defining feature. He was as much concerned with sound and mood, with color and composition. Over at Columbia, Woody Herman, with his optimal rhythm section of Ralph Burns, Billy Bauer, Chubby Jackson, and Davey Tough, was already turning out the Burns and Hefti hits that would establish the Herd as the finest swing band of all time. Kenton wasn't even inclined to compete for that honor. He wanted to be the best, but on very different terms, with a distinctive orchestral sound, and a post-war modern music that would be as different from anyone else as Duke Ellington had been in the past. "Southern Scandal" was an important step along that evolutionary path.

Aided by Universal's extraordinarily vibrant recording technique, the orchestra sounds big, bright, and ballsy, wonderfully impressive in 1945, and still "modern" in big-band terms even into the next century. Buddy Childers' scream-trumpet tops the high-powered brass near the start, in direct contrast to the calming interplay between Stan's piano and Max Wayne's bass. Freddie Zito's aggressive trombone solo came to be seen as a Kenton trademark, perfected in future bands by the likes of Kai Winding and Milt Bernhart. But most of all, "Southern Scandal" defies convention, combining elements of swing within a rigid, formal framework. The critics, sensing a further erosion of their traditional reference points, hated it. Kenton fans loved the juxtaposition of the two styles, the intensity of the beat, and the polished, incisive orchestral performance. This was artistry on the cutting edge of modern music, and it took the jazz world by storm, provoking controversy wherever it was played.

In retrospect, 1945–46 are the years when Kenton had the greatest personal impact not only on the *sound* of the band, but also the *music* played. Once Pete Rugolo joined the team, Stan's own abilities were such that he was unable to compete with the complexities of the more advanced music. But by then Stan had clearly defined the orchestra's route, and had won over public support. The future might not always be easy, but if Stan wanted it, that there would be a Kenton orchestra in the years ahead seemed certain.

# 5.

# A New Beginning

## (1945)

During the summer of 1945 Stan was giving serious thought to the future direction of the orchestra. With the end of the war came a desire for change. Public acceptance of the more daring modern bands was growing, the Woody Herman Herd setting a lead, and Kenton became increasingly convinced this was the time to return to the jazz course he had largely abandoned when joining Bob Hope in 1943. As Kenton dramatically phrased it in a famous quote that helped cement his own reputation among fans as a virtuoso of deific proportions: "I remember one morning in Boston, I woke up and I said to Gene Howard, 'Gene, I think the Lord must have spoken to me last night. The clarinets are out. We need a mood—a JAZZ mood.'"[1]

"So the five clarinets backing the boy singer went," Al Anthony remembered. "I never did like their sound, nor could I make any sense of what we were doing, playing fast figures in a very high register: it sounded like we were playing exercises. We lead players are a particular breed of people—we don't hear things the same way as a soloist. But Stan liked my work, and the way I interpreted the book, although many times I didn't really have a good feeling of what I was doing. The music then was very different from some of the later bands. We didn't swing, and I didn't really like the music, but Stan, being the person he was, convinced me to stay. He said the reed section was mine to do what I wanted, and true to his word he meant it.

"I told the section to make their phrases by listening to me—the lead man. Later, I had the idea of not using any vibrato on certain passages, and this gave sort of a choral effect, which Stan liked, though you needed really good players to play in tune. Stan liked deep heavy reeds, so let me tell you about Gioga—we never called him Bob you know. Stan called him 'Jaegus'—old friendship name I guess. He got a big, pure baritone sound, always in tune and a very consistent player. Gioga gave a lot of bottom to the sax section—what more could a lead man want!

"When Bob Cooper first joined he was very young, and not quite strong enough. All the charts were different, so he was taking time to adapt. Needless to say, with confidence and experience, Coop became somebody—and how! But in 1945 Stan had eyes for Vido Musso. He'd been after Vido for a long time, but Vido was always working, and this band was not like Dorsey, Goodman or Herman. Remember, Stan didn't swing, so Vido had his doubts." (Underlining by Anthony.)

Then Musso had a change of heart. For many, Vido's florid tenor is the representative solo voice of the "Artistry" band, which would have been unimaginably different without his overwhelming talents. Al Anthony is generous in his assessment: "I had no problems with Vido. He was a powerhouse player, we respected him for it, and he blended well into the section. And Vido wasn't selfish, he gave Coop a chance to find himself, and helped by giving Coop solos on many of the jazz charts."[2] (Cooper was clearly learning from Vido, and Bob's solos on many broadcasts of "Eager Beaver" are so Mussoish it's difficult to tell them apart—very different from Coop's later reputation as a leading player of the West Coast cool school.)

A major addition to the brass arrived when Ray Wetzel (formerly with Woody Herman) came in for John Carroll at the Paramount Theatre in New York. Ray was a triple-edged talent, since he not only shared the lead with Buddy Childers, but was a capable jazz soloist and comedy singer. More genial than the sometimes irascible Buddy, Stan told me Ray played his fair share in shaping the future sound of the Kenton trumpet section. According to Milt Bernhart, "Ray and Buddy shared the trumpet lead equally. They were such good friends that was never a problem, and the lead parts went back and forth. Buddy didn't always say things that were diplomatic, he spoke his mind. So sometimes he'd hurt people's feelings, and that's the way he was, so he didn't make it with the rest of the band like Wetzel did. Ray was just a good-natured guy, while Buddy was more of the boss. Buddy gave orders to the rest of the players, and there wasn't a lot of argument; he'd been there longer, and he just kind of slid into the role."[3] Nevertheless, it was Wetzel who sat in the central trumpet chair traditionally occupied by the lead player. But the rapport between Buddy and Ray was such that many years later Childers would say, "Ray Wetzel was one of nature's noblemen, a wonderful, wonderful guy. A great trumpet player and a great musician. He was a complete human being."[4]

Eddie Safranski got his chance because Max Wayne was suffering from heart problems that compelled him to quit the band. Stan was desperate to replace Max with a bassist equally gifted, and solicited

Safranski, whom he'd heard playing in Hal McIntyre's band. Safranski welcomed the opportunity of playing in the more challenging Kenton orchestra, but agreed to the move only after McIntyre gave his personal blessing. Eddie Safranski proved to be the ideal Kenton bassist: not only a good time-keeper, but an inventive and imaginative player who saw the instrument as a harmonic as well as a rhythmic voice. Eddie enjoyed an immediate personal rapport with his leader, resulting in many titles opening with piano/bass solo interplay, like that pioneered on "Southern Scandal." In the words of Noel Wedder, "Stan often said God smiled on the orchestra when Eddie Safranski wandered by. His work on 'Concerto to End All Concertos' still sets the standard which all subsequent Kenton bassists aspired to reach."[5] Nevertheless, according to Shelly Manne's biographer Jack Brand, Shelly would voice an opinion that Safranski didn't swing hard enough on the rhythm numbers, one of so many similar dissensions between drummer and bassist over the years it is hard to believe they could all have been coincidental. Stan's requirements were very different from those of the average jazz leader, and a passion for swinging was not always his top priority when appointing rhythm section players.

With the change of musical emphasis came a need for new charts. Gene Roland made one of his perennial reappearances in New York and was rehired by Stan as staff arranger. It was Roland's substantial orchestration of "Just A-Sittin' and A-Rockin'" (recorded on October 30, 1945, at Radio Recorders, now being used by Capitol in place of the smaller MacGregor studio) that gave June Christy her first chance to prove her jazz pedigree with a superior song. Little deference is paid to Ducal tradition in this modern-sounding interpretation of the Ellington-Strayhorn standard, and June escapes the O'Day analogy to prove conclusively that hers is a unique vocal styling ideally suited to the Kenton band. "Artistry Jumps," the up-tempo rewrite of Stan's "Theme," is geared for sheer musical excitement, including a savage solo from Vido Musso, while the final side recorded on this seminal session completes the trilogy of Kenton compositions (along with "Eager Beaver" and "Southern Scandal") that did so much to establish the band's popularity among jazz fans. "Painted Rhythm" is a simple little tune, which would have sounded quite different in the hands of Glenn Miller (smoother) or Woody Herman (looser). The difference lies, as always, in the rhythmic attack, and also in the incisive brass and the tight "edge" to the band. These are the characteristics that set Kenton apart, made him separate, and unique. They are the foundations upon which the Kenton Sound is predicated.

I would judge this came about by necessity as much as choice. The band had been established around Stan's writing, and "swing" in the accepted sense had never been part of Stan's vocabulary. It simply wasn't in his genes. Many will disagree, and Johnny Richards has rightly pointed out that there are many different types of "swing." But the musicians recognized what they regarded as a deficiency, though most were content to remain silent, because Stan was well-liked, a good employer who paid top wages, and his star was on the ascendancy. As he became more popular, so by association did they.

Kenton's problem lay in finding other arrangers who were prepared to write in his style. It is fascinating to speculate how well the band would have fared, or how it would have developed, had Pete Rugolo never left his native Sicily to settle in California at the delicate age of five. Certainly the music would have been very different. It is intriguing to realize that this most American of all composers was by birth 100% southern European. Pete's talent was genetic, but the form it took was due entirely to his environment, and exposure to American music from an early age. It is also instructive that though he was thoroughly schooled in the classics, and had exceptionally been admitted to the all-female Mills College so that he could study with the French composer Darius Milhaud, Pete's major interest was always in "popular" musical culture.

Rugolo had first enjoyed Stan's music during army service, and had even submitted some charts for Kenton's approval based on the band's old, staccato style. Stan particularly liked an ensemble piece with the odd name "Opus a Dollar Three-Eighty" (a title Pete told me had no special meaning),[6] and resolved to bring Rugolo into the band as soon as he became available. Clinton Roemer had a real insight into the work of the various arrangers, because he copied so many of the post-war charts that were written on the West Coast. "I first met Pete in November of 1945 at the Hollywood Palladium," says Roemer. "He and his wife Jan had come down from Northern California, where he was still in the army, to spend a few days with the band. He must have been given an assignment at that time, because he returned as a civilian a week or two later with an arrangement of 'Embraceable You' that I copied on November 26. 'Never Too Late to Pray' followed on December 4. I recall being at the rehearsal for the latter, and the arrangement was something that no one had ever heard the likes of. This was Pete's style from the beginning, and was very different from anything Kenton was writing at the time."[7] But Stan loved the semi-spiritual "Never Too Late," with its off-beat, dissonant introduction, and recorded the title twice, for both Capitol and MacGregor transcriptions. (What singer Gene Howard thought of this sudden change of style is not known!)

The first Rugolo original in Roemer's copy-file is a feature for Ray Klein, dated January 1946 and called "Song for Trombone." The title was just one sign of the close compatability emerging between Kenton and Rugolo. Not for Pete a tricky title like "Clever Klein": both men preferred the more sober image reflected by a serious title for their music. But the rapport between the two went much deeper than their selection of song titles. A strong, enduring bond of friendship and empathy was formed that lasted a life-time, with none of the bad feeling that sometimes existed between Kenton and his later arrangers. I believe the reason was two-fold.

Foremost was the contrast in their characters. Kenton was headstrong, impulsive, forceful, Rugolo quiet, compliant, unassuming. There was no clash of personality, no ego striving for superiority. Rugolo admired Kenton to the point of veneration, a respect that remained undimmed by the passage of time and changing circumstances, and was always willing to accede to Kenton's requirements. Secondly, the two men were equally committed to their music, a common dedication that surpassed all other issues, and enhanced their mutual respect. Rugolo felt himself fortunate simply to be allowed to write without restrictions (something that rarely happened in dance bands), and Kenton was so excited by Rugolo's work he was happy to give Pete that freedom. As Pete said, "I could arrange the way I wanted to, and even compose originals and know they'd be heard. And Stan never said, 'Don't do it that way,' or 'Do it this way.' He was willing to try anything as long as he felt the writer really meant what he was saying."[8]

Gradually, Kenton came to see Rugolo as the band's "artistic" writer, and Roland the "popular" arranger who produced the more commercial music. Roland wasn't pleased at being pigeon-holed, and probably felt excluded by the growing bond between Stan and Pete. It was Gene who produced the hits like "Tampico" and "Shoo Fly Pie" (which reached eighth place in Billboard's Top 20), and enabled Stan to say, "We had kind of a struggle until the end of 1945—gradually the money coming in was a bit more than the money going out."[9] With all the acclaim that is rightly heaped on Rugolo, Gene Roland's influence and effect on the band's music should never be under-estimated.

The band filmed several musical shorts in the Forties, but was only ever featured in one full-length movie, and that was strictly a Columbia B-picture programmer. *Talk About a Lady* (originally *Duchess of Broadway*) starred Jinx Falkenburg and Forrest Tucker, and seemingly Stan plugged neither of the two principal songs from the film, though both had the makings of a hit. "Avocado" is in the "Tampico" genre by the same writers—Allan Roberts and Doris Fisher—with vocal by June, Gene, and the band (Stan is dressed in full Mexican garb, wearing a wide sombrero on his back); while "I Never Had a Dream Come True" is a pleasant enough ballad. Doubtless Stan had his reasons ("Avocado" is pretty corny, though Joe Greene's "I Been Down in Texas" isn't exactly Mozart!), but one might have expected the tunes to have featured in the band's repertoire while the film was playing local theatres. There isn't a single broadcast of either song that has surfaced, let alone anything for Capitol's phono or transcription labels.

The newly formed Capitol Transcription Division was similar to the MacGregor label, in that it supplied 16-inch discs playing at LP speed, for use only by radio stations. Many otherwise-unheard titles have been made available on Mosaic from this source, including a magnificent solo by the versatile Jimmy Simms on "Solitude." (It was Simms in very different mode doing the scream trombone at the end of "Painted Rhythm.") Simms may have been a Bill Harris disciple, but it still amazes how many undervalued jazz musicians there were during the big band era.

Stan once said, "If a leader doesn't have the same musical outlook as his drummer, he's got no band."[10] The percussion chair has always been pivotal to the band's success, and required a man with extraordinary skill, strength, and stamina to move the Kenton monolith. Stan could tell within minutes whether a drummer was going to make it in his orchestra. On the face of it, Shelly Manne was the last person you'd expect to fit; during 1945 he'd been active in the bebop movement Stan didn't much care for, recording with Dizzy Gillespie for Guild, and leading a bop-oriented quartet on New York's 52nd Street.

But Stan saw beyond Manne's immediate role to the musician beneath. "One night," said Shelly, "Stan came into the Three Deuces where I was playing in my own quartet with Allen Eager, and he said he was having drummer problems and liked the way I played, and would I like to join his band?" Manne knew full well that Kenton's was not a bebop band, but then Shelly never was a fully-fledged bebop drummer. "I thought Kenton's was an important new band," said Shelly, "and I welcomed the opportunity to express myself creatively within the context of an orchestra that was stretching the boundaries of big-band jazz. And Stan encouraged me to experiment, not only with rhythms, but also to approach the drums from a more melodic viewpoint." [11] Shelly proved to be the ideal Kenton drummer, and stayed (give or take the odd hiatus) for the next six creative years.

Around the same time in early 1946, the line-up of the famous "Artistry" orchestra moved closer to completion when Freddie Zito quit the trombones, and was replaced by another iconic Kenton figure, the Danish-born Kai Winding. Though Winding would exert a profound and enduring influence on the sound of the trombone section, he was not universally popular among his peers, and Al Anthony for one seems to have preferred the lead work of Ray Klein: "When Freddie Zito left, Ray Klein took over the lead on ballads, and Kai Winding played lead on all the other charts. What a beautiful sound Klein brought to the ballads! All lead men of quality affect the sound of a section—guys in the section copy the lead man's sound without realizing it. That's why when Kai played lead, the trombones sounded so different than when Ray was leading—you never heard a section change sound and timbre so much. Didn't sound like the same section at all!"[12]

The days when Stan would be turfed out of a ballroom half-way through the contracted period were now long gone, as venues competed to attract the band's attendance. The road remained a hard grind, but was compensated by longer bookings, such as the recent eight spectacular weeks at the Hollywood Palladium, the band's fourth major appearance at the West Coast's premier dance spot. At the end of the first month, the Palladium management reported that Stan was breaking attendance records, with the second and third weeks grossing $37,000 and $36,000 respectively. Small wonder that Look magazine in its January 8 issue prophetically nominated Stan Kenton as "Top Band of 1946: the Orchestra most likely to hit the top during the coming year."

# 6.

## The Arrival of Rugolo

### (1946)

Not all long engagements were as welcome as the Hollywood Palladium. There, the band might get day-calls for rehearsals, recording, filming or benefits, but mostly the work was at night. Theatre dates were another matter. In a routine exclusive to the USA, at theatres the band performances alternated with a film throughout the day, as Stan recalled: "The theatres were awfully hard work. We used to do between 5 and 7 shows a day, and the pay was good, but it was just too difficult physically. We worked the Paramount several times, and the first show went on before 9, and the last show got off at 1 a.m., so it was less than 8 hours between the time we finished and the time we had to be back on stage blowing again."[1]

The sheer monotony of waiting around between shows, with no opportunity to leave the theatre for any length of time, did have one positive result for Ray Wetzel, who came up with an idea for a catchy tune that he appropriately called "Intermission Riff." Many writers have pointed out that the theme is identical to a riff used just once near the start of "Yard Dog Mazurka," a 1941 Gerald Wilson composition for Jimmie Lunceford. I have no knowledge of Wetzel ever being queried about this, but in any case, Wilson discards it after a single statement, so that in "Mazurka" it remains undeveloped. Al Anthony recalled, "Between shows at the Paramount Theatre in New York, Wetzel and the guys would blow to get their chops in shape. Wetzel got a riff going, and a few days later a few trombones joined in. Boots came up with a reed counter-melody, and over the weeks we kept adding and adding, all head stuff, and voila! We had a great chart that we played on shows and finally recorded."[2] Readily recognizable, and a great vehicle for ever-changing solo improvisations, "Intermission Riff" became an essential part of the Kenton Experience from that day onward. It remained in the book to the very end, and is rightly revered by Stan's fans as a classic.

A more formal score by Kenton himself that never received its proper acclaim was Stan's 1943 arrangement of the evergreen "More Than You Know." Frequently updated during the Forties (lastly in the summer of 1947 for the Progressive Jazz debut), the chart was not flashy enough to generate excitement, and was never issued commercially until Capitol appropriated it from their Transcription label. Cut in July 1946, this version proceeds directly from the piano/bass introduction into a saxophone soli movement of such authority it remains a living testament to Kenton's writing ability and Al Anthony's alto expertise. Wetzel plays a perfectly straight trumpet solo before the big orchestral conclusion to a musical experience of outstanding poise and beauty.

But Kenton's charts were not sufficient on their own. Every band needs variety, and in early 1946 Gene Roland supplied that demand. Surprisingly, Stan failed to plug Gene's inventive arrangement of Mel Torme's sophisticated modern-blues song "Four Months, Three Weeks, Two Days, One Hour Blues," despite Christy's gorgeous performance. Gene's is a bop-influenced chart that features a spectacular trumpet riff not unlike that heard on Dizzy Gillespie's "Good Dues Blues," though Gil Fuller's arrangement for Musicraft was not recorded till five months later, so Roland may well have been the originator. Whatever, bop did not turn Kenton on, which may be why "Four Months Blues" received so little exposure. The Capitol rendition is the only recording I am aware of.

When Roland was around the band, he invariably got the itch to play. "Gene first showed up in 1944, when the drugs problem wasn't quite as serious, or Stan wouldn't have used him," observed Milt Bernhart. "Gene was talented, and Stan recognized that and went for it. And Roland was able and resourceful; he played in the trumpet section in 1944, and in 1946 he produced a valve trombone and they put him in the trombone section."[3] Buddy Childers' assessment of that situation was less than generous: "Gene was very gifted, but he was a real pain. He kept insinuating himself into the different sections, but he never played *with* the sections. He just messed things up."[4]

In 1946, Kenton was planning his first Capitol album. Seventy-eight rpm jazz albums were unknown in Europe, but in America they consisted of three or four ten-inch shellac discs, housed within thick cardboard covers, usually with attractive technicolor cover designs and copious notes and photos. Expensive to produce, an album recognized that an artist had "arrived." Stan wanted an original for Christy, again in the blues idiom, but which avoided the routine lyrics and clichés. Gene came through with "Ain't No Misery in Me," and on the strength of that asked Stan for a raise, which was refused, causing Roland once again to quit. "Gene simply caught Stan at a bad time," Bob Gioga commented, "and I knew that given time to think it through Stan would change his mind. Roland knew that too, but he wanted a move, and this was his way out."[5] Gene returned to New York, and organized the first four-tenor saxophone band (with Stan Getz, Al Cohn, Joe Magro, and Louis Ott), which later became the Four Brothers sound commonly associated with Herman and Jimmy Giuffre, but which really owes its origin to Gene Roland.

"Over the years, Stan gave Gene a lot of leeway," concludes Milt Bernhart. "He wrote a lot of things so fast that you could tell they were throw-aways. And then Stan would get pretty angry, and tell him, sometimes in front of everyone, 'That's a piece of crap!' If Gene had a genuinely good inspiration, something really worth-while, you'd know the difference, you'd hear it. It was a matter of how long he took. 'Ain't No Misery in Me' was a very fine arrangement. I admired Gene for his writing and originality, like the Latin-American 'Ecuador.' The things Roland wrote for trombones were very playable . . . I recognized Gene's ability, but as a person he was impossible, really."[6]

Gene's departure left the field wide open for Rugolo. At the start of 1946, broadcasts were filled with the charts of Roland and Kenton; by mid-summer, the book was dominated by Rugolo's arrangements, and would remain that way for the rest of the decade. Pete of course was writing within criteria already set by Stan. The *identity* of the band—its sound and rhythmic approach—was already established. What Rugolo brought to the band was a distinct *direction*.

Stan had already hinted at the course he wanted to take with compositions like "Opus in Pastels" and "Production on Theme," but found writing the more advanced music hard. To Pete the skills came naturally, readily, instinctively. "Pete Rugolo was the architect of the Stan Kenton band," observed Allyn Ferguson. "Pete had the academic background that Stan lacked."[7] Bill Russo put it even more succinctly: "Rugolo was able to create Stan's vision in concrete form."[8]

Clinton Roemer recalled that Rugolo, never an assertive individual, was lacking in confidence when he first joined the band (reportedly on a weekly salary of $150). He sought constant reassurance from Stan, and looked to Kenton for support and encouragement. "When I first started writing arrangements," Pete told Terry Vosbein, "for the first six months or so I tried to write like Stan, not simple things, but more his style, and he told me I didn't have to do that, I should write anything I wanted."[9] "We wrote a few things together," Rugolo told Gene Lees. "'Collaboration' was one, but most of the time he just left me alone. He said, 'You know what to do.'"[10] Pete named me just three titles written in unison with

Stan: "Artistry in Boogie," "Collaboration," and "Theme to the West." The fact is, that as he wised-up that Rugolo's abilities far out-stripped his own, Stan was soon content to leave work on the coal-face to Pete.

Of the three titles named by Rugolo, "Collaboration" is by far the most significant, and itself went through an amazing metamorphosis. First conceived and orchestrated as an exciting, up-tempo flag-waver, featuring turbulent saxophone voicings in counter-point with the brass, it seems Rugolo realized the theme would be better served at a slower tempo, and rewrote the orchestration as an impressive concert arrangement for Kai Winding's sensitive trombone. Both versions were recorded for Capitol, the first remaining unissued until the Mosaic release in 1995, by which time no one could recall the circumstances of the rewrite at all.

"Little by little," Rugolo recalled, "I started bringing in the more modern stuff, and at first the guys in the band weren't crazy about it, because they said it didn't swing. They liked Basie. But slowly they came around. The trumpet players especially had never seen writing like it, where they would have to come in at different times and all that, and after a while they started to enjoy the challenge. Saxophones were funny too—people like Vido Musso, who was not a good reader, he'd count on Boots Mussulli to tell him when to come in, 'cos I was writing for the saxes with everybody coming in at different times, not all five of them together.

"I'd bring in some of these progressive arrangements, and the guys had never played anything like that before. They'd say, 'Hey, I have a wrong note here,' and I'd say, 'No, I want you to play it like that.' They were used to playing all the old-time things, and I introduced these new ideas to Stan. He played everything open in the early days, and I liked to experiment with different timbres and tone colors. I'd put maybe two trumpets in a Harmon, one in another kind of mute, and leave one open, opening up all kinds of tone colors. Stan was wonderful, he never changed a note. He thought the more modern the better."[11]

"Pete was the perfect person for Stan," asserted Bill Russo, "and the band played his stuff better than it ever played the rest of us [in later years]. It's because even with the outstanding players involved, [the 1946–'48 edition] wasn't a swing band, and it would be a preposterous assumption for that band to think it was."[12] And Rugolo confirmed: "Truthfully, a lot of the guys didn't like my arrangements, because though there were some people in the band that liked modern music, others just liked swinging, Basie-type things. And they would balk because we played so many of my things that didn't really swing. They weren't supposed to swing, they were supposed to be concert pieces."[13]

As for Stan, he affirmed many times that as far as he was concerned, "swing" was not a priority. John Tynan once asked Kenton to confirm that in his opinion swinging was not an essential ingredient in jazz. "No," Stan replied. "It never has been."[14] And Red Kelly, who played string bass for both Stan Kenton and Woody Herman, once said of the two leaders: "Woody didn't trust anything that didn't swing. Stan didn't trust anything that did."[15]

My own belief is that Stan's music was diluted when he was persuaded to play conventional "swing." There's a private 1972 recording of "Stompin' at the Savoy" with Nat Pierce on piano that swings like the clappers. It's good music. But it's not good *Kenton music*. If the listener wants a swing band, he should turn to Count Basie. Or Buddy Rich. Or Woody Herman. Kenton's music is at its best when uncompromised by unnecessary concessions.

Throughout the Rugolo era (roughly 1946–1948), the myth was maintained that Pete and Stan were sharing the writing equally, in a partnership akin to that of Ellington and Strayhorn. In reality, the alliance was similar only in the compatibility of the two men. Milt Bernhart was always an intelligent observer behind the scenes: "In much of the Rugolo-Kenton writing partnership, Stan might suggest something, and that's about as far as it would go. The man with the pen in his hand was Pete. Stan never had the score paper and was writing something. He stopped doing that. I had the feeling that he didn't mind, because he considered that was a chore he could easily dispense with. If he had an arrangement in his head, he'd have liked somehow to have been able just to project it onto paper. But that wasn't possible, so it was no problem for him to have Pete do the writing. And if Stan had suggestions, Pete would respond, one way or the other, and that's how they meshed."[16]

It wasn't until many years later that Rugolo broke his silence: "Stan might sometimes come up with part of a theme, but more often the actual melody was my own work. Then many times Stan and I would discuss a piece at length, and write what we called a 'menu' or 'map,' such as piano intro, Vido 1st eight, saxophone chorus, Kai solo, and build to a big ending. And then I would go away and write the arrangement, though often as the work progressed I'd have to change radically from the original design. At other times Stan and I would agree about the need for a particular composition, such as a drum number to feature Shelly, and we'd exchange ideas, and then I'd write the piece the way I thought it should be." "But as for Stan actually writing any of the notes, he didn't do anything when I was with the band. Stan was always so busy promoting the band, he never had the time to write any more."[17]

Because of all the conflicting reports, I posed the question directly to Rugolo whether he or Stan ever literally completed each other's orchestrations, and Pete gave an unequivocal one-word answer: "No." That nothing was done to dispel the notion that this was a common-place occurrence was due to Rugolo's easy-going nature and respect for Kenton, and to Stan's reluctance to surrender his traditional writing position within the band. Clinton Roemer dismisses the notion in his characteristically blunt way: "If there'd been two hands on any arrangements, the transition would have been like night to day."[18]

The fact remains that a number of the compositions (though never the orchestrations) were credited to both writers. It wasn't unusual for bandleaders to demand a share of the composing credits (and hence the royalties) in exchange for their band playing the piece. (Charlie Barnet and "Skyliner" is a well-chronicled example.) But I am certain that was never Kenton's motive. Rather, the band had been built upon his own writing, and it was going to take time for him to be ready to accept that his role had been overtaken by others. Clinton Roemer confirms that view: "I believe Kenton must have felt the need to take some of the credit for the change in style that Pete had brought to the band."[19] Very few composers would have so easily acquiesced, but Rugolo simply didn't care. "Pete was a sweetheart," Bill Russo told me. "I mean, I'm not a terrible person, but I'm not quite as complaisant as Rugolo."

Rugolo's formal training and innate capability enabled him to integrate classical elements from Bartok to Stravinsky into the music, along with an unprecedented emphasis on dissonance and different time signatures, all the while retaining a jazz feeling without reliance on a 4/4 beat. And Stan was able to tweak Pete's charts, knew instinctively how a piece should be played, and then feed it into his own orchestra so that it came out pure Kenton. In a role comparable with that of the famous classical conductors, Stan's direction and authority lay behind every fresh conception that the band created.

But Stan undeniably needed Pete (and the many writers who followed him) in order to work his magic on music that was radical and fresh. Bill Russo comments on the enormous influence Kenton had on his composers: "Stan's encouragement of his arrangers was powerful and convincing—he got people to do things they might not otherwise have done. He always tried to get the best out of people and frequently succeeded. Pete Rugolo was the perfect person for Stan, because Pete was one of the first to apply an extensive symphonic or non-jazz compositional technique to the jazz orchestra. Rugolo was without doubt the initiator of Third Stream Music."[20] Stan and Pete preferred the term Progressive Jazz.

# 7.

# The Artistry Orchestra

## (1946)

Whoever initiated the name "Progressive Jazz"—and evidence points to Rugolo—the term did not come into immediate widespread usage. The 1946 band was referred to by the more established title "Artistry in Rhythm," and remains perhaps the most popular of all the Kenton orchestras. That was certainly the view of Bill Russo: "I was infatuated with the Artistry orchestra, I was thunderstruck and amazed by that band. In some ways I think it was the greatest of all the Kenton bands, which is not received opinion at this moment."

The fine-tuning of the Kenton Style and Sound was completed in 1946. "We were trying to standardize a manner of playing—a conception of how the music should be played," Stan explained. "The arrangers would write a piece of music, then we'd stand up in front of the band and 'sing' it, until the guys would catch on as to how we wanted it played. I felt we should standardize it, so that when the band had a piece of music in front of them, they'd pretty well know how they were going to treat and interpret it. Wetzel was a big help, and we found that if Ray couldn't sing it, it couldn't be played. I'd ask Ray to sing the intro of an arrangement, and I'd say, 'You guys hear that, now do it.' By 1947 the conception became standard, and it hasn't really changed much since 1947. All our rhythmic principles and so forth that we applied then have applied ever since. Wetzel was not only a great first trumpet player, he built other trumpet players. He would take young guys and instil confidence in them, until all of a sudden he'd made a first trumpet player out of them. We were all very fond of Ray and had tremendous respect for him."[1]

"And the higher the trumpets played," noted Bernhart, "the more Stan wanted. Stan wanted the trumpets to be in the stratosphere. It was really a matter of getting five trumpet players that could play high."[2]

Probably because the section was only four strong until Skip Layton joined in the fall of '46, the trombone sound was the last to be fully developed. As Phil Herring noted, "We have five trombones, and nobody else does, which makes it special. And really if you listen closely enough, you'll find that the band is actually centered around the trombone section. It's the sound that Stan likes, I think."[3]

The catalyst who brought about this permanent development in the structure of the orchestra was Kai Winding, who built the section into an extension of his own lyrical, yet forceful solo style, as Milt Bernhart confirms: "Kai Winding was the lead trombone in 1946, and without question the most important player in the band at that time. His style was unique, and Stan wisely allowed him much freedom. Even when playing lead over the section, Kai would change figures and inflections as his feelings dictated, and we all got pretty good at anticipating this and following him. It was kind of a game, like a steeplechase. Sometimes Kai would even become nettled because we had second-guessed an especially intricate variation on the original part, but it certainly kept us on our toes."[4]

Bill Russo, who wrote so well for the trombones himself a few years later, explains: "Kai Winding's influence came from within the band. Probably more than any other player Kenton has had, Winding influenced the way the orchestra played. He formed the trombone section into an expansion of himself; he somehow got this section of unwieldy instruments to play with speed and lightness and flexibility and with very subtle inflections. This was a soloistic approach to ensemble playing, and it spread to other sections of the orchestra."[5] (This soloistic approach wasn't quite as radical as Russo might seem to suggest. Kenton had advocated the idea often, and applied it himself, especially to the saxophones, since 1940.)

Kai's next big contribution was over the use of vibrato within the band. Echoing Anthony's concept for the reeds, Kai explains: "Before I went with Kenton, most brass sections used lots of vibrato—big, fat wah-wah tone. I didn't much like vibrato. Still don't. I got the trombones blowing very pure, very straight, and pretty soon the rest of the band was doing the same thing. Instead of a sweetish, melodious quality, we had this tremendous zing, a kind of open blare that hit the audience right between the ears." (That famous Kenton "wall of sound"!)

Nor does Winding overlook the importance of Stan's qualities of leadership: "Kenton gave us our heads. There were no rules at all. . . . And the more far out the better. He really was hot in front of a band. Pete Rugolo used to bring in his arrangements to rehearse before Kenton took over. Pete was a very quiet, well-mannered guy, but he knew his work, and he knew everyone else's too. He'd rehearse us and it would sound fine. Then Kenton would charge in, shouting and swearing, and he'd get us so excited we'd blow our heads off. He was terrific."[6] Of course, Kenton "gave everyone their heads" because Rugolo and the section leaders were producing exactly the sound and the music he loved—and the public was eating it up. Let anyone deviate, and I fancy they'd have been collecting their cards before they could have uttered the verboten word "Bebop"!

Milt Bernhart explains the final part of the equation: "Pete Rugolo had been trained as a symphonic composer, and he decided to write for the trombones in a choral style. He spread out the voicings so that there was a large distance between the top and bottom horns. That spread of notes is the exact reason for the distinctive sound. Plus, Kai Winding played lead with less vibrato than normal, obtaining an almost symphonic sound. In the years that followed, whoever played lead it became the unwritten law that this style was to be the standard operating procedure. And so it was. Myself, Bob Fitzpatrick, Bob Burgess, Kent Larsen, Dick Shearer—we all carried on that particular style of leading the trombones, even though none of us really played the same way at all. It was the way Stan wanted it."[7]

On a personal level, Milt felt far less gratified: "I sat next to Kai in the section, and he seldom spoke to me. I didn't challenge Kai in any way, but he was not very friendly. So when Skip Layton came on the band, taking solos and sometimes leading the section, it struck Winding hard, and he resented it. He was very unhappy about the introduction of a player who could go beyond anything that he could do. Obviously that's a threat, and I don't think Kai ever spoke three words to Skip. Kai was special as a trombone player, but he didn't have the endurance to play all the lead in that band. When we played a dance date that lasted maybe four hours, somewhere in the middle of the evening he'd begin to get a rasp and miss most of the notes, and then slam his horn down after we'd played something. He was a prima donna, and I was not too thrilled about that. It got so bad that Skip, Harry Forbes, and I all independently offered our resignations to Stan around the same time. We hadn't discussed it together, there was no conspiracy, but Kai was just not showing us any kind of respect. Stan promised he'd talk to Kai, but whatever Stan said it didn't change anything."[8]

The cause of Winding's behavior may have been partly because despite his achievements, he was not gaining total personal satisfaction from his role. Kai was at heart a bebop player, as he explained: "Kenton's was a very exciting band, and interesting in many ways, but it wasn't a straight-out, swing-type, cooking band with the emphasis on soloists, and it wasn't as bop-oriented as other bands."[9]

None of this dissension in the ranks shows in the music that flowed from Rugolo's pen. "Willow Weep for Me" became the first song with Kenton to become a permanent part of the Christy canon. As her voice matured, June would technically sing the number better in future years, but as so often with jazz, this first recording remains the definitive version. June's sensitive vulnerability, Winding's mournful trombone, and Rugolo's masterful Debussy-styled orchestration fuse so well that "Willow" became the perfect example of virtually a new art form, in which a jazz mood could be expressed by means of implied tempo rather than an explicit beat.

Shelly Manne was a drummer of two parts. Nothing gave him more satisfaction than swinging a big band, but at the same time he was fascinated by Kenton's conception of the drums as a melodic instrument. Stan wanted a drums feature that would showcase Shelly as part of an integrated orchestral composition, rather than the mindless drum solos that most bands promoted (and which Shelly himself hated). Manne worked closely with Rugolo to produce "Artistry in Percussion," which Stan loved so much he revived the Stravinsky-influenced composition in 1972 for another of his favorite drummers, John Von Ohlen.

Kenton changed the title of "Artistry in Bass" to "Safranski" out of respect for his gifted double bass player. It's a fleet demonstration of Eddie's skills, and a full-scale celebration of the piano-bass duets that opened so many arrangements from this period. Safranski's accomplished performance benefits from his early classical training, as he bows and plucks his way through Rugolo's impressionistic composition.

Copyright restrictions prevented an outright performance of Ravel's "Bolero," so Rugolo wrote an original utilizing the rhythms of this Spanish dance, building from a quiet beginning to a fiery finale, with graceful contributions from Musso and Winding en route. With typical modesty, Pete comments, "I just wrote a simple thing, but it builds pretty good."[10] (He named it "Artistry in Bolero.")

Rugolo was equally adapt at writing modern arrangements of the many standard tunes that filled the "Artistry" book, like "I've Got the World on a String" and "Peg O' My Heart." Equally often it was the exhilarating performances that turned more mundane material ("Across the Alley from the Alamo," "The Spider and the Fly") into minor works of art. And Stan got into the act by updating some of his earlier arrangements.

"Concerto to End All Concertos" must be one of Kenton's finest personal achievements, so-titled because Stan wanted to make fun of the many jazz tunes being called "concertos" at that time. This two-part work features a strong, melodic theme at its core, with a secondary, up-tempo march acting as a foil, and it is the difference between these contrasting motifs that accounts for much of the tension and release in this richly textured composition. Part One is much the flashier, with a beautifully apposite solo from Vido Musso, followed by Wetzel's shout in the stratosphere, and an awesome Mussulli solo of such fleetness it appears to glide effortlessly from his horn. But the best is yet to come, as each section in turn defines the Kenton Sound via sectional soli on the main theme: the full-toned, vibratoless voice of the magnificent trombone choir led by Kai Winding; a gorgeous saxophone stanza, with the widest possible spread between Gioga's deep baritone and Al Anthony's alto lead; and the pure, perfectly blended trumpet trio probing Stan's paraphrases of the melody. And finally, a return to the up-tempo theme and a rousing flourish to wind things up. "Concerto" remains to this day a major contribution to Modern Music, and arguably Stan's most ambitious original composition.

I asked Bernhart why only three trumpets were featured on the sectional solo: "When Stan wrote it in 1942 he had only three trumpets, and that's how it stayed. It's orchestrally effective as a trio . . . The three horns playing quietly and without vibrato get a kind of extra-terrestrial feeling that Stan envisioned. Add one more trumpet, and the result might come dangerously close to Harry James."[11]

And Buddy Childers recalled, "My biggest satisfaction with the band was managing to play things like the trumpet trio from 'Concerto to End All Concertos.' It was hard, because it starts so soft, and then it goes up to high F and gets very loud, and then comes back down again. And that's the way it should be played. I think to this day that the record we made in 1946 was by far the best presentation, although the one you always hear is from *Kenton in Hi-Fi*, but to my taste there was not nearly as much soul in that."[12]

Riding on Kenton's coat-tails, Vido Musso's career was at its peak, thanks especially to a hit recording of "Come Back to Sorrento" from Stan's *Artistry in Rhythm* album. The musicians hated this over-blown schmaltz, but it hit the public fancy, and Stan called for it often. Regardless of his lack of leadership qualities due to an inability to connect verbally with an audience, plus a business acumen the size of an amoeba, Vido determined this was the time once again to form his own band, and gave Stan his notice, leaving the way clear for Red Dorris to rejoin Kenton.

In one sense, Red was as much a casualty of war as those physically harmed, insofar as the hero of the 1941 band was now a bit-player, unable to regain his past position. Milt Bernhart spells it out: "I was in the army with Red Dorris, and Red had a bad drinking problem. By the time he got back to Stan in 1946 he had lost everything. Red demanded his job back on the GI Bill, so Stan had to take him, but he wasn't that thrilled. So Red came back on, but he couldn't really co-ordinate, and there was immediate trouble. His playing just wasn't up to it. And he'd go out at night still in his uniform, and come back the next day with stains all over his clothes. Sitting on that stage with a band that was usually immaculate, that really did it for Stan. Red was a good jazz player, a little bit like Ben Webster, he could get that raw sound, and if he'd kept his brain he might have been able to make it work. But it was the booze, he was drinking all the time. It had started even back in 1941, but he was younger then and could cope better."[13] Red split after a few months, ending up in a Dixieland group, by which time Musso's band had inevitably folded, and by mutual agreement Vido was welcomed back into the Kenton fold.

According to the Kenton publicity machine, the men in suits at Capitol had passed down an edict that Gene Howard was to make no more recordings, which effectively meant he was out of the band. Gene would have known full well that Kenton must have been consulted first, and that Stan agreed with Capitol's reasoning that Howard-the-dance-band-crooner no longer jelled with the band's growing reputation as a jazz outfit. Gene was naturally devastated, but Stan softened the blow by offering him a post in charge of promotion and publicity, and the ex-singer retained strong links with the band until 1954.

Herb Jeffries was touted as replacement for the band's important upcoming date at New York's Paramount. As always, the official explanation of why it didn't happen (that Jeffries was unable to break his Exclusive recording contract) doesn't tell the full story, as Herb revealed: "I didn't really want to belong to a group, especially if I could make more money as a single. And there was a little pride involved—I wanted to see if I could fly on my own."[14]

Even without Jeffries on board, Milt Bernhart says, "The Paramount Theatre in the Fall of 1946 was a momentous engagement for Stan. It was a big show, lines around the block for the first couple of weeks, because the program was very interesting, with Stan, June Christy, Nellie Lutcher, The King Cole Trio, and the motion picture was *Blue Skies* with Bing Crosby and Fred Astaire. So you can imagine, that's a blockbuster. We played to full houses every day—5 or 6 shows. We always played the things that the people wanted to hear: 'Concerto to End All Concertos,' 'Lover,' 'Collaboration,' and Shelly on 'Artistry in Percussion.' It was a good band show, and very demanding. 'Concerto' was an impressive composition in itself, but especially on that stage with that lighting;

they'd spotlight the soloists, and in the second part bring the lights up and down for the various sections—it was about as good as it got."[15]

Even so, Stan was aware that however good the band sounded live, it was by the sound of its recordings that it would be judged and remembered. He wanted to create the big, fat sound of the sections on records at a time when recording skills were far from the sophisticated techniques of today. So Kenton involved himself in every aspect of recording, trying new ideas and supervising the technical side as well as the creative, as Capitol producer Bill Miller recalled: "I was never directly involved with Stan until 1945, when he moved from the MacGregor Studios on Western Avenue to Radio Recorders on Santa Monica Boulevard. I was however a Kenton fan, and hence attended most of the sessions produced by Lee Gillette and Jim Conkling, and Stan and engineer John Palladino were a very inventive recording team.

"Stan told us, 'You've got to find a way to make the saxes sound big and gutsy.' So we put a ribbon mike about six inches above the floor, and the guys stood around that. When we first miked the saxes the mike was up high, and the sound was going up, but this new technique gave us the middle and bottom saxophone sounds which were missing when the saxes were picked up in the old, conventional way. But it was Kenton's loud, high brass which gave us the most trouble, as too many of our components were not distortion-free, as they are today."

The problem was overcome by using the echo chamber device installed at Radio Recorders, which added artificial reverberation, causing an otherwise "flat" sound to resemble the depth of sound heard in a large hall. As Stan phrased it, "We could have held the volume of the band down, but then we wouldn't have created the sound we wanted. By using the echo chamber, Capitol's engineers were able to record the brass with the wide, open sound we were after. It's almost as if you're standing right in front of the band, and there's no sound in jazz that's any more thrilling than a sound that is positively recorded like that."[16]

Both in person and on records, the Artistry music sounded RIGHT. The musicians knew it, and the audiences instinctively sensed that this band was HOT. The best of Stan's music had a magical, almost mystical quality, that exerted a profound influence on impressionable youngsters. It touched their inner selves and colored their lives in a way that defied rational explanation. I know, because I was one of them. The brassy excitement of "Machito," the wistful sadness of "Willow," the robust romanticism of "Collaboration," would sear the subconscious in such a way that the music remained an integral force for the rest of life. Glenn Miller might be remembered for nostalgic reasons. Kenton was an heroic figure, on a creative plane far removed from that of mere dance music.

The year 1946 was in fact good in general for modern bands. Many added the odd "progressive" piece to their library (like "Sherwood's Forest" by the Bobby Sherwood outfit), but several pursued a more persistent modern policy. The most successful was Stan's old "adversary" Woody Herman. Audree Kenton confirmed there was an intense and personal rivalry between the two leaders. Stan envied Woody's acceptance by the critics, and his vocal popularity, while Herman yearned to be a concert attraction like Stan. To this end, Woody's chief arranger Ralph Burns wrote the extended works "Summer Sequence" and "Lady McGowan's Dream," and to show he was serious about these ambitions, Herman achieved a first by engaging that most eminent of all modern classical composers Igor Stravinsky to write a piece especially for his band, though "Ebony Concerto" attracted very mixed reviews.

Other bands fared less well commercially. Dizzy Gillespie was attempting his first (and some think most musically successful) foray into big-band bebop, notable for such Gil Fuller charts as "One Bass Hit" and "Things to Come." The short-lived Earle Spencer band came superficially closest to the Kenton approach, with an unashamedly copy-cat style that never did establish its own identity, but seemed rather a caricature of the genuine article. The most seriously progressive band of all, which carved a genuine niche in the idiom, was that led by Boyd Raeburn. Chief arranger George Handy ("Dalvatore Sally," "March of the Boyds") was a gifted original, as were Ed Finckel ("Boyd Meets Stravinsky") and Johnny Richards ("Man with a Horn"). In 1946 the Raeburn band was probably musically even more advanced than Kenton, but without Stan's staying power. Boyd had failed to build a fan base, and he recorded for Jewel, a small label without Capitol's publicity channels or distribution network. Milt Bernhart played briefly with Boyd in the summer of 1947: "It was a challenge far beyond Kenton, and much more demanding. The only thing wrong with the Raeburn band was that very few people were coming to hear it."[17]

Within a very few years, each of these bands had either thrown in the towel, or reverted to a more danceable music. Only Kenton would remain defiantly progressive well into the next decade.

# 8.

# Artistry off the Rails

## (1947)

**As 1947 dawned, Stan Kenton had** achieved just about everything he had set out to accomplish in music. Stan had every reason to be satisfied, but below the surface problems were accumulating. For six years almost without a break, Kenton had driven himself at a pace that would have exhausted most men within a month, and for the first time in his life he was feeling tired. The constant travelling, lack of sleep, snatched meals, and ever-present cigarettes were having their effect. Once they reached a hotel the guys could often relax before that night's performance, but for Kenton it meant another round of radio shows, intensive interviews, personal appearances. Everyone wanted a piece of Stan Kenton.

On top of that, Violet was giving him grief. They had planned the orchestra together, but for Violet the dream had turned sour, for the simple reason the couple had no home life together. Stan was constantly on the road, and even the short periods he was able to sleep over, his mind was as much on music as marriage. Violet had become a grass widow, and their daughter Leslie can hardly have known who her father was. Now Violet was hassling Stan that if their marriage was to last, somehow he had to spend more time with her, and that demand was incompatible with leading a road band. Kenton was truly between a rock and a hard place.

Medical advice was that Stan should take a complete rest or face a total breakdown. In his own words: "The pressure was such that I was never at home. I began to worry a great deal about my family. I felt my marriage was going on the rocks. I began to blame the band. We had been going at such a great pace, I felt like I wanted to take time out to patch up my marriage."[1] *Down Beat* put it even more bluntly, saying Kenton "is on the verge of a nervous breakdown, as a result of six years of steady work at a grueling pace to push his band to the top of the name list, a condition aggravated by worry over the divorce suit recently filed by the wife on the coast."[2]

When it came to a contest between band and family, music usually won. With the orchestra booked solidly for months ahead by binding contractual commitments, Stan decided he had no option but to continue as planned. He tried to convince Violet this was the right move, to throw off his exhaustion, and continue with the normal routine.

Having unseated Gene Howard from the crooner's chair, Stan now decided he wanted to experiment with a vocal group, an attraction more commonly associated with dance bands than a jazz unit, leaders in the field being Glenn Miller's Modernaires and Tommy Dorsey's Pied Pipers. (True, Woody Herman had his Blue Flames, but they were so ineffectual as to be instantly forgettable.) Kenton cast envious eyes on Mel Torme's Meltones, a hit with Artie Shaw's band, but they weren't available, and anyway Stan always preferred originality over the obvious. Dave Lambert was hired to organize a new group, a surprising choice in view of Dave's bebop background. Lambert elected to go with the usual four guys and a girl, and Stan named them The Pastels, after his famous saxophone composition.

The result was a highly professional vocal group, slightly more "husky" than the Modernaires, but one that broke no new ground in the idiom in the way The Four Freshmen would do a year or so later. Stan would complain they lacked a jazz phrasing, but in fairness the material they were given was generally not of a jazz nature, and was clearly designed with the aim of producing hit recordings.

Much care went into the making of their first record, a calypso novelty called "His Feet Too Big for de Bed," but it bombed, and it was the ballad B side "After You" that instead became a minor Kenton classic, and was recorded with the band in later years by both The Modern Men and The Four Freshmen. "I was commissioned by Stan Kenton to organize The Pastels, and write their first book of arrangements," Lambert confirmed. "I sang with them only on the occasion of their first recording date, because Don MacLeod, the last member to join, had not been with the group long enough to learn the arrangements, hence my participation. Once they left New York immediately after the record date, my work was done, and Pete Rugolo took over as vocal coach."

The Pastels came closest to a jazz sound on the (professionally unrecorded) Ellington classic "Just Squeeze Me," and Capitol's "By The River Ste. Marie," but they failed to register with the public, and in terms of hard cash represented by five extra pay packets, were not a good investment. They lasted a scant three months with the orchestra before Stan let them go. The group returned to New York and oblivion.

"His Feet Too Big" is today more noteworthy as the first occasion on which Stan augmented the band with extra Latin musicians on bongos and maracas. Jazz bands in the past had often toyed with the Latin idiom, but Kenton was the first leader to realize the vast potential offered by these forms of rhythmic expression. Gillespie and Kenton supporters have long argued over which of these bands initiated the trend, but there is no denying that Stan was the first on records, and there is also a major difference in that Dizzy accentuated the Afro side and Kenton the Cuban aspect of Afro-Cuban music. Also undeniable is the fact that Stan continued to make more extensive use of the Cuban influence over the years than any other jazz orchestra. Latin rhythms became an integral part of the band's vocabulary.

If it was the band of Noro Morales that first alerted Stan to the Cuban potential, it was Machito's orchestra that sealed the pact. Stan related: "It was the beginning of 1947 when I first heard genuine Afro-Cuban music . . . a band by the name of Noro Morales. Rugolo and I went to this place called the Embassy Club in New York, and there was this back room where the band was playing and people were dancing. It seemed at first I heard things that sounded like Woody Herman, and then I heard music that sounded like us, and then like Ellington. One guy was dancing by the band, and he said, 'If you think this is good, you go hear Machito!'"[3]

So Stan did just that. According to Milt Bernhart, "Stan went to hear Machito's band up in Spanish Harlem, and he came in raving the next night about what he had heard: the Latin rhythm. Machito's was a very jazz-oriented band, they had a full brass section, they all came from Cuba, and they played very authentic, Cuban-style, which Stan had never heard before. It was quite new in New York at that time, shouts and screams in the brass section, a couple of young trumpet players, and the rhythm—each guy played the same instrument all the time, no doubling, the maracas guy played nothing but maracas, and so forth. Stan found it very exciting, and we made the record soon after named for and dedicated to Machito."[4]

Pete Rugolo was as enthusiastic as Stan, and was indeed probably the one who pointed Kenton in the Latin direction in the first place. "Machito" was Pete's first serious excursion into the idiom, and it also gave him the opportunity to exploit Skip Layton's extraordinary technique. Skip had demonstrated his exceptional range previously on Bobby Sherwood's "T-Bone for Two," and could play at least one octave higher than the trombone's normal range.

"Machito" is written in song format, and could have made a very pretty ballad. (In the album *Artistry in Voices and Brass* it actually becomes "Daydreams in the Night.") It is Rugolo's scoring that turns the tune into an up-beat, Latin-tempoed spectacular, though the suave and polished Kenton ensemble is a million miles from the raw, rough image of the actual Machito orchestra. The breathtaking finale was envisaged in out-line by Pete, but invented in detail by Childers and Layton. According to Buddy, "I wrote the duet ending to 'Machito' at Pete Rugolo's request. Pete said, 'Write something for Skip Layton and yourself in the upper register that's comfortable for you both. Make it spectacular but play-able.' I've never received credit, but the ending was my idea."[5]

Capitol recorded "Machito" twice, the second time largely because Kenton realized the work would sound more authentic with additional Latin instrumentation (so taken for granted today it is difficult to appreciate how radical the move was in 1947), and brought in Ivan Lopes on bongo drums and Eugenio Reyes on maracas. The rhythmic enhancement brought about by these extra musicians is striking.

Because Stan had Kai Winding as featured trombone soloist, Skip Layton was generally restricted to showing off his high-note technique, as on Ken Hanna's arrangement of "How Am I to Know." Skip solos twice, but it's as much a duet feature for Kenton and Safranski as it is for trombone. Milt Bernhart was on the recording date: "Ken Hanna was playing trumpet and writing a little when I joined the band in September '46. Stan really used Ken as a writer when he needed last-minute assistance. Hanna didn't mind, he had Rugolo to get past, so Ken was a second-line arranger. If Rugolo was busy, Hanna wrote really well for the band. Stan didn't know quite what to do with 'How Am I to Know,' and it was barely played, even on a dance job. It was very difficult, and certainly different with Skip playing the lead part. But Kai resented this terribly, it took away from him, and he was the star. For that reason alone we didn't play it much outside of the record.

"The only thing wrong about records for Skip was that visually, if you see what he's doing, that's impressive. But on record his trombone playing three octaves higher simply sounds like a trumpet, which isn't going to make anybody sit up and take notice." (By common consent, Milt's "three octaves higher" is an exaggeration. It's possible Skip could reach two octaves higher, but one is more likely. Cf. Terry Vosbein and Don Reed.) Milt continues: "Skip had a gimmick: he didn't tongue the notes. His tongue was not in the way, something about his throat that he was born with, so he could open it up, and the air came from way down in the stomach (probably like Pavarotti sings—there is a similarity). But you had to be impressed if you were a trombone player, and even a non-musician is going to find it extraordinary. So, he leads the trombone quintet on this very demanding chart of 'How Am I to Know,' playing double-time, and a lot of things that he had to play were way beyond anybody's range, nobody had ever done it, but Skip made it."[6]

Perhaps to appease the voices in the band that claimed Rugolo's writing didn't swing, Pete prepared a long piece (by 1947 standards) running for four and a half minutes that allowed the band to cook. Pete's imaginative title was "Rhythm Incorporated," though for some bizarre reason Cap preferred the rather tasteless "Capitol Punishment." Actually based on the boppers' favorite "How High the Moon," "Rhythm Inc." swings as hard as the '46–'47 band was ever likely to, with Safranski driving the beat, and Manne dropping bop bombs, as Stan's young lions let their hair down in a succession of exceptional solos. It all winds up with breathtaking brass riffs dominated by Layton's unparalleled artistry, which caused the unsuspecting *Down Beat* reviewer to comment, "The human voice that acts as an accessory to the brass in the final screamer is exhibitionistic to be sure, but marvellously effective." *Metronome* was better informed: "The outstanding noises are from trombonist Skip Layton, who swings the entire brass section with his high trumpet-like wails that are nevertheless controlled and in tune." But typically, neither magazine gave the recording their highest rating, which it deserved.

The band was working harder than ever, some nights featuring a two-hour "Stan Kenton in Concert" before a seated audience, and then playing a further two hours of music for dancing. As they began yet another exhausting cross-country tour, not only Kenton was showing signs of cracking up. On April 13 in Mobile, Alabama, June Christy lost her voice completely and had to return home for recuperation, leaving Stan without any singers at all. What especially incensed Stan was the fact her husband Bob Cooper (they'd married in January 1947) insisted on going with her. It all came to a head at the University of Alabama in Tuscaloosa on April 16.

Milt Bernhart recalled, "We were doing one-nighters, crossing New Mexico and Texas with a lot of night-riding, and long distances between locations, and by the time we got to Alabama . . . well, I wouldn't have known that Stan was ready to crack-up, because he didn't show it . . . The date at Tuscaloosa was a concert as I remember, and the curtain came down, and Stan stood in front of the band and he said, 'This is our last night. I'm breaking up the band tonight. The bus will be going to Chicago, and anybody who's going in that direction, if you'd ride with the bus I'd appreciate it, the rest we'll transport you where you come from.' There was a deathly quiet and we all look at each other. Holy cats! This came as a real surprise."[7]

Shelly Manne differs in detail but not in essence: "We were down south in Alabama, and Stan was just so tired from working so hard, he decided one night to throw the whole thing up in the air and take a good rest. There we were in this beat hotel, not knowing what was going to happen, and Bob Gioga came to us and said, 'Well, it's over!' Just like that, and everybody's mouth dropped open, and we got on the bus and made our way back to wherever we started from."[8]

Everyone received two weeks' salary in lieu of notice. Kenton made the news official in a Western Union telegram to Tom Rockwell at GAC in New York, which Rockwell must have made available to *Down Beat*, as it was reproduced in the issue dated May 7, 1947, under the headline "Kenton Too Ill to Go On, Plans Up In Air." Stan had written, in the usual shorthand of telegraphic messages: "Had to break up tonight. Couldn't go further. Am terribly sick. Please notify everyone in the office. As ever. Stan."

That Kenton was exhausted and disturbed to the point of disorientation cannot be doubted. He entered the local hospital for some R&R, then discharged himself to drive home to LA, still in a very confused state of mind. In Arkansas Stan came upon some timber workers sawing and hauling wood, which looked a pleasant occupation, and applied to join them. He was turned down, and resumed his journey. Violet was certainly mollified by the sacrifice Stan had made by abandoning his orchestra, and agreed to take him back, insisting at the same time that he consult a psychiatrist. Stan complied, and later claimed that the treatment had marked a changing point in his life: "Psycho-analysis made me less afraid, I became more sure of myself, and it seemed to remove a lot of inhibitions that I had had to cope with. In other words, I became much more out-going and less fearful, in both my personal life and my music."[9]

The marriage was temporarily saved, but musical ambitions were certainly not changed. Kenton recovered his strength and energy faster than had seemed possible, and by mid-summer was actively planning his return to the band business, though not to the status quo where he had left off. This time he contemplated an orchestra which concentrated on concert music, with as few dances scheduled as possible. The prospect excited Rugolo as much as Stan, and the pair spent many hours at Capitol Records planning the new band. This time the "Artistry in Rhythm" tag would be downplayed. The new music would fly under the unconditional banner of "Progressive Jazz."

# 9.

## Progressive Jazz

### (1947)

Several leading members of the Artistry band failed to respond to Stan's open invitation to rejoin. Christy was very uncertain, but was persuaded by Carlos Gastel she needed more band experience in order to succeed as a single. Vido Musso's rejection was initially seen as a blow, but soon came to be recognized as a blessing. Woody Herman's new Herd was opening frontiers with the Four Brothers saxophone sound led by Stan Getz, and the Musso/Mussulli duo would have seemed decidedly old-fashioned by comparison. Instead, the partnership of Bob Cooper and Art Pepper heralded the modernity of West Coast cool, while the piercing tone of George Weidler's lead alto more than compensated for any loss of volume.

As Pete Rugolo told it, "Vido was more or less the old school, Coleman Hawkins, that type of thing. When Coop took over the solos, he was just the opposite, he was from the Stan Getz school, and that's what those guys liked. Previously it had been pretty much the older school of playing, trumpets from the Roy Eldridge school and people like that, but after Gillespie came in all the guys started trying to play like Dizzy. But we always had high trumpet players; they could all play up to high Fs and Gs, that's why I was able to write everybody screaming with unisons up there. I was very lucky that the guys were so good!"[1]

Kenton liked loud, and he made sure he got it, by adding Al Porcino to returnees Childers and Wetzel: the only occasion the band carried three lead trumpets at the same time. And Rugolo knew just how to obtain the maximum volume on scores like "Soothe Me," noted by *Down Beat* as "probably the loudest ever." Nevertheless, the strain on the players was such that they had to wear abdominal belts in order to avoid a hernia.

Milt Bernhart moved over to first trombone. Though Milt wasn't such an assured improviser as Winding, he more than compensated with his gorgeous tone, described by the English trombonist Roy Crimmins as "The greatest sound I've ever heard on a trombone. I would rather have

Milt Bernhart's tone than all the speed of Watrous or Fontana."[2] Eddie Bert was a fresh face on jazz bone, a young swing/bop player whom Stan believed had potential after hearing him in the Red Norvo band.

Despite the return of Manne and Safranski, the biggest changes occurred in the rhythm section. Until now all guitarists in the band (principally the long-serving Bob Ahern), had been strictly rhythm players, and Stan had no plans to change that, until he heard Laurindo Almeida. A recent émigre from Brazil who spoke no English, Laurindo did speak some Italian, so Pete Rugolo acted as interpreter, and recalled, "Almeida introduced himself to us and sat down and played, and he was good. I remember him playing 'Laura' and some classical pieces, and he told us how much he wanted to play with a jazz orchestra. He impressed us so much that Stan hired him on the spot, and we wrote music to feature him with the band."[3]

The Latin influence was reinforced by the permanent addition of Jack Costanzo on bongos. Costanzo had no language difficulties; his problem was he didn't read music. Eddie Bert relates that "when he came on the band he did just what he heard. There were no parts. He just played what he thought would fit the situation. He had the taste, and I guess Rugolo picked up on what Jack was doing and wrote the bongo parts that way."[4]

At first intended to play only on the Latin numbers, it became clear during rehearsals that Costanzo had a unique role as an integral member of the rhythm section on most titles. Whereas later bands used conga drums simply as an extra rhythmic impulse, Costanzo uniquely employed his bongos more sparingly, and hence more effectively, to enhance the momentum and mood of a composition, the only time I have heard Latin drums extensively used in a jazz band in this way.

Kenton supplied the vision: a fusion of jazz with classical and Latin devices, creating a new, American concert music. Rugolo supplied the charts to fulfill Stan's conception. The most radical change was rhythmic, with greater reliance than ever before on material without a regular 4/4 "swing" beat, the metrical patterns ranging from 5/4 to 7/4 and 3/4, giving much of the music a classical timbre, taken to extremes on titles like "Impressionism," "Monotony," and "Rhythms at Work." Kenton was equally enthused by his experiments into Latin music on "Cuban Carnival," "The Peanut Vendor," and the four-part "Prologue Suite." To Stan the rhythm instruments were never the "toys" the trumpet section rather condescendingly called the claves, cowbell, maracas, scratcher, tambourine, etc. they were frequently called upon to play, backed by the authentic Latin flair of Laurindo Almeida and Jack Costanzo. Both these men were steeped in the rhythmic traditions of South America, and introduced crucial changes to the character of the band. They endowed the music of Progressive Jazz with a persuasive Latin flavor, and the music is enriched by their presence.

While others played minor roles (Bob Graettinger's "Thermopylae," Ken Hanna's "Somnambulism"), it was a freshly enthused Rugolo who filled the Progressive Jazz library. The musicians may have preferred the lighter charts like "Pete's Riff" (recorded as "Metronome Riff") and "Pepper Pot," but it was the heavy music Pete enjoyed writing, and which impressed Kenton the most, giving rise to the term "Monster Music" from Stan's detractors.

Certainly it was music that did not fit easily into an accepted category, that spurned improvisation in favor of carefully formulated structures—even many solos were written out—and which relied on sounds and senses as much as melody or harmony. As such, it was not too far different from the objectives of Bartok or Stravinsky, except that Rugolo always maintained an essential jazz feel. In the end, the dissonance and discord proved unacceptable, not only to the critics and musicians, but also to a majority of the fans. It is certainly true that much good music has been spurned during the lifetime of its creators; and at the age of 93 Pete Rugolo remains among us into the summer of 2009. When Kenton is revived in 100 years, I hope it is "Prologue Suite" that prevails, rather than "The Peanut Vendor."

Two pieces represent the extremes of Stan's new music. "Impressionism" is one of the most classical in design, the mood throughout solemn and intense, but bound to jazz by subtle rhythmic phrases and a written duet between George Weidler and Bob Cooper. Stan agreed with Pete's assessment that it was among his best and continued to play the chart well into 1952. More genial is the Latin-flavored "Cuban Carnival" with additional Latin instruments (conga, timbales, maracas) imported from Machito's orchestra. "Carnival" establishes its authenticity as the rhythm instruments enter in turn, culminating with the full frenzy of the fiesta's orchestral climax highlighted by Al Porcino's screaming trumpet.

Many titles fused the two aspects of Progressive Jazz, most effectively by Rugolo's four-part composition, originally recorded as "Stanba Suite" (an amalgamation of "Stan" and "samba") but changed to "Prologue Suite" because it served as an introduction to the new American music that was Kenton's ultimate goal. Pete's most ambitious achievement, and employing every device in the Rugolo canon, "Prologue Suite" was usually played as a first-half concert closer, and was regularly well-received by audiences. Both Kenton and Rugolo are credited as co-composers, but the music has Rugolo's credentials all over it, and Pete told me, "It was Stan's idea to write the Suite, but the music was mostly mine."

Rugolo recognized the unique talents of newcomers to the orchestra and utilized their skills in specially written feature compositions. George Weidler, husband of Doris Day, had already introduced a fresh, classically inclined conception of saxophone playing into the band through his position as lead alto. His powerful sound and unfaltering technical control animate "Elegy for Alto," written in 5/4 time to create an ad-lib effect, though in fact every note was written by Rugolo.

Jack Costanzo's bongos feature in the fleet, exhilarating "Bong Riff" (played at greater length in concert than on the Capitol recording), while Laurindo Almeida, truly a virtuoso on concert guitar, displays his talent on the beautiful "Lament." Both men play a vital role on many pieces, exemplified on the classically inspired "Fugue for Rhythm Section," featuring only a six-man rhythm team of piano, bass, guitar, drums, bongos, and maracas played by Rene Touzet. The percussionists are introduced first and as the melodic instruments enter (guitar, piano, and bass), each is in turn accompanied by one from the opposite section, until all are playing contrapuntally. "Fugue" is an ingenious concept, a complex fusion of this early music technique with modern instruments.

June Christy was at first ill-served with a succession of novelty-type numbers— "Curiosity," "He Was a Good Man," "I Told Ya I Love Ya"— while Rugolo struggled to find a way to involve her in the new music. The breakthrough came when Pete rearranged "Lonely Woman" (originally a Milt Bernhart trombone solo) as a vocal feature. Abstract throughout, with never more than an implied beat, and full of modern dissonance and harmonies, Christy relishes the challenge of this intricate chart. Kenton loved her strong performance, and encouraged Rugolo to arrange more songs in similar vein ("Over the Rainbow," "I'll Remember April"). Then as a coup de grace, Stan decided to go one stage further, and have June recite a dramatic poem against an abstract musical background. Stan chose the verse (by Audrey Lacey, a young college student), but as usual allotted Rugolo the composing chores.

"'This Is My Theme' bothered June," recalled Bob Cooper, "because there were no lyrics, just spoken words, which she had to recite to Pete's orchestration, and she told Stan she didn't want to do that, because she felt so uncomfortable. But we rehearsed it enough for June to really know the piece of music. Stan was adventurous, and that's what he wanted the band to be, out in the forefront of creating new music, so he was just trying everything."[5] Christy insisted on recording behind a screen, so the band wouldn't see how embarrassed she was: "And I made Stan promise me I would never have to perform that work in public. He gave me his word, and I never did."[6] Listening to the seven takes (several incomplete) it took to record "This Is My Theme," it's fascinating to hear June grow in confidence and authority as Rugolo coaxes the perfect performance from her. The poem is intended to convey feelings and moods rather than a story, and June recites with dramatic sensitivity against Pete's appropriately abstract orchestral accompaniment. "This Is My Theme" is an absorbing experiment, a complex fusion of words and sounds that preceded the 1950s vogue for jazz and poetry by several years, but it was one that would never be repeated.

In concert, some 50% of the music actually emanated from the Artistry book, which was more conventional jazz, at least by comparison, and audiences tended to receive everything played with enthusiasm, so that Stan could easily delude himself that fans were accepting "Impressionism" as fervently as "Artistry Jumps." Capitol knew better, especially after the release of the band's second album, *A Presentation of Progressive Jazz*, containing eight sides of the heaviest music, and with the most musically detailed notes ever attached to a popular album. It sold well enough on the Kenton name, but not in the same major league as the previous *Artistry in Rhythm*. On singles, Capitol soon learned to pair a "Thermopylae" with "The Peanut Vendor," a "Theme to the West" with "Curiosity." Best sellers of all were two "jump" numbers back to back. Already Carlos Gastel and the suits at Capitol were getting nervous, to the extent that Stan's announced album release of *Prologue Suite* was cancelled altogether. The four movements were not linked thematically, so it was relatively easy to give them separate titles and pass them off as individual pieces, to be issued piecemeal over several years:

Part 1 became    Introduction to a Latin Rhythm

Part 2 became    Chorale for Brass, Piano and Bongo

Part 3 became    Abstraction

Part 4 became    Journey to Brazil

Thus was Rugolo's major work emasculated, but the truth was "Machito" and "Lover" sold records. "Monotony" and "Thermopylae" did not. Stan had to accede to a degree, but such was his own conviction in the new music, he believed he could carry the people with him. And he did, but not in sufficient numbers. Even musicians like Milt Bernhart were skeptical: "Stan decided he wanted concert music, not Stravinsky, but something like that, non-directional, impressionistic, modern American music—forget about the dance floor. That music to me was pretentious, not a lot of fun to play, and tough on audiences. But Stan kept banging away, he wouldn't let up, though during a concert there would certainly be enough accessible music so the audience wouldn't leave early. But I didn't get a lot of enjoyment out of some of those charts, and nor did most of the other people."[7]

According to Eddie Bert: "When it came to Progressive Jazz, Stan had something in mind that he wanted to do, and I think he more or less did it. But that band swung as well. We were playing the Kato Ballroom in Mankato, MN, and we were squashed together, elbows touching and all that, and the band started swinging. And Stan stopped us. He said, 'Gentlemen, this is not Basie. This is Stan Kenton.' And we were looking at each other like, 'Wow! We finally got it off the ground, and he stopped us!' But we did play arrangements that swung: 'Harlem Holiday,' 'How High the Moon,' and 'Unison Riff,' though I never heard Stan swing on piano, it was more like sounds. When he did play rhythm piano, it didn't add very much. He played more for mood and effect."[8]

Some numbers from the Progressive library did make it into the permanent book—generally the least progressive! "Interlude" originated at the tail-end of Artistry, but is associated with the late '47 band, a melodic ballad in song format, with lyrics added later by Bob Russell. As Rugolo recalled: "One time we were playing a hotel for dinner-dancing around 7 o'clock, and the owner wanted some softer music while people were eating, so Stan asked me to write some simpler arrangements, muted brass, piano solos, and so forth. That's how I came to write 'Interlude,' which I thought was just going to be used for dinners, but as it worked out it became a popular song. Very few of the things I wrote ever sold much, and I think I've made more money out of 'Interlude' than any other piece. All the other stuff I wrote for Stan, I get small statements, but not a lot of money. I never made a penny, ever, on any of my own Columbia or Mercury albums!"[9]

Neal Hefti's bebop arrangement of "How High the Moon" became a standard for June Christy that she sang for the rest of her career. Audree Kenton elaborates: "June and Bob were nice people together. Most of the things that sounded so improvised with June were ideas that Bob [Cooper] had worked out for her. He always coached June, and the things that sounded so spontaneous when June did them, like the bop vocal on 'Moon,' were often taught her by Bob. He deserves more credit than he got—Bob was always there in the background."[10]

But it was the improvised "Peanut Vendor" that gave Kenton one of his most durable hits of all. Stan wanted to make some records with Machito's rhythm section, and brought in a copy of the sheet music to a rehearsal. According to Milt Bernhart, "Stan began the riff at the piano, Shelly Manne picked up the rhythm, and I played the melody from the sheet music. We fashioned a head arrangement that first night. Trumpets did something, but not as much, it wasn't so elaborate. The trumpet figures came from Buddy Childers, Ray Wetzel joined in, and it built from there, until a month later we were ready to record. Machito brought along some rhythm players from his band, and they were very good. Shelly was probably the most excited person in the studio, because he'd taken an interest in Cuban rhythms, and was really in his element. He enjoyed every minute of it. I couldn't imagine what had gotten into Stan to make him decide this old war-horse was going to amount to much—but it did, and in a very big way."[11]

Never committed to paper, the repetitive rhythms and high-blasting trumpets of "Peanut Vendor" formed a mesmerising combination, and while the interpretation continually changed over the next 30 years as different bands all sought to add their mark, the basic ingredients remained constant. To the end, audiences felt cheated without a taste of peanuts at some point in the program. In 1947 Stan would have regarded "Peanut Vendor" as little more than a novelty, far inferior to the complex Rugolo music. It was Kenton's cross that throughout his career, so many of his followers preferred the frivolous to the serious.

The Progressive band's first extended engagement was in its way as ill-fitting as the Roseland Ballroom had been in 1941, but New York was still the prestigious Big Apple, and with venues competing for Stan's services, GAC naturally accepted the most lucrative offer: a four-week booking in the Century Room of Manhattan's Commodore Hotel. Accounts of the date are contradictory. Probably the truth lies somewhere in between. Michael Levin's contemporary report in *Down Beat* was positive: "First week's engagement was a healthy 2,700 covers. Thing which characterized the Kenton opening and the band's performance since, was its enthusiasm. Not since the halcyon days of the Herman Herd have so many men on a stand played so much so loud with such apparent pride and enjoyment. Not in some years has a hotel crowd stood around a bandstand, watched avidly, cheered, applauded and yelled at everything the band did. This is the first time a band has fought back, said THIS IS OUR MUSIC. IF YOU DON'T LIKE IT, DON'T COME! The people are coming and liking it."[12]

Fifty-five years later, Noel Wedder painted a very different picture: "The Century Room was not a particularly up-beat engagement. No one danced while I was there: in fact, there was very little excitement. The audience, sparse as it was, comprised mainly the upper East Side carriage trade—people who felt the need to participate in everything new, whether they enjoyed it or not. During the set there was very little belching forth of the brass, which I assume was a request from the Commodore management. It was evident by the look on Stan's face, and the continual lowering of his hands to keep the sound down, that he and the band were not having a particularly enjoyable time."[13]

A correspondent identified only as Vic shared his recollection, and evidently caught a very different set from Noel: "It was a miraculous experience! I still have a mental picture of June, in this fabulous evening gown, glowing like a human jewel as she stood before the band. I remember being knocked out by the solo work of Milt Bernhart and Art Pepper, and the spectacle of Shelly Manne 'chopping wood.' But the most overwhelming sensation was the huge sound, the power of that band—like nothing I'd ever heard before. I walked out of that plush Century Room on Cloud Nine, and a convert to the world of Kenton forever."[14]

Eddie Bert played there every night: "We worked the Commodore Hotel in New York for a month, and they tried to get us to play in cup mutes and all that, and it didn't work. I mean, you couldn't play those arrangements in mutes, so we just opened up, real loud. There was a big mirror at one end of the ballroom, covering the whole wall, and Al Porcino would look longingly at all that glass and yell, 'Let's bust that mirror tonight!' We never managed it, but the high trumpets one time did break a mirror at the Adams Theatre in Newark, New Jersey."[15]

These were halcyon times for Stan Kenton. No leader had ever striven harder to reach the top, and that he had done so playing a brand of music more advanced and adventurous than any band before him only added to the achievement. Devotees around the world, many of whom had never heard the band live, let alone met Stan personally, felt a loyalty, an obligation, an affection for this man that went far beyond the ordinary. His music, often created at great personal sacrifice, had marked our lives, and our gratitude was enduring.

And then James Petrillo, president of the American Federation of Musicians, pulled the plug for the second time, ordering a blanket ban on all commercial recording, which effectively silenced posterity's chronicle of this very fine orchestra. It was a blow from which Kenton would eventually recover, but which heralded the end of the big band era for ever.

# 10.

## The Lost Years

(1948–1949)

In 1948 people still wanted to dance, and Stan soon found his plan to concentrate exclusively on concerts unworkable. He blamed a lack of suitable halls, overlooking the fact that had there been the demand, promoters would soon have found the necessary venues. So in essence the band still carried two separate books, dance and concert, though at most dances a portion of the time was devoted to a mini-concert.

Many new charts were added during the year, but being unable to record, most of the comparatively few broadcasts that survive are dominated by the older scores in order to plug the Capitol platters. Despite the band's popularity, AFRS inexplicably neglected the orchestra during 1948, so that most of the new music has been lost for ever, unless a hidden cache should unexpectedly emerge. Titles like "Convertible," "Double Whammy," and "Oogaga" remain no more than names on a band-book listing.

Pete Rugolo remained Stan's indispensable chief arranger, at a time when few of the younger musicians were unaffected by the influence of Bird and Diz on modern music. "Stan didn't like bebop at all," Pete told Terry Vosbein. "I wasn't too crazy about it myself, but I liked to keep up with new ideas in jazz, so I tried to keep the guys happy and wrote a few bop things, but Stan . . . hardly ever played them. I always traveled with the band, Stan wanted me around all the time, and at dances during the last set he'd leave the stand and I'd sit in on piano and play some of the bop things, and he didn't care. I played more like Count Basie-type piano, Stan was so heavy with his Earl Hines style. One of the things I wrote was a tribute-piece called 'Dizzy-Like,' which became 'Artistry in Gillespie.'"[1] It didn't end there, because Pete then rewrote the chart altogether and rechristened it "Design for Brass," but Stan still didn't dig it, and in 1950 gave the score to Vic Lewis, who recorded it for Parlophone (EMI).

Other bebop scores from the Rugolo pen include "June's Bop," a scat vocal for Christy, a reworking of Parker's "Yardbird Suite," and an original called "Three Bop," which Pete changed to "Three Mothers" when Herman's "Four Brothers" chart by Jimmy Giuffre hit the headlines. Under either title the composition was a no-holds-barred bopper featuring Pepper, Conte, and Coop, and the nearest Stan ever got to sounding like the Gillespie band (hear it on Tantara's *Revelations*). When Rugolo rearranged the theme for the 1948 Metronome All Stars small group he renamed it "Overtime" (because of the length of the session), and it was this title Charlie Barnet used when he recorded the big-band chart for Capitol in 1949.

More to Stan's liking was "Theme for Alto," an atmospheric ballad for the full-voiced George Weidler, which Stan recorded in 1951, though by then Weidler was long gone, and an unhappy Bud Shank was called upon to take his place, despite the difference in their styles. At least as impressive was an intense companion-piece for Milt Bernhart's trombone called "Hambeth": a combination of Hamlet and Macbeth, with some of the most trenchant use of dissonance ever conceived. Milt recalled: "The title 'Hambeth' was a joke, a play on words, indicating that I'm a ham actor. We didn't play it a lot, we couldn't record in 1948, and it wasn't a melodic number, it was based on harmonies and movements. I didn't feel comfortable with it, so it just kind of got lost in the shuffle."[2] The only known recording, a 2009 version produced by Terry Vosbein, shows Milt was certainly not exaggerating, though a much simplified Rugolo arrangement featuring Johnny Keating and retitled "Theme for Trombone" was recorded in 1950 by Vic Lewis.

If we are all losers from the Petrillo recording ban, no one's career suffered more than that of Bob Graettinger, who had joined as staff arranger in the fall of 1947. Because of Graettinger's non-conformist lifestyle and the unconventional nature of his music, a mystique has grown around him that almost defies rational explanation. One thing is clear: Kenton and Graettinger stuck together like limpets, Kenton because he was so smitten by Bob's writing; Graettinger because no one but Stan would have dared to play his music in public.

Kenton himself was a man of strong feelings and emotions, and I believe he heard in Graettinger's work an intensity and passion—a SOUND—that gratified his senses. Bob's writing was hard, crisp, skillfully constructed, energetic and LOUD—all the "masculine" attributes that Kenton most admired. Above all, Graettinger elevated Progressive Jazz to its final, logical conclusion—totally different, truly original, often incomprehensible. Better than any other writer, he fulfilled Kenton's aspirations to establish a New American Music.

Bob first burst upon the scene with his 1947 recording of "Thermopylae" (mis-spelt "Thermopolae" by Capitol), presumably named in honor of the Spartans who died defending this narrow Greek pass against the invading Persian army in 480 BC. The somber composition is bereft of solos, or even relief from the repetitive theme and clashing panoply of brass fanfares, and it is hard to deny the opinion of Robert Morgan, Graettinger's biographer, that the work is "Totally depressive, and in the final analysis a weak piece of music."[3] Nevertheless, Kenton told me, "I fell in love with this thing Bob had sent me called 'Thermopylae,'"[4] and Eddie Bert (not noted for his promotion of non-swinging styles) commented, "I was at the rehearsal when 'Thermopylae' was auditioned. We started playing, and I got chills from listening to the trumpets and what they were playing in back of me. It was a good piece of music."[5]

With Stan's encouragement, Graettinger set about writing his magnum opus, which he called "City of Glass." Premiered at Chicago's Civic Opera House on April 20, 1948, the story told by Art Pepper in his autobiography *Straight Life* has become part of Kenton folklore: "It was a miracle we got through 'City of Glass,' an incredibly hard musical experience. Bob conducted it, a tall, thin guy about 6 foot 4. He looked like a living skeleton conducting, like a dead man with sunken eyes, a musical zombie. He took us through it, and he finished and he turned around to the people and he nodded, and the people didn't do nothin'. The place was packed, we'd played the shit out of this thing, and now there wasn't a sound. The audience didn't know what to do."[6]

Some nine minutes long, discordant, cacophonous, and without any discernible melodies, "City of Glass" left a majority in the audience stunned and bewildered. Seeing their discomfort, Kenton leapt center-stage while gesturing to the band to rise, and by spreading his arms wide to the audience indicated that what they had just heard was *great*, and it was *over*. The dutiful but polite applause that followed was far from the standing ovation Pepper recalled in his memoirs.

The musicians were as unimpressed as the fans. Eddie Bert related: "It wasn't like a trumpet section and a trombone section, everybody was playing different parts. You just had to follow the music as best you could—I didn't know what the heck I was playing, you just played what was written. I don't know if anybody could figure it out, but it wasn't jazz as I understand it."[7] Milt Bernhart was of a similar opinion: "'City of Glass' didn't belong in a jazz band, because it didn't resemble jazz in any manner, shape or form. It was writing for a symphonic orchestra, but it would have to compete with Samuel Barber or Alban Berg, and anyone else who wrote in a linear, non-melodic, polytonal style. But I don't think Stan had ever heard these guys, because as far as he was concerned, Graettinger was the first." After this inauspicious reception, "City of Glass" was duly mothballed, and never repeated for the rest of the year.

Instead, Bob concentrated on arranging standard ballads for the dance library—except that in Graettinger's hands the arrangements were far from standard! Milt Bernhart again: "One was 'Autumn in New York,' and another was 'You Go to My Head.' Stan and everybody in the band felt very highly about them, they were very enthusiastic. Bob's scores certainly were different, we hadn't anything in the book that resembled these arrangements. Bob took those songs, and he created a new slant on the melodies. We were playing them at dances, but I don't know what the dancers thought. They could hear the melody I suppose, but Graettinger's way with a melody was very advanced, and the arrangements took strange turns and were full of surprises. But not nonsense—it was new and original, but it all seemed to hang together and make sense."[8]

But Bob will never be accorded the proper acclaim for this most prolific period of his career, for the simple reason that unlike Rugolo (with Kenton), Ralph Burns (Herman), George Handy (Boyd Raeburn) and Gil Evans (Claude Thornhill), the contemporary recordings aren't there to establish his reputation. Graettinger had the misfortune to thrive during the one year of that wretched recording ban, and his sounds died on the ballroom walls that absorbed his music. In most cases, all we have are live recordings revived in the 1990s by the Dutch Ebony Big Band, which professional as it is, cannot compete with the incomparable Kenton band of 1948.

Graettinger's daring harmonic and melodic complexity is literally breathtaking. One of Bob's techniques was to have a soloist play the melody very straight, almost deadpan, while the orchestra ran riot around him. On "I'm in the Mood for Love" it was George Weidler playing the straight man, a difficult role in view of so much accompanying dissonance, in one of Bob's most audacious arrangements. The turbulent introduction is a mini-composition in itself, but Graettinger also creates moments of beauty: at the end the trombones rise out of the crescendo with a really lovely choral voicing.

Such contrast (largely missing from Bob's originals like "Thermopylae") adds greatly to the success of these "dance" arrangements. There's tension and release on "I Only Have Eyes for You," as Graettinger piles layer upon layer of sound until the orchestra seems about to implode upon itself, until relieved by the melodic solo trombone (played in 1948 by Harry Betts). The one title revived and recorded by Kenton in 1952 was "You Go to My Head," with Bob Burgess in Betts' original role. By no means the most daring of these charts, even so the opening dissonance, which provides the arrangement with much of its distinction and originality, proved unacceptable to 1950s audiences, and this feature was often dropped from live performances.

"Graettinger was kind of a strange boy," recalled Pete Rugolo. "Bob wrote some great things, but he didn't care what people thought. He was just living with some strange gal [Gale Madden], and smoking it up with the weed and stuff. His arrangements were so different, and really far-out, much more modern than my writing. Bob just wrote anything he felt like. Every so often he'd bring something in, like his arrangement of 'You Go to My Head,' and it was very difficult at first, because it was so unusual. But when we got it together it was good, and Stan loved it."[9]

The personnel in 1948 remained remarkably stable. Shelly Manne left in April, complaining that he was so tired from the exhausting schedule, that when he finished work at night he felt as though he'd been chopping wood. The talented Irv Kluger took his place, but when Manne returned in November, *Down Beat* took advantage of the remark to produce a cover photo of a stern-looking Stan, arms folded, standing over Shelly as he wields an axe to a wood-pile. It was all great publicity for the orchestra.

The other important newcomer was Conte Candoli, who was perhaps best known for his role as Gillespie disciple in Charlie Ventura's "Bop for the People" group, to the extent that Stan was reluctant to give him solo opportunities. "I was all set to leave," Conte told me, "and it was June Christy who told Stan: 'Conte's a fine jazz player, you want to let him blow some.' And when she said that, Stan added solos for me on tunes like 'Intermission Riff.' I laid off the bebop and made it a little more like Roy Eldridge, and Stan liked the way I played immediately, and I decided to stay on."

There was a constant dichotomy between what the fans wanted to hear ("Eager Beaver," "Peanut Vendor") and what Kenton wanted to play ("Impressionism," "Somnambulism"). Carlos Gastel was one among many who urged Stan to tone down the avant-garde and please the public, to the extent that the couple finally split in Tucson on June 9, after an angry exchange of words (duly reported in the press as "amicable").

According to Bernhart, Gastel had set up a deal that offered Kenton the chance of a life-time, to star in a radio series sponsored by Ford, which Stan turned down because he wouldn't have complete control over the content. This was the last straw for Carlos, who (in the jargon that music papers employed in 1948): "Tried to induce Kenton to tinkle terp arrangements to hold a larger following. Biz on several recent concerts in south-west has been blowzy. The pair couldn't see eye-to-eye on the reason, so they parted."[10]

By this time, Kenton no longer depended upon Gastel's savvy to the extent he had in the early years, and Gastel had established such a large stable of stars that he no longer had the time or the need to manage Kenton's affairs as he had once done. According to Audree Kenton, "Carlos and Stanley disagreed about many, many things, not only the Progressive orchestra. They fought a lot during their association. Stanley was an idealist, he believed in the concerts, but Carlos was more commercial than Stan could ever be. They disagreed about so many things—their fights were famous."[11]

Bob Allison, who became Stan's nominal manager, was the complete opposite of his predecessor. The bulk of the responsibility fell to Kenton, which was exactly how Stan wanted it: he consistently hired inexperienced people to administrative positions, knowing they would rely on his advice and judgment. Inevitably some of Stan's appointments worked better than others, but the man increasingly in control of his own destiny was Stan Kenton.

Coming up three days after Kenton's acrimonious break with Gastel, was a prestigious concert at the vast Hollywood Bowl ampitheatre on June 12. Stan would play the Bowl many times during his long career, but often as part of a package. This was his first appearance as the sole attraction, a huge responsibility for a jazz band. In the event, the concert was a triumph. *Down Beat* reported an attendance of 15,000, with a gross of $26,000, half of which went directly to Kenton, and $6,000 to promoter Gene Norman.

Milt Bernhart related: "I would have to remember that concert well, because I was married the next day in Las Vegas. The concert was telecast live in Los Angeles, an absolute first of its kind, the medium being relatively new. It was a big thrill, a perfect combination of a magnificent outdoor ampitheatre, sold out, and with many Hollywood celebrities in full view. I remember being thunderstruck at seeing Burt Lancaster and Red Skelton in the audience. The band was in excellent form, and the whole thing was a one-of-a-kinder."[12]

The entire concert was recorded by AFRS, and issued in its "Just Jazz" series. In truth, Stan played safe with the program, probably a wise move in view of the huge audience, by no means all of whom can have been dedicated fans of the band. Few of the avant-garde instrumentals were played, with an emphasis on Artistry music and a surfeit of comedy material. (Stan regularly featured the routine on which he sang "St. James Infirmary" with comic interruptions from band members, as well as Wetzel's humorous vocals such as the very funny if slightly off-color "Trees.") Bob Graettinger was not represented at all. But the band rose to the occasion, and as one review put it, "Stan Kenton reached a peak in the presentation of his Progressive Jazz at the Hollywood Bowl. Artistically it was a success, commercially a triumph."[13]

After a respite in July, playing weekends only at Stan's "home ballroom" the Balboa Rendezvous, the band was back on the road playing mostly dance dates, necessary to keep the orchestra working. As Pete Rugolo remembered it, "Around mid-1948 I wrote a lot of really commercial dance arrangements, soft things with muted brass, of standard tunes like 'Blue Moon' and 'Don't Blame Me.' Stan started playing the things at dances, but they were very simple arrangements, just for the purpose of playing at hotels or for dancing. They weren't recorded, but they were good, with a lot of piano solos. Stan liked to start off everything with the piano."[14]

A November 7 dance date at the National Guard Armory in Washington D.C. would attract no special attention were it not that the event was one of the few to be recorded that year, by the talented recording engineer Jimmy Valentine. Few of the newer arrangements were played, but otherwise unheard titles include Rugolo's tribute to June, "Styled for Christy" on which she doesn't sing a note (Tantara); the chaotic "African Nightmare"; and Ken Hanna's chart for Christy "This Is Romance" (Dynaflow). The only Graettinger orchestrations are "You Go to My Head" and a Christy vocal on "Lover Man," suggesting (admittedly on very incomplete evidence) that Bob's charts played only a minor role in the band's repertoire.

At the start of December, during the middle of a balls-breaking run at the Paramount Theatre, Stan announced his intention to temporarily disband. He was both frustrated and exhausted. Frustrated because of his inability to record throughout the whole year (coincidentally the recording ban was lifted simultaneously with the band's break-up), and the fact his concert expectations had been only partially accomplished; something he blamed on "Booking agencies that attempt to book specialized bands such as ours into normal dance-band jobs."[15] Exhausted by the constant grind of one-night-stands and the sleep deprivation caused by the need to promote his band near-on 24 hours a day. Perhaps he had under-valued the services of Carlos Gastel more than he had anticipated!

By the middle of the month, Kenton was planning to abandon music altogether, and take up psychiatry instead. He seemed undeterred by the prospect of years in medical school, and entering a new profession about which he knew very little. At his age—Stan was 37 on December 15—the impracticality of such a plan should have been too obvious to contemplate, indicating Stan was in a very confused, disoriented state of mind.

By Christmas Kenton was resolute, and wired all his band-members of his intentions. The following telegram to Bart Varsalona is dated December 24, 1948: "Have definitely decided against reorganizing. Am going to retire from the music business as a band leader. I appreciate most sincerely our past relationship and want to wish you the greatest for the future. As ever. Stan."

Despite all his achievements, and the band's impressive financial position, Kenton had come to the conclusion that his present orchestra had gone as far as it could in the prevailing conditions. It was time for Stan to take stock, time for another pause in his life-long pursuit of musical excellence.

Stan Kenton was a man of two parts. He truly loved Violet, and one side of him desired a normal home life with his wife and daughter. But the other side, to be with his band making music, was stronger—and that inevitably meant traveling the country, and being away from LA for months at a time. In 1949 Violet came first for a while, and in February the Kenton family left the States by boat for an extended vacation in South America.

It was during that period of relaxation that Stan came to his senses, and realized his future lay not in medicine but music, and he became restless to return to California. The family visited Brazil and Argentina, reneged on a half-formed plan to tour Europe, and returned to the States in May.

Stan explained his change of heart: "There wasn't any place to play our music. There were no jazz clubs then, and in the ballrooms all they wanted was dance music. I thought I'd passed my peak. I'd had psychiatric therapy, and like a lot of people who get the psychiatric bug, I got so I wanted to take up medicine myself, and become a psychiatrist. But when the smoke lifted, I realized that all I wanted was music. There was still a lot to do."[16] Violet, incensed at his decision, and still bitterly opposed to his career in music, set about divorce proceedings, which were finalized in February 1950.

During Stan's absence, Capitol Records had groomed Charlie Barnet to take his place on their roster, an indication of how important Progressive Jazz was to the label in 1949. Presumably Capitol made Barnet an offer he couldn't refuse, because the "Mad Mab" was not the most logical choice, being a known swinger and a Duke Ellington devotee.

Charlie's Capitol band was by no means a typical Barnet orchestra and was heavily into bebop, though he also played progressive-type charts donated by Kenton from his own library. Best of these were two Capitol-recorded vocal arrangements written by Rugolo at the tail-end of 1948. Trudy Richards does a passable imitation of June Christy on the inspirational orchestrations of "Gloomy Sunday" and "Ill Wind," the latter the more subtle with its especially ingenious use of conga drums. Stan's generosity was not entirely one-sided, since in 1950 he borrowed the Dennis Farnon arrangement of "All the Things You Are" that Barnet had recorded to feature Maynard Ferguson. But Barnet's excursion into modernity failed at the box office, along with most other similar orchestras as the cold wind of change blew through pop music, heralding the end of the big band era.

Stan appeared not to notice. His band had been one of the biggest earners of 1948, and his heart was still set on concert music. This time he was determined there would be no compromises. His next orchestra would be the most ambitious, and certainly the largest, of his entire career.

# 11.

## Innovations in Modern Music

### (1950–1951)

**By 1950 big bands were disappearing fast.** Those that remained generally cut down in size or diluted their repertoires. The new Herman Herd was a pale shadow of the glory days at Columbia and Capitol. It was against this backdrop that Kenton and Rugolo planned their greatest adventure yet: a 40-man concert orchestra complete with a 17-piece string section. The sheer audacity took the music world by storm. There was also a widespread consensus that though Kenton was certainly not lacking courage, he was also out of his mind. GAC certainly thought so, and refused to bankroll the tour. Stan was obliged to book the orchestra himself, a task delegated to Bob Allison working from the Kenton office.

The project was planned towards the end of '49, and the new slogan "Innovations in Modern Music" adopted, neatly avoiding the categorization jazz or classical. As well as new scores from Rugolo, Stan cast his net wide: "I chose composers whom I respect, and who know what I can do. I told them they have complete freedom in whatever they write, but that I expected integrity. All I said to them was, 'What would you write if you had the chance to create the greatest thing you know how?' I want everybody to be a part of the thing. We need contributions from every source."[1] (An important concession on Stan's part, because for the first time he was recognizing the fact that the Kenton orchestra was much more than a vehicle for his own musical expression—something he had never quite accepted when Rugolo's charts dominated the book. All the same, Gene Roland smarted because he wasn't commissioned to be among those included!)

George Kast was hired as concert-master, and he selected the string players from among the finest in Hollywood, and who expected remuneration commensurate with their status. But Kenton always traveled first class, and the jazz players were of the same standing. Stan's first words on hearing Maynard Ferguson's ear-bending trumpet in 1948 had been, "He's mine!" but at the time Maynard had been under-age and unavailable. Now Stan got his way. Maynard was "resting" in his hometown of Montreal in Canada, and was happy to get the call. With the high-note man settled, Buddy Childers accepted the lead and touted for Shorty Rogers on jazz. Stan was initially reluctant because of Shorty's association with Woody Herman, but Buddy persisted, and "once Shorty was with the band, Stan adored him, and who wouldn't?"[2]

With the ever-reliable Milt Bernhart in situ on trombone, Stan brought in two new young players who would play increasingly vital roles in the years ahead: Bob Fitzpatrick and Bill Russo. Bill was brought in because "Pete Rugolo had heard my rehearsal orchestra in Chicago, and he liked what I was doing and told Stan. So Stan phoned me, and I was out there in the first week of January 1950, along with Maynard Ferguson. We were both 21 years of age, a very exciting moment in my life, and I think his too. I was amazed at the level of playing. The string players were among the best I've ever heard in my whole life." Or as Paul Weston put it, "Where did Stan get these men? They're among Hollywood's best. He must be paying them a lot of money."[3] Milt Bernhart for one was annoyed to find it was in fact roughly double his own salary!

For the first time, Stan decided he needed the saxophones to double extensively on other reeds. Art Pepper was fluent on clarinet, Bob Cooper multi-talented on oboe and English horn. Lacking was a flutist, and Buddy Childers suggested a young alto player named Bud Shank from Charlie Barnet's band. "Two weeks prior to the audition," related Shank, "I really practiced a lot, and I still didn't play flute very well. But it was enough, so I got the job, and then started sweating it out!"[4] Two other newcomers to Kenton's world were chosen because both had played with symphony orchestras but were drawn to jazz. John Graas (French horn) would become a leading exponent of the West Coast idiom, while Don Bagley (double bass) with experience in the Los Angeles Philharmonic, could play with the other strings, or swing along with Manne on the rhythm numbers. And June Christy, now a star in her own right, agreed to return with her own recital and pianist, strictly for the duration of the concert tour.

Excitement mounted as the new music started to drift in, unheard, untried, untested: "Amazonia" (from Laurindo Almeida), "In Veradero" (Neal Hefti), "Cuban Episode" (Chico O'Farrill), "Trajectories" (Franklyn Marks), "Jolly Rogers" (Shorty Rogers), "Solitaire" (Bill Russo), "Incident in Jazz" (Bob Graettinger), "Soliloquy" (Johnny Richards), "Mirage" (Pete Rugolo). Kenton was forced to admit these scores exceeded his own musical education and technical understanding, and the orchestra had to be rehearsed by the composers until everyone was familiar with the music and Stan could assume his conducting role.

A major task during ten days of intense rehearsals was to weld together the classically trained string players (who rose to their feet in deference to the conductor when Kenton arrived for the first rehearsal), and the jazzmen (who probably barely noticed Stan's entrance!). Though confronted by a thousand problems all requiring instant solutions, Stan was overwhelmed by the strength and range of the music: so different from the stumbling beginnings at Balboa a mere ten years previously. Nowhere were classical devices tacked onto jazz in an artificial way; the composers had integrated the different idioms into a unified whole. This music went "beyond jazz," using musicians and techniques from both schools to produce an original, uniquely American art-form.

After a semi-public "workshop rehearsal" in Los Angeles' Philharmonic Auditorium on January 30, the orchestra moved into Capitol's Melrose Avenue Studios, the first Kenton phono recordings since December 1947, and the first to be made on tape. Some 16 titles were recorded in five lengthy sessions, and as Stan put it, "The Capitol people were with me all the way. I remember hour upon hour in the studios, and there was no thought of how much it would cost; the thought was only to make the finest recordings that we knew how."[5] (Of course, Stan is speaking for himself; the "Capitol people" might have put a slightly different slant on things!)

The full public debut of Innovations in Modern Music for 1950 was at the Palomar Theatre in Seattle, Washington, on February 9. Ted Hallock covered the event for *Down Beat*, and did Kenton proud: "In my opinion, our language is completely inadequate to cope with what really happened when Kenton's assemblage blew, plucked, scraped and pounded the most significant collection of sounds ever heard in an American hall of music. Seattle's vast auditorium (5,000 capacity) held 3,000 people, the majority of whom knew exactly why they were there. Sections filed in singly, to hesitant, tense applause. But when Kenton walked on stage, the crowd went crazy. He acknowledged applause mildly, and leaning towards the string section, gave the downbeat for 'Artistry in Rhythm.' The strings began a short tremolo introduction, and I thought the Theme had been emasculated until Kenton turned to the brass and screamed NOW!! When en masse the 39 musicians played Artistry's first Fm 7, it sounded like a combination of all the enthusiasm you can imagine has ever existed, plus the God of Music patting everyone concerned on the shoulder reassuringly, murmuring: 'Everything is all right again.'"[6]

Some of the dance bands had used strings in the past (including Artie Shaw, Harry James, and Glenn Miller), but frequently only as a background cushion of sound more suited to the sweeter side of the book. Kenton's conception was quite different, and he encouraged his composers to adopt an exploratory attitude towards the section. The arrangers knew Kenton wouldn't want a Kostelanetz-schmaltz (perversely, Stan's own "Theme for Sunday" came closest to that), and wrote accordingly. By using no vibrato the strings have become "Kentonized," and produce a hard, brilliant tone that matches the familiar resonance of the Kenton brass. In Stan's words, "The idea was to get the strings playing in a jazz manner, as modern jazz musicians, and steer clear of the old European way of playing. And we did some very interesting and very successful things with strings."[7] (Particular examples would include "Cello-logy" by Almeida, "Gregory Bemko" by Russo, and "House of Strings" by Graettinger.)

No one described their reaction to the music better than Buddy Childers: "I adored it. This was the first time I really, absolutely, and with all my heart, loved the music that we were playing. It was such a thrill. Such a great, great musical experience. It was a challenge to us as players to accomplish the proper playing of the music. We were like guys in a regiment in war, they become really close, and that's pretty much what it was like. It was really tough. But there was also a tremendous sense of achievement."[8] In reality, it took a while for the string players and the jazzmen to meld socially, especially as it required two buses to transport the orchestra between dates. The string-men traveled in one, termed the School Bus (because the musicians were always reading), and the dance band in another, known as the Balling Bus, because the guys there were more likely to be sharing a jug than a book! But once the tour started, the two worlds merged, most certainly on stage, which is where it really mattered.

Milt Bernhart also truly defines the impact of Innovations with his very personal description of the New York concerts on April 8–9: "First of all, Carnegie Hall even at this late date is a name synonymous with prestige and achievement. But in 1950, with an orchestra that did bridge a gap between jazz and symphonic music, before the most highly sophisticated kind of musical audience, in the city that was certainly the music capital of the world—well, that was something else. The feeling of walking stage front, and playing the featured solo on 'Solitaire' with knees knocking, heart beating wildly, but living through it, hearing the applause, feeling the elation—how else can it be described except as the biggest thrill a lifetime can offer."[9]

Artistically the zenith of Stan's entire career, the concerts were persistently dogged by negative reviews, which could be generally translated into: "I didn't understand the music, and don't know what to say about it." Though Margaret Hartford in the *Hollywood Citizen-News* dated June 4, 1950, did turn the genre into something of an art form when she wrote: "June Christy has a distinctive, urgent style and a throaty contralto that sounds like an inspired newsboy, mortally wounded." Faced with such undiscerning criticism, Innovations soon turned into the commercial disaster the business men had predicted. Classicists wanted nothing to do with a jazz band, and the strings turned off many a "floating voter" among the jazz fans. The orchestra did well in the largest urban centers, playing to packed houses at New York's Carnegie Hall, Chicago's Civic Opera House and the Hollywood Bowl (where the press reported an attendance of 14,000, and a gross close to $25,000). But too many of the smaller cities covered during a four-month tour drew only half-full houses. Apathy hung in the air, and heavy losses were incurred. Kept under very close wraps at the time was Stan's overall financial deficit of a small fortune estimated at $125,000. (And that of course was in 1950 money.)

Capitol worked hard on the new Kenton album, and had it ready by March 1950, half-way through the tour, in an attempt to maximize sales. Release was made in all three current formats: 12-inch 78 rpm, 7-inch 45rpm, and 12-inch LP. But despite excellent production values and extensive promotion, Capitol's *Innovations in Modern Music Volume One* did not break any sales records. There would be more Capitol-Kenton albums with strings, but like the term "Progressive Jazz" before it, the name "Innovations" was banished from the Capitol lexicon. Volume Two never left the station.

Kenton's bank balance may have been depleted, but at least he had the satisfaction of a unique artistic experience, and the recordings for posterity to cherish. Private tapes were also made of several Innovations concerts, some preserved on CD. Not unexpectedly, Shorty Rogers was the writer closest to conventional jazz. His "Jolly Rogers" sans strings was a straightforward swinger (Stan had called it "An Expression from Rogers," but Capitol soon changed that), but Shorty also enjoyed writing for the full orchestra: "The piece named after 'Art Pepper' was the first time I attempted to write for strings. Art was something special, and this piece seems to have a life of its own. Even though I've heard it countless times, I have to confess I'm still thrilled each time I hear it."[10]

Stan had been using the Dennis Farnon arrangement of "All the Things You Are" recorded by Charlie Barnet to feature Maynard Ferguson, but had to stop when Jerome Kern's widow threatened legal action.

Maynard's high-register trumpet solo was one of the orchestra's big attractions, so Shorty stepped in and wrote an original named after Ferguson: "In one day, while we were on the road in Lincoln, Nebraska. I went to the YMCA and found a room with a piano. But the 'Art Pepper' piece took several days, and is still one of my all-time favorites. In fact, that was the most important period of my life as far as writing goes."[11]

The orchestra's top attraction was June Christy, who provided relief from the barrage of unfamiliar music with some of her hit songs (including the evergreens "How High the Moon" and "I'll Remember April"), but whose big number was the new Pete Rugolo arrangement of "Lonesome Road." No writer was better than Rugolo at blending the formal, classical aspects of Innovations with the spirit and excitement of big-band jazz. On "Road" the dark, brooding mood of the introduction is in vivid contrast with the up-tempo middle section and its exhilarating trumpet flights. Every now and again you know Maynard Ferguson is among the personnel. But the star is Christy, who suppresses the sexuality in her voice in favor of a classical purity of tone that is in perfect harmony with Rugolo's intentions, and almost resembles an instrumental solo. June is faultless in this very demanding role, the finest partnership of voice and orchestra that Kenton could ever have hoped to achieve.

Some of the compositions were descriptive, none more graphically so than Rugolo's "Mirage." In concert, the lighting was choreographed to the depiction of the gradual formation, full realization, and slow disintegration of this visual fantasy. During the opening passages, while snatches of strings and woodwind introduce the theme and create the illusion of a mirage forming, the orchestra was bathed in a red glow. This was transformed into a flood of white light as the climactic brass explodes, and the full orchestra reveals the expanse and splendor of the complete mirage. Then, as the vision begins to fade, the musicians played in near darkness, until at the end one realizes it was only a delusion, and the lights flashed bright again. Special credit is due to Shelly Manne for his skilled percussion work, a drummer so sympathetic to Kenton's ideals he would never be eclipsed.

Franklyn Marks was a studio composer dedicated to breaking down the traditional restrictions of classical music. "Trajectories," which usually opened the concerts, describes Franklyn's impressions as he watches a galaxy of shooting stars, employing Latin rhythms and pizzicato strings in constantly changing rhythmic patterns to achieve his vision. "It was very satisfying to compose for Stan," Marks told me, "and some of my best writing came out of that, but it was working in the Walt Disney studios that made me a living."[12] Franklyn's "Evening in Pakistan" (or "Kenton in Karachi" as one wag termed it) was appropriately exotic, sensitively portraying the mysterious world of minarets and mosques via a bolero beat and extensive use of tambourine and finger-cymbals.

Unsurprisingly more abstract in concept was Bob Graettinger's "An Incident in Sound," which Capitol retitled "Incident in Jazz." Despite their use of dissonance and modernity, the other composers all display a sense of order and symmetry in their writing, which Graettinger spurns. Bob's work lacks a sequential pattern, is deliberately asymmetrical, and despite the lively theme and jaunty tempo is never frivolous, due to the atonal orchestration. Like many Graettinger charts, the piece ends on a contrastingly tranquil note. "'Incident in Jazz,'" commented Ted Hallock, "is modern music, heart deep."[13]

Quite unlike the blazing excitement of *Cuban Fire* and similar extravaganzas that are associated with the name Johnny Richards, "Soliloquy" is a subtle, sensitive creation, and the unbiased listener cannot help but be impressed by Richards' total control and command of all the opportunities offered by the large orchestra. Johnny's career was the reverse of many of his peers, as he left a lucrative but sterile livelihood writing for motion pictures to pursue the much more risky but rewarding vocation of a career in modern music.

Of the compositions that are unreservedly Latin in flavor, the most searching and exploratory is Chico O'Farrill's "Cuban Episode" (originally and more effectively titled "Cuban Fantasy"). Featuring Carlos Vidal's conga drums and fiery vocal, "Episode" is a multi-tempoed creation that combines dark-hued rhythms with the incisive Kenton brass in a passionate combination of the two cultures. Much lighter in tone is Neal Hefti's "In Veradero," named after the location in Cuba. Defined by a lightly hypnotic Latin rhythm and exciting orchestral work, Hefti's tuneful melody makes this one of the more accessible compositions, featuring Bud Shank's nimble flute and a beautiful tenor solo by the late, great Bob Cooper.

"Salute to the Americas" had its title clipped by Capitol. One of Rugolo's most powerful compositions ever, this emotionally stirring, multi-tempoed flag-waver (actually more reminiscent of Iberia than South America) made the perfect concert-closer, as witnessed by Noel Wedder: "The hush of silence as the final strains of 'Salute' floated skyward was followed by thunderous applause. Audience reaction was awesome, and sometimes lasted 5 or 6 minutes. As Stan turned toward the audience, holding both them and the orchestra in the palm of his hands, the beatific look on his face said it all. He knew, as everyone else knew, they had just been taken on a musical journey that would last a lifetime."[14]

In retrospect, few would disagree that over 20 years earlier Paul Whiteman had made a more durable impression on "legitimate" music than Stan Kenton. Any half-decent classical records store will feature the original Whiteman orchestrations of George Gershwin's "Rhapsody in Blue" and Ferde Grofe's "Grand Canyon Suite," while the collector will find Kenton only in the jazz department. Unlike Whiteman, however far-out Kenton might go, he rarely left his jazz roots, and Third Stream music (of which Innovations was a forerunner) was a tributary of jazz. Audiences decide, and music-lovers made clear there was room only for two main styles: classical (principally of European origin) and jazz (itself the indigenous American music). Kenton's aim was always to extend the boundaries of jazz, and it is as a jazz band-leader that Kenton's reputation will ultimately stand or fall.

Despite his losses, Kenton was reluctant to abandon Innovations, and was determined there should be a second tour. "I've burned my bridges," Stan had screamed in a banner *Down Beat* headline; now he hastily built a pontoon and refinanced by playing a much more accessible form of music with the jazz-band nucleus, and accepting a dance tour that GAC was happy to organize. There was even a hit recording of "Orange Colored Sky" in conjunction with the Nat Cole Trio.

Stan still needed a touring singer, and when no suitable girl could be found, Milt Bernhart suggested Jay Johnson, whose deep, manly Herb Jeffries-styled voice was in sharp contrast to his boyish, clean-cut appearance. Stan's appetite for original songs saddled Jay with some inane recordings ("I'm So in the Mood" was the worst), but on standards his excellent diction and precise intonation are heard to perfection. According to Bernhart, "Stan thought the world of Jay, and took it really badly when he was killed in a motor-cycle accident in 1954. Everybody at the funeral was busted up. Stan broke down and cried."[15]

Meanwhile, Kenton was himself struggling to come to terms with the band's looser, lighter styling, occasioned by the new personnel and the 1950s context. Stan still hankered after the Artistry sound, as Bud Shank related: "He approached me one night after the job, and asked, 'Uh, Bud, can you start playing the old book more like George Weidler?' I replied, 'Okay Stan, I'll try.' That's all that was said. The next night I played exactly the same way I had before, and never heard another word from Stan on the subject."[16] "When Stan tried to play the old arrangements it didn't work, because of all the changes in personnel, and Stan finally realized that."[17]

Not that the new book was necessarily better than the old one. Stan's "Easy Go" was swingier than "Painted Rhythm," but it was also less substantial. Rogers' "Viva Prado" was brash and flashy, but it lacked the depth and deftness of "Machito." The original Kenton style was diluted, because this was a band in transition, in search of the best alternative. Ready cash remained short, and Stan's decision to postpone Innovations II was determined by the luxury of a six-week booking at the Hollywood Palladium commencing February 20, 1951. Like all ballrooms in the post-war era, the Palladium was well past its glory days but remained the West Coast's premier dance hall, so it did Stan's reputation no harm that he attracted over 16,000 paid admissions during the first week, a figure that *Down Beat* noted stacked up well compared with more conventional bands like Freddy Martin and Jerry Gray.

Almost as controversial as the Kenton music were the red and grey plaid jackets designed by the French fashionista Jacques Fath. Distinctive they certainly were; dignified they were not. "Tacky," opined Ralph Blaze; "I hated them," said Bob Cooper.[18] But perhaps they suited the general mood of spontaneous good humor and relaxation that pervaded the Palladium engagement, as evident in the almost nightly CBS broadcasts from the dance spot. Kenton soon attained a finely tuned rapport with announcer Bill Baldwin, and allowed his sidemen to "improvise" with scat-vocal effects on "Painted Rhythm" and "Southern Scandal"; Milt Bernhart's very funny spoken epilogue to "Laura"; up to four "Leap Frog" endings tacked onto "Eager Beaver"; and an extempore version of "Artistry in Rhythm" in march tempo!

Milt Bernhart comments: "The band by now had settled in. There hadn't been many changes in the players, and there was kind of a feeling of coming together that only happened if everybody was there every night, so that all the parts were played, and people were allowed to add little turns and things, so that it loosened up. Most bands were pretty strait-laced, and Bill Baldwin, the compere at the Hollywood Palladium, didn't quite know what to make of us. Comedy in Stan's band kind of developed so that it looked like it was being done for the first time. If it wasn't extemporaneous-looking it would have lost its interest for Stan quickly. But he wanted the audience to enjoy the evening, and he knew that some laughter wouldn't hurt. Shelly was very good, he never felt restrained, and I guess I added my quota."[19]

Most of the Palladium broadcasts were preserved, some by AFRS, and selections have been released in very reasonable audio on a range of labels. The music is easy to listen to, generally light in character, but loaded with fine personal contributions from the talented soloists. Distinctive to these broadcasts are extended versions of "Minor Riff" that feature fascinating improvisations from Wetzel, Rogers, and Alvarez in varying solo orders.

Meanwhile, the IRS was chasing Stan for unpaid tax bills, and as Kenton told me, "It was the first time I'd ever been in a jam with them. I needed a hit record that would sell, something that would be more generally appealing, which is when I came up with the idea for 'September Song.'"[20] Commercial, yet still musical, with beautifully voiced choruses from the trombone and saxophone sections, as well as the band vocal, "September Song" worked, reaching 20th in Billboard's Top Twenty, quite an achievement for a big band in the musical climate of 1951. It was quickly followed by "Laura" and later by "Tenderly," both doing well, but neither achieving the iconic status of "September." Gene Howard and Jay Johnson added to the vocal strength, though as Milt Bernhart noted, "Several guys were left out, because they would have destroyed it. Art Pepper for one never sang, he wasn't even going to try."[21]

Another trend-setting arrangement from the Kenton pen was "Street of Dreams," because it defined for the first time the orchestra's new ballad style. "Street" allows for impressive sectional soli, with emphasis on the saxophone writing at which Stan excelled. The chart became a fixture in the book, and was played at dances and concerts until the end. In later years the piece became even more of an alto saxophone feature for the likes of Ray Reed and John Park, than the relatively brief Art Pepper solo on the 1951 recording.

Maynard Ferguson remained a star attraction on tunes like "The Hot Canary" and his name-piece from the Innovations repertoire. Anyone has to respect Maynard's dexterity in the upper register, which he ascribed to natural ability rather than any special technique, though I personally prefer Ferguson's work in the section to his feature solos, recordings which (in Maynard's words) often were "Made definitely for commercial purposes: to make money."[22]

As were Gene Roland's arrangements. "Gene was kind of off the wall," said Eddie Bert. "He'd disappear, but then all of a sudden if he needed some bread he'd show up. And every once in a while he'd write something that was a classic."[23] Such a number was a tune Gene called "Shed House Mouse," which Stan changed to "Jump for Joe," in recognition of Joe Rico, a Buffalo, New York, disc jockey. Roland's catchy riff and Pepper's melodic alto made "Jump for Joe" a favorite with the fans, and ensured the tune a permanent place in the Kenton hall of fame.

More complex was Roland's "Riff Rhapsody," with a Latinesque mood not hinted at in the title. Canadian collector Fred Augerman described the piece in a way that illustrates his deep emotional ties with the music:

"This is the Stan Kenton orchestra that I love. The haunting trombone of Milt Bernhart, as only he could get that lonely sound, the muted trumpet of Shorty, and a brief but dynamite solo by Bob Cooper. After Coop finishes, the crashing dissonance and screaming brass that so typified the band's sound, the power is just awesome, and if you can listen 'through' the brass, there's Bob Gioga, just blowing his brains out on the bottom end. All the Kenton elements are in that arrangement."[24]

By September, Stan was intent on disregarding everyone's advice that he was committing economic suicide, and began organizing the second Innovations tour. He knew that to fail to keep his word would be to break faith with his followers, his musicians, and most of all to himself. This time the intense excitement in the industry that Innovations I had created was missing, and so also was Stan's right-hand man. Pete Rugolo, who had been a vital part of every Kenton endeavor since 1945, had left to try his luck in the studios, and Stan must have felt like he was missing his right arm. Bill Russo attempted to fill the breach, but Russo—intellectual, independent, ambitious—was never going to offer the same support nor enjoy the same rapport with Kenton that Rugolo had achieved.

At the same time, in a very real sense Rugolo represented yesterday's music, and if Kenton wanted to move ahead, he had to find fresh blood. Unfortunately, on this occasion, Russo (who had recently thrilled Kenton with his dazzling "Halls of Brass") didn't quite fulfill his potential. Stan's conception vocally was to treat Christy's voice as an instrument, and his own name-piece "June Christy" had done just that. Russo's attempts to introduce the concept into standard songs "Gloomy Sunday" and "One for My Baby" resulted in rather clumsy orchestrations that received little attention. "Ennui" was a carbon copy of "Solitaire," but truly innovational was the outstanding "Improvisation."

"I was trying to incorporate early 20th century classical music into the jazz idiom," Russo told me. "The idea was to have four people improvising simultaneously, and I think ideally a little less restrictively than we did it in the large orchestra. But we didn't have too much time to think about it, we really needed more rehearsal time, and we had to find out what would work by experimentation on the job. The second idea was that Stan as conductor would also improvise, by bringing in the orchestra at what seemed to him the appropriate times, but as it turned out that didn't work too well." Because of so much improvising on the spot, the quality of the work varied between performances, and was probably anathema to Kenton, who liked everything worked out in advance and performed to perfection on every occasion.

Most popular among audiences were the less avant-garde compositions: a brilliant Latin "Samana," named by Manny Albam after his birth-place in the Dominican Republic, and the very jazz-oriented "Coop's Solo" and "Conte Candoli" (a reworking of "Round Robin") from Shorty Rogers. But for Kenton, the plaudits fell to Bob Graettinger, who had rewritten his 1948 "City of Glass" as a 17-minute four-part composition for large orchestra, though only one Movement (usually "Dance Before the Mirror") was ever played at concerts. What Graettinger had not done, was make his composition any more comprehensible to the average listener; indeed, the addition of strings made it even more difficult. Kenton blamed lack of rehearsal time for not performing the full Suite, but equally likely is the fact he didn't want half his audience walking out midway through a concert.

Despite playing only the larger cities with a two-month schedule only half as long as Innovations I, even smaller audiences than before demonstrated the limited demand for music that straddled the jazz/ classical divide. With losses soon mounting to equal 1950's estimated $125,000, Stan introduced popular hits into the concerts, including "Peanut Vendor," "Opus in Pastels," and "September Song" complete with band vocal. At Seattle, immediately after a cool reaction to "Reflections" from "City of Glass," the band featured the vaudevillian "Blues in Burlesque," with Manne's raucous vocal and Ferguson's squealing trumpet playing to tumultuous applause. Kenton's frustration can only be imagined, and he cannot be blamed for trying to stem the financial outflow, but the "concert dignity" to which he aspired isn't easy to sustain alongside such antics.

Fully aware that Innovations had come to the end of the road, and in an act of ultimate defiance, at the conclusion of the tour Kenton committed innovational hari-kari by insisting the concert orchestra record nothing but Graettinger music, including the complete "City of Glass." Stan's clout at Capitol was backed by the unstinted support of his personal friendship with President Glenn Wallichs, but in an industry that counted success only by sales figures and the number of units sold, producer Lee Gillette must have reflected that "Glass" was going to do nothing to raise his own reputation among the Capitol hierarchy.

Gillette attempted to sugar the pill with attractive cover art-work and a descriptive "explanation" of the music (supposedly written by Graettinger himself) on the liner, though any attempt to link this narrative to the discordance heard on the record was doomed to futility. Sales were limited to Kenton completists, most of whom tried in vain to hear in the music something of the quality that so appealed to Stan himself. I well remember a second-hand dealer at one of Murray Patterson's Rendezvous conventions holding up an LP of *City of Glass* and declaring, "There's never any need to examine this one for wear—it's never been played more than once!"

While audiences simply reacted with their feet, a kind of romanticism grew up around Graettinger that protected him from the criticism of his peers (many of whom "understood" Bob's music no better than the fans). Graettinger's total lack of interest in material possessions leading to primitive living conditions, his method of writing music using colors to illustrate the different instruments, and his total dedication to his music above all else, ensured the admiration of other musicians. Many alumni preferred not to commit themselves about "City of Glass," but Bill Russo, whose experience extended to both jazz and classical idioms, was unequivocal: "I have to say I have developed a clear-cut aversion towards music that isn't helpful of society—music that I regard as selfish and personal and negative. Essentially, 'City of Glass' is typical of the total waste of so much art in the 20th century. I am not enamored of any music like 'City of Glass.' Mozart tells us there is an organized, harmonious world available to us, and Bob is telling you there's a tortured, difficult world, and you're not going to sort it out."

There is never complete unanimity about music as controversial as "City of Glass," only a strong consensus. Asked by English collector Colin Goodall for his view, Buddy Childers was typically explicit: "Either you do not have the intellectual capacity to appreciate the music, or it is bullshit." So Colin asked Buddy for his opinion. "It's bullshit," Buddy replied.[25] Kenton always vigorously defended Graettinger in public, but in later years even Stan had his private doubts. Joel Kaye once asked him about "City," "And this is my recollection of what Stan said: 'Well, I'll tell ya, it was either the greatest music the band ever presented, or the biggest pile of crap we ever played, and I still don't know which.'"[26]

Thereafter, Stan continued to slip in the odd Graettinger composition during recording sessions, until he had enough music in the can for a second 10-inch LP. *This Modern World* was more varied but equally lacking in jazz emotions, with the exception of a feature for Maynard Ferguson that Stan called "A Trumpet," since Graettinger was now declining to name any of his pieces himself. For years Kenton enabled Bob's survival by subsidizing him with a small retainer, but with his health already in decline by 1954, Bob's output dwindled, and he spent the last years of his life in seclusion working on a "Suite for String Trio and Wind Quartet" that was still unfinished in 1957 at the time of his death from lung cancer at the age of 33. He was already a forgotten figure, and the only musicians who attended his funeral were Stan Kenton and Pete Rugolo. Bob's had been a life in turmoil—almost an "Artistry in Tragedy." As Bud Shank put it, "Most of us who knew Graettinger figured that he died of a broken heart. He lived entirely in his own little world. He could never find anybody to understand him."[27] I'd hazard no one came closer than Stan Kenton.

There were several consequences resulting directly from the failure of Innovations to pay its way, not least the damage to Kenton's own reputation. He was no longer seen within the industry as infallible, the man for whom everything he touched turned to gold. And secondly, many of Stan's best-known sidemen defected from the band to settle in California, attracted by the climate and the prospect of well-paid work in the TV and movie studios. Men like Shorty Rogers, Bud Shank, Bob Cooper, John Graas, and Shelly Manne became central to the West Coast Jazz movement of the 1950s, a style of playing that favored cool understatement, and with as much emphasis on experimental composition as solo improvisation.

Kenton himself, in the words of the song, had to pick himself up, dust himself down, and start all over again—which he did with such success that the next few years are viewed by many as the most productive of Stan's whole career. If Innovations itself was in the long term a Mirage—a Street of Dreams—it bequeathed a legacy of recordings which alone establish Kenton among the most distinguished leaders of twentieth-century music. In Stan's view, "The Innovations Orchestra was a great thing artistically, but believe me, we wound up with a financial fiasco you wouldn't believe. The orchestra wasn't successful—I had just taken on too big a challenge. But I have no regrets. It was sort of a noble failure."[28]

# 12.

# New Concepts of Artistry in Rhythm

(1952)

Kenton literally couldn't afford to sit around. Records were an artist's life-blood, and during lengthy discussions, his colleagues at Capitol pointed out that while the advanced music had failed to sell whatever tagline he called it by, reissues of the easier, earlier music were moving fast. At the same time, people like Musso, Christy, and Rugolo had moved on, and it was impossible to recreate the "Artistry" band, even if Stan had wanted to spend the rest of his life regurgitating "Eager Beaver" and "Southern Scandal." A new, readily accessible musical policy was imperative, but exactly what form that might take was unclear.

Within weeks Kenton had put a new orchestra together. Some continuity was ensured by the return of alumni Childers, Candoli, Fitzpatrick, Russo, Bagley, and Gioga, but as Howard Lucraft put it: "The new band's mostly a bunch of previously unknown but very talented youngsters."[1] Stan had high hopes for his new vocal discovery, a deeptoned singer with little previous professional experience named Jerri Winters, perceptively described by Don Reed as "Sounding like a cross between June Christy and Sarah Vaughan, if you can imagine that."[2] But Jerri had the appeal of neither, her records didn't sell, and she left after some four months. (Her successor Helen Carr fared even worse, with only a four-week stretch.) Fortunately Kenton had more success with his musicians. Dick Meldonian, an under-rated alto sax player, narrates: "Stan made a call to my house trying to locate drummer John Markham, as he was forming a new band and Shelly Manne had left. So I asked Stan if he could use me, and he said to come down for a rehearsal. Herbie Steward and I played the alto saxes. But Herbie decided to stay with Harry James, so I recommended Lennie Niehaus for the other alto chair. He came in, and Stan dug him as you know."

Kenton was bound to be impressed by the fluency of Niehaus, who made the fast runs at which he excelled seem too easy to be true. Lennie concedes, "I think I was a more cerebral player than Charlie Mariano.

94

My influences were Charlie Parker and Lee Konitz, and I like to think my sound is a combination of the two. I've been compared to Paul Desmond, and I really appreciate the way he played, but I don't see myself sounding like Paul. He played on one level, like a person talking in a monologue."[3] (An appraisal which at times has also been levelled at Niehaus himself.)

"Stan encouraged me to write," says Lennie. "I scored a couple of vocal arrangements for Jerri Winters, and I did 'Pennies from Heaven' for the dance book, that Stan later recorded. In 1952 I also wrote an original that I called 'Birdhaus.' It was a bebop number, named after Charlie Parker naturally, but also the last part of my own name. Later Stan turned it into a solo vehicle for Lee Konitz, where he played the melody that I had written for the entire sax section. So Stan opened it up and called it 'Solo for Alto' and let Lee stretch out."[4] Then in late April 1952 Lennie's career was rudely interrupted when the draft landed him in the army, his place eventually being filled by Vinnie Dean. (Though Niehaus would return with a vengeance!)

Another significant newcomer in the sax section was Charlie Barnet-graduate Bill Holman. When they first joined, both Russo and Holman were regarded more as potential young soloists than composers. That would soon change, though Holman in particular could well have made it as a soloist if he hadn't proven himself such a spectacular arranger. "I was always a little bugged about my own playing," Bill told me. "It wasn't the way I wanted it to be, and there's so many great soloists around, I figured I was just taking up space that could be better utilized by somebody else."

John Markham didn't take the bait, so Stan followed a suggestion of Boots Mussulli and contacted Frankie Capp. "The first thing Stan asked me," Capp related, "was what size cymbals I used. Stan was a cymbal freak. He liked big, loud cymbals. It's not my idea of a good sound, huge cymbals that cover everything else up, but anyway, I joined in February 1952. I came out to LA, and we rehearsed at the Florentine Gardens."[5] No chair in the band caused Kenton more anxiety than the drums. The wrong drummer really irked and soon found himself replaced, as happened with Capp. Kenton wanted Stan Levey, a burly ex-boxer, but waited until he'd found Capp a position in Neal Hefti's band, a much smaller, lighter outfit. "That's how much Kenton thought of me," said Capp. "Wasn't he a gas!"[6]

Gradually, the arrangers and musicians exerted their influences, and it all started to come together as a cohesive plan to feature a more swinging style of music than ever before, but with Kenton holding a tight grip on the reins. Stan certainly had no intention of becoming a Bogus Basie or Mark II Herman, but he was sufficiently convinced to give it a go. And thus was born the New Concepts of Artistry in Rhythm: new, futuristic ways of updating his most popular period from the past.

The first tangible evidence came from Bill Russo in the form of a minor blues which Stan named "Bill's Blues" in recognition of its author. Because it's a jazz piece played at a fast lick, the work has been wrongly described as a "riff," whereas in fact it is a complex, contrapuntal composition with a strong melodic line (a fact emphasized by Russo when he rearranged the piece in 1962 for his London Jazz Orchestra, which dissects the theme at a slower tempo in a quieter, almost classical context). Candoli and Niehaus both take choice solos on the Kenton recording, while Russo always insisted the trombone was Fitzpatrick (though some believe it to be Russo himself).

But the real catalyst who changed the band's music forever was Gerry Mulligan. Gerry was introduced to Stan by Bob Graettinger, the pair having met through their mutual friendship with Gale Madden. So when Graettinger told Kenton that Mulligan was likely to produce the type of music he was looking for, Stan listened. Gerry's Chet Baker Quartet fame was still ahead of him and he needed the bread, but the fact was, he wanted to have his cake and eat it. Having sold his scores to Stan, Mulligan wanted to retain creative control over the way they were played. Kenton was having none of it, so theirs was not a cordial relationship, and lasted a scant three months. The music itself was much more enduring.

"Limelight," "Swing House," "Walking Shoes," and "Young Blood" may not have been archetypal Kenton, but from a jazz point of view Mulligan's charts were without peer. The change was just a little too radical for Stan, especially since they came with a heavy dose of Attitude. Kenton's opinion of music was always strongly motivated by his rapport with the writer. Thus he could express incomprehension as to why Mulligan's charts were so popular with the band (and the fans!), while at the same time emphasizing his deep appreciation of the very similar scores penned by Bill Holman (whom he came to regard as the musical son he never had).

"Mulligan's charts were a lot of fun to play," commented Lennie Niehaus, "because we had a lot more freedom to do what we wanted. By thinning out the lines and making them less cluttered, Gerry softened the sound of the band. It was like Bach, contrapuntal, and the moving parts would weave in and out of each other, so that lightened up the sound, and helped the band to swing in a different manner. We have

Gerry Mulligan to thank for that. He led the way for Holman and myself, and maybe a few other arrangers. The guys in the band thought it was great, but Stan needed a lot of convincing."[7]

So when Stan took over rehearsing the arrangements, he immediately "Kentonized" the music, with faster tempos and louder shout choruses. Mulligan heard his visions vaporizing before his ears, and strenuously objected, leading to a massive clash of egos. (Not helped by eye-witness reports that at this time Mulligan's behavior was every bit as odd as Graettinger's; the only difference was that Bob was delivering the music that Stan lived for, whereas Gerry was not!) "I like jazz that is easy and quiet with a subtle swing," commented Mulligan. "I was very much surprised with 'Young Blood' the way Kenton did it. I hadn't visualised it with so much fire and drive. But I suppose it wouldn't be Kenton without that desire to shout."[8]

Immediate beneficiary of the Mulligan influence was Bill Holman. "My first arrangements the band played were 'Deep Purple' and 'Star Eyes,' both for the dance library. But I loved Gerry Mulligan's charts so much, the next thing I wrote sounded just like what Gerry had been writing, so Stan never used that one at all. But I was playing all of Gerry's arrangements—or at least, the ones Stan was using. So I really got to pay attention to what made up a great writer's charts.

"But Mulligan was not interested in becoming a Kenton arranger. He just wrote his kind of music for Stan, and there was no compromising. In my case, I wanted to write for Stan Kenton, so I spent many months just trying to figure out how I was going to do it. And when I did start writing for the band, it was not quite like Gerry, but there was a whole lot of influence there. Stan made it plain from the start he didn't want any Count Basie-type swing charts, and I knew I didn't want to write Progressive Jazz, so I had to find some kind of middle way that would keep us both happy; and eventually I did. And it was heavier, more massive than the things that Gerry wrote, but that's because of who I was working for."

According to Noel Wedder, "Holman and Stan carried on a 'love-hate' relationship for years. Of all his arrangers, Stan was closest to Bill, which didn't stop them from quarrelling. Their arguments over scores were legendary. But Stan saw Holman as the son he'd always wanted. Charming. Self-effacing. Determined. Stubborn. A take-no-prisoners attitude. But above all, extremely talented."[9] With the last comment at least, the musicians agreed to a man.

"When it comes to writing," said Bill Trujillo, "Holman's got a way of simplifying things. He'll write one unison line, and a counterpoint. When you play Bill's charts you feel happy. They just hit you right. They *swing*. The way he does things is different from any other arranger, like a big band playing as a small group."

Opined Bill Perkins: "I would say Bill Holman's music was the best-liked by the band. The secret? Taste and voice-leading. Bill Holman wrote the book on voice-leading for big bands."[10] And Phil Gilbert: "I think Bill Holman is the greatest composer/ arranger alive or dead. Just listen to the prolific body of work he has done. He has written masterpieces for his own band, countless singers, and the likes of Terry Gibbs and Stan Kenton. It is a thrill to play his music. If you ask anyone, in any section of the orchestra, how they like their part, the answer is 'Perfect!' No boring parts, ever!"[11]

It's hard to quarrel with such unanimous praise, which could fill a book. Certainly over the years Holman wrote great charts for Stan, but whether Bill was the *best* writer of *Kenton-styled* music is quite another matter. Musicians who play the music sometimes have different views from audiences who listen to it, as do composers who write the more progressive-type orchestrations. Such a man is Pete Rugolo: "The guys really loved Holman's music, because he wrote everything swinging away. They were good charts, and great to play I guess, but musically to me they all sounded more or less the same. As an arranger, I like to hear something new coming out, some nice chord changes. I got Bill Russo on the band, and he was very much my type of arranger, 'cos he liked to write modern music. After I left, Russo wrote a lot of really good concert compositions."[12]

Along with Holman, Russo became the dominant voice in the New Concepts band. Richards wasn't quite ready yet, and neither Graettinger nor Roland ever set the style of the orchestra. While Russ Garcia told me Bill Holman had a very high IQ, "Willis" (Holman's middle name and the name used by other musicians) was always one of the guys, socially as well as musically. Bill Russo, on the other hand, was an academician, with a penchant for using long words the guys had never even heard before let alone knew the meaning of. Even worse, his music *didn't swing*. "Hard-nosed, he was," said Bill Perkins. "Russo sometimes seemed to write difficult things just for the sake of being difficult. However, in retrospect the recordings of some of his arrangements remain as some of the best music Kenton ever produced."[13]

"I felt a deep discomfort being with the Kenton 'dance band,'" Russo confided. "The guys didn't really like anything except Count Basie in whatever form it took, so to be continuously around that band and share only their interests in women and liquor was difficult." Bill's manner and speech suggested an intellectual superiority that was alien to the average jazzman. Even Kenton felt wary in Russo's presence, and despite their similar taste in music, the two men were never close. In personal terms Stan felt insecure with Russo, the man who was producing the music he preferred, and a closer affinity with Holman, who wasn't.

"Kenton was very supportive and protective of me," Russo continues, "so that if I wrote something that the band didn't like, he would defend me. At the same time, Stan was never entirely comfortable with me, because I was the bright, young person who was most like him. I didn't realize that until many years later. So I did feel a sense of loneliness and isolation, and I think to a certain extent I was looked upon as a burden. Stan's nerve was weakening after Innovations—there was a failure of nerve. And I think it was partly because neither I nor Johnny Richards could be quite what he wanted. What he wanted was Pete, he'd relied on Pete for so long, and Pete could do it, but Pete was no longer available. Also, I don't think Stan knew quite what course he should follow, instead of capitulating to the Basie elements on the band. They were very strong, all the beboppers that Stan had never had before, and they exerted a very strong force on the band—in my opinion a negative force."

Under different circumstances Stan would have agreed, but now his finances were a constant reminder that too much adventurous music can damage your wealth. It was the NBC radio network that came to his rescue, or more specifically, one NBC executive who was a Kenton fan. Bob Wogan's proposal was to broadcast the band on a sustaining basis in a regular, 30-minute weekly program from whichever location they happened to be playing. Wogan promised Stan the best audio engineers NBC could offer, and even more importantly, the freedom to choose his own format and program without NBC interference.

The results were serendipitous. *Concert in Miniature* ran for around 18 months, was picked up by AFRS, and supplemented by frequent *Concert Encore* broadcasts. Though introduced by an NBC announcer, the largely unscripted shows were hosted by Stan himself, whose often rambling introductions endeared him to the many big-band jazz lovers who tuned in regularly, eager not to miss a single show. All were widely recorded, the best "unofficial" copies being by hi-fi enthusiast Jerry Haendiges, who has made a majority available in good quality CD format. Previews began in April 1952, with the first official *CIM* coming from Kitchener, Ontario, on June 3, and the last known live broadcast in the series airing November 3, 1953.

The impact of the *Concerts in Miniature* (announced as by "Modern America's Man of Music") provided Kenton with fresh impetus to build his band into an aggregation that matched his title. Stan often preferred to build his own stars, but that took years to accomplish, and now

Kenton needed immediate results. There was an open chair for Maynard Ferguson in the trumpet section, and Stan's favorite high-note man returned in July, after his first attempt to form his own band floundered. The only drag was that Maynard's wife, singer Kay Brown, came as part of the package. Kay may have been a looker, but another June Christy she was not, and Stan kept her well away from the microphone on his *CIM* broadcasts. During a six-month stay she made only one record with the band, Gene Roland's "Lonesome Train," which was a derailment to start with.

Bob Fitzpatrick had a temporary fall-out with Stan, and Bob Burgess came in as lead trombone. Burgess was nicknamed "Butter" because he played so smoothly, and was introduced as "an artist" by Stan on the *CIM* for July 22. For the jazz trombone chair, Stan recruited Frank Rosolino, a player with amazing facility and an individual style. Everyone appreciated Frank's easy-going attitude and good humor. That Rosolino had hidden depression was not apparent until many years later, when he shot his young sons and killed himself. In the words of Bill Perkins, "Frank came on with a fresh sound. On the surface he was always funny, and his playing was ebullient, never dark, never mournful. My playing gets mournful, because that's my nature, and we know now Frank had an incredibly tragic dark side also."

And then there was Lee Konitz. Not that there was any comparison between them, but if Vido Musso represented the Kenton Sound of the Forties, for the Fifties the personification must surely be Lee, a major soloist in his own right, and one of the few true jazz originals. Says Bill Russo: "Lee was an inspiration to write for. He sustained me. He had a sense of the line and how to play that was very comfortable for me. He made things that I wrote acceptable to the band, that would not otherwise have been acceptable. By contrast, Lee was pretty negative towards me. Lee has been negative towards me for 50 years now. He likes me personally, but there's probably no more than a couple of things I've written that he may have liked . . . Lee treated me in exactly the same way as he does today—total condescension! I treat him with the greatest respect! I dragged Konitz into the band kicking and screaming—I don't think he wants to think about that anymore. He was very reluctant to come on the band, partly because he knew he was going to get into so much trouble with Lennie Tristano and his colleagues."

Konitz indeed remembered it a little differently: "I was surprised to get a call from Stan Kenton. He told me he was trying to get more of a jazz band together, and mentioned Richie Kamuca was joining. I was raising a family and needed a steady job, and the thought of making $175 a week was monumental to me. I intended staying on the band until Christmas, and getting a little bit out of debt, and then going on my way. By Christmas I was in debt to the band, so I stayed for another year!

"It was a unique experience, though I generally prefer to play improvised music, and for the most part Stan's was an ensemble band. So when there was a solo you played everything you knew in 32 bars, because you might not get another chance for a while. Today I am very pleased when I hear the things I played with Kenton. I think Lester Young did some of his most meaningful playing with the Count Basie band, and I don't compare myself with Lester, but with Kenton I was in a situation that brought out certain aspects of my playing that won't come out with just a rhythm section or whatever. Overall I feel proud of the body of work I produced with Stan, and I am delighted to have had that experience. The camaraderie, and whole life investment that goes into that kind of a situation is unparalleled, so it was a memorable time."

Some alumni remember that Kenton seemed in awe of Konitz, and treated him with unusual deference and respect. Says Russo: "Lee had a strong sense of his own worth. He was easily the best improviser in the band, maybe the best improviser ever, and I think in some ways Lee's very best playing was with Kenton; so he had this awareness of his own power, and received the best treatment from both Stan and the audiences."

The belief that some of Konitz' finest work was with Kenton is justified and widespread. Said Conte Candoli: "Lee Konitz was very important to us. I think Lee did some of his best playing *ever* with Kenton. He was something extra, a real force in that band." A view echoed by Bill Perkins: "Bill Russo's music is not player-friendly, but the music's worth is proven when you listen to it—the records show just how good it is. Lee Konitz hated Russo's music, and he hated the band at the time, and yet Buddy Childers and I both agree, perhaps the most brilliant saxophone playing Lee ever did was with that band, playing Bill Russo's arrangements. The combination inspired him to peaks that I've never heard before or since."

Perk is exceptionally perceptive. While Konitz plays well on the looser Holman charts, the greater discipline required to meet the restriction imposed by Russo's more structured frameworks serves as a challenge, and spurs Lee to unsurpassed heights of creativity. (Try Capitol's "My Lady," "Lover Man," or "Improvisation.") Finally, Holman himself came up with the best explanation for Lee's inspired work with Stan: "I've always said that some of the best playing Konitz ever did was on the Kenton band. A lot of people think that. It was hard to play with that band—being so big the time wasn't always the greatest, it would slow down and speed up, and it was loud! So I think the band just needled Lee a little bit, and made him a little angry, and it came out in his playing; he was a little more aggressive than he was before or has been since."

Richie Kamuca was a fabulously cool tenor man, who joined the same day as Konitz (August 26) on Stan Levey's recommendation. Richie was not a fluent reader at the time, so he roomed with Holman, who brought him up to speed with a crash course. A good-looking guy, Kamuca was a real hit with the girls who followed the band. The story goes that once both Rosemary Clooney and Johnny Mathis were in the audience, and both had their eye on the same prize for the night! Bill Holman summed Richie up as "A tried and true Lester Young person. But Richie had his own sound that nobody else had, and he had this light, airy way of playing. He wasn't trying to break the boundaries or anything, he just wanted to have fun, and he wanted to swing."

Stan Levey gave up his own combo to join Kenton. Despite his small-group bebop connections (Levey had been the drummer in Charlie Parker's first trio with Joe Albany as far back as 1944), Levey soon proved himself versatile enough to fit into the big-band drum chair, and became the driving force of Kenton's rhythm section. A big man physically, Levey had the essential power and strength, and reputedly managed to break several cymbals during his time with Kenton. Record producer Dick Bank told me Levey (who had a reputation as a superb time-keeper) wasn't impressed by either Bagley on bass or Sal Salvador on guitar, and had a hard time holding the section together and driving the band at the same time; this is something supported by Levey himself, who commented, "When I was with Stan, the rhythm section was not the greatest, because a couple of players had an agenda of their own. In other words, they were not good team players, which made it difficult because it put most of the work on my back—it was a hard job but we got it done."[14]

Stan wanted to make the public aware of all these highly rated (and expensive!) jazzmen in his team, and hit upon the novel idea to familiarize them via a recording he called "Prologue." Johnny Richards wrote the music illustrating each man's individual abilities, while Stan wrote the narration introducing each segment. The guys were not let into the plan beforehand, because as Bob Burgess recalled, "[Bill Putnam] was doing the mixing, Johnny Richards was rushing back and forth with the vodka flowing, and we didn't see the music before we played it. None of us even knew the recitation was going to exist, but Stan went to great pains to describe the orchestra and what he felt about the individuals in the band."[15] And Conte Candoli confirmed, "We didn't have a clue at the time what it was all about, but that was normal. It was Johnny who had to do the editing and put it all together. The completed 'Prologue' was phenomenal, it really credited the musicians in an innovative and dramatic way. But Stan loved the people in his band. He'd bring us down front and let us announce our own songs, and used our names every time he could." The closing bars of "Prologue" with Stan's jubilant voice shouting "THIS IS AN ORCHESTRA!" above the rising orchestral tumult and Maynard Ferguson's piercing trumpet, leave an indelible impression.

Several days of intensive recording followed "Prologue," producing a collection of "New Concepts" which are uncontestably exceptional, one of the benchmarks against which all other recordings may be judged. More than any other factor, they elevated Stan's status and prestige at a time when he needed it the most. Jazz fans in general loved Mulligan's "Young Blood" and "Swing House," both strong compositions providing substantial frameworks to accommodate the band's battery of soloists: Candoli, Konitz, Kamuca, and (on "Swing House") Rosolino.

Sal Salvador recalled that "Invention for Guitar and Trumpet" came about because "Stan had the idea for a piece featuring Maynard and myself one night when I was riding in his car along with Bill Holman, and he told Bill to see what he could come up with. Bill wrote a great piece of music, the hardest I ever had to play. Maynard and I rehearsed it all the time, and when the record came out it really brought my name to people's attention."[16] But Holman disagreed, insisting that the work was not typical of what he wanted to write: "My conception was just forming when I wrote 'Invention,' and I didn't have a solid direction of my own. I don't really like it at all, though it earned me more money than anything else I wrote for Stan!"

If the pieces Russo composed to feature the soloists have anything in common besides the excellence of their writing, it is that they were unanimously disliked by their recipients! Bill could write swing music, but he frequently brought classical elements into his work, which is what gives his charts a special Kentonian flavor, while at the same time turning off the very musicians he is writing for. Frank Rosolino told Don Reed he didn't dig "Frank Speaking," because the background writing was "too fussy." Conte Candoli told me, "I didn't like 'Portrait of a Count' at first, but I changed it a lot, and instead of the written melody I asked Russo to write out the chord changes, so that when I played I sort of made up my own melody. And over a period of time we kinda worked it out, and turned it into a nice number that I was happy about." (Not exactly a ringing endorsement of the Kenton title with which Conte is most closely associated. After that I didn't dare ask about the much more abstruse "Poem for Trumpet" Russo composed for him!)

Perhaps out of sheer devilment, Russo pulled out all the stops on Konitz's specialty "My Lady," causing Lee to wonder whether he could even improvise efficiently on the piece. "I looked it over," said Konitz, "and there was a chord change every two beats. I knew Bill wasn't one of the best trombone players, so I asked him if he'd tried to play the piece. He said he'd played it through, so I figured if he could play it, I must be able to play it too!" And of course Lee did, beautifully.

Russo's use of trombones as a rhythmic device on "23°N-82°W" (the co-ordinates of Havana) wasn't quite as original as he might profess. Manny Albam had used the technique previously on "Pan-Americana" (Charlie Barnet, 1949), but when I raised this with Bill, he neatly deflected the issue. Whatever, by opening with the bones and emphasizing their use in this rhythmic manner, Bill certainly created a highly novel and exciting Latin-American chart. Instantly recognizable, this was the piece that really attracted people to Russo's writing, and was good enough to be revived by Stan for the Seventies bands.

But Russo's greatest achievement was his rescoring of "Improvisation" for the smaller orchestra. This time the central motif was not a four-way improvisation, but instead, "I gave the central role to Konitz, who was the most elegant and eloquent of any of us. We recorded Lee late at night and sent most of the orchestra home, and I was very happy with the way the recording turned out," Russo said. Konitz himself picked "Improvisation" as some of his best work for Kenton, though he did question Salvador's creativity: "I wish Sal had felt a little freer to make the accompaniment more interesting. He made it more difficult for me to find attractive melodies to play." (Billy Bauer was Lee's ideal guitar player.) The contrast between Lee's plaintive alto and the massive Kenton brass-led "wall of sound" is an overwhelming experience that confirms "Improvisation" as the crowning achievement of the Kenton-Russo-Konitz partnership.

During 1952, Capitol Records celebrated their 10th anniversary with a special gold-labelled promotional LP *Capitol Cavalcade 1942–52*. Kenton was represented by excerpts from two of his successes from the Forties: "Eager Beaver" and "Tears Flowed Like Wine." But that music was from an earlier era. Throughout 1952 Stan had single-handedly built a rejuvenated orchestra from the ashes of Innovations, a forward-looking band for the Fifties that once again placed Kenton at the top. As Stan used to say, "If we're going to have a swing band, we're going to have the *best* swing band."[17] And without a doubt, he did!

# 13.

# If It's Tuesday, It Must Be Belgium

## (1953)

**Kay Brown quit in January 1953** in search of unfulfilled movie stardom, leaving Stanley to search for a new singer. June Christy recommended Chris Connor, whom she happened to hear on a Jerry Wald broadcast (though Chris' main big-band experience had been with Claude Thornhill). "Stan sent for a demo of mine," Chris related, "and I guess he liked it, because next thing I got a call from George Morte [Stan's road manager] asking if I'd like to join the band. That was the biggest thrill of my life. To sing with Stan's band had been my dream ever since I started singing. Even before I performed with the band in public, we recorded at Capitol, and that scared the hell out of me, but Stan was very sweet and handed me the sheet music, and we went on to record 'And the Bull Walked Around, Olay!' that Joe Greene had written."[1]

"Bull" was essentially just that, a nonsense ditty with band vocal chorus that Kenton hoped might hit the jackpot in the same way as "Tears Flowed" and "Tampico" had done for O'Day and Christy respectively. But times had changed, and "Bull" deservedly sank like a stone. Despite this initial setback, Kenton was very impressed with Connor's voice, whose jazz style was already fully developed when she joined the band, and wisely allowed Chris in future to sing exclusively the better type of quality song which afforded full scope for her talent.

Very much a member of the "cool school" of vocalizing, Chris closely resembles Christy, and is actually technically probably the better singer. Connor invariably sounds very much in control, by no means impassive, but always composed and unruffled. She lacks Christy's emotional range and sense of vulnerability. Stan once commented that "Anita O'Day was the original, the purest one. You couldn't trace her style back to anyone else. But with Christy and Connor you could see the line back to Anita. All three had the ability to communicate directly with the listener's subconscious." And as for singing flat, Kai Winding insisted that Christy and Connor "Had far better pitch than most other singers. It's just that

105

their voices were so uncluttered; with little vibrato they had nothing to hide behind."[2]

Connor's impact may be judged by the fact that though she sang with Stan a bare five months, she is still very much remembered as a Kenton vocalist. In the view of Mark Masters, "I believe that if ever there was a combination of arranger and singer that was meant to work together, it was Bill Russo and Chris Connor. His warm dissonances and cool style were the perfect mate for Chris' lush voice." Russo wrote the arrangements for most of Connor's songs, from the plaintive "Nobody Knows the Trouble I've Seen" to the Latin-flavored, exhilarating "I Get a Kick Out of You," and commented: "Stan would say, 'Write a piece for voice that we can really sell; let's do this and get a good single out with Chris Connor.' Sometimes I'd suggest a song, but often Stan would come up with the titles. I'd write an arrangement, and if he didn't like it, he might say, 'That's fine, but we'll use it next year!' Partly by which pieces he chose to use, Stan exerted a great influence on us, both directly and indirectly."

Occasionally Joe Greene turned out a more musical song than his more frequent novelties, and along with "Soothe Me," "All About Ronnie" must rank as his best. Certainly Stan dug "Ronnie," and he already had a recording in the can arranged by Johnny Richards for Jerri Winters, but now he wanted a version by Chris so that the issued recording could be duplicated live, and charged Russo with writing a new orchestration. I don't know if Capitol 2511 could be termed a "hit," but it certainly turned the song into a standard for both Stan and Chris Connor, who sings what could easily be the over-sentimental lyrics with cool sophistication. Joe Coccia and Kenton both wrote later arrangements for the band, while as Chris said in 2002: "'All About Ronnie' was a wonderful song that became my signature tune, and I'm still singing it today."[3]

Despite her success with Stan, Connor quit early in July. *Down Beat* described her departure as "abrupt and without notice," the official reason being poor health. Kenton told me, "Chris was very good with the band. She's a good singer, and everybody liked her, but she became terribly homesick while we were on the road playing near Cleveland. She came to me one night and said, 'I don't think I can stand another hour. I've got to get back to New York.' And so I had to let her go."[4] With singers now ruling the pop charts, they no longer needed to spend years with dance bands in decline before striking out as a single, though as Chris recalled: "I knew it was the wrong thing to do, I should have stayed much longer, but my short time with Stan had gained me enough recognition for me to go out on my own. I owe Stan a great deal. He was one of the most beautiful men I have ever met, completely dedicated, and a gentleman on top of it."

With ballroom bookings an essential part of the band's itinerary, Stan was intent upon updating the dance book in the same way he had the jazz. The job fell to Bill Russo, Holman having shown little aptitude in that direction. The Russo Sound, most readily distinguishable through Bill's plangent scoring for the trombones, adapted particularly well to tuneful standards like "Sophisticated Lady" and "April in Paris." Along with Rugolo's, Russo's was arguably the finest dance library the band ever boasted, and with plenty of space for solo improvisation, was equally well suited to listening as dancing. Russo's writing, even on the up-tempo titles, always radiated a certain gravitas, was never flippant or superficial. It demanded attention, and was richly rewarding in return.

Even Lee Konitz, usually a stern critic of Bill's charts because he disliked the classical elements, was moved to be generous: "Some of the nicest writing that Bill did were those standards for the dance library. In fact, I very naively asked Bill if he had really written those arrangements himself, or if he'd shipped them out to a student: Bill just laughed." And as Lennie Niehaus said at Rendezvous in Britain 2000: "The dance arrangements Russo wrote for Kenton were fine. Stan didn't really like mutes, but Bill would write one trumpet in a straight mute, and one in a cup mute. Bill Russo brought a whole new sound into the band."[5]

The best of Russo's very jazz-biased "dance" book was recorded on two 10-inch LPs called *Sketches/Portraits on Standards*. Several ballads were written specifically to feature the soloists, including Lee Konitz' exquisite performance of "Lover Man," Bob Burgess on "Over the Rainbow," and Frank Rosolino's "I Got It Bad." But the "dance" chart that has attracted the most attention in retrospect is the up-tempo "Fascinating Rhythm," which Bill himself considered to be one of his most successful: "I added material derived from the song, and I changed the melody in some important respects and altered the rhythm of the piece. The song itself is very elegant, hip and modern, and the whole design fits together very well. In fact, Lee Konitz doubts that I wrote it because it's so good—which only a school friend going back to age 13 could get away with! Both Lee and I were interested in the Tristano style, music that was written but sounded more like a jazz soloist, and some of that came through in 'Fascinating Rhythm.'"[6]

Equally arresting is the modernizing of Duke's "Sophisticated Lady": notice how well Russo builds the arrangement to introduce Lee's poignant alto solo. Also striking are the light, airy swing of "I've Got You Under My Skin" and the unusually slow tempo of "How High the Moon" (which was how the song was intended before the boppers appropriated it), because neither Stan nor Bill much liked bop, and Russo wanted to escape the usual bebop associations. As Joel Kaye declared, "Some commercial albums are also artistic successes, like *Sketches on Standards*. Those Bill Russo arrangements are just works of art, as well as having a pretty good popular appeal."[7]

*Sketches* also contained two non-Russo charts, one being the celebrated "Pennies from Heaven" by Lennie Niehaus. The orchestration is so smooth it seems to float, but it's the feisty trumpet solo that really catches the attention. Conte observed, "I frequently get compliments for my solo on 'Pennies from Heaven.' People tell me that's one of their favorite trumpet solos. I remember I didn't feel at all well on the day of the session, so I didn't really feel like playing at all, and it just became a lucky take." Don Reed sums up popular sentiment when he says: "I have never heard Conte play a better solo than he did on 'Pennies from Heaven.' I think that is one of the all-time great trumpet solos."[8]

Gerry Mulligan had an arrangement of "Begin the Beguine" in the book, but the chart on *Sketches* is by Stan. Whether Mulligan knew the authorship I don't know (arrangers were not noted on the LP liner), but in any case Gerry got his revenge for Stan's criticisms of his work when he wrote, "I was walking by a record shop in Hollywood one day when I saw a Kenton album with 'Begin the Beguine' listed on it. My gosh, I thought, he's recorded [my arrangement]. So I went in and listened and found it was another arrangement altogether. The one I'd written was not as a beguine, but rather a simple four. The one on the record was, in my opinion, quite without character."[9]

With Ms Brown out of the band, in February Maynard Ferguson again got itchy feet, and moved to Paramount Studios, which doubtless paid a higher salary than Kenton could afford. Big-band veteran Ernie Royal (Basie, Ellington, Herman, Hampton) came in, renowned for his all-round trumpet ability as well as his high-note skills. At the same time, Bob Gioga decided it was time to quit the road. Bob had been with the band non-stop since its inception in 1940, an invaluable friend and long-time road manager to Stan, and a valued player in the saxophone section, all points seized on by Milt Bernhart: "Gioga and Stan first played together in the early '30s, and became best of friends from that point on. Bob was a very good and rarely noticed bari sax man—just listen to the records. But on top of that, as road manager for years and years, his loose sense of humor kept things relaxed on and off the bandstand. He was important to Stan for that reason alone, but he played good and deserves a lot of credit for the development of the Kenton sax sound."[10] Bob's short-term replacement was Henry Levy, later to achieve recognition under the name "Hank" Levy as an avant-garde writer for Don Ellis and Stan Kenton.

With Richie Kamuca set to leave in June, Kenton wanted a big name to replace his star tenor player, and took a risk by hiring one of the leading soloists in the business. Jack "Zoot" Sims was a gamble for Stan, not because his musicality was ever in doubt, but because his reputation as one of Woody's original Four Brothers gave him the autonomy to behave in a quirky, unpredictable manner; and he was another strongly independent character who might well close ranks with swingers like Konitz and Holman to kick against the traces and question Kenton's musical policy. That there was something of an adversarial situation is indicated by a story Stanley told: "Sometimes Zoot was with me, and sometimes he was in league with the band. He would say to me, very indignantly, 'What are you looking at us for? We're making it!' But at other times he would say, 'Why can't you guys get it right? Stan can't put up with this!'"[11]

Whatever, Kenton clearly thought it was worth the hazard to have another master-player the equal of Lee Konitz on the band; and the musicians certainly were inspired by Zoot's presence, and appreciated Stan's determination to build the very best band money could buy. Konitz expressed his own admiration for Zoot: "I feel that the people who have been really outstanding in some way introduced something into the vocabulary of jazz, or in the actual sound and structure of the music, that was unique. Zoot Sims had a very special feeling for the melody, a very special feeling for the rhythm of the piece, and a very special sound."

Nevertheless, I feel it would be wrong to suggest Sims galvanized the band in the way Konitz had before him. He did not make the same immediate impact, and did not stay long enough to impose his personality on the music. To my knowledge, Zoot rarely made public pronouncements about his experiences with Stan. In many ways, Russo and Holman were like chalk and cheese, and both seemed to harbor very different opinions on many aspects of Kentonia. Russo stated at Rendezvous '96: "Zoot Sims was once asked how he liked playing with Kenton, and Zoot said, 'Yeah, I really had a great time with Stan's band.' But not everyone will accept that—it's a truth people don't want to believe, because it flies in the face of popular myth."[12] On the other hand, Holman somewhat enigmatically stated on a 2000 radio broadcast tribute to Sims (who would have been 75 years old had he not died from cancer at 59): "Musically, it was a stone around Zoot's neck. It was an impressive band, but not a 'fun' band, because there was this conflict between Stan and the guys. They wanted to play a style of no-holds-barred swinging jazz, whereas Stan insisted we played straight eighth notes, and the two conceptions didn't really come together very well."[13]

That was of course Holman's view, though he doubtless spoke for several members of the band as well. Whatever, arrangements were now flowing freely from the Holman pen. "Bags" (a feature for bassist Bagley) was one of the first, followed swiftly by "Hav-A-Havana," "Frivolous Sal," "The Opener," and "Theme and Variations." "'Bags' came off very well I thought," said Willis, "and that made me realize that possibly I did have a direction I could follow to write for this band that would satisfy both Stan and myself." How closely Bill came to Stan's ideals is open to doubt. In trombonist Don Reed's opinion, "Holman did not write what Stan wanted, but Stan was open-minded enough and smart enough to realize that what Bill wrote were great things that would help the band."[14] One point not in question was Kenton's disapproval of some of Holman's titles. Stan never did like tune titles with puns, or which he thought degraded the music. So names like "Hav-A-Havana" and "Frivolous Sal" were frowned upon, and even worse was the onomatopoeic "Boo Boo Be Doop." "Stan could never bring himself to say that one," commented Bill. "It didn't fit the image. He preferred titles like 'Artistry in Cosmic Radiation.'" (Not strictly true: Kenton did on occasion announce "Boo Boo," though with distaste; and Stan's own titles were almost aways brief and to the point, often named after a featured artist or instrument.) Also beyond doubt is the band's appreciation of Holman's charts. When asked to choose a number to play themselves, it was sure to be one of Bill's—often the aforementioned "Boo Boo Be Doop"!

The highlight of 1953, and one of the peaks of Stan's career, was the band's first tour of Europe, though not all the musicians would remember it that way. Mounting excitement was tinged with some apprehension. No one really knew how the band would be received on the Continent, and a big disappointment was the refusal of the British Musicians Union to allow the band to appear in the UK, which housed one of the music's biggest fan bases, judged by record sales. The Union believed American bands in Britain would result in a loss of work for their own members without reciprocal tours by British bands in the States, for which there was little demand. (For the record, Kenton did get to play for US servicemen at Air Force bases Sculthorpe and Burtonwood, as these were technically American territory.)

Two band members were not looking forward to the trip. Sal Salvador could not bring himself to fly the Atlantic, and was replaced for the tour by Barry Galbraith, who was actually the superior player. The other defaulter was Ernie Royal, officially because of nerve problems with a muscle in his upper lip. However, Conte Candoli, who should know, told me, "Royal was not too happy with his role in the band, and consequently when Stan was getting ready to go to Europe, Ernie decided he wanted to stay in New York. People have said he had a sore lip or something, but on the contrary he just wanted to quit the band and stay home." Royal's loss was a blow, but with Buddy Childers on lead, and Conte and Don Dennis to take the solos, the section could carry Don Smith and Ziggy Minichiello (an ex-band-boy) without any real damage.

After Chris Connor's sudden departure, Stan didn't have a singer and he felt it essential to take a vocalist with him to Europe. He knew it was June Christy who above all others was best associated with his music, and June agreed to return for the duration of the tour, as a star attraction with her own recital. As Conte Candoli remembered it, "Christy was a great gal, and a dynamic force in the band. She really contributed, and a lot of people came just to see June. Her best buddy on the European tour was Zoot, they were hanging out everywhere together." And June herself told me, "That first European tour was one of the most thrilling experiences of my life. Everywhere we played it was SRO, and we were overwhelmed by the acceptance and great love and appreciation that the Europeans have for jazz."

Indications had been that the orchestra would be well-received, but no one was quite prepared for the acclaim and near-idolatry that followed the band, and Stan in particular, as they played the Continent for a month, opening August 22, 1953, in Copenhagen, Denmark, where "The response was almost unbelievable. They screamed, applauded and stamped their feet with an ovation that could well have turned into a riot," according to Howard Lucraft.[15] That same date a phone call from Stan's mother in Hollywood told him his dad had just died from leukemia. Stan grieved, but there was no question of his returning home; too much was at stake. The grind had just begun, as the band traveled through Denmark, Sweden, Germany, Holland, Belgium, Switzerland, France, England (US bases only), Ireland and Italy. In scenes reminiscent of the Beatles furore a decade or more later, and for perhaps the first time in his life, Kenton realized the mass adulation of A-List, film-star status: lionized, revered, honored, cheered, and acclaimed across the length and breadth of Europe. "From start to finish," said publicity manager Gene Howard, "we found the most enthusiastic crowds we'd ever played to. There were near riots in almost every town. In most cases, police barricades were necessary to prevent crowds storming backstage. In one

German town they broke down a wall and practically disrobed their 'champion' before police reinforcements could quiet the mob. Sometimes Kenton would have to stay in his dressing-room for two hours after the concert before the stagedoor crowd could be thinned out."[16]

From all over Europe came enthusiastic reviews of the concerts, with Zoot Sims the soloist most often singled out for special praise, closely followed by Konitz, Candoli, Rosolino, and Stan Levey. But almost every writer agreed that the real star was the band, disciplined, powerful, and swinging as never before. Howard Lucraft made the interesting comparison that in 1943 at the Berlin Sportpalast it was Hitler who had received the organized roars of thousands of young Germans as he denounced the "Decadent American culture." From the very same podium a decade later, Kenton was greeted with louder, freer, and happier cheers as he announced, "A great force in jazz—someone you all know about—Miss June Christy!"[17] In fact, Kenton apart, perhaps June received the keenest personal reception of all. Then approaching her peak form with a series of unique albums for Capitol Records, June blended her recital with several of her best-loved Kenton standards ("Willow Weep for Me," "How High the Moon"), with some of her current hit singles ("Great Scott," "My Heart Belongs to Only You"), and sometimes previewed her as yet unreleased signature song "Something Cool" to rapturous applause (though how much European audiences could make of the song's story-line sung in English with an American accent is a moot point!).

Such was the clamor for tickets, extra concerts were laid on, and even the normally uncomplaining Kenton said, "It isn't the one-nighters that get you down—it's the two-in-one-night stands. On many occasions we had to play one town at 6 o'clock, then pack up and drive 50 or 75 miles and play another town at 11."[18] Inevitably, as fatigue set in and the appreciative audience reaction became less self-motivating, some of the musicians began bitching. They were used to life on the road, but this was a harder grind than ever experienced before, and even in the hour of triumph, seeds were sown that would eventually lead to the band's downfall. Conte Candoli told me, "That was a *hard* tour. We did two concerts a day for a month, sometimes in two different towns. We didn't know that was going to happen, and we didn't get any extra pay—we were on a fixed retainer." "The promoters never counted the money, they made so much," observed Stan Levey. "They just used to shovel it into bags."[19] The trouble was, none of it was coming the musicians' way! (Whether Kenton himself received bonuses is unknown to me.)

Though for many in Britain who made a windswept journey across the Irish Sea, the Theatre Royal concerts in Dublin were the tour's high-spot, both Bill Russo and Stan Levey have opined that of all the European performances, the peak was at the Alhambra Theatre in Paris on September 18. Even Stan had been apprehensive of Paris, where the French fans had the reputation of preferring trad jazz, and of voicing their disapproval of music they disliked in no uncertain manner. The band accepted the challenge, and Paris accepted Kenton, with a standing, shouting ovation that was overwhelming, from the wild opening applause to the closing shouts of "Bis! Bis!" (Encore). "The band caught fire the night we played Paris," Levey told collector John Loeffler. "It was hands down the best concert of the whole European tour."[20]

The entire Paris performance is released on Jasmine CD, the music a mixture of "New Concepts" and older Kenton classics, but even the earlier works assume a fresh veneer, because this is a different-sounding orchestra, and because of the dramatic change in solo styles. "Eager Beaver" and "Intermission Riff" have become solo vehicles for the fleet, melodic inventions of the incomparable Zoot Sims. But Zoot is also outstanding at a slower tempo, and his sweeping, searing series of notes that illuminate "Concerto to End All Concertos" are soulfully impressive, resembling a deeper-toned Lee Konitz. One might question whether Zoot's light, pulsing swing is best suited to the Kenton brand of music, but there is no doubt his phrasing, tone, and technique make him a readily identifiable, original tenor-sax player.

By the end of the tour everyone was weary, but the strain on Kenton was greatest of all. Incessant interviews, countless broadcasts, meeting with fans, dinners with dignitaries, on-the-spot decisions, were all extras that left Stan "So tired my legs trembled, and I could hardly stand or sit with any comfort."[21] But instead of even the briefest respite, the band flew back to the States via Iceland on September 24, arriving in New York the following morning, and unbelievably went straight into rehearsals for a live TV show that same night, and the following day played two prestige shows (8:30 p.m. and midnight) at Carnegie Hall. At age 41 Kenton was still young enough to throw off his tiredness and appear to recover from probably the most triumphant, and certainly the most strenuous tour he would ever experience. For Stanley such mass acceptance was the oxygen of life, and provided him with superhuman resilience that superseded mere fatigue.

A three-week residency at Birdland at least avoided travel, but in preparation to follow was another exhausting tour termed Festival of Modern American Jazz that involved some of the greatest names in the business. Package tours were nothing new in themselves; the difference with this one was that the stars would play not with their own groups, but accompanied by the Kenton orchestra in new arrangements specifically scored by Russo and Holman to showcase their individual talents. Signed to appear were Dizzy Gillespie, Stan Getz, Slim Gaillard, Candido Camero, and June Christy, plus the Erroll Garner Trio playing on their own. The tenor of the entire show was set on musical worth presented in a serious manner, as "Len" wrote in *Down Beat*: "There wasn't a single lull, the pacing was almost faultless, and the music was as consistently interesting as anything since the early days of Duke Ellington's annual soirees."[22]

The Festival entourage traveled in two buses, and on the night of November 10, both buses set off to travel through the night to arrive in good time for their next date in Pittsburgh. Stan was in the "guest" coach when the larger bus carrying most of the band members crashed at speed into the rear of a tractor-trailer truck on the Pennsylvania Turnpike. Perhaps the miracle is that during four decades on the road, this was the only accident of any significance, and even on this occasion there were no fatalities. Most seriously injured were road manager George Morte and Conte's wife Peggy Candoli. Out of action were Ziggy Minichiello and the trombone section. Conte Candoli recalled: "It was at night, totally dark. The bus driver fell asleep. My wife was three months pregnant, and she broke a vertebra in her back. Bob Burgess and Frank Rosolino suffered facial injuries, and everyone was badly shaken. Nasty accident! George Morte was in the front seat, and was thrown right through the windshield. They took us to an emergency hospital nearby. I stayed with my wife, and both she and the baby turned out fine, but I left the band after that and we went back to my home town."

Those not injured thought that at least they'd have a brief respite to recover, but had reckoned without Stan's steely determination that the show should go on. A phone call to Chicago, where Russo had retired to write for the band, and Bill flew in with a relief trombone section of local Chicago musicians. Likewise Lee Konitz, who had remained in New York to celebrate his daughter's birthday, rushed back. There may have been a seat or two empty when the curtains parted at Pittsburgh's Syria Mosque Theatre on November 11, but the concert went ahead as planned.

Any satisfaction Stan may have felt was short-lived. The crash was the final straw that broke the spirit of a band already demoralized by sheer fatigue, and the unceasing grind of the one (or even two)-nightstands across Europe and America. Stan had simply driven his men too hard. "The greatest Kenton band to date is virtually finished," wrote Howard Lucraft, quoting Buddy Childers as saying, "I don't know what the heck is happening. Neither does poor Stan. I seem to be the only guy staying with him."[23]

Out immediately were Candoli, Burgess, and Rosolino (though Frank would return in 1954). Sam Noto, a proficient trumpet soloist out of Billy May's band, replaced Conte, and would stay for almost five years, without ever attaining Conte's stature. In place of Burgess, Stan was fortunate to tempt back Bob Fitzpatrick, whose dedication brought much-needed stability to the decimated trombones. Meanwhile the new section needed breaking in, which led directly to the departure of Zoot Sims, as Bill Holman related: "Instead of laying off for a few days after the accident, we had to work double hard to rehearse with the new trombones. So Zoot said, 'We know our parts, why do we have to rehearse because they don't know theirs?' Stan said, 'Because I say so, Jack!' And they went back and forth like this for a while before Stan said, 'I think you'd better give your notice, Jack.' And Zoot said, 'Okay, you got it!'"[24]

Coming in was one of the finest tenor players ever to grace the band. Bill Perkins had been playing with Woody Herman when he got the call. "My first impression was one of complete confusion. I didn't even have a rehearsal, it was a very last-minute thing after the road accident, and I just struggled through this very complex and difficult repertoire. And then I went out and tried to play a solo, and I got lost completely, because I'd never played before in such a loud band. It was hard to orientate yourself, and I was very wet behind the ears, very inexperienced. Stan was very courteous and attempted to put me at my ease as much as possible, and I remember Lee Konitz was still in the band. Lee never said anything to me for about four weeks, and then finally we were working in some club, and he said, 'Well, I see that you can play after all.' And those were the first words Lee ever spoke to me!"

After Sims went, the band simply unravelled, piece by piece. Bill Russo wrote more for a short while, but his playing days were over as he realized his future lay as a leader-composer. "I felt I couldn't do what Stan needed," said Bill. "It was becoming a swing band, and I wanted to do things my own way."[25] Konitz stayed until the middle of December: "I finally left when it just wasn't that rewarding any more. I wanted to be back in a small band."[26] No one was quite going to replace the originality of Konitz, but Charlie Mariano came as close as any. Charlie spoke Bird's language rather than Lester's, but by the time he joined Kenton he had extended the idiom with a poise and emotion of his own making. "Mariano is one of my all-time favorite players," said Bill Trujillo. "I hear him play, and I want to cry, I want to laugh. He is total passion, and I think that's what music is all about. Playing from the heart, and the soul."

The most fractious parting was that of Bill Holman. Stan had already gone well over half-way to meeting Bill's demands, and tunes like "Zoot" (for Sims) and "In Lighter Vein" (Konitz) were well outside his usual boundaries. In a heated confrontation Holman argued that Kenton should surrender the last vestiges of his traditional style, and become a straight-ahead swing outfit. Stan would effectively surrender control of his own band and become essentially the Bill Holman orchestra, a scenario to which Stan could not possibly accede. So Holman, already upset by the loss of both Sims and Konitz, quit as well, though the two men would mend fences sooner than seemed possible at the time.

Within the space of a month Kenton had watched his dream band disintegrate before his eyes after one tragic act of carelessness. The stress and strains must have taken their toll on Stan's stamina, but it certainly wasn't visible on the surface, as he struggled to rebuild his band. The effects such devotion to his music would have on Stan's long-term health, at that point still lay many years into the future.

# 14.

## "Kenton Presents Jazz"

### (1954–1955)

After a short breather, the Festival of Modern American Jazz reassembled in January 1954 minus Slim Gaillard and Stan Getz. Slim's comedy spot was replaced by the less-than-frivolous alto of Lee Konitz, whose demeanor had frequently suggested his rightful place was featured artist rather than mere band member. Getz was serving a spell in prison for drug use. The irony is that Getz' position was filled by Charlie Parker, an even more notorious user of banned substances.

Kenton's attitude to illegal drugs was unambivalent—he didn't want them on his band—but as much because of the bad publicity a bust would bring than because he failed to recognize some sort of stimulant was often necessary to make tolerable the grind of "The Road." His own vices were legal—cigarettes and vodka—but at the same time he often tolerated known addicts on the band. Gene Roland is a prime example, and in 1948 he had fired the little-known but talented trombonist Parky Groate, while retaining the services of the equally culpable Art Pepper. Several guys in the '70s indicated to me that "weed" (marijuana) was quite widely practiced, and so long as you didn't make it obvious, Stan turned a blind eye. At the very least, Stan's attitude made the guys careful, and hence less likely to be detected.

Whatever, the anti-bebop Kenton now had the art's two leading exponents—Bird and Diz—playing with the band at the same time, though never together; each had his own spot on the show. Stan had always admired Parker's playing, but by 1954 Bird's excesses meant he was well past his prime, and was actually within one year of his premature death at age 34. Conversely, Konitz was at his peak, and Lee told me, "One day I ran into Max Roach, and he told me, 'The word is out that you're cutting Bird.' Of course, I'd come back to a situation I was familiar with, and Parker didn't have that advantage. Plus, he was juicing. After that, Dizzy took Bird aside and told him, 'This young ofay is cutting you, you'd better get on top of it.'"

The normally disorganized Parker had arrived with only one arrangement to play, the Joe Lipman big-band chart on "Night and Day." After Bird declined to be featured on a retitled "Zoot," because he felt it was too closely identified with Sims, Kenton commissioned Holman to rush through two arrangements for Parker, and a couple of weeks later Bird was happily playing the super-fast "Cherokee" and the contrasting ballad "My Funny Valentine," both ideal designs to showcase America's alto ace.

Despite the competitive situation, Konitz and Parker became close. "Bird was a very friendly man," commented Lee, "but he could also be crafty. I had lent him $10, and one day as we boarded the bus I asked him if he could pay back the loan, and he said OK, and the first person that came on the bus he asked to lend him $10, and he gave it to me! One time, Charlie asked me to stay with him at the black hotel, and I was very touched. We had adjoining rooms, and he asked me to join him with my horn and we talked a little bit about my low register, and played 'Donna Lee' together. But Bird wasn't in good shape, he could hardly get through it."

Bill Perkins confirmed: "Bird was very close to his last legs on that tour, and sadly most of the time he was pretty stoned. But on those rare nights, say one out of seven, when he was not completely stoned on drugs, Dizzy always knew and would be standing in the wings, listening to Bird play. Because the stoned Parker could still play (he'd done it all his life, sadly enough), but when he wasn't stoned it was just absolutely awesome. So I treasure that memory. And when he wasn't stoned Bird was the warmest, kindest individual—no hip talk, no jive talk from him—he was very, very well-spoken, a very intelligent man with a lot of knowledge, as well as the greatest saxophone player that ever lived."

Kenton was aware of Bird's vulnerability: "Charlie was a magnificent humanitarian, with a great feeling for people, and he was most dedicated to music. We spent a great deal of time together on that trip, because we were touring the south, so I kept Charlie with me to protect him from any kind of abuse. We rode together mile after mile, and had a long time to get acquainted. He was hooked of course on one thing or another, but he managed to show up and make the dates—he wasn't unmanageable or anything like that. Charlie got what he wanted out of life, I think."[1]

At least two of the Festival concerts were recorded: Gene Norman has kept his Shrine Auditorium performance well under wraps, but the Wally Heider Portland (Oregon) recording of February 25 has seen several releases, notably on Status CD. The question of unofficial "bootleg" issues presents a moral maze with no ready solution. Kenton was in favor of collectors exchanging recordings, but against individuals profiting from his music. Yet, what good comes from secreting historically important, perishable recordings that no one will ever hear? Sales of jazz music performed perhaps 60 years ago are too small to warrant the expense of official release, and diminish by the year as older enthusiasts pass on. One thing is certain: the studio recordings will always dominate, but we would all be losers in the study and enjoyment of the jazz we admire without the efforts of music lovers behind labels like Tantara (Bill Lichtenauer), Astral Jazz (John Loeffler), Mr. Music (Wayne Knight) and Dynaflow (Steven Harris) to bring us "live" recordings from the past in the best possible digital sound.

Kenton had always intended to disband after the Festival tour ended, but first there were important records to be made. Stan wanted to capture both Bird and Lee on Capitol tape playing the special arrangements written for them by Bill Holman, but Charlie's manager Norman Granz vetoed Parker's participation, so Konitz did the session on his own, playing his three "Festival" charts ("In Lighter Vein," "Lover Man," "Of All Things"), plus one of Bird's: "My Funny Valentine." It's impossible to know what form Parker might have been in that evening of March 1, 1954, had he been allowed to play. The results might have ranged from stupendous to disastrous, or any point in between, which may be one reason why Granz was disinclined to allow Charlie to record outside of his own artistic control. Konitz is his usual brilliant self, a master-musician at the top of his form, but inevitably after 18 months of recording with Kenton he does not carry the "novelty" appeal of Bird.

There was room in the Kenton repertoire for arrangers as disparate as Holman and Russo, and *Kenton Showcase* featured charts by both men in equal measure, music that remains outstanding for its integrity, originality, and versatility. Willis told me, "I wrote the *Showcase* charts during 1953 when I was still with the band. And after I'd left with some bad feeling, I figured that was that, but the next thing I knew, Stan came to town and he was recording an album of my music. And this was my first experience of somebody who was that big, who'd do that, and not say, 'Well, we had a fight, so he's out.' I did attend the *Showcase* sessions, but I didn't have much input. On 'Kingfish' I did something about the ensembles, but most of the time I was just a spectator."

Which was probably for the best, because Bill was still not happy with Stan's interpretation of his music: "Even on the *Showcase* album, the band didn't have a very solid swing concept, because Stan was always yelling for straight eighths, and I was always writing swing time. Poor

Buddy Childers, who was responsible for the phrasing, tried to satisfy us both with a middle ground, and it just came out sounding weird."[2] What Holman really wanted was his own band, which he eventually attained. Kenton liked the eighth notes played "straight" (exactly as written, without room for flexibility), because it imposed a rigidity that restricted the sensation of swing, and this was his trademark, a vital part of the Kenton Sound. Nevertheless, the band certainly pulsates, moves, swings (whatever you want to call it) to my ears on tunes like "Fearless Finlay," "Kingfish," and "Solo for Buddy." Perhaps the most Kentonish of all Bill's *Showcase* titles is the rather heavy-handed Latin spectacular "Hav-A-Havana," and the most distinctive the cleverly devised "Theme and Variations" (though it's likely Willis would have counted off at a slightly slower tempo than Kenton thought appropriate).

Whereas Holman's writing serves largely as a springboard to launch the solo improvisations, Russo's carefully crafted compositions more often use individual voices to develop his designs. Holman works strictly within a jazz framework, is easy on the ear, and is readily accessible. Russo casts his net much wider, with music that is deep, sometimes somber, and demands the listener's total commitment. It is much closer to the Kenton ethos.

"Egdon Heath" is a brilliantly described miniature, the swirling early morning mists created by sections of the orchestra playing in counterpoint, while Bob Fitzpatrick's mournful trombone defines the main theme. Dave Schildkraut's atmospheric alto surveys the desolate landscape by day, before the evening haze descends to close the scene. "I think 'Egdon Heath' was one of my best compositions for Kenton," said Russo. "I like the procedures that I used, with the melody being imitated in various ways, and I like the jazz feel of the double time. I named the piece after *The Return of the Native* by Thomas Hardy. I never saw Egdon Heath, but I was very moved by that book."

"Thisbe" was adapted for trombones and rhythm from an unused 1950 Innovations composition "Pyramus and Thisbe," named after the mythological duo in Shakespeare's *A Midsummer Night's Dream*. There are echoes of Bill's "Improvisation," with the Fitzpatrick-led bones replacing Konitz, while Bob Lesher's guitar hovers around the edges, and also by the rapidly accelerating tempo that concludes the work. If the mood is generally melancholic, so was Russo: "'Thisbe' is named after a lady with whom I was infatuated, but who was not available to me."

Trombones are also the dominant section in "A Theme of Four Values," a brooding, mystical piece that develops into a powerful climax. For years no one could fathom Russo's enigmatic title, which is again inspired by Bill's personal life: "I was enchanted with an English ice-dancer, who was also a painter, and she had just explained to me the notion of values of painting, not just colors, but gradations of colors, so I used the words in the painting sense."

Even Russo's lighter pieces, like "Blues Before and After" and "Sweets" are ingeniously designed, the latter described by Bill as "The most main-stream piece I ever wrote for Kenton." Originally titled in homage to the Oakland (CA) ballroom of that name, so many people assumed it was named for Harry Edison that Bill later changed the dedication.

The *Showcase* music brought to a head the two factions within the current Kenton orchestra. Almost to a man, the musicians and the critics praised Holman at Russo's expense, and I doubt the two men had a great deal of esteem for each other. I have no knowledge of Russo ever directly criticizing Willis, but he frequently deplored the "Basie elements" within the band, and there is no question Holman was the leader of that move-ment. Holman himself was less constrained: "Russo's writing wasn't jazzy enough for me. He kind of had one foot in the Progressive Jazz camp, and the other foot in his own kind of thing, and I think he was afraid to write something that would sound common, like a lot of typical jazz figures; he always wanted to be a cut above that, and I think you have to get down and dirty if you're gonna write jazz charts."

The music of both writers has survived well, and is highly regarded, because both wrote with passion and integrity. Holman is universally recognized as the ideal swing arranger, setting a standard to which lesser writers aspire but rarely achieve. Russo may have fewer admirers, but few would deny his craftsmanship. Bill Perkins commented: "The music's worth is evident when you listen to it—it's great!" And Jiggs Whigham perceptively observed: "Bill Russo's music has a real dark character, the voices are very dark. It's unique, a little esoteric, and I like it a lot." After *Showcase* Russo quit Kenton altogether to pursue an independent career. His music will be missed.

By 1954, West Coast Jazz was at the peak of its popularity, and as a major Hollywood label Capitol belatedly realized it should be cashing in on what had become big business for firms like Contemporary and Pacific Jazz. Searching for a sales gimmick, someone came up with the idea of linking a series of recordings with the name of California's most popular big band, Stan Kenton. The plan was enthusiastically endorsed by Capitol executives Glenn Wallichs and Alan Livingston, as well as Stan himself (temporarily bandless for much of 1954).

Thus was born the Capitol subsidiary label Kenton Presents Jazz, with Kenton charged to record established stars of his choice, and to discover fresh modern jazz talent. Not surprisingly, Stan favored alumni from his own orchestra, and initial small combo sessions supervised by Kenton included as leaders Frank Rosolino, Bill Holman, Bob Cooper, Boots Mussulli, and Sal Salvador. A ringer was the leading West Coast pianist Claude Williamson, and invited was Lee Konitz, who declined on the advice of his manager George Wein.

Generalizations are dangerous instruments, and there are always exceptions, but many of the sessions turned out extraordinarily slick music, with faultless musicianship, but seemingly rehearsed to the point of extinguishing any jazz flame that might have set the music alight. In jazz, meticulous perfection and absolute accuracy can seem like lethargy and lack of involvement. One longs for improvisations that take chances, that strike out with passion and conviction, and break the tedium. The odd thing is that such bland, vapid music is precisely the sort Kenton was most critical about, and which was certainly not typical of the best of West Coast Jazz.

The only new group Stan discovered was the very commercial Al Belletto Quintet, a vocal/instrumental group, which it was presumably hoped might emulate the success of the Four Freshmen, but which failed to make the big-time however liberally Kenton recorded them. I don't know how much pressure was placed on Stan by the Capitol hierarchy, but with few exceptions (notably the highly acclaimed Serge Chaloff Sextet's *Boston Blow-Up* and Bob Cooper's experimental *Shifting Winds*) the entire KPJ series was predicated on smooth, marketable music aimed at the widest possible audience and which failed to fully satisfy any. A few of the later dates were not supervised by Kenton at all, even though issued under his badge, and the label was discontinued altogether in 1955 after Capitol was purchased by EMI.

In September 1954 (after acting as MC at the first Newport Jazz Festival July 17–18) Kenton returned to what he did best, leading his own orchestra for the second Festival of Modern American Jazz. This time the aim was less ambitious, as the other artists played without any Kenton involvement: Charlie Ventura's Quartet with singer Mary Ann McCall, Shorty Rogers and his Giants, and the Art Tatum Trio. Guitarist Johnny Smith was backed by the Kenton rhythm, and Candido played in the band.

The most important newcomers were Max Bennett on bass and Mel Lewis on drums, two relative unknowns at the time, but who unlike a lot of Kenton's rhythm partners had a mutual respect for each other's work. Mel always acknowledged that he made his name during his association with Stan Kenton, and Ralph Gleason was prophetic when reviewing a

Festival concert when he observed that "Mel Lewis might give the Kenton band more swing than it has had since the days of Shelly Manne."[3]

A highlight of Stan's Festival performance was the orchestra's version of Russo's "Improvisation," restructured to feature the two altos of Charlie Mariano and Lennie Niehaus, fresh out of the army. As Lennie saw it: "Charlie Mariano was more Bird, and I was more a combination of Konitz and Parker. We were all influenced by Charlie Parker's notes, but I played them in a different style. It was fun to play together with Mariano. I'd go up to the microphone first and play a solo, and then Charlie would join me, and we'd play several minutes of simultaneous improvisation. Charlie was a little more funky than me, but he's a great musician."[4] Despite the strong line-up, this second Festival entourage attracted lower attendances than the previous tour, perhaps because the special appeal of top soloists playing in concert with the Kenton Orchestra was lacking. The closing performance on November 21 marked the abrupt end of the Festival series.

Kenton enjoyed public appreciation of his music, but never cared much about the awards and plaques that accompanied fame and success. He was grateful for the recognition, but regarded the trophies as expendable. However, I believe Stan was genuinely moved at being voted into *Down Beat*'s Hall of Fame in December 1954, the third such winner in the magazine's popularity poll, and ahead of such names as Ellington, Goodman, and Parker. In Stan's own words: "I was flattered, because only two men had been there ahead of me. One was Louis Armstrong, whom I certainly believe is the father of all modern jazz. And the other of course was Glenn Miller, who was known and loved by most of the world. So when 'Stan Kenton' was voted the third member, I felt thrilled to think that I was recognized and even thought of in the same breath as Armstrong and Miller. There are certain unsolicited things that happen that mean a great deal to you, and I didn't take being elected to the *Down Beat* Hall of Fame lightly at all—I appreciated it very much."[5]

Kenton's popularity was recognized and feted by his record label. For some months Capitol producer Bill Miller had been working on a de luxe four-LP album, which was named *The Kenton Era*. Intended as a celebration, the title also hinted that Stan's day in the sun was coming to an end, as indeed proved correct in terms of mass popular appeal among the nation's youth. Multi-LP boxed sets were rare in 1955, but as Jack Tracy phrased it: "Capitol's *Kenton Era* is certainly the handsomest and most striking album of its kind yet to be issued. Previous releases can't compare to this one in cover design, or in the integration of art work, photos and music."[6]

The box cover was indeed the most distinctive ever conceived, a metallic silver silhouette of Kenton's face, almost cartoonish in its characteristics, yet brilliantly drawn and instantly recognizable, with just "The Kenton Era" in red and silver and the Capitol logo, set against a black background. The music (all previously unreleased) was a mixture of Capitol studio recordings and live performances acquired at considerable expense, portraying the entire range of Stan's orchestral career, from Music City in 1940 to Paris in 1953. (Why one of the then-unissued Konitz solos from March 1954 wasn't included is anyone's guess, but then it's always easy to snipe at other people's choices in collections of this nature.) The specially recorded "Prologue" featured Kenton's narrated history of the band to date, backed by a montage of musical excerpts from the band's past, with a shorter "Epilogue" looking to the future and a final, fresh recording of "Artistry in Rhythm."

Capitol placed all their promotional effort behind the *Era*, including a 2000-copy issue to disc jockeys of a special LP containing eight selections from the set, the full album sent to national critics, and special window displays at retail level. (I still recall the imported album in splendid isolation gracing the picture-window of HMV's London store in Oxford Street.) Primarily a prestige production, I don't know whether the *Era* turned a profit, but the box was snapped up by Stan's fans, and artistically remains a distinguished tribute to a great musician at the peak of his career.

It would be wrong to classify *Duet* as controversial; not enough copies were sold to warrant that description. The problem lay not in Christy, who was in excellent voice, nor the splendid selection of standard songs, but in Kenton's heavy-handed piano. When June was band vocalist, she would sometimes wander over to the piano, microphone in hand, and she and Stan would together make musical love. Stan's piano would sympathetically accompany June as she sang of unrequited passion, perhaps "Body and Soul" ("My heart is sad and lonely") or "I Got It Bad" ("Never treats me sweet and gentle, the way he should"). Probably Bill Miller, a long-time Kenton enthusiast and June's producer at Capitol, had something like this in mind when he proposed an album of Christy ballads with Stan's solo piano accompaniment.

But Kenton relaxed and at ease on a single song towards the end of an evening's engagement was very different from Kenton up-tight and taut, recording an album in Capitol's studios. Stan was always afflicted by nerves, becoming tense and anxious when the recording microphone exposed his piano at length, and he compensated by over-statement. Furthermore, *Duet* was an album of equals. June had risen in popularity through her exposure with Kenton, and Stan undoubtedly felt he now had to take equal prominence, a premise at odds with an accompanist aiming to simply support a star singer. That the pair could jell is proven by live recordings, but Christy was indisputably a jazz singer, while Kenton was essentially a concert pianist, and in *Duet* the combination too often becomes a battle of coexistence, rather than a meeting of minds.

June was not happy with the results: "Frankly, I was not at all satisfied with *Duet*, and I don't think Stan was either. Using solo accompaniment can result in a monotonous sound. It doesn't have to be that way, but in this particular case I think it's true."[7] Decoded, June implies that Stan's over-emphatic piano is at fault. Bill Miller told me: "The *Duet* album was the only time I recorded Kenton personally, and Stan had quite a time with the piano accompaniment, as he always tightened-up when the recording light went on. The results were pretty good musically, but the record was not a success and sold very little." In retrospect, the addition of bass and drums might have forced Stan to adopt a more conciliatory line, but Miller had a difficult task; as Christy's producer he couldn't afford to appear to take sides, or risk riling Kenton, who was the more important artist to Capitol at the time.

The normally Kenton-defensive Noel Wedder was emphatic in his assessment: "The album featuring June with Stan playing solo piano was a huge mistake. Stan was incapable of backing her up like her long-time accompanist Joe Castro. The pairing of the two together as solo artists just did not work."[8] The poor public response seemed proof that Stan's real instrument was his orchestra, and deterred him from venturing a second attempt to record his piano work at length for the best part of two decades.

# 15.

## Stompin' at the Savoy

### (1955)

**The two most influential chairs** within a jazz orchestra are filled by the lead trumpet and the drums. Previously, Buddy Childers had been willing to follow Holman's lead and "change the direction of the band," but Stan Levey had sided with Kenton, so an alliance had been lacking.[1] In 1955, there was no such division between Al Porcino and Mel Lewis. "Porcino and Lewis were kind of tight," noted Bill Holman, "so Stan sort of turned the band over to Al and Mel as far as the direction was concerned. They set about getting the band to swing, and had the guys playing really close to a true jazz feeling. I think that was the most swinging band Stan ever had."

So Porcino and Lewis carried the orchestra with them, including a Stan Kenton apparently swept along by the general enthusiasm, to the extent that he appointed Bill Holman head arranger. For the first time since becoming a bandleader, Stan stood back and to a large extent allowed this unofficial triumvirate to assume control. Al Porcino was straw boss, a very fine lead trumpet player, but also a born malcontent, always pressing for personnel changes, and telling members how to play their parts. "Even when the band was roaring, he never seemed completely satisfied," said Max Bennett. "What Al really wanted was to be leader of his own band."[2]

Like Al, Mel Lewis could also be opinionated: "I was the bad guy in the band. I used to get on to everybody who didn't pull their weight. People said the Kenton band never swung, but it swung all the time I was there, and that had something to do with *all* the players in the band. I didn't play any harder with Kenton, and that band was as blasting as any band you ever heard. I just didn't find it necessary to be loud—I don't push a band, I cushion it. Woody Herman offered me a job when I was with Kenton, but Stan's band offered more musical satisfaction. We never really sounded like Woody, though we started to get a little close. Really, we became a Bill Holman band."[3]

Holman was the man providing the grist for the mill, the arrangements without which the best band in the world could not function, and bassist Bennett is one among many who credit Stan with giving Bill a completely free hand: "Holman had the most influence of anyone, and the band sounded best when it was playing his charts." "I was writing a lot of vocal scores," noted Willis. "They were among the first arrangements I wrote to back a singer, and it was fun doing them."

Holman was writing for Ann Richards. Stan didn't exactly "discover" Ann himself (Hollywood song-writer and vocal-coach Eddie Beal made the introduction), but she may be the reason for his musical relaxation, because he soon found himself "in love" (or at least infatuated) with his young singer, then aged 19 as opposed to Stan's 43. Ann reciprocated, though whether out of regard for Kenton or to further her career in music is a moot point, and the couple married in Detroit on October 18, 1955.

Ann Richards was principally a "pop" singer with jazz inflections, and was never in the same league as Christy or Connor. I preferred Ann during her early years, her voice clear and crystalline, and without the shrillness and affectations that marred her later work. Richards sang on and off with the band until 1961, and bore Stan two children, Dana and Lance, but theirs was never a marriage made in heaven, and the final straw for Kenton came when Ann displayed herself in public by posing nude for *Playboy* magazine, without telling Stan in advance. A Kenton lady did not demean herself in this manner without paying the consequences, and divorce quickly followed. Richards enjoyed some success as a single act, but her appeal waned as her looks faded, and she seemingly committed suicide in 1982 at the tender age of 46, a sad end to what had at first seemed a promising career.

Stan wrote Richards' initial arrangements himself, aiming for a hit with dogs like "Falling" and "A-Ting A-Ling" that failed on every level. Never a prolific composer, Stan was now essentially the band's "commercial" writer. His last "serious" compositions had been "Shelly Manne" and "June Christy" a full five years earlier. Overall, Stan left the "heavy" music to his arrangers, as Max Bennett pointed out: "At the risk of making a lot of enemies, I'd have to say we liked Stan's own arrangements the least. Of course, he'd written a lot of things which sold and were popular, but musically and structurally they fell considerably short of Holman's and Mulligan's arrangements."

In 1955 Ann was lacking experience but never sounded better than on Bill Holman arrangements like "Black Coffee" and "The Thrill Is Gone." But far more significant than his vocal charts was Holman's commission from Stan to rejuvenate the library with a book of standards in concert-length orchestrations, arranged as he saw fit. Kenton gave Willis complete freedom, knowing full well that whatever Bill came up with, being by Holman, at their heart they would have a sense of unfettered swing. At the same time, it is noticeable that Stan had placed certain constraints on Bill, insofar as the mandate restricted him to arrangements of other people's compositions. Holman's originals were light and fluid, but often largely indistinguishable one from another. I'd hazard Stan was keen to find out how Bill's undoubted arranging abilities would fare when applied to stronger melodies than he routinely composed himself.

The results surpassed anyone's expectations. Two years on from his first inauspicious "dance" charts, Holman's arranging skills had matured beyond all recognition. It is no exaggeration to say Bill's concert scores took the band by storm. First to arrive were "I've Got You Under My Skin," "What's New," and "Between the Devil and the Deep Blue Sea." Unlike anything he had ever written before, Bill had dissected each of the melodies and reconstructed them in such an individual way that they had become an extension of the Holman persona, recompositions in their own right. Kenton was certainly impressed, if a little cautious. "It wasn't really Stan's cup of tea," observed Bill Perkins. "Stan was more Wagnerian in his taste. He liked the heavy music the best."

Undoubtedly the most popular and influential of all these up-tempo charts was the celebrated "Stompin' at the Savoy," which Bill wrote at Stan's specific request. The arrangement has achieved an iconic status, and become so synonymous with Holman he still has to play it regularly over fifty years on. "'Stompin' at the Savoy' has become so popular," said Lennie Niehaus, "that I kid Willis about it. I tell him that's his 'Intermission Riff'—the piece that keeps being called for. 'Stompin'' had become rather stilted since the Benny Goodman recording, but Willis elongated the melody, and made it sound fresh and different. He gave it a new life."[4]

In 1973 Stan chatted about "Stompin'": "Bill Holman is inclined to be a bit cynical, it's in his personality. For instance, he would write a wonderful piece of music like 'Stompin' at the Savoy,' then there's that little cadence on the end that is actually corny . . . I know when we rehearsed 'Stompin'' I said, 'Bill, what on earth did you put that thing on the end for?' And he said, 'Well, I just wanted it, take it out.' And I said, 'No, we're not going to take it out, we're going to leave it on.' He used to make light of things he'd do, like giving those ridiculous titles. But he's not so much that way any more—he's settled down."[5]

It was into this heady atmosphere that Dave Van Kriedt found himself plunged. A veteran writer from his days with the experimental Dave Brubeck Octet (1947), Van Kriedt was hired by Stan as much for his arranging skills as his tenor sax. But Dave was intent upon combining jazz with symphonic music, and he found the 1955 Kenton orchestra an alien climate. Lennie Niehaus explains: "Dave Van Kriedt was a good tenor player, but he wasn't a Bob Cooper or a Zoot Sims. Dave was really into composition. One arrangement we played a lot was 'Why Do I Love You,' and it was very linear, but not like Mulligan. It was much more involved, and the second half was arranged as a fugue. So Dave asked me why the band didn't like his arrangements, and I had to tell him it was because of his style. If you listen to Brubeck and Desmond with the quartet, they played very compositionally: they played simultaneous improvisation. They sound like a Bach invention. And Dave came out of this Brubeck school, but a majority of the guys in the band just wanted to play swinging figures. You really had to read Dave's music in order to play, and each individual part didn't swing, it didn't flow. I thought they were good arrangements, but I knew why the rest of the band didn't enjoy playing them. They just weren't fun to play. Dave Van Kriedt really came to Kenton several years too late. He was in the right band, at the wrong time."

By the summer of '55, Holman switched tack a little to write music featuring individual soloists—initially the ballads "Yesterdays" for Bill Perkins and "Stella by Starlight" for Charlie Mariano. Both arrived just in time for inclusion on the album called *Contemporary Concepts*, which Mel Lewis explains almost wasn't recorded at all: "In 1955 the critics were saying the Kenton band was swinging for the first time in its history. The band had a fresh, light feeling to it, and credit was being given to me—the new, young drummer on the scene—and to Bill Holman's writing. We had acquired a road manager named Bob Martin, who used to be a jazz disc-jockey. He was a wonderful guy, and when we got to the Blue Note in July Martin said to Stan, 'You know, you really should record this music while it's fresh and while the band is sounding so good.' And Martin talked Stan into it, he even went and booked the studio time, he did everything, so Stan gave in and we did it. And if you notice, Stan doesn't play a drop of piano on it. He didn't really want to do this album, because it was not typical Kenton music. And Holman did one helluva job, this was what really made him somebody; and it made Mel Lewis also—this was really where I got my recognition. The reviews of the album were spectacular from all the important critics—Nat Hentoff, Ira Gitler, Martin Williams, even Leonard Feather. It became the most swinging album Stan ever made, but it swings in a different way. It's not like Woody's band, with that hard, forceful thing that they had, and it didn't have the Basie 4/4 relaxed swing. This was bebop, but not like Dizzy's bebop band. This was much more sophisticated musically."[6]

Holman himself has disputed that his music should be described as "bebop," but terminology apart, the general thrust of Lewis' assertions cannot be questioned.

Bill Perkins talked to me further about the sessions: "Bill Holman's arrangements were masterpieces, but those recording dates were frustrating, because Ann Richards spent so long getting her songs right, there wasn't much time for the jazz charts, which had to be recorded more or less straight off, and we were very unhappy about that. And some of that music only came in that week, so it was cold. I mean, the first time I played 'Yesterdays' was on the record session, and I was totally befuddled by it—I was very unhappy with the way I played. But that record has done more for me than any other, so maybe people like it because I was just going on my instincts alone. The chart is timeless, and it has the Holman mystique, the darkness, because Bill's personality is on the dark side, and I think that's the thing that captured people. Bill does write plenty of happy-go-lucky light things, but 'Yesterdays' has an undertone, a brooding quality." Something also revealed perhaps in Perk's own playing, because as Holman said, "I wrote 'Yesterdays' with Perk in mind. I'd known his playing for several years, and I wanted to reflect his individuality."

Just like Perk, because of the lack of rehearsal time, Charlie Mariano was very dissatisfied with his solo on "Stella by Starlight," which has also come to be recognized as a masterpiece of invention. If Mariano's language is bebop, he has taken Bird's vocabulary and extended it with a poise and emotion strictly of his own making. Kim Richmond says of Charlie's two-tempoed tribute to "Stella": "It is the passion in his playing that reaches me, and that I hear on the 1955 Kenton recording. Mariano is someone who produces music from the heart."[7] And Lennie Niehaus hears "A slow, almost Brahmsian quality in 'Stella by Starlight.' And when I first heard it, I thought, 'Wow! Where did this come out of Willis?' Because I had never heard him write anything like that before. I recorded 'Cherokee' for the album, and Mariano had 'Stella by Starlight,' and I think Charlie got the better deal. 'Cherokee' is a great arrangement, it swings, but it isn't 'Stella,' and it was very difficult every night at that fast tempo to come up with something new."[8]

Despite experience in the bands of Woody Herman and Lionel Hampton, Carl Fontana was yet another musician who earned his reputation with Kenton. Fontana joined in time for the *Contemporary* sessions, but too late for Holman to write for him personally, so Stan had Mulligan's "Limelight" modified from its usual multi-solo status to feature his new trombone star. Carl's showcase debut remains one of his finest solos on record, with Fontana firing notes like a machine-gun on autopilot in a stunning display of virtuosity. Holman later came up with a graceful "Polka Dots and Moonbeams" to spotlight Fontana's ballad style, and a typically uncomplicated Holmanesque swinger dedicated simply to "Carl." Fontana was one helluva talented trombonist, in Bill Perkins' opinion: "A breath of fresh air. His musicality was just superb. The shading of his playing, his taste, his sound, his articulation—all are unique. Many people have followed him, but he still stays a giant."

Because the Chicago-recorded *Contemporary Concepts* sessions were set up so hastily, there was no time to inform Stan's producer Lee Gillette in Hollywood, and in the rush Stan overlooked the courtesy of explaining afterwards, with the result that the pair became estranged for over a year. Dave Cavanaugh produced Kenton's albums in 1956, until Lee and Stan reached an accommodation, and Gillette resumed his role as Stan's ally and producer at Capitol Records.

Because he wasn't in the public eye, Lee Gillette's importance as Stan's record producer is often over-looked. From an early dislike of Kenton's music, Lee grew to love the band, and Stan relied heavily on Gillette's expertise, which exceeded that of many producers because he could read a score. Bill Wagner was manager of the Four Freshmen, who also recorded for Capitol, and he opined, "Lee Gillette was one of the neatest guys that ever lived. I always said if I could be 10% as good in the booth as Lee was, I would be very, very happy."

Possibly the least said about the CBS-TV summer replacement show *Music '55* the better. Kenton acted as MC, but to the general public he sounded stiff and labored compared with the slick announcing to which they were accustomed. Certainly CBS hired top names each week as guests; jazz artists included Duke Ellington, Count Basie, Ella Fitzgerald, Dave Brubeck, and Lena Horne, which is perhaps the very reason a majority of viewers preferred to patronize Arthur Murray on the rival NBC!

Stan explains: "CBS needed someone to head this *Music '55* thing, but there were a few aspects that were kind of bad about it. The New York Musicians' Union wouldn't let me use my own band for a start, so my orchestra was out on the road, and Johnny Richards organized a special group of guys in New York. It was a good band—some of the men had been with me in the past—but I would rather have used my own orchestra, because we were playing together all the time. Also, I didn't have much to do with the production side, because I was away on the road, and every Tuesday I'd fly into New York from wherever I was to do the show, and right after it was over I'd fly back out again.

"So CBS was quite interested, but after three or four shows they became aware it wasn't going to succeed, because there wasn't enough popular appeal in it. There were good guests booked each week, and they would get quite excited over the marquee value of a group of artists, but they'd not bother over the production values of the show. They felt names were enough in themselves, and by the time I flew in, it was too late to change anything that had been planned. So, CBS lost interest, and we just ground out the ten weeks and forgot about it."[9]

By the end of 1955 Stan was becoming disillusioned with the "swing thing," but had no alternative with which to replace it. He sought a compromise by making quite comprehensive changes to the instrumentation. In the words of Mel Lewis: "The Christmas vacation always gave Stan a chance to revamp the band if he had any new ideas. And in 1955 he did. Charlie Mariano had left, and instead of replacing him, Stan brought in two French horns, and revoiced the saxophone book with the horns, so the part wouldn't be missing. And then he cut down the trombones to three tenor trombones and one bass trombone, but added a tuba. Trumpets remained at five, though Vinnie Tanno started playing flugel horn a lot of the time."[10]

Al Porcino was not a happy bunny: "Invariably with Stan it was the same thing. For a while it would be beautiful, we'd be swinging along so great I could hardly believe it was a Kenton band. And then one night Stan would suddenly realize it wasn't his band any more. It was *swinging*. And then we'd quit playing the swinging charts and start playing something far out, or 'Intermission Riff' and all those goodies. It was that way in 1955 when we had a whole new library of beautiful music by Bill Holman, except that it took Stan a little longer to get tired of swinging that time. I don't want it to sound like I'm putting him down, because I love the guy. We just didn't want to play the same kind of music. He always said he'd leave the swinging to Woody and Basie."[11]

Bill Holman said much the same thing: "The band had been swinging as never before, and one day, I don't know what came into Stan's mind, whether he felt the band was getting away from him or what, but he fired Bob Martin, and he fired Al, and he told me to quit writing. And that was the end of that era." It had to happen. Never, even in the hey-day of Progressive Jazz, had the orchestra been called the "Pete Rugolo Band," in the way the guys were naming this band after Bill Holman. In actuality, the repertoire did not change overnight, as Al and Bill seem to imply. The Holman influence would remain dominant during the coming year, but to the dismay of some and the delight of others, by his subtle changes in instrumentation, Stan Kenton had in effect given notice that he was reclaiming ownership of his own orchestra.

# 16.

## Fuego Cubano!

### (1956)

Bill Perkins for one wasn't best pleased: "In 1956 Stan brought in a couple of totally inept French horn men. They were both legit players, and they weren't very good. Julius Watkins—he knew how to play jazz, but these guys just loaded the band down. I was the first tenor, but I had to play the part of the second alto, which meant I had to play high all night. I hated it! Stan had four saxes against twelve brass, and it was just terrible."

Kenton had consulted with Lennie Niehaus before making the changes, but only over the details, not the principle, and Lennie knew the futility of arguing with the boss once his mind was made up—especially if you wanted to keep your job! "I'd have to say I preferred the five-man sax section," Lennie told me. "We sure learned to play hard and strong, because to keep up with all that brass was not easy."[1]

The concept of French horns in a dance band was certainly not new. Boyd Raeburn had employed them in 1946, and Claude Thornhill as early as 1941. Even Harry James frequently used a horn in place of a fourth trombone. French horns brought a unique subtlety to a band's sound, and added a richness and depth to the ensembles. But they could not "shout," and for this reason Kenton would ultimately find them lacking. But for the moment he was enthusiastic, and employed Holman to rescore the older arrangements to include the new instrumentation. What Willis thought of the changes can be imagined, but a job is a job. Even musicians had to eat, and too many fine jazzmen ended up driving a cab, or working in retail outlets.

New lead trumpet was Ed Leddy, a fierce, strong, and accurate player, but without Porcino's maverick tendencies. "Ed had enormous stamina," commented Don Reed. "He played the lead on every piece, night after night, and never made a mistake. That is really an amazing feat."[2] Also back was Sam Noto, a double threat along with Vinnie Tanno in the jazz solo stakes. Mel Lewis remained on drums, but new on bass was Curtis

Counce, one of the few black players prominent in the West Coast Jazz movement (others included drummer Chico Hamilton of Quintet fame, and multi-talented reed player Buddy Collette).

The first big project of 1956 saw Stan returning to his roots, with the Capitol album *Kenton in Hi-Fi*, which rose to No. 13 on Billboard's pop albums chart. Stereo was still in its infancy, but monaural technology had improved beyond all recognition since the Forties, when the great Kenton/ Rugolo classics had first been made, and the album concept was to re-record these hits in the best possible mono audio. Stan used the nucleus of his present band, but brought back Vido Musso and Milt Bernhart to rec-reate the authentic solo sound. Trombonist Don Reed still picked out Carl Fontana's solo on "Intermission Riff" as one of the all-time great trom-bone solos ever recorded by the Kenton band—and he's right![3]

As Bill Holman's influence waned, arrangers Joe Coccia and Johnny Richards filled the void. It is clear from speaking with the musicians that most if not all regarded the changeover as a retrograde step, not least because neither man possessed Willis' innate sense of swing. They brought a more formal, tighter orientation back to the orchestra, which is exactly what Kenton intended. And both wrote specifically for the new instrumentation, giving the horns their own, distinctive parts.

Joe Coccia was Principal of a High School in Cranston, Rhode Island, and had been writing for the orchestra since 1942 without getting much played in public. Kenton believed his arrangers should be wholly com-mitted to music, and family man Coccia was unwilling to surrender the security of his teaching post to travel with the band full-time. Now Stan put aside his reservations, as Joe relates: "It was a challenge, as I had never written for that mixture of instruments before. My assignment was to write for the dance book, mixing horns with the saxes, while the tuba had to be playing a lyrical line like the trombones. This was of course pre-mellophoniums, and I believe the horns may well have served as the catalyst for adding the mellophonium section four years later."[4] Coc-cia features the horns to excellent effect in some of his most distinctive arrangements: "All About Ronnie," "When I'm with You," "I'll Stand By" (all issued on Tantara's *Revelations*). The titles seem to have had a short shelf-life however, and their low-key, almost Thornhillian characteristics may have been a little too restrained for Kenton's total approval.

On March 4, 1956, the band with its full complement left New York aboard RMS *Queen Elizabeth*, bound for its second European tour. But this time the first destination was Britain, following successful negotiations with the Union for a reciprocal tour of America by Ted Heath and His Music. Kenton's debut concert on English soil was at 2 p.m. on March

11, in London's vast Royal Albert Hall, the atmosphere electric as the capacity crowd greeted Stan's first-ever appearance leading his orchestra before a British audience in their homeland. The English jazz "establishment" was uniformly anti-Kenton, and everything he stood for, but individual writers and musicians could not disguise their excitement and admiration for the powerful precision and outstanding musicianship of this fine orchestra and its distinguished soloists.

The program consisted of a mixture of older "classics" and the more recent Holman charts, including a brand new "Royal Blue" named especially for the UK tour, and one very fresh composition by Johnny Richards which really set the audience roaring (and I was one of them!) called "El Congo Valiente." Of the soloists, highest praise went to Perkins, Niehaus, and Fontana.

My own references from this and other UK concerts note that Perk surpassed himself with a beautiful free-flowing solo on "Out of Nowhere," including a subtle quote from "Sweet Eloise" in the tail. I like the ingenious way Bill includes snatches from other songs in his solos and cleverly extricates himself (it's rare to find "Yesterdays" without such a spot), but when I once mentioned it, Bill grinned sheepishly, like a kid caught with his hand in the cookie-jar: "I try not to quote from other songs in my solos. If you do it too much you're full of clichés, though everyone does it a little bit: Diz and Bird both did. These things come to me on the spur of the moment, I don't think of them ahead of time, because if you try to pre-plan it always bombs. When you step out to play jazz, hopefully that magic will take over—or maybe not!"

To what extent Niehaus had that magic is a constant source of debate. Reaction to Lennie was double-edged: amazement at his control and fluency, coupled with disappointment at a lack of passion and involvement. Trumpet player Phil Gilbert does not mince his words: "Lennie Niehaus is a well-educated musician with good technique on the alto sax. He can play very fast and very slow, and in the end his solos are emotionally barren of passion. A perfect example is 'Stella by Starlight,' which was given to Lennie when Mariano left. Two very different musicians: one an artist, the other given to playing meaningless scales and flourishes, leaving one wishing for space and tenderness. Even his writing is cold."[5]

Lennie himself was well aware of such brickbats: "I don't know what people wanted to hear from me that would make it more emotional. Did they mean more funky? I could never figure it out. I'd be playing my heart out there on the stage, and critics would complain of a lack of passion, and write things like, 'Great technique, but emotionally bland.'

Well, I took chances all the time, but they just happened to come out without mistakes. Maybe I should play some wrong notes, but how can you do that? Why should you want to? Everybody has a soul, and what is soulful to one person might not be soulful to another."[6]

My own conclusion is not that Lennie's playing is emotionless, but that the emotion is all on one level, with no highs and lows, and little variation in intensity. In a sense, Lennie is a victim of his own technical efficiency. He makes it all seem too easy, and never has to struggle to reach his goals.

No one disagrees that Carl Fontana was an extraordinarily gifted trombone player. His regular feature solo on Holman's delicate "Polka Dots and Moonbeams" is both technically adroit and stunningly creative. Much like Rosolino before him, Carl is an individualist with his own unique sound, whether it's in relaxed ballad mood, or shooting notes at high velocity on fast-tempo titles.

For 33 days the band toured the length and breadth of Britain, from the southern seaside resort of Brighton (Sussex) to Glasgow (Scotland) in the north, almost invariably playing two separate shows each night. Not every house was SRO, but things were going fine until disaster struck on (coincidentally) April 1, as a result of which Spencer Sinatra and Jack Nimitz were unceremoniously bundled back to the States. Kenton cited "excessive fatigue" as the reason, when in fact the boys seemed to have too much energy for their own good! With the reeds already reduced to four players by design, the band therefore lost literally 50% of the saxophone section overnight. With all due credit to the English replacements, no band can experience such a dramatic turnover in personnel without suffering some loss of cohesion and character as a result.

Stan had warned his men that being the first American band to play in Britain since Teddy Hill in 1937 would place them firmly in the glare of world publicity, and to be on their best behavior throughout the tour. How Sinatra found the time during the band's busy schedule is a mystery, but somehow he became closely involved with the girl-friend of English jazzman Ronnie Scott. No big deal perhaps, but as Phil Gilbert remembered it: "Spence was not only hanging out with Ronnie Scott's chick Joan, they were also messing around with drugs. Stan would never tolerate any drugs, pot or anything. So when the chick's mother called Stan and threatened to blow the works, he was fearful the tour would be ruined by bad publicity, and fired Spence and Jack on the spot. We all remember it well, because they were both fine players, and the morale of the band went low as they left. Sadly, Spencer never conquered his habit with drugs, and committed suicide around 1970."[7]

Other sources tell much the same story, though the details differ. Jack Nimitz names Scott himself as complaining to Stan (*Jazz Journal*, December 1977), and tuba player Jay McAllister in Bill Lee's biography of Stan involves Scotland Yard (the police!). Clearly Kenton was under intense pressure (the full facts will never be known), and took the drastic action he thought necessary to placate injured parties and avoid a drugs scandal. The irony is, Joan followed Sinatra to the States, where the pair were married; so true love conquered all, at least in the short term!

Lennie Niehaus adds that "In all fairness to Jack [Nimitz], he was not involved with Sinatra's problems, except for the fact that they roomed together. We all knew that Jack was OK, he was just guilty by association, but Stan sent both of them home. After that it seemed like every time I looked around there was a different saxophone player in the band, and that meant another section rehearsal, and here we were on the road, in Europe, riding around on buses that weren't the greatest, playing two concerts a night. We got several players like that, but mainly it was Don Rendell and Harry Klein."[8]

"I was terrified when I first joined," recalled Rendell. "The music was absolutely impossible. It went by at such speed, page after page, completely black with dots. Tremendous Bill Holman arrangements, and I felt I had no chance. But after a couple of nights it got a little better. Lennie Niehaus was a very warm guy on lead alto, and I also got a lot of help from Bill Perkins, who was very modest and shy. After a few days, Stan opened up the arrangements to fit us in. For instance, Bill Perkins had been taking the whole solo on 'Intermission Riff,' but they fitted me in to duet with him. These Kenton guys didn't just read an arrangement, they interpreted it, so sometimes they weren't playing exactly what was written, and that resulted from a lot of rehearsing and playing together. I was particularly impressed by the emphasis on time, it was incredible."[9]

A second crisis occurred when the band left England to tour continental Europe, and Ed Leddy fell ill. Most reports cite pneumonia. Phil Gilbert graphically described what followed: "Ed Leddy normally played all the first parts. Ed was a gentle, respectful guy, and everyone loved him. He was our teacher, and we all followed his instructions with reverence. So when Ed suddenly became ill the day we left for Norway I was devastated. All at once Sam and Vinnie scrambled over the lead parts, and we struggled with four trumpets for two weeks or more. We damn near fell apart. The whole band lost its edge, especially after the replacement of two saxes in England. Sam took over and we survived, but just barely. Raggedness and pitch problems bothered me, and dissension arose within the section. Sam did not have the sound or the stability of

Ed Leddy. We were rudderless. A month after Ed's illness he was strong enough to be playing the whole lead book again."[10]

Kent Larsen sums up Stan's second European tour with a spirited reminiscence: "England was cold and rainy, we did 60 concerts in 33 days, we ate ham sandwiches until they came out of our ears, and we had a complete ball: the audiences were super! The Continent was just as hectic as regard to schedules, but it was a joy meeting and playing with so many wonderful musicians. The five days each way on the *Queen Elizabeth* were a thrill, just like a paid vacation. By the time we got back to the States, I'd spent more money than I earned, we found that Elvis was the biggest thing on records, and the band spent a week in New York recording *Cuban Fire*."

What Kenton hadn't explained was that "El Congo Valiente" was just one of a number of extended compositions Johnny Richards had written featuring the Latin-American idiom. What Kenton didn't know at the time was that the complete *Cuban Fire* collection was destined to become the most musically popular and iconic album of his whole career. Stan's concept had been simple enough. Despite his enthusiasm for Latin rhythms, he'd often been chastised by Cuban musicians for not being sufficiently authentic in their use. Johnny Richards (family name Cascales) was Mexican by birth and spoke fluent Spanish, so Kenton commissioned John to spend time in New York with the Latin players and learn how to combine their genuine rhythms with North American jazz. "And then," Stan told Johnny, "I want you to create a Suite, but I want you to abide by all the rhythmic rules that those Latin guys have."[11]

As painstakingly recorded for Capitol, *Cuban Fire* was an outstanding achievement of immense proportions. Not only did it kick-start Richards' career, leading to his becoming one of the most vital composers in modern jazz, the album also gave a significant boost to the Kenton orchestra, becoming that rare combination, a success in both artistic and commercial terms. *Cuban Fire* was music that reached a new stature and dimension. Highly dramatic—some would say grandiose—passages are tempered by periods of sheer beauty and repose: as on the opening "Fuego Cubano" which begins with a flurry of high-powered excitement and brooding menace, but soon relaxes under the calming influence of the main theme statement played by a Larsen-Noto duet.

Most memorable of the six dances is "El Congo Valiente," because of its distinctive theme, stated at the opening by French horns. The difficulties inherent in Richards' writing are well illustrated by "La Suerte de los Tontos," on which the horns have to start the piece "cold." There's a Wally Heider recording from the Macumba Club later in the year, on which the horns fluff the introduction four times, and don't get it right even on the last attempt. On another Macumba date Stan makes the horns repeat the intro because of clams, and ironically explains it's a difficult thing to play: "Because it's hard to understand the title—something about the Sweat of the Horns!" (Correct translation: "The Fortune of Fools.")

Richards makes liberal use of the band's complement of soloists on every movement of the Suite (which, incidentally, does not include "Tres Corazones," despite the liner notes to the CD release). All perform with vigor and passion, but my personal pick would go to Bill Perkins, despite stiff competition from Lucky Thompson, whom the band had picked up in Paris, and who would depart right after the recording. Perk's fine tone and ability to dovetail his ideas with John's music are beyond reproach. Throughout, Richards uses the soloists to develop his compositions rather than engage in free expression, and solo performers are compelled by the dynamics of the music to work within this controlled melodic framework. Doubtless many of the musicians would prefer the freedom of improvisation allowed by the Holman/Mulligan-type charts, but Richards had such command of the orchestra, and has composed melodies of such outstanding merit, he gained the respect and (sometimes grudging) admiration of everyone involved. Under Stan's leadership the band plays with great energy and flair: the battery of Latin percussion instruments added for the occasion complement but never overwhelm the orchestra, however crucial they are to the success of the Suite.

Mel Lewis explains: "Willie Rodriguez had organized a special rhythm section playing specific instruments that would go along with the South American rhythms that Johnny had researched before he wrote the music. Johnny had rehearsed them before we even got there, and now they had to learn to blend with a jazz drummer and tympani. Tremendous care and effort went into every aspect of the *Cuban Fire* recordings, which became one of the finest works of Johnny Richards with the Kenton band."[12]

Carl Fontana was generally an unaggressive, laid-back guy—perhaps a little too much so in career terms—but all that changed when Carl discovered Curtis Counce had been "courting" his wife. Phil Gilbert told me, "Carl is from the deep south—Monroe, Louisiana—and prejudice in 1956 was still strong—it still is when a black guy hits on a white chick who is married to Carl Fontana! Word leaked out in June when we got to the Blue Note in Chicago, and one night before the first set we heard that Carl was looking for Curtis, and if he found him he was going to kill him! Pretty strong stuff! Counce was warned that Fontana was looking for him, and was told to leave town right away. Which he did. Don Kelly's wife was also involved somehow, and Counce, Carl, and Don all left the band that night, and three new guys sat in to open. The hole Carl left was immense, musically and emotionally. The band never got another trombone player that came close to Carl. NEVER! We didn't miss Curtis or Don for long."[13]

Stan himself was responsible for another furore, when he sent an intemperate telegram to *Down Beat* stating his "complete and total disgust" at the results of the 1956 Critics' Poll, which placed Count Basie top of the Big Bands, and 13 out of 15 of the Established Star categories were won by black musicians.[14] Leonard Feather promptly raised the stakes by inferring this represented racial prejudice on Stan's part, and though Feather would completely retract the insinuation four years later, it was inevitably the initial censure that stuck.

Kent Larsen was Stan's road manager at the time, and he told me, "We were on our way from Detroit to Crystal Beach in Ontario, Canada, when Stan read this particular *Down Beat* poll. His reaction was that there were several great [white] jazz musicians whom the critics had overlooked. He subsequently sent a wire to *Down Beat* voicing his dismay at this lack of recognition, and the possibility of a racist attitude *on the critics' part*. One of the issues Leonard Feather brought up in reply was that Stan had either token or no black musicians in his band, but I'm sure that your research has shown different. I recall trouble in getting black musicians the same hotel accommodation as the rest of the band in southern parts of the USA, and on one occasion the whole band left a restaurant outside of Washington D.C. one morning after most of us had already ordered, because the management would not serve Curtis Counce."

The big bands were a product of the 1930s, when racial segregation was at its worst, and all the touring bands had always been predominantly black or white. Of the "big four" in the declining years of the big band era, Woody Herman and Stan Kenton were largely "white," Count Basie and Duke Ellington mainly "black." Both Stan and Woody had always carried a sprinkling of black musicians, and likewise the odd white musician was often found in the Count and Ducal ranks. In fact, Stan respected a musician for his ability, regardless of color, as shown by the evidence:

FACT—Stan on countless occasions lauded and praised such artists as Louis Armstrong, Jimmie Lunceford, Earl Hines, Benny Carter, Charlie Parker, Dizzy Gillespie, Count Basie, and Duke Ellington.

FACT—Stan regularly employed black musicians in his band, beginning with Karl George in 1943, and was generous with feature spots for the better soloists.

FACT—Stan always went out of his way to ensure his black players were treated fairly while travelling with his band "on the road."

Bill Russo gives just one example: "When Ernie Royal was on the Kenton band in 1953, Stan would not permit Ernie to seek separate lodgings in a black hotel, usually of lesser quality than white hotels. When we played the southern States, Stan would enter the white hotel alone, and register for a double room for himself and Ernie. For a white man to share a room with a black man in the South in 1953 was very dangerous. Stan's conduct was the act of a decent and courageous man, not the act of a racist."[15]

A couple of critics (Bill Coss at *Metronome*, and Michael Levin at *Down Beat*) did point out there was absolutely no evidence to justify Feather's comments, and Nat Hentoff wrote that "Stan is as free from prejudice as any man I know." Mel Lewis puts the whole trumped-up charge in perspective: "At around the same time Stan got put down for so-called racism, we'd had in the band Curtis Counce on bass, Julius Watkins on French Horn, and Lucky Thompson on tenor. It offended them when Stan Kenton got put down. They liked him. Stan just felt that the white musician was getting the short end of the stick. He probably was right, but then the black jazz musicians had been getting the short end of the stick forever. He just said the wrong thing at the wrong time, and people loved to jump on him."[16]

The two weeks in November at San Francisco's Macumba Club have acquired a special significance because Wally Heider recorded the band's performances almost every night. The big, booming baritone saxophone of Pepper Adams dominates these dates, turning Pepper's presence from a footnote in Stan's discography into a major event (and showing how recordings, or more often a lack of them, can distort musical history). Adams takes no more than his fair share of solos, but seems to fill more space because he bestrides the band like a colossus, and his are the solos that remain in the memory when others have faded. Like many jazz artists, Pepper preferred playing in combos to a large orchestra, but just as a precious jewel may be enhanced by its setting, so a superior soloist may be uniquely inspired by the challenge of a choice arrangement in a big-band setting, a point proven by Adams with his many Macumba interpretations of "My Funny Valentine." (Try Magic's *Live at the Macumba Club*.)

The Macumba band plays lively, joyful jazz. Much of the music had been Capitol-recorded, but often in a more inhibited format; live recordings catch the band in a more relaxed, less formal light. On November 3, somehow the band can't close "Jump for Joe," causing Stan to ask, "Anybody know how this thing ends?" Lennie Niehaus plays a stupendous alto on "Cherokee," with a truly amazing coda, while a really long solo bonanza on the head arrangement of "Take the 'A' Train" includes an amusing excursion by Jay McAllister's tuba, and Don Bagley quotes liberally from "I'm Beginning to See the Light." On November 4, Perkins has a field day with quotes, including "Chloe" during "Swing House," "Toy Trumpet" as he's "Stompin' at the Savoy," "La Cucuracha" comes "Out of Nowhere," and "I Don't Want to Set the World on Fire" while serenading "My Old Flame." Stan evidently approves, because he sums it all up with the comment: "Perk—we dig you!" Stan also congratulates newcomer Archie LeCoque (trombone) on the excellent way he has settled into the band, and Kent Larsen on his expert handling of the lead trombone chores.

"At the end of 1956," said Mel Lewis, "we took our Christmas vacation, and I got a call from Stan saying he was going to Australia, but he's only taking a nucleus, and hire guys down there. Now I knew that was going to be a catastrophe! And frankly, I also knew he was going to drop the Holman approach, and revert to the traditional style of Kenton band again. It was going to get heavy, and I wanted to swing, so I decided I didn't want to be involved. When you're a jazz musician, you've gotta move on!"[17]

Stan indeed knew it was time for a change. The Macumba date had not been a financial success, and subsequent one-nighters had been light in attendance. The younger generation regarded the big bands as old hat, yesterday's music, and had moved away to rockers like Elvis Presley and Bill Haley, whose "Rock Around the Clock" set pop music back towards the Stone Age (a direction it's been travelling in ever since!). Good songs with sophisticated lyrics would almost disappear, and the decent singers went with them. Hollywood stopped making the traditional, spectacular musicals, in favor of cheaper, tawdry vehicles for Presley and the like. And as more and more ballrooms became bowling alleys or high-rise condominiums, the future of the big band playing music for grown-ups became very bleak indeed. Only the most renowned orchestras with an established fan following would succeed in staying afloat in the years ahead. Fortunately for us, and although he would have to make many concessions, Stan Kenton was one of the few.

A rare shot of Stanley in his early teens with parents Stella and Floyd, and sisters Erma Mae and Beulah. Stella was very much the matriarch of the family. *Courtesy of Stella E. Kenton.*

Violet and Leslie, 1941. *Courtesy of Jack Hartley.*

Stan began his career playing piano in numerous dance bands, here the 1935 Russ Plummer orchestra appearing at the Rendezvous Ballroom, Balboa, California. *Photo by Crail-Grand Studios, Hollywood, California.*

Looking every inch his 6-foot, 4-inch tall, Stan was almost 30 years old when this photo was taken in December 1941. *Photo by Robert N. Allen Jr., San Bernardino, California.*

Stan's first "working" band played the Hollywood Palladium between November 25 and December 31, 1941. During this engagement, America entered World War II after the Japanese attacked Pearl Harbor. Personnel from left to right: Trumpets: Chico Alvarez, Frank Beach, Earl Collier; Trombones: Dick Cole, Harry Forbes; Saxophones: Jack Ordean, Bill Lahey, Ted Romersa, Red Dorris, Bob Gioga; Rhythm: Howard Rumsey (b), Al Costi (g), Marvin George (d)   *Photo courtesy The Stan Kenton Collection, University of North Texas Music Library.*

By 1946, "Artistry in Rhythm" had established Kenton as one of the most popular bands in the land. Surrounding solo-ist Buddy Childers at the Meadowbrook, Cedar Grove, New Jersey, in February 1946 are John Anderson and Ray Wetzel (trumpets), Gene Roland, Milt Kabak and partially hidden Bart Varsalona (trombones), Vido Musso, Boots Mussulli and Al Anthony (saxophones).   *Courtesy of Jack Hartley.*

Surrounding Stan in this February 1946 shot are Boots Mussulli (alto), Bob Gioga (baritone), Al Anthony (alto), Eddie Safranski (bass), Bob Cooper (tenor), Vido Musso (tenor) and Bob Ahern (guitar).  *Photo by Charlie Mihn.*

Capitol producer Jim Conkling with anxious-appearing June Christy, Stanley, and Pete Rugolo. Kenton laid the foundations for Progressive Jazz, but Rugolo was the architect who brought the plans to fruition.  *Photo by Gene Howard.*

Milt Bernhart named Kai Winding as the most important soloist in the Artistry band. He's accompanied by a top-notch saxophone section of Vido Musso, Boots Mussulli, Al Anthony, Bob Cooper, and Bob Gioga. *Courtesy of Jack Hartley.*

In 1947, the Progressive Jazz orchestra brought Kenton the same sort of admiration and large crowds enjoyed in later years by over-hyped rock groups. Here June Christy pauses in mid-song while the band plays "Over the Rainbow." *Courtesy of Jack Hartley.*

Art Pepper (pictured here in 1951) brought his "cool" sounds into the band in September 1947, while Bob Cooper also adopted a similar style, giving the Progressive Jazz saxes a completely different complexion from the Artistry orchestra. *Courtesy of Jack Hartley.*

A large string section expanded the orchestra to some 40 musicians for the Innovations in Modern Music concert tours in 1950 and 1951. June Christy sang in both years, this date being in Grand Rapids, Michigan, on October 12, 1951. *Photo by Robinson Studio, Grand Rapids.*

Maynard Ferguson solos on his name-piece with the inter-Innovations "dance" band, actually a top-class jazz orchestra. The sax section now comprises Bob Cooper, Art Pepper, Bud Shank, Bart Caldarell, and Bob Gioga. Most of the guys loathed the distinctive red and gray plaid jackets, but they certainly caused controversy. *Photo by Stan Peterson.*

Jerri Winters, pictured in an informal pose with June Christy, sang with the New Concepts band in 1952. *Photo by Gene Howard and Associates.*

Three important members of the New Concepts trumpet team: Conte Candoli, Buddy Childers, and Don Dennis. Dennis was a very capable jazz soloist, but was over-shadowed by his team-mate Conte.   *Photo by Dale Stevens.*

New Concepts of Artistry in Rhythm at the Rustic Cabin, Englewood Cliffs, New Jersey, in November 1952. Shown are Bill Holman, Lee Konitz, Vinnie Dean, Richie Kamuca, Tony Ferina (saxophones), Bob Burgess, Bill Russo (trombones), Don Dennis (trumpet). Ferina was subbing for a vacationing Bob Gioga at the time.   *Courtesy of Jack Hartley.*

Though she sang with the band for only five months, Chris Connor made a big impression in 1953, second only to Christy herself, and moved on to a highly successful solo career. *Courtesy of Jack Hartley.*

Near the end of the band's first fantastically successful European tour, Stan played two concerts at the Theatre Royal, Dublin, Ireland, on September 20, 1953. Trumpets: Don Smith, Conte Candoli, Buddy Childers, Don Dennis, Vic Minichiello; Trombones: Bill Smiley, Keith Moon, Bob Burgess, Frank Rosolino, Bill Russo; Saxophones: Tony Ferina, Zoot Sims, Lee Konitz, Dave Schildkraut, Bill Holman; Rhythm: Stan Levey (d), Barry Galbraith (g), Don Bagley (b), Stan Kenton (p) *Courtesy of Jack Hartley.*

Lee Konitz on alto sax, described by Bill Russo as perhaps the finest improviser ever to play in the Kenton band. *Courtesy of Jack Hartley.*

Stan's piano idol Earl "Fatha" Hines and June Christy laugh at the joke. *Photo by Bud Berman, courtesy of Bill Daly and Associates.*

Stan married Ann Richards soon after she joined the band in 1955, giving him two children: Dana Lynn, born in 1956, and Lance in 1958. Ann sang with the band on and off (but mostly off) until 1961, the year the couple divorced. *Courtesy of Jack Hartley.*

A sombreroed-Stan poses for the camera during a short tour of Mexico in June 1960. *Photo by Armando Moreno.*

After Pete Rugolo, Johnny Richards was probably the writer whom Stan admired the most. John's 1956 "Cuban Fire" has acquired iconic status in the orchestra's library. *Courtesy of Jack Hartley.*

Nat "King" Cole and Kenton were personal friends, and recorded together twice for Capitol Records. "Orange Colored Sky" (1950) was a big enough hit to be re-recorded in 1961 stereo, but "Steady/My Love" (1960) failed to hit the jackpot. *Courtesy of Jack Hartley.*

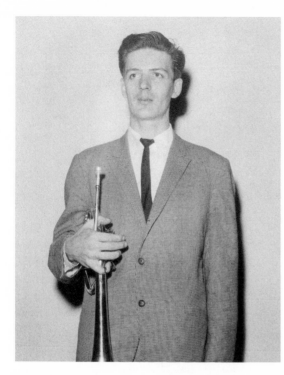

Disliked by most of the musicians, but widely accepted by the fans, the mellophoniums were one of the most controversial innovations Stan ever introduced into the band. English-born Ray Starling was the most fluent soloist on the instrument during 1961–1962. *Courtesy of Jack Hartley.*

The mellophonium section from May 1963: Bob Faust, Tony Scodwell (lead and soloist), Dick Martinez, and Bob Crull. That's John Worster on bass. *Courtesy of Tony Scodwell.*

Four-fifths of the May 1963 trombone and sax sections: Trombones: Jim Amlotte, Ron Meyers, Jiggs Whigham, Chris Swansen (Dave Wheeler not shown); Saxophones: Archie Wheeler, Steve Marcus, Gabe Baltazar, Ray Florian (Joel Kaye not shown) *Courtesy of Tony Scodwell.*

Dee Barton brought a very original trombone style to the band in 1961, before switching to drums in 1962. During the Sixties, Dee's writing was also an important asset. Also shown in this May 1963 shot are: Trumpets: Dalton Smith, Ronnie Ossa, Bob Behrendt; Trombones: Jim Amlotte, Ron Meyers, Jiggs Whigham, Dave Wheeler. *Courtesy of Tony Scodwell.*

Stan's last full-time vocalist, Jean Turner sang with the band throughout 1962 and 1963. This unposed shot portrays Jean and two unloved mellophoniums. *Courtesy of Jack Hartley.*

Gene Roland was the only arranger to write for Kenton in all four decades of the band's existence. *Adventures in Blues* by the mellophonium orchestra is one of Gene's most popular albums. *Courtesy of Jack Hartley.*

Between Neophonic concerts, Stan led his own dance band in the later Sixties. This shot was taken at Lambertville, New Jersey, on June 7, 1967: Trumpets: Jay Daversa, Bob Scilatto, Larry Ford, Carl Leach, Mike Price; Trombones: Jim Amlotte, Dick Shearer, Tom Whittaker (Andy Munthe and Graham Ellis not shown); Saxophones: John Mitchell, Alan Rowe, Ray Reed, Bob Dahl, Bill Fritz, all playing Latin "toys" *Photo by Jack Hartley.*

John Von Ohlen, nick-named "the Baron" by Stan, was a vital asset to the band between May 1970 and February 1972. *Courtesy of Jack Hartley.*

Mike Vax, a leading member of the trumpet section between 1970 and 1972, solos at Rockaway, New Jersey, on November 8, 1971. *Photo by Jack Hartley.*

Stan proudly displays a billboard advertising his first Decca album (released on London in the US), recorded at Croydon, England, on February 10, 1972. *Photo by Bourdon Studios, Inc.*

Dick Shearer, who played in every Kenton band between 1965 and 1977, solos on "Bon Homme Richard" at Sheffield, England, on February 12, 1973. *Courtesy of Peter Hall.*

John Park, probably the band's finest soloist during the entire 1970s, solos on "Street of Dreams" at Bristol, England, on February 16, 1973. That's Ramon Lopez on conga drums. *Courtesy of Peter Hall.*

Stan brought his band to the UK again in September 1973. These three shots by Peter Hall are from Club Fiesta, Sheffield, on September 10, 1973: Trumpets: Gary Pack, Mike Barrowman, Dennis Noday, Paul Adamson, Mike Snustead; Trombones: Bill Hartman, Lloyd Spoon, Dick Shearer, Dale Devoe, Mike Wallace; Saxophones: Kim Park, Richard Torres, John Park, Mary Fettig, Roy Reynolds; The rhythm section is not shown, but comprised Stan Kenton (p), Kerby Stewart (b), Peter Erskine (d), and Ramon Lopez (Latin) *Courtesy of Peter Hall.*

Trumpets give all they've got to outblow "The Peanut Vendor": Mike Snustead, Paul Adamson, Dennis Noday, Mike Barrowman. Gary Pack is not shown. *Courtesy of Peter Hall.*

Stan in good spirits brings the concert to a close with "Malaguena." The band liked playing in clubs where space was limited, because then they played in "stack" formation rather than Stan's preferred "spread." *Courtesy of Peter Hall.*

Stan Kenton towards the end of his career, his problems clearly etched on his face, but still the kindly gentleman he ever was. *Courtesy of Jack Hartley.*

# 17.

## Back to Balboa

### (1957–1958)

Standard songs composed by Duke, like "Solitude," "Mood Indigo," and "Sophisticated Lady," performed and recorded daily by artists world-wide, assured Ellington a steady income to supplement his band earnings. Kenton had no such fall-back, and knew he had to trim his sails. French horns and guitar were out. A fifth trombone replaced the tuba, but saxes remained at four, making life no easier for Niehaus and Perkins, while the bass and drums literally comprised the regular rhythm section.

A top-selling LP would help depleted revenues, and Stan decided on a group-vocal album along the lines of the highly successful Four Freshmen (whom Kenton had helped propel to popularity). However, Stan preferred not to call in favors and use the Freshmen themselves, as that would have incurred split royalties, but instead to groom a similar group himself, which was his first big mistake of 1957. Stan's manager, Margaret Sharpe, was a member of the famous Roger Wagner Chorale, and she knew that four men from the choir had been rehearsing after-hours as a Freshmen-styled pop quartet termed the Modern Men, and suggested them to Kenton.

To turn an amateur vocal group overnight into a professional unit capable of competing with the Freshmen or the Hi-Lo's was way beyond Kenton's abilities on his own. In 1947 it had taken the combined talents of Dave Lambert and Pete Rugolo to coach the Pastels, and even that group hadn't exactly taken the world by storm. The strained, tense voices of the Modern Men were not helped by the very straightforward, unambitious Kenton backing arrangements, which lacked the lightness of touch and dexterity Pete Rugolo had brought to such Four Freshmen classics as "Love Is Just Around the Corner," or "The Last Time I Saw Paris." The result over a whole LP is monotonous and flat, so that Ann Richards was coaxed out of retirement to provide a contrasting sound on three songs; in fact her featured vocal "Softly," on which the Modern

Men are confined to background "oohs" and "aahs" is one of the album's brighter moments.

Plans for the group to tour with the band were dropped when *Kenton with Voices* predictably bombed at the box office, even Howard Lucraft commenting, "The LP should be called *Voices with Kenton* —it's practically all voices and hardly any Kenton."[1] Even then Stan was reluctant to admit failure, and a young writer named Roy Pritts penned some arrangements that were used for the Men's occasional appearances at the Rendezvous later in the year. Trombonist Don Reed summed the group up as, "Poor in every way you can think of. Mainly their intonation, especially the lead singer, was bad. They had no warmth or feeling like the Four Freshmen, whom they were trying to imitate. I do remember we were embarrassed when we had to back them up."[2]

Jerry McKenzie was only 22 when he joined on drums in June '57 at the Blue Note in Chicago, replacing Reed Vaughan whom Stan had found wanting. As a Kenton fan, Jerry knew the music well and "Performed with such ease he might have been playing with the band for ever. At the end of 'Theme and Variations' he played exactly the same fill that Stan Levey did on the recording. Stan was so pleased, you could see the relief and satisfaction in his smile," according to Don Reed.[3] Seemingly, Jerry was more problematic when new music came in with which he wasn't familiar. As Phil Gilbert noted, "Then Jerry didn't hold the band together—he held on to it for dear life!"[4] Nevertheless, together McKenzie and returnee Red Kelly on bass formed a substantial rhythm section that served the band well.

Stan now embarked upon the difficult double act of balancing what was primarily a dance band with keeping happy the hard-core Kenton fans. Concerts such as the July 5 Newport Jazz Festival (issued on Pablo CD as *Stompin' at Newport*) were the exception, and mainly the band scuffled around the nation's remaining ballrooms, forced in the main to stick to dance music which stayed close to the melody and the meter, though played with such panache and style, and with so much solo space, it is impossible not to be impressed. But some nights they plumbed the depths, as Don Reed recalls: "One time we played the Officers' Club at Parris Island, and they kept asking for waltzes and polkas, and we thought, 'Why in hell did they hire Stan Kenton if that's all they want?' But Stan accommodated them. He had Sam Noto and the rhythm section play some waltzes and polkas, and that satisfied them. Stan was that way—if things weren't going well, he wanted to do something to put it right."[5] Despite his dislike of nostalgia, Stan must have sometimes longed for a return to the days not so long past when enthusiastic crowds had cheered his experimental music to the rafters.

Even in the current economic climate, Kenton remained intent upon improving the sound of his band, and decided to add a fifth man to strengthen the reeds. But even that wasn't straightforward, as Bill Perkins recalled: "We kept telling Stan to add another sax, so eventually he did. But instead of the logical second alto, he added another baritone, which was like sinking the *Titanic!* Stan was looking for a different sound, and a leader has different priorities from the sidemen."

One way or another, Perk was experiencing a difficult period in his life. "When I first joined the band," says Archie LeCoque, "Bill was a pretty happy guy. Then he got deep, nobody could understand what was going on with him, he was going through some kind of mental or emotional hassles, till he finally refused to say a word to anybody on the bus. He just sat in his seat and stared straight ahead, and never took part in anything. Finally, he got a rain parka. (You put it over your head and except for a little hole at the top for your head to stick out, it covers the whole body.) Well, he'd wear this parka but without his head sticking out the hole, so there'd be this weird lump sitting in the seat, and he'd be under it. And then he found this great big piece of driftwood, and he set that in the seat next to him, so all you could see was this canvas-covered lump in one seat and a piece of driftwood sitting there. It looked really bizarre to anyone coming on the bus, and they could never figure out what it was. They'd ask, 'What's that?' and be told, 'Oh, that's Bill Perkins under there.'"[6] (Bill was, of course, going through a temporary phase. You couldn't have wished for a more modest, pleasant, well-adjusted person than the Perkins Tony Cox and I met with in 1998.)

Stan had Kent Larsen playing lead trombone and Archie LeCoque the jazz solos, while there was general agreement in the band that the roles should be reversed. I liked LeCoque's raspy trombone, a little like Tommy Dorsey but with more emotion and grit, and found his solos very effective, but Archie fancied his role much more as a lead player. As first trombone, Kent had problems with the high register, and didn't have a big sound up there, or always hit the high notes accurately. "I sat right next to him," said Don Reed, "and sometimes I had a hard time hearing him. We were all very unhappy with the situation."[7] However, even Reed admitted that Larsen always became very nervous taking solos on record dates, and frequently messed up, which may well be why Stan preferred to keep him on lead. In 1995 LeCoque and Reed were reminiscing together: "You know," said Archie, "we really gave Kent a lot of support. I believe we made Kent sound a lot better than he was."[8] Nor is that view confined to these two friends. Jim Amlotte told me, "Larsen wasn't really a lead player— he didn't have the range or the ability. But

Stan overlooked the clams, because Kent was a jolly guy, the sort that Stan liked very much."

Noel Wedder confirmed: "Kent Larsen was movie-star handsome and a charming son-of-a-gun who made it his business in life to make everyone around him happy and up. Like a lot of talented musicians, Larsen had a pleasing singing voice, and knew something about pitch and staying in tune. And he had enormous stage presence when he sang—a very upbeat, extroverted guy that women flocked to like a magnet. This was not lost on Stan, who during the late '50s was doing everything possible to make inroads into the dance-band market."[9] Archie LeCoque sums Larsen up as "An excellent road manager, and a darn good jazz trombonist. A very happy-go-lucky guy, Kent died at a pretty early age [48], but lived two swinging lives doing it."[10]

Very little new music was coming into the library, but the quality if not the quantity of the charts written by Wayne Dunstan (tenor sax) stood out. The beautifully arranged "When Your Lover Has Gone" was featured often but never studio-recorded, perhaps because Wayne was one of the band's "bad boys." "Wayne was really easy-going, just a beautiful guy," said LeCoque. "He'd get up to all kinds of things, on the long hops especially. He'd get everybody laughing."[11] But not necessarily including Kenton, and Don Reed was a little more specific: "Wayne Dunstan got busted for using pot, so Stan fired him, and Richie Kamuca took his place."[12]

What exactly Stan was thinking, when he decided to lease the Rendezvous Ballroom in Balboa and operate it as a resident base for the band, defies logical explanation. Even in the palmy days of 1941, all the dance-spots in southern California's coastal resorts had closed for the winter, so how Stan imagined he alone could keep the Rendezvous open in the frosty climate for dance bands of 1957 is beyond belief. No doubt he longed to settle down, and certainly he had a sentimental attachment to the Rendezvous, but sentiment has no place in business. I've no doubt he was advised against the plan, but employees who opposed Stan once his mind was set did so at their own risk (of losing their jobs!).

"We completely renovated the place," said Stan, "had a new sound system installed, new furnishings and so on, and established it as a home for the Kenton band. It was my idea to play there for periods, and when we went on tour have another band come in to replace us."[13] *Down Beat* reported that the Rendezvous cost Kenton $158,000 to lease, around $75,000 to remodel and furnish, and that opening date would be December 13, 1957.

Stan wanted an album on the market heralding his move as quickly as possible, and recorded at the Ballroom in October. Joe Coccia was scheduled to revive the dance library, but his album didn't stand a chance. For one thing, Joe was heavily restricted by his commission. Accustomed to writing more experimental music (my own favorite Coccia chart is the lively Latin feature for Archie LeCoque's trombone "Nightingale"—Status 108), Joe was required to write easily recognizable dance music around two and a half minutes long. Even worse, although Wally Heider would record the band frequently at the Rendezvous with complete clarity, Capitol with all their sophisticated technology couldn't get it right, and came up with the most flat, lifeless audio of any Kenton album they ever recorded. The band seems listless and tired, devoid of any joy or vitality, with Perkins' tenor in particular sounding hollow and empty—faults not heard on Heider's recordings of the same charts from the same venue.

Jim Amlotte summed up the album as "Good for dancing. Those charts were danceable music, which is what Stan wanted at the time— nothing creative, nothing new. Looking back at them now, I think they were a little watery, more simplistic than some of the other arrangements. I remember Joe's 'Spring Is Here,' and I enjoyed playing that better than the *Rendezvous* album." And Bill Perkins got it right when he told me, "The location sound on those recordings wasn't good, it tended to make things drag. When the album came out it just sounded empty. And Coccia's dance arrangements were heavy, they didn't swing. But don't get me wrong—Stan should have used Joe for his concerts, because he was a good writer, but not for dance music."

Even Coccia himself wasn't pleased with the results: "Recording in the empty ballroom resulted in a sound quite different from the one I expected. And I was particularly unhappy with some of the takes, especially 'This Is No Laughing Matter.' If I had been present I would probably have been able to suggest tempo and musical adjustments, but I was 3000 miles away on the east coast. I am happiest with the two originals Stan permitted: 'Two Shades of Autumn' and 'Desiderata,' and even there I would have liked some changes. Whenever I hear the album now I become more dissatisfied with what I wrote, and I wonder why Stan even recorded some of that material."[14]

Bob Curnow liked the originals too: "On 'Two Shades of Autumn,' Coccia uses horns in pairs. For instance, there are a number of spots where two different trombones are playing a duet that winds in and out of the texture. Within the trumpet section, he'd use three trumpets doing one thing, and two doing another in counterpoint. There's a lot of that going on, and it's very different—not the first time it was done, but very characteristic of Joe's writing at that point." "Desiderata" features Kenny Shroyer, in Phil Gilbert's words, "Probably the best bass trombone player I have ever known, a free spirit with a very loose and flexible style, and fine intonation. He got into the studios and became a valuable session man."[15]

"It was December 13, 1957, that we opened at the Rendezvous," Don Reed recalled, "and that was a grand night, with June Christy, Nat Cole, and the Four Freshmen, and they all came in and did their show for nothing, just to get Stan going on this thing. And we had a good crowd, but then every night after that the turnout just kept getting smaller and smaller . . . "[16] Stan had psyched himself up into believing his efforts were going to rejuvenate the ballroom business, but in retrospect he was much more realistic: "I should've known that opening night it was the kiss of death," he told Carol Easton. "Because when we used to play one-nighters at the Rendezvous, we'd have anywhere from 3000 to 4000 people. And that night, with all that powerful box-office attraction, we had only 2,400 people in attendance."[17]

Kenton wasn't wrong. The demoralized band was soon reduced to playing weekends only, and even that was a disaster. "The apathy of the young people regarding our music was disheartening," commented Jerry McKenzie. "I remember one Saturday night—I counted 36 people!"[18] Sunday afternoon "Concerts on the Pacific" were better attended because Stan brought in local college students for free to ensure an audience for the "Monitor" broadcasts pre-recorded by NBC.

Hopes were placed on a Kenton-financed TV show on local Los Angeles station KTTV, but this too flopped, failing to find a sponsor or a national outlet. Archie LeCoque recalled, "The format was all music, featuring the band and soloists, and Jan Tober sang with us at Balboa for a few weeks until Ann Richards could come in after having Stan's baby. [Lance Kenton, born January 15, 1958] But you know how it is—people don't want to sit for an hour and just listen to music and watch the musicians, and the show folded after just six episodes."[19]

As usual, Phil Gilbert tells it straight: "The band went into Balboa with lots of hope and expectations, only to have it all shattered within a few weeks. We played weekends only, and nobody came to hear us. The place could hold over three thousand people, and the average 'crowd' was 20 or 30 displaced persons. Stan was baffled. Didn't know what to play. A young guy dancing cheek to cheek with a chick he'd like to score with can't handle a screaming trumpet section missing notes because they just had four days off (without pay), in an empty ballroom that has the acoustics of an armory! We got paid for three days, about $120 each week. And this went on for months!! [If accurate, this is actually very generous. When Don Reed joined the previous year, he told me his weekly pay packet, for a full seven days' work, was also $120.] Stan was losing thousands of dollars each week, and was drinking a lot. Cracked up his Porsche one foggy night on his way home, broke some ribs, and Pete Rugolo conducted for a couple of weeks while Stan recovered. Morale was very low all over. A band used to seven nights a week playing one-nighters cannot perform well with three days on and four days off!

"Red Kelly and Jerry McKenzie and I hung out together most of the time and enjoyed the beach-bum existence. We lived in different little pads in Balboa. Most of the guys commuted to LA, 50 miles one way. With all this time on our hands, I bought a new MGA and drove it all over southern California, drank a lot of beer, and smoked a ton of pot. Stan was a very likeable, considerate leader, but he also had his personal problems with his women, and the bottle and cigarettes. The Balboa Band was only a shadow of the great bands he'd had. His world was crumbling, but he did come back with some very good bands for a while, till the bottle and time ran out."[20]

Capitol taped a second album in the ballroom, and the engineers managed a little better, though the sound is still echoey and disengaged, and the stereo tapes were canned in favor of the mono recordings. None of the music was newly written, and the best charts dated back to 1956 and the French horn band. (Stan brought in two horns for the session.) Marty Paich was never on Stan's full-time staff, but when he did produce a chart for Kenton it was something special, and "My Old Flame" had already become a classic. "Marty was one of Hollywood's great arrangers," noted Phil Gilbert. "His ballads were unique in their harmonies and extraordinary originality. I still remember the feeling I got when we rehearsed 'My Old Flame' at Zardi's. After all the moving moods throughout came the classical climax, and I thought, 'My God, that's gorgeous.' Everyone was stunned."[21]

"Rendezvous at Sunset" (originally titled "Evening") reflects the romantic face of Johnny Richards, and is one of the loveliest original ballads in all of jazz. Whatever the mood, Richards' music post-*Cuban Fire* has substance and symmetry, and nobody wrote more effectively for the French horns within a jazz framework. Towards the end of "I Concentrate on You" the horns rise out of the orchestral timbre in a truly gorgeous surge of sound. (A talent not lost on Kenton when it came time to form the mellophonium orchestra in 1960.)

The five Richards charts without horns Johnny told me were written "several years before they were recorded." Richards' biographer Jack Hartley dates them as 1955, but anyway it was before *Cuban Fire*, and the Latin rhythms are definitely not authentic, sounding tacked on rather than an integral feature. They would not have been welcomed at the time by the "Bill Holman band"!

Don Reed noted that "Stan liked Johnny Richards. I think he was Stan's favorite arranger, but those scores were so demanding physically on the band, because the trumpets were constantly screeching. Everybody was playing loud all the time, long sustained notes that blared, and the arrangements didn't swing."[22] And Phil Gilbert is typically blunt: "Richards was a highly educated musician with great orchestrating skills, but he was also very disturbed and drank heavily. *Cuban Fire* was his best, and he wrote some nice ballads like 'The Nearness of You' and 'The Way You Look Tonight' with no explosions or head-on collisions. We did not enjoy his *Back to Balboa* charts at all. I hated them. Too hard, and to what end? Uniting those tunes with Latin rhythms was no help at all."[23]

On the other hand, Jim Amlotte was unexpectedly positive: "I really liked those Latin charts on 'Begin the Beguine,' 'Out of this World,' and so forth. Johnny Richards is one of my favorite composers, but his music taxed you to the end. To Johnny, nothing was unplayable, and his music was challenging: very, very challenging. Richards put his arrangements together so well. Some guys will say there's too much tension, but this is what I like. Some things are going to swing, and some things aren't, but as long as there's a pulsation, that's enough for me. They don't all have to be Basie-type swing."

Stan persevered at the Rendezvous until early April 1958, when the continued drain on his finances forced him to call a halt. He had lost as much money as on an Innovations tour, but without the corresponding artistic achievement. "After that failure I had really to sit down and assess what had happened," Stan reflected. "That was a good band, but I realized there just isn't enough Kenton following to support a venture like that in a huge ballroom—it was impossible, because there were just not enough people interested in what we were doing. So out of the window went my plans to provide a home for the band, and I once again wound up terribly in debt because of all the money I had spent in trying to activate the ballroom. Why, I went through $125,000 in four months down there, and it was just terrible."[24] (And Stan winced at the memory, even as he ruefully laughed.)

In retrospect, one wonders how Stan could ever have expected this particular venture to come to a different ending!

# 18.

## Standards in Silhouette

### (1958–1959)

Stan did what he always did when the going got rough: he set about writing himself a hit record, though by 1958 it had to be an LP rather than a single. His first thought was to repeat the success of "September Song" with an album of band vocals, but after a couple of sessions Lee Gillette must have pointed out that while a single song might have made it in 1951, the monotony of 12 band vocals in succession was not going to hit anyone's jackpot. So Stan tried repeating an even earlier success with a saxes and rhythm album, but the magic was missing. The music dragged, and in the Seventies Clinton Roemer rejected the tracks for Creative World release, noting, "These titles are very weak in comparison with the 1941 saxophone numbers."[1]

In Kenton's case it was third time lucky, though even that nearly went awry. He wrote a dozen quality arrangements of standard ballads for the full orchestra, emphasizing trombone section soli, which nearly fell apart on the first session. As written, the lead trombone didn't solo as such, but he did feature the melody while the other trombones played sustained harmony underneath. "Kent Larsen was playing lead," related Jim Amlotte, "and he couldn't make it all the way through the first number—it was just clam after clam. The guys in the section had to play it over and over, and pretty soon nerves started coming apart. So Archie and I both tried the lead part, and we both clammed, and Archie's a fabulous player, but he hadn't played for several days and wasn't up to it. So when Stan saw that none of us could make it, he got into a huddle with Lee Gillette in the booth, and decided to play the lead on piano himself, with the trombones playing underneath him. And after that the whole album was done that way."

The LP wasn't intended to be jazz; it was meant to have wide appeal to a broad audience, and it succeeded in its intention to make money, both for Kenton and for Capitol. But most listeners will be unaware of the circumstances under which the album was made, and will judge the music on its merits alone. Each arrangement on its own is a gem, but the writing is formulaic, so that after several tracks the titles all seem to merge together into bland repetition. The music screams out for improvised solos to relieve the tedium, and give the titles individual identity, but there are none. Live audiences often fared better, for Stan would often surrender his piano spots, to Niehaus on "End of a Love Affair," LeCoque on "Early Autumn," or Rolf Ericson on "How Deep Is the Ocean."

With an obvious debt to Shakespeare, Capitol publicized *The Ballad Style of Stan Kenton* as "The Taming of the Crew," a tag that must have met with Stan's approval. Whether or not his hard-core fans wanted the music "tamed," Kenton was certainly pleased. The writing was in no way demeaning, yet both the scores and his piano playing had been accepted by the general public, and Stan thereafter termed himself a "romantic writer." I remember discussing *Ballad Style* with a long-term fan who defended the album, but rather spoiled his case by adding, "It makes excellent background music during dinner-time conversation." Stan was of course adapting to current conditions in the pop music business, but "background music" had never been what Kenton was all about.

*Ballad Style* set a trend for the next dozen years, insofar as Kenton was often forced to make his music more lyrical, and rarely included jazz solos in his own writing. I asked Jim Amlotte for his observations: "My feeling is that Stan omitted horn solos for commercial reasons, and the color of just one solo piano. Stan needed the exposure, though he always got the frights when he had to record, even the one-finger things. On the road he often used one of the jazz soloists in place of piano, and you could do that at a dance, rather than put it on tape and sell it commercially. I think the concept came from Gillette, who really gave Stan good advice to help maintain his progressive image, but don't get too far out—let's make it a little on the commercial side, but with the Kenton band sound."

Phil Gilbert was typically caustic, but as a long-term Kenton alumnus, his views should not be suppressed because they are contentious: "Stan wrote all the charts on *Ballad Style*, but commercial music that sells to a mass audience does not have to be dull and boring, and this was! That album is also a clear representation of Stan's prowess at the piano. On all the songs he plunks one quarter note after another, playing straight melody one-finger style, showing no pianistic style or emotion. Very little technique. When Stan attempted a 'jazz' chorus on maybe 'Intermission Riff,' it had no character, no creative ideas—just chug-chug-chug, bang!"[2]

Pete Rugolo was having a hard time getting started in the studios, and was experiencing "writer's block," so to help him overcome a difficult period in his life, Stan suggested that Capitol record a pair of melodic, string-laden albums featuring many of the Forties "classics" that had built the band's reputation. Pete's writing was planned to be "Hollywood" professional, a notch above Muzak, but in no way innovative or experimental, and Capitol seized eagerly on the idea, delighted that their maverick artist was not intent upon promoting some new far-out scheme that was certain to lose money.

Though released as Stan Kenton albums, in fact the project was entirely Rugolo's. Stan did no more than play a little piano on a couple of titles, and that may have been dubbed in afterwards. Milt Bernhart led the trombone section that augmented the strings, and he told me, "I don't associate Kenton with those sessions at all—I'm not even sure Stan was there, Pete Rugolo was totally in charge. Pete writes very well for strings, but they wanted only easily listenable music. Sometimes I hear those albums played in supermarkets!"[3]

Noel Wedder commented: "Album sales and royalties are very important to an artist, and rather than let them slowly evaporate by depending solely upon limited sales to a small if loyal jazz audience, Stan did what he had to do to expand the universal appeal of the orchestra. Both Stan and Pete felt that the thematic material was extremely strong, and would transcend any undue criticism that might compare the music with Mantovani or Jackie Gleason."[4] Nevertheless, it is those "jazz albums" that remain in Capitol's active catalog well into the twenty-first century, not the popularity contests that in the long term proved to be nothing but a minor distraction.

The idea for an album of show tunes came from Lee Gillette, but the concept was developed by Kenton, who wanted a riff or rhythmical pattern heard throughout each orchestration. He assigned the writing to Lennie Niehaus, who came up with a happy, bouncy collection that probably would have sent Stan running for the hills a decade earlier, but which suited his purpose very well in 1958. The battle now was for sheer survival in a hostile environment. "It wasn't like the old road-band days," said Archie LeCoque. "Now it was a scuffle. We played any place—ballrooms with 300 people that could hold 4,000—just to keep going. None of us had any money. It was a bad time, and Stan was searching for something that would sell. Lennie's *Stage Door Swings* had nice arrangements, and everyone seemed to enjoy playing them."[5]

That was probably because the music flowed, and was easy to play. The band saw the arrangements for the first time on the recording dates, and played them through "cold" without any problems. "Lee Gillette was our A&R man," said Lennie, "and he told me *Stage Door Swings* outsold a lot of Stan's albums that were put out around that time. 'Ev'ry Time We Say Goodbye' was a very pretty tune and turned out really well, and Stan would often close at dances with 'The Party's Over.' I think the most easily recognizable riff was based on 'Intermission Riff,' which you'll hear behind Archie's trombone solo on 'Lullaby of Broadway.' 'Hey There' was very popular at the time, and 'Whatever Lola Wants' was sort of a novelty tune. There was an expression the guys used to say: Whatever Lola Wants, Stan Gets(z)."[6]

What wasn't clear from Capitol's potboilers was that Kenton was using the extra revenue to improve his orchestra by bringing in new blood, best heard on live recordings. The band privately recorded in November 1958 at Keesler Air Force Base in Biloxi, Mississippi, is lively, precise and sharp, far more enthusiastic and alert than the moribund Balboa outfit, the best CD audio incontrovertibly being on Astral Jazz. Jerry McKenzie is kicking this crew with a new-found confidence and authority. He is propelling the band, providing the buoyancy to turn weight into power, and embellishing the music with his own percussive nuances.

Bill Trujillo was providing Perkins with real competition on tenor sax. These two "Bills" often sound very similar, and in fact it is even more hazardous to differentiate between this pair than it was Perkins and Kamuca. (It's Trujillo adding style and flair to Keesler's very fine versions of "Kingfish" and "Intermission Riff.") But it was the trumpets that Trujillo raved about to me: "Frank Huggins was the real lead player. He was splitting the lead with Billy Catalano, but Frank had that sizzle. Bud Brisbois was the high note artist, and could play all the high notes, and that's why Stan liked him. He was just a natural, like Maynard. And in Jack Sheldon we had a top jazz artist. Jack always played good, always. He was a West Coast trumpet player, out of the Miles Davis/Chet Baker bag, a very lyrical, melodic player. Jack wanted to be a comedian, and sometimes at a dance Stan would let him roam free around the stage, telling jokes and making people laugh."

A hint of Sheldon's humor is heard at Keesler (remember it was an A.F. Base) when he announces his solo feature "Everything Happens to Me"; a pause, then in a droll voice, "I was in the Air Force too!" But it's Jack's trumpet that really sets this band alight. Trujillo is right that Jack is West Coast cool, but his playing is stronger and sharper than Baker, with a rounder, fuller tone that I find much more emotional. Sheldon's solos are exciting and adventurous, and often elicit a spontaneous round of applause denied some of the other players.

Larsen and LeCoque are splitting the trombone lead, though Archie played whenever the band recorded, because Kent would tense up and goof the high notes. But LeCoque also had his insecurities, and persistently played down his solo abilities. Stan clearly admired Archie's gravelly, resonant tones (as do I), and featured him frequently, on upbeat numbers like "Intermission Riff," as well as the "Early Autumn"-type ballads to which he was especially suited.

Once again Stan caused surprise in the ranks, by switching to two bass trombones, thus finally settling the standard Kenton instrumentation. "I wanted more depth, and a tuba doesn't have the flexibility and fluidity,"[7] Kenton explained. Stan loved his high trumpets, but he also liked a strong foundation with the "bottom" sounds. The sidemen generally didn't like changes; it upset the balance to which they were accustomed. "We're finally getting there," joked Bill Olson. "It won't be long before we have five bass trombones. And the other quip going round was, It's gonna be a fight to see who's going to play lead bass trombone!"[8]

With the band in better shape than it had been in some while, all that was required was a revitalized book, and that was about to come from veteran Kenton arranger Gene Roland, and a new, fresh young talent named Bill Mathieu.

Capitol got in on the act by recording ten new Roland charts "live" before an invited audience on the penultimate night of an extended engagement at the Tropicana Hotel in Las Vegas (February 2, 1959). The band enjoyed Gene's arrangements because they swung and weren't too deep—Roland didn't do deep—though after Holman, Mulligan, and Niehaus, without quite the same relish as the 1940s band had felt; very few alumni ever named Gene Roland as their favorite arranger.

Stan had hired Gene in the hopes he would come up with a hit for the band, as he had in the past, but that didn't happen. Instead, Roland provided a book of lightweight "swing" charts which, though fine in themselves, lacked that distinctive Kenton trademark, and would have been equally well suited to any other big band, something Stan acknowledged when jocularly announcing "Random Riff" as "An arrangement we are breaking in for Woody Herman" —as if! Much of Gene's "Tropicana" music was "in the vernacular of Herman" (as Kenton phrased it), whether originals like "Puck's Blues" and "Home Journey," or fresh variations of jazz standards ("Tuxedo Junction," "A String of Pearls") to the extent that Stan refused to sanction release of the completed album on the grounds that the audio wasn't up to standard.

In reality, the Tropicana technology was excellent, and everyone knew Stan had blocked release because of the perceived similarities to Woody. "The Tropicana was a happy album," commented Niehaus, "and a little more swinging than much of Stan's music, to the extent that

Kenton didn't think it sounded like his band."[9] Stan eventually relented after Kent Larsen (who joined Capitol as a producer in March 1960) had remastered the music. "Needless to say, it was a labor of love," said Kent, "and subsequently sold quite well."

Bill Perkins finally quit the band just prior to the Tropicana booking, his tenor chair filled temporarily by Richie Kamuca until John Bonnie could come in. In my years of research, I have never found anyone say a bad word about Perk, or fail to praise his playing. Of all the many accolades he received, perhaps the most bountiful, when Perk passed away in 2003 after many years battling with cancer, came from Mike Vax: "Perk was one of the best and most helpful musicians I ever worked with. We will miss you, Bill, but the band in heaven just got a LOT better."[10]

Also taped at the Tropicana was the first-recorded arrangement by newcomer Bill Mathieu of "This Is Always." Mathieu differed in many ways from your average jazzman: a well-educated, highly literate, intellectually minded philosopher, he would soon produce one of the most enduringly efficacious albums in the Kenton oeuvre. A sample of Mathieu's perspicacity is his account of the battle for the lead chair that erupted between Billy Catalano and Frank Huggins: "Billy's time was better, but Frank had the chops. On the night of February 1, Billy punched Frank on the stand, strode to his room, and packed his bag. Stan kissed Billy smack on the lips and said, 'You'll be back.' But Billy was gone for good. Another player, Joe Burnett, was sitting in the trumpet section by next afternoon, and of course, Frank Huggins was playing lead. In big bands—the Kenton band especially—the first trumpet job belongs to the strongest warrior. In cases of internecine warfare, Stan would often fuel the struggle with intimate encouragement to both parties, then step back and let the stronger man win. This did not seem cruel at the time."[11]

When Jack Sheldon left in February '59, his chair was taken by another under-stated jazz trumpet, though Rolf Ericson had a slightly harder edge to his playing. Born in Stockholm, Rolf was a leading member of the current Swedish clique before finally settling Stateside in 1952. Almost simultaneously, Jim Amlotte moved over to bass trombone, and Jimmy Knepper made the section a potent solo force with LeCoque and Larsen already in the team. "Jimmy only stayed with us for a short time," said Archie, "but whenever I could I gave my solos to Jimmy, and later in the year to Don Sebesky, because I liked listening to them play."[12]

That Jerry McKenzie should be succeeded by a drummer named Jerry McKenzie is a coincidence which in fiction would be greeted with derision. The second McKenzie was recommended to Stan by McKenzie I, who relates, "My successor was a young chap originally called Jerry Lestock, but he changed his name to McKenzie because that was his mother's maiden name, and her divorce from Lestock necessitated the switch back. This of course was a source of great confusion and embarrassment for both of us. Jerry (Lestock) McKenzie later became a policeman in the Detroit area."[13]

McKenzie I played with Kenton just the one time, from June 1957 to February 1959. McKenzie II, on the other hand, returned several times, so future references will always be to him. His residency in 1959 was brief; the band found him a cocky kid, unwilling to accept advice, and harassed him into quitting. "McKenzie II suffered greatly," commented Noel Wedder. "The guys were constantly on him for not 'kicking time.' He had a tendency to play very tightly and not take chances."[14] Jerry's successor, Jimmy Campbell, was much better received. "Jimmy kicked the band harder," noted Bobby Knight, "and the band had a much better swing feeling with him. However, if you knew Stan, that wasn't necessarily the feel that he found the most satisfying."[15] As noted, a slightly maturer McKenzie II would be back!

Though he would remain on the arranging staff, Lennie Niehaus' long tenure on alto was coming to an end, with Lennie's wife demanding to know whether he was married to her or to Stan Kenton! Incoming Charlie Mariano was a fair exchange, and as Bill Trujillo noted, "Lennie was a big influence on the section because of the way he played. We followed the alto player, and we matched his vibrato and phrasing. So when Charlie Mariano came on, it was a totally different thing. Charlie was more aggressive, and he played with more volume and fire, so we had to come up to match his playing. If you really listen, you'll hear the difference."

Stan was paying Bill Mathieu $60 plus bed and board, but Bill was finding it hard to meet his own aspirations. He longed to write rhythmic music and join the arranging elite of Mulligan and Holman, but nothing seemed to come out quite right, and rather than try to fix the faults, Stan preferred to simply junk the charts altogether. An exception was the Latin "What Is This Thing Called Love," heard on Tantara's *Revelations*, a good arrangement, but a genre already well exploited by Johnny Richards and others.

Jim Amlotte explained why Bill's early pieces didn't make it: "Stan made up his mind about a piece of music very fast. One take, one playthrough, and that was it." Bill's breakthrough came when Mathieu found his own voice in San Francisco, though not in the swing style he had been aiming for. Recomposition was certainly not new to the Kenton band.

Graettinger had practiced the art in 1948, Russo (Mathieu's friend and mentor) in 1953, and Holman in 1955. But Bill discovered an entirely new approach to recomposing standard ballads at the same time as he discovered San Francisco: "Separated from the band and on my own in an enchanted city, an innate joy broke the surface like a gulping fish. Music poured through. I wrote an arrangement of 'The Thrill Is Gone' that I knew was good."[16] Kenton too knew a good score when he heard one. "That's a beautiful thing, Bill," he said. "What's next?"

Mathieu remained behind in Chicago after an engagement at the Blue Note to continue his writing. "Willow Weep for Me" and "Lazy Afternoon" joined the growing number of arrangements, and one afternoon in the well of the band bus Stan casually remarked, "Bill, why don't you start thinking in terms of a record of your music?" At just 22 years old, Mathieu would be Kenton's youngest arranger to have an album of his own charts.

With such an incentive, Bill's inspiration took wings. During a two-week stay at the Steel Pier in Atlantic City, the band rehearsed "I Get Along without You Very Well," "Django," "Lonely Woman," and "Ill Wind": "Stan is genuinely pleased. Everyone has a seaside glow. The band is swinging. Charged layers of cymbals and brass sift through the ocean air. Success is easy!" These were the halcyon days, before realization set in. By August the material was complete.

When Dalton Smith was taken ill, Stan asked Bill to fill in, "just for a few nights." Mathieu was an adequate trumpet player, but not up to the standard of the Kenton book. At first his peers were sympathetic, but when Bill failed to improve and his run was extended into an indefinite time-frame, their compassion turned to resentment at having to carry a passenger in their section. Mathieu wasn't strong enough to record with the band, and Stan brought in replacements to fill the gap.

*Standards in Silhouette* was a triumph, different from anything else the band had ever played, yet uniquely Kenton in sound and style. The album rates alongside *Cuban Fire, New Concepts*, and *Innovations* as one of Stan's indispensable, all-time, great orchestral achievements. Mathieu has reconstructed these popular melodies with intricate care and detail. He extracts fragments from the songs and weaves these themes with his own motifs, using both sections and soloists, often in counterpoint. Short fill-ins by individual instruments (as well as featured soloists) are used as an integral part of the structural jigsaw. Especially exciting is the way the brass crescendoes arise unpredictably, and often end unexpectedly, allowing a more peaceful but always appropriate statement to emerge from the melee. And the momentum is sustained without a lull over nine songs of concert duration, affording a consistency, a unity of style, that gives the music its own identity, so that it resembles a Suite.

Many elements fitted together to make *Silhouette* so perfect. Mathieu's charts are of course the foundation, but the music could not have come together the way it did without Stan's experience and expertise, and the orchestra's understanding of Bill's intentions. Every credit is due the principal soloists, who loved this music to a man. "Absolutely gorgeous," said Bill Trujillo. And Archie LeCoque (outstanding on my own favorite: "I Get Along without You Very Well") confirms: "I think my solos on *Standards in Silhouette* were the best work I did with Kenton. Bill Mathieu wrote such beautiful charts you didn't really have to stretch out too much, you just stuck close to the melody and the arrangements took care of everything else."[17] And Bill himself adds: "I was very happy with all the soloists, but particularly Charlie [Mariano]. His playing, especially on 'Django,' provided the spark and the jazz authenticity that the album needed."

As soon as Mathieu's album was successfully in the can, the band plunged into recording Gene Roland's Latin-inspired *Viva Kenton!*, which contained some nice arrangements ("Mexican Jumping Bean," and "Mission Trail," with robust John Bonnie tenor sax), but also some trite, corny band-vocals ("Chocolate Caliente," "Cha Cha Chee Boom"), and which probably outsold *Silhouette* by two-to-one. Mathieu himself was also having self-doubts: "From over my shoulder an unseen disappointment brought me down. My music wasn't as good as Bill Russo's, or Gerry Mulligan's, or Bill Holman's. In the end I accepted the victory with no parade." Russo had warned Mathieu in a letter that "Stan will not be deceived by simulated or incomplete loyalty," and now Bill ruffled even Lee Gillette by referring to his music as "juvenalia." What Mathieu failed to appreciate was that by demeaning his music in this way he was by extension challenging the judgment of the leader he most admired, and who had endorsed his creations so enthusiastically.

Without pausing for breath, the band now entered into a five-week series of concerts (Capitol-recorded at Purdue University) with June Christy and The Four Freshmen termed "The Stan Kenton Show." Almost all the numbers have been better played on previous recordings, an exception being the Christy/Freshmen vocal on "September Song." June had a cold and was even huskier than usual, but this only adds to the emotion she pours into her singing. Mathieu admits he was still very naive, had never yet in his life been stoned (on anything), but during that tour, "More than anything else I saw booze. Christy, Bob Flanigan, Jimmy Campbell and Stan were the officers of a kind of drinking club, and a fearful amount of alcohol was consumed. Each night Stan drank his quart of Scotch, and the night I realized this was dark. I couldn't discuss it with anyone, my prudery being as obnoxious to my peers as their vices to me. I was lonely, disenchanted, tired, and the worst player in the band."

The ending was probably as inevitable as it was obvious. The concert *Silhouette* scores were *too good* for audiences in 1959, and were of only limited use for live play. Kenton replaced Bill in the trumpet section, and one afternoon gently drew the youngster aside and said, "'I think you should leave us now.' I fought for my position as a writer, but Stan knew what he was doing. He knew how unhappy I had turned. He had given me what he could, and drawn out of me what he could. He'd been paid; I'd been paid. I knew this work was finished."

At Mathieu's request, Stan wrote a letter of recommendation to Duke Ellington, and for a while Bill arranged for Duke. "It Don't Mean a Thing" and "I'm Beginning to See the Light" are on Columbia's *Piano in the Background.* But Ellington and Sweetpea were an impossible act to follow, and after that Bill "stopped collecting bandleaders," and moved on to a career in alternative forms of music though always retaining a jazz influence. By 1997, when Michael Cuscuna asked me to write the liner notes for the CD release of *Standards in Silhouette,* Bill gave me freely of his advice, and in retrospect was intensely proud of his Kenton writing, which has indeed weathered the years like the finest music does. Many of the Mathieu quotes herein derive from an unpublished dissertation on his Kenton experience, written by Bill in 1988. "Counting the Ways" is the most erudite, perceptive insight into the Kenton psyche I have ever seen. Like the best music, it requires—demands—several studies for complete comprehension, but it amply rewards any reader willing to make the effort.

The year 1959 had been a time of mixed fortunes. Some nights the band packed them in at ballrooms, and other dates were attended by audiences of less than three figures. "I made the mistake," related trombonist Bobby Knight, "of asking for a raise when we played a one-nighter in Blue Mountain, Kentucky. Stan said that he'd pay me the receipts for that night instead. Since I was making $155 a week, I was afraid to take him up on it!"[18] (Average weekly salary at the time was $175, but as an unseasoned newcomer, Knight was on the lower rung of the pay-scale ladder.)

The "Road Show" tour with Christy and the Freshmen was tough:

Ross Barbour: "It was hard. There were a lotta miles between jobs. The guys would get sullen. They'd get quiet. They'd get grumbly."

Bud Brisbois: "Being stuck on a bus that long can break you mentally. I saw guys leave the band playing less well than when they started. Others would find the means to get through it—drinking, pot, poker. Some guys would drink cough syrup."[19]

Bill Mathieu: "Towards the end of the tour, the band began collectively to lose it. Mean little fights were common, and patches of weeping sprang up unnoticed, like weeds."

Kenton had endured these conditions for two whole decades, and would do for two more. The miracle was that each night the band would appear on the stand, well turned-out, united and alert, ready to play the hell out of their music and please the Old Man. Some would claim that Stan's greatest claim to fame was his contribution to jazz education, which began in 1959 with the "Kenton Clinic" at Indiana University with the aim of helping youngsters achieve their musical goals through study and practice with some of the best teacher-musicians in the land. The number and scope of these Clinics would grow almost annually thereafter, until they became an indispensable part of the band's itinerary. But for most, Kenton's greatest legacy was the music he endorsed. "The thing that most impressed me about Stan was his leadership," declared Jim Amlotte. "That and his desire to make people aware of his music. I think that was the biggest thing in his life. It had to be that."

# 19.

## The Restless Searcher

(1960)

It must be coincidental, but Kenton greeted the start of every new decade with a fresh initiative. In 1950 it had been strings and concert music. By 1960 Stan needed the dance halls to survive, and anyway he couldn't begin to afford the luxury of a large string section. French horns had already been found wanting, changes had already been made to both saxophone and trombone sections, and Stan loved his high trumpets too much to meddle with them. He needed a whole new sound, but was at a loss to know how to proceed. Old friends Gene Roland and Johnny Richards were recruited to offer advice.

Meanwhile the band kept working, as did Stan's sense of humor. After "Love for Sale" on January 25, 1960, Kenton acknowledges the prolonged ovation from what sounds like a large crowd at Cal-Poly State University, and observes: "It's very nice of you to react that way. I do however want to advise you that jazz musicians are different than musicians of other forms of music. When they hear a lot of applause they immediately start thinking in terms of money and all sorts of things that are unbecoming to a non-profit organization such as this!"

"Love for Sale" itself had been one of those "sleepers," and a rare example of Kenton failing to recognize a potential hit. First written by Rugolo in 1948, the chart had been initially neglected by Stan; but Pete persisted and rearranged the score in 1950 to include the Innovations strings, which is when the title started to take off, sufficiently to persuade Stan to record it later that same year with the dance band nucleus. The driving rhythm and Harry Betts' compelling trombone attracted the fans, already intrigued by the unusual "false" ending that lulled unsuspecting audiences into premature applause, since after a brief pause the Latin rhythm restarted with repetitive energy and vigor before the big orchestral climax. When the Capitol single started to sell and fans began requesting the title, Stan admitted his error, Rugolo's belief in the chart was vindicated, and the number remained in the book from that day on, until

"Love for Sale" became almost the equal of "Peanut Vendor" in the Kenton Hall of Fame.

At Tacoma, Washington, on February 5, the band featured two orchestrations from the *Ballad Style* album. "The Night We Called It a Day" is played as originally written, with trombone section lead instead of Kenton's piano, in my opinion to the arrangement's benefit. Bobby Knight takes the feature role on "Early Autumn," in one of the most facile, delicate bass trombone solos I have ever heard, even if he does end the piece with the more traditional sound of a bull-frog in heat.

An important arrival in April was Hawaii-born Gabe Baltazar: "I loved the single alto line-up, because I didn't have to blend with a second alto, though I did have to be versatile to play both lead and the jazz solos. I guess I came more from the hard-bop school than the cool West Coast sounds, and I had to whip the section together so they would follow my phrasings. I'd been used to using vibrato, but Stan soon stopped me: 'Hold it Gabe, we don't use vibrato!' and I got to love to play straight. Every once in a while we'd play 'Opus in Pastels,' and that was the only time I got away with a little vibrato, and the Old Man kind of smiled and gave me an OK look. Stan's saxophones had sort of an organ sound, the way the voicings were written. That saxophone voicing was his trademark, his signature, with a tight, closer voicing than the more open spread in use today.

"Marvin Holladay helped me a lot when I first joined. He advised me how to run the section and helped me settle in. Marvin was a powerful player, and a lively, energetic person, with a lot of pent-up energy that came out in his playing. He went out there and he just barked right into that horn. Of course, there were also times when he played very pretty, in a reflective mood, very low-key. He had a lot of technique in his baritone."

A second, more contentious arrival in the section during 1960 was that of veteran tenor saxophonist Sam Donahue, regarded by some in the band as an "old-fashioned" player. It's noticeable that Stan was escaping from the "cool" West Coast-style sax sounds that had never really been his thing, back to the deeper, Hawkins-Musso tones that had always been his preference. Donahue possessed exceptional technique on his horn, and could play high notes with ease, which really bugged Bud Brisbois when Sam would effortlessly squeal out the top notes at the ends of tunes while Bud was straining up there, and busting a gut to achieve the same effect.

During the summer the band played Mexico for a week, drawing small audiences but plenty of visits to the bathroom as "Montezuma's

Revenge" took its toll. But really the band was marking time in 1960, while Stan decided how to proceed. He knew the orchestra had been drifting for several years, and a fresh impetus was essential, but at the same time money was tight, and any changes had to embrace as wide an audience as possible. "At the beginning of the year," Stan explained, "I became very restless with the sound that the band was getting. Johnny Richards and I both agreed it was time to work over the instrumentation of the band. We felt the development of new instruments and new tonal colors was long overdue."[1]

First thoughts were to expand the saxophone section, deleting the alto altogether, and have Gabe Baltazar on soprano lead. Stan experimented with a section of up to ten players, but unsurprisingly this proved unsuccessful. So Stan then gave Gene Roland carte blanche to find a new brass instrument to add to the orchestra, and Gene put together a team of four E-flat (alto) trumpets, an idea that was also nixed, because according to Stan, "It was impossible to distinguish any difference between them and the conventional B-flat trumpet section. We then tried the miraphone— something in the order of a German cornet—but we quickly abandoned that because of the muddled sound it produced. And after experimenting for two days with flugel horns, we were ready to give it up completely."[2]

Finally, the Conn instrument manufacturers at Elkhart, Indiana, learned that Stan was interested in locating a new brass instrument, and came up with a possible solution. Since the mid-Fifties, initially at mellophone player Don Elliott's request, they had been working on a new version of the mellophone, which had the bell facing forward, rather than the traditional backward direction. Conn's rather radical invention featured trumpet-style valves, but with the circular tubing of the mellophone and a forward-facing French horn bell, and thus had something in common with all three instruments. Pitched in the key of E-flat, the Conn people called their hybrid the mellophonium.

In consultation with Johnny Richards, Stan convinced Conn that if he was to feature their new instrument, they had to change the tuning slide to play in the key of F, which delivered a more distinctive sound. It also rendered the instrument almost impossible to play in tune, but Kenton was insistent, and conscious of the invaluable publicity Stan's use would bring their horn, with some misgivings Conn made the necessary alterations. Other than that adaption, stories that abound to this day that Stan "invented" the mellophonium himself are totally untrue. As Kenton himself said, "We had them send some instruments to us, and Johnny Richards and I became terribly excited with the sound of the mellophonium. It had an identity of its own, it was something that bridged the gap between the trumpets and the trombones, and we started to look for players."[3]

Which wasn't easy, because for all their sometimes free-wheeling life style, jazzmen can be surprisingly conservative when it comes to changing the status quo. Trumpet players took most naturally to the mouthpiece, but the initial lead of the four-man section was classically trained French horn man Dwight Carver, and that came about purely by happenstance: "I was living in a bachelor apartment on Santa Monica near Vine in Hollywood. About three or four doors from me next to the *Down Beat* magazine office was a rehearsal room where various groups would rehearse from time to time. One fall day in 1960 I realized that my idol Stan Kenton was rehearsing there, and one of his trombones was missing. So at Stan's suggestion I went down the street and got my 'ax' and sat in with my French horn. After the rehearsal, Stan and Johnny Richards approached me and asked if I would be interested in playing mellophonium in the band.

"My first reaction was: 'Why not the French horn?'

"'Have an open mind,' was Richards' reply.

"So a few days later Stan and John brought two or three mellophoniums to my apartment, for me to select one and familiarize myself with. They put me at my ease, saying that Gene Roland was interested in the horn, and telling stories to illustrate what an amusing and interesting character he was. Richards told one about Roland almost being caught in a pot party vice raid, where Gene quickly and casually escaped arrest by sliding down a laundry chute. What surprised me was to see Stan laughing about that particular story, seeing as how he was so dead against any of his band guys having any connection with drugs. Anyway, the upshot was I found myself a member of the Kenton orchestra as lead mellophonium player.

"In the early stages everything was experimental, and there was a myriad of problems. Firstly, the mellophonium itself was compromised simply because the E-flat horn had been modified to make it into an F horn. That is bad enough in the middle register, but in the higher register it is a bloody disaster, and some of the notes were impossibly out of tune. And secondly, no one was sure how to write for the mellophoniums as a section. Even the 'Old Man' himself was groping in the dark. The whole project must have taken some real financing. It was another of those innovational experiments like 'City of Glass' that only Kenton would have the balls to do."[4]

By September Stan felt the band was ready to record, though the first mellophonium section was very pro tem, comprising Dwight Carver,

Kenton alumnus Joe Burnett, studio trumpet player Bill Horan, and a young student from North Texas State University, Tom Wirtel. Why Kenton, surrounded by all the talent in LA, chose to fly in a novice from Texas who had to return to his studies immediately afterwards is unknown, but Stan had a long and happy association with the university, and later in the year when Sam Noto quit unexpectedly for family reasons, Stan again recruited a North Texas student, Marvin Stamm, for a three-week stint, and was so pleased with his performance he promised Marvin a seat in the band as soon as he graduated in 1961. Tom Wirtel didn't know who had recommended him to Kenton: "All I remember is getting a surprise call from Stan to go to Los Angeles for some recording dates. Of course, I was thrilled, and Stan was very helpful and put me at my ease when I arrived. All of the mellophonium players were really put on the spot, because we were charged with learning a new instrument in just ten days. And none of the writers was going to write easy stuff for us. We had to come up to the level of everybody else, and do it right away.

"We had no place to practice in the hotel, but Dwight Carver had the bright idea to take our horns out into the countryside and get our act together. By the time of the recording sessions we were a well-rehearsed section. And it's a good thing too, because the rest of the band was very apprehensive of the whole idea of including mellophoniums in the orchestra. At the first rehearsal, someone commented that we read our parts better than any of the other sections!"

There was nothing especially new about the music itself, but the mellophoniums certainly introduced a fresh, distinctive flavor into the sound of the band, with the versatile Johnny Richards the most adept at integrating the horns in an orchestral setting on "Malibu Moonlight," "El Panzon," and "On the Wagon." Gene Roland wrote a couple of typical swingers, with "Lady Luck" containing the only mellophonium solo on the dates, played by Gene himself, and stylistically harking back to Freddie Zito's 1945 trombone on "Southern Scandal"! The most unusual piece (still unissued as I write) is "Midnight Tales," a band vocal with a menacing mood and restless urgency, very different from the lyrical "September Song" genre. Kenton's writing would set the tone for other arrangers to follow. There's one exciting moment between vocals where the mellophoniums leap out and hit so hard it leaves the listener tingling.

Even so, the sessions were problematic, as explained by Dwight Carver: "This was a new world for everyone, Stan included. I was having my problems learning on the job, and everything came hard for everyone. The horns were so bad at least they were consistently bad, and many times we were out of tune, but fortunately on the unisons we were at least in tune with one another, and that way it sounded kind of intentional."[5] Kenton decided the mellophoniums needed more time to break in, and for a joint tour with Count Basie (billed as "The Greatest Bands in Jazz," with the two leaders alternating top spot on publicity posters), Stan carried a single mellophonium played by Gene Roland, giving time for Gene to become more conversant with the horn and its solo possibilities. As Noel Wedder put it, "Stan and Johnny may have hit upon using the mellophoniums and handling all the grunt work to make them viable, but it was Roland who gave the instrument life and proved what a lyrical instrument it could be."[6]

If the band had reacted badly to earlier changes in the sax and bone teams, their reaction to being joined on a permanent basis by a brand new section of four mellophoniums is unprintable. Their antipathy was equalled only by the mellophonium players themselves, who regarded the instrument as a freak, with uncontrollable pitch problems, and were there only because they wanted to play for Kenton. The trumpet section felt especially vulnerable. Not only was their traditional position at the top of the pecking order under threat, most mellophonium players were frustrated trumpet men themselves, with eyes only for moving into that "legitimate" section directly, and for whatever reason, a trumpet chair became open.

In point of fact, over three years only one man, Keith LaMotte, ever actually made the transition, as he relates: "I think I have a unique perspective, having played mellophonium from the start of the 1961 band, and trumpet throughout 1962. There is no question that the horns were difficult to play, and there was resistance at the outset from some of the musicians in the band—but not because of any lack of effort by the mellophonium players. We had many section rehearsals, plus we worked hard with Dalton Smith, Fitz, and Gabe to make the section tighter, more musical, and more a part of the ensemble. Naturally the horns were the target of good-natured jokes and needling by the other sections: they were new, not part of the traditional Kenton sound, odd-looking, and they did have intonation problems. But Stan wanted the mellophoniums to be successful, and we all worked our butts off to please him and the rest of the band."[7]

Dwight Carver certainly did his best in a difficult situation, but was handicapped by his background: "My main difficulty as section leader was that the ex-trumpet players did not match my French horn tonal concept. At times they would wipe me out with their brassiness. I think they generally regarded the mellophonium as a stepping-stone to something else, but I am sure that most were also proud to be a part of this pioneering ensemble. I know that is what kept me going."[8]

And Joel Kaye confirmed: "I liked the mellophoniums a lot, despite the serious problems with intonation and volume. But a fair number of the band didn't like them, because they were so much louder than the other brass instruments. Fitz especially seemed to have his problems with the mellophoniums."[9] Noel Wedder has confirmed that Bob Fitzpatrick was indeed highly critical, and unfairly blamed the players rather than the instruments, reportedly threatening Carver with physical retribution if he didn't "pull his section together," and even conducting his own rehearsals with the reluctant mellophonium players;[10] while Bob Behrendt quotes Fitz as likening the sound of the mellophoniums to "A bunch of stampeding, pregnant elephants." Carver was actually placed in an impossible situation, because while the band would have preferred him to exert more authority and force his team to tone down their act and follow his softer sound, Kenton wasn't renowned for his moderation, and through his own writing actively encouraged the section to "shout."

The mellophonium players didn't always help their own case, and made up jokes at their own expense: "I left my mellophonium on the back seat of my car hoping it might get stolen, but when I returned not only was my ax still there, someone had placed a second mellophonium next to it!" Or, "Perfect pitch is the ability to toss a mellophonium into a toilet from 40 yards without hitting the lid." On occasion the band exercised their displeasure, such as the time when all four mellophoniums were reportedly found floundering at the bottom of a hotel swimming pool. (Legend has it Stan did a Queen Victoria, and was most certainly "not amused.")

But perhaps more importantly, audiences and fans, and even the critics, in general approved of the mellophoniums. I think you have to possess a musician's keen ear to pick out the faults, and that applies to unedited, live recordings as much as carefully planted Capitol product. Gabe Baltazar is of the same mind: "When the mellophonium section settled in after being on the road for a few weeks, it kind of jelled, and blended with the brass and saxes. When you're playing within a band you hear things differently from what you hear in the audience. The listener won't hear the problems like the musicians, because we're right in there trying to play and blend at the same time."

Kenton himself was like a man who'd won the lottery; his gamble had paid off! The mellophoniums had achieved all he had hoped for and more. In unison they could whisper like a breeze or roar up a storm. They could blend with the other sections or rise above them like "exultant Valkyries," while the ever-adaptable Gene Roland had proved the instrument's solo potential. The enlarged ensemble enticed Stan to write with more enthusiasm than in years, but recognizing his limitations, he concentrated on the dance library and allocated the jazz work to Richards and Roland.

A new start required a new tag-line, and Stan somehow came up with the unwieldy "New Era in Modern American Music," which was too long for anyone to remember. Even the term "New Era" never became common usage, and by universal consent the band was called simply the Mellophonium Orchestra. By whatever name, with unprecedented backing from Capitol, 1961 would prove one of the most rewarding years ever in the annals of recorded Kentonia.

# 20.

## Four of a Kind:
## The Mellophonium Orchestra
(1961)

Kenton wrote the first mellophonium albums himself, believing that as leader it was his responsibility to point the way—though it's unlikely Johnny Richards required any instruction. Both Stan and John liked their music splashy, and tended to have the mellophoniums play too high, where they were most vulnerable and less likely to blend with the other sections. By common consent of the alumni, Lennie Niehaus and Ray Starling wrote for the M-horns in a lower register, where they effected a better orchestral blend and were less likely to play flat (but by definition were also less loud and hence less distinctively prominent). The new band's first release, *The Romantic Approach*, was a replica of *Ballad Style* with the added bonus of the mellophonium sound, but also the same drawbacks. However, before that Stan had recorded an album of ballad arrangements in concert style which Capitol scrapped altogether. When producer Michael Cuscuna investigated in 2004, he found the raw tapes exactly as recorded, unmastered, unedited, and unchecked for balance, without even any A-takes indicated. Reports in 1961 were that the sessions were junked because the M-horns were so out of tune as to be unissuable, but no one could understand how they were able to improve so rapidly within days. It was not the mellophoniums that changed, however, but the writing; Stan had written long passages so high that the M-horns couldn't cope. When the register was lowered even a little, the faults were less apparent.

That wasn't the only drawback. What Capitol's top brass wanted for their dollar was an album with broad appeal that would attract plenty of radio play, and DJs liked a running time of around two and a half minutes. Stan had stretched out to an average double that length ("Street of Dreams" actually plays for 7:25!) but in so doing had created his best ballad writing ever. "Theme for Sunday," with the stark sound of the mellophoniums replacing the Hollywood-styled strings from the 1950 score, never sounded better, and the sectional writing is truly gorgeous.

170

But such concert-length creations cry out for contrasting solos, and these are lacking, other than Kenton's own very elementary, one-finger-style pianisms. The album fell between two stools, being neither sufficiently commercial for popular appeal, nor jazzy enough to attract other than the hardest-core Kenton fans. Also apparent is that Kenton was very dependent on the melodic allure of his material to make this writing effective. "Winter in Madrid" does not have the same sophistication as standards like "April in Paris" or "Body and Soul" (both live on Tantara) and falls flat. Stan was about to find this out for himself when he started to write his Christmas music.

Most contract artists sooner or later record a Christmas album, but with Glenn Wallich's authority fading, Capitol's executives were deeply apprehensive at the prospect of their "progressive" maestro offending America's religious faction with a sacrilegious collection of Christmas music. And as Kenton made clear to Lee Gillette, who suggested the idea in the first place, he wasn't about to start playing "Rudolph the Red-Nosed Reindeer" or similar Mickey Mouse music. Gradually the concept took shape for Stan to write an album for brass and rhythm of Christmas carols in modern design and interpretation, and the project got the green light.

Stan started to write in identical style to that he had used for his ballad work, but carols were a different type of music altogether, and as Jim Amlotte so aptly put it, "The style that worked so well on standard ballads was just not that interesting when applied to religious music. He needed help in that line, and realized Ralph Carmichael would be the perfect person to do those Christmas songs. Realistically, Ralph's arrangements over-shadowed Stan's writing. Carmichael put a lot of creative thought into his arrangements, and introduced a sense of joyousness lacking in Stan's very somber 'Christmas Medley.'"

Ralph Carmichael was in fact an ordained minister, but, said Stan, "He's also a very wild, spirited guy who enjoys the high life, and a very talented person musically."[1] Ralph confirmed: "I was a long-time fan of Stan's, so I was thrilled to get the opportunity to work for him. I ended up writing most of the music, with Stan mainly confined to the 'Christmas Medley,' which we ran down on the first date. That didn't work out well, and Stan scrawled an expletive over the score and said he'd rewrite it for the next session. He wasn't happy with that either, but it was too expensive to remake a third time. I tried to be sensitive to the spirit and message of the original compositions, while painting the charts with some Kentonian colors. I conducted on the dates because I was the only one familiar with the charts, and we all had fun—someone thoughtfully bedecked the microphones with red and green crepe paper to create a Christmas atmosphere. After the album was completed, Kenton, Gillette, and I celebrated at the old Formosa Cafe in Hollywood, and I remember Stan roaring, 'Well, Carmichael, if this is what it takes to celebrate Jesus, count me in!'"[2]

Carmichael's spirited approach introduced a sense of fun and adventure that pervades the whole album, essentially by his rhythmic devices and use of percussion effects (tambourine, finger-cymbals, sleigh-bells) and—dare one say it—on titles like "Good King Wenceslas" and "God Rest Ye Merry, Gentlemen," a sense of swing. The LP was selected by both *Billboard* and *Variety* as the Christmas Album of 1961, and with its special annual appeal, remains in Capitol's active CD catalog.

If Carmichael had made effective use of the mellophoniums in his charts, Johnny Richards was like a kid let loose in a candy store. On *West Side Story* the horns alternately swoop and shriek or play with a soft-toned caress, but always remain an essential feature of Richards' incisive writing, at times increasing the dramatic tension, but on ballads like "Maria" tempering the excitement with a warm lyricism that endows the music with exceptional grace and beauty. There is no denying John's music was not universally well received. Those who had come to Kenton via Mulligan, Holman, and Roland resented the lack of "swing" and preferred Manny Albam's more conventional Coral renderings of Leonard Bernstein's music. But many more fans with deeper Kenton roots via Rugolo, Russo, and Innovations recognized in Richards a logical extension of that heritage, and embraced the depth and dynamism of his music with undisguised enthusiasm. The creativity and boldness displayed throughout the ten selections of *West Side Story* clinched Richards' reputation as a master arranger. It was with good reason that Stan lovingly referred to Johnny as his (musical) "brother."

"I loved playing Johnny's music," said Jerry L. McKenzie, "and so did Stan. *West Side Story* was probably the toughest album I ever recorded, and I can still vividly see Johnny Richards standing in front of the band, rocking back and forth talking to the rhythm section, inspiring the orchestra to generate the feeling that would make his music happen. John's music is very brass heavy, and it's difficult for the drummer to drive the band in that situation, but Johnny wanted that grandiose sound, and once that band got rolling with the mellophoniums and the whole brass section blowing together, it was absolutely incredible."[3]

Noel Wedder recalls the *West Side Story* charts as "Brilliantly constructed, but a travail to play. Very complicated. John was also a super-perfectionist, and insisted the music be played note for note, with particular attention to the dynamics, especially important on the ballads 'Maria' and 'Tonight.' I remember John telling Dalton [Smith] as the orchestra thundered through 'Prologue' that he was playing a note wrong. Dalton shook his head in amazement and asked, 'How in hell did he hear it, with everyone playing their asses off?' Dalton quickly learned, as did everyone else, that John had superb ears."

A problem arose when it became clear during rehearsals that jazz trumpet player Ernie Bernhardt wasn't up to the job. "Ernie could sing," commented Noel, "and he was a dynamite arranger, but as a jazz soloist he was terrible, and that is not over-stating his ability."[4] Stan wanted Marvin Stamm to fly out to California for the sessions, but when that proved impractical, "Stan asked Conte Candoli to do the record, and as we all know, Conte is one of the best, and as always he did a beautiful job," said Stamm.[5]

Released in bold headlines as KENTON'S WEST SIDE STORY on front and back cover, the LP remained in *Billboard's* top-100 album chart for 28 weeks, peaking at sixteenth in November 1961, and won the 1962 prestigious Grammy award as the year's best big band album. Though Stan in general did credit his arrangers far more generously than most bandleaders, Richards' name is very sparingly displayed on the LP jacket, despite the importance of his writing to the album's success, so that it was easy for the casual observer to believe Kenton had played a more active role in creating the actual music than was really the case. But Stan was Capitol's contract artist, not Richards, and it was in the label's interest to promote the Kenton name. Any "blame" should be attached to Capitol, not Kenton.

With four albums in the can, the mellophonium orchestra made its official public debut with a four-week engagement at the plush Riviera Hotel in Las Vegas on March 29, 1961. The mellophoniums were generally well received by the most prominent critics:

John Tynan: "Utilized to telling effect, both in section and in the jazz solo work of Gene Roland." (*Down Beat*, July 6, 1961.)

John S. Wilson: "Their presence gives the Kenton band more scope and balance than it has had for many years." (*New York Times*, September 16, 1961.)

George Simon: "An overall effect that blows all before it with its sheer musical brilliance and excitement." (*New York Herald Tribune*, September 23, 1961.)

A study of the personnel reveals competent soloists—Jack Spurlock trombone, Gene Roland mellophonium, Gabe Baltazar and Sam Donahue saxes—but few of the top echelon names previously associated with a Kenton band. This orchestra had to rely more than ever on its ensemble sound and the notoriety/curiosity attached to the mellophoniums. Dalton Smith on lead trumpet wasn't the hottest high-note stylist the band ever carried, but he honed his section to perfection, and worked in close rapport with Bob Fitzpatrick to improve the dynamics of the band: hence their aversion to the unpredictable mellophoniums. And the solo strength in the trumpets was bolstered immensely in May 1961 after Marvin Stamm graduated from North Texas State University (now University of North Texas). The band's most distinctive soloist, Stamm's restrained style and limited range (resembling a more animated Miles Davis) was not the type of trumpet Kenton usually favored, but a reliable, creative solo voice (or at least, one whom Stan could afford and who was willing to endure long tours) was becoming ever harder to find. Stamm's individual trumpet sound often resembled that of a flugel horn, though both Joel Kaye and Marvin himself have confirmed that this was never the case, as "Stan did not care for the instrument," said Marvin.[6] In Gabe Baltazar's opinion, "Marvin Stamm had a great ear. He didn't know too much about chordal changes when he first joined, but his ear was so sensitive, he could feel the tones and notes right away. I liked his solos, he had a nice feel, and he was sort of loose. I'd say he was influenced by Miles, but Marvin had the chops to play both high and low notes and improvise too."

Carl Saunders joined the band "When I was 18, just out of High School and couldn't sight-read that well." But he was proficient on trumpet even then, and was in his own words, "A Stan Kenton freak." Being young and inexperienced, he also did not command a high salary. (According to Noel Wedder, most of the sidemen were getting just $125 a week.) His mother Gail Bradley had known Stan since the Thirties, and made the introductions. As there was no vacancy in the trumpet section, Stan offered Carl a place with the mellophoniums, and as Carl says, "So what's an 18-year-old kid to do? I took the gig on mellophonium, and that was April 1961. The M-horn does have a distinctive sound, but it's not as good as the French horns they were replacing. We played pretty good as a section, but the parts weren't really swinging stuff, it was more those background French horn-type parts, so it wasn't really that much fun to play. And the rest of the band frowned heavily on the mellophoniums. We were just kind of in everybody's way, but Stan was very supportive—the mellophoniums were his baby."[7]

Like Stan himself, Sam Donahue was a veteran of the swing era, and his style had little in common with the younger, bop-influenced soloists like the two Marvins, Stamm and Holladay. But Sam's Hawkins-inspired tenor was impressive, except when he started squealing in the upper register. Gabe Baltazar confirms: "Sam Donahue had been a bandleader himself, and he had a very powerful sound, like a Vido Musso. I had to really get after him to phrase my way, because he had his own style of phrasing. With solos I wouldn't bother him, but in the section he'd be sticking out almost like a sore thumb sometimes, because he had such a powerful sound. Sam could play very high for a tenor, and when he would play too many high notes Dalton Smith used to get really disturbed. But Sam and I were good friends, we had a nice rapport going."

As another of the older players, Jim Amlotte also recognized Donahue's worth: "I often wondered why Stan wanted Sam in the band, but listening to him I used to tell the younger players, 'It might be old school, but every note Sam plays is within what the chord is, he doesn't go that far out. You can learn something from this guy.' Sam played with a maturity that doesn't happen when you're getting started. Stan respected Sam Donahue, respected him a lot."

Stan must have spent a small fortune on the new arrangements that now filled the book, some 200 in all divided between the jazz and dance libraries, though I doubt all were in use at the same time! And that doesn't include the many charts that didn't get past the first rehearsal. One can only wonder what musical merits the many Roland scores like "Chameleon Suite" and "The Bone and the Horn" may have possessed, because they seemingly did not enter into Stan's "New Era." Not even the eight albums recorded for Capitol in 1961 could begin to accommodate all the new music, which relied heavily on Lennie Niehaus' dance library. "I took it upon myself to concentrate on the dance book," said Lennie, "because I felt that was where the band was weakest. There was a need for new arrangements which sounded like Stan Kenton, but which people could dance to. So I made that my special project, and it was fun to find all those good tunes which I'd always wanted to arrange. I just kept writing and shipping 'em off to the copyist, and he'd send them on to Stan on the road."[8]

In fact Lennie wrote too quickly for each to have an individual originality, but the guys loved playing them because they flowed easily and weren't too far out. These opinions are from a musician's point of view:

Gabe Baltazar: "Niehaus' style of writing is more contemporary than Kenton's. Stan used very close harmony, which was popular in the

'30s and '40s. Lennie would open it up more, and use more moving, contrapuntal lines, almost like Bill Holman. Lennie leans more towards swing: he lays down a background behind you that makes you feel good, and helps you play a little more artistically."

Joel Kaye: "Lennie Niehaus was a better writer than Stan, a better orchestrator, and he wrote some really swinging music. Lennie wrote fine saxophone soli, and the things he wrote back in the '60s sound just as great today—he's just a very good writer."[9]

Dwight Carver: "Compared to Stan's stilted style, Niehaus' arrangements had a built-in sonority and smoothness. However, Lennie's charts also had a uniformity and conventional quality about them, and lacked a feeling of exploration in my opinion."[10]

Two of the best Niehaus scores are also the jazziest. According to Niehaus himself: "'Just in Time' is a very fast tune the way I wrote it, and I elongated the melody and changed the pattern. On 'It's All Right with Me' I had the bass sax, the tuba and bass trombone playing a riff on the melody as low as they could go. It was something you could only do with that combination of instruments, and I thought it worked out well." When Lennie spent longer working on a chart, his ballads were also something special: "'It Might as Well Be Spring' is a nice, long tune, with beautiful chord changes, and it really gives an arranger something to work with. I gave it to Sam Donahue, because he was an old friend of Stan's, a marvellous tenor player from the Don Byas/ Coleman Hawkins school, and he was perfect for the solo on that song. Another favorite tune of mine is 'Moonlight Becomes You,' and Marvin Stamm takes a very nice solo on that one."[11]

When the band regrouped in July after a short break, Gene Roland had departed on one of his perennial escapades, and his chair was taken by a tall, gangling newcomer born in London, but who had moved to the States with his family when he was 16. In Stan's words, "Ray Starling is a fine mellophonium player, a helluva pianist, and a very talented writer. He's very enthusiastic about life, about everything, he walks around on top all the time. He's wild, and fun to be around."[12]

In Carl Saunders' opinion, "Dwight Carver played very beautifully, but he wasn't really a jazz player, he didn't have that natural swing thing. But Ray Starling was full of music, a swinging, heart-burning piano player, and when he played mellophonium he filled up his horn with music. He had fire and energy and intensity. I thought he was great."[13] So did Stan, and within months Ray was the new lead mellophonium player and Dwight had moved to one of the lower chairs.

Few alumni have displayed more insight and perception into the inner workings of this band than Joel Kaye, who explains: "Ray Starling had been playing mellophone with Sal Salvador's big band around New York. Ray had chosen the mellophone long before Stan incorporated the M-horns into his band, so he had some real comfort in playing that instrument. He felt that was his voice. Ray played the trumpet, but on trumpet he sounded anaemic, and you wouldn't believe it was the same guy, because when he played the mellophonium he was just so bold, so authoritative. He made such a statement it was just amazing. He loved the mellophonium, and he played it like he loved it, you could tell. Ray's technique far outstripped Gene Roland's, and Ray had such a catalog of ideas that he could execute, any time. Ray was very conscious of the intonation, and could keep the guys in line; he had the discipline, and the comfort level on the instrument where he could really do things. His solos were truly outstanding, and he was a real spirit."[14]

Dee Barton joined at the same time as Starling, with a trombone sound almost unique in its guttural styling that sounded not dissimilar to a solo mellophonium. Barton had been a member of the North Texas university band that also included Marvin Stamm, Archie Wheeler, and Tom Wirtel, and came to Stan's attention via the North Texas Lab Band recording of Dee's "Waltz of the Prophets." Barton made much more of an impression on his peers when he later moved to drums than as a bone player, Carl Saunders commenting: "Dee played like a walrus going berserk on the trombone." (I think Carl's walrus-comparison refers to his sound, but it could have been because of Dee's long, drooping moustache which resembled the mammal's whiskers!)

Barton's was the brave new voice among the composers, bringing with him both "Turtle Talk" and "Prophets" from his student days at North Texas. "Turtle" was Dee's nickname for Tom Wirtel (who had been called upon to play mellophonium on the September 1960 sessions), and the intriguing, dissonant "Turtle Talk" was dedicated to Wirtel, even though at North Texas it had been a trumpet feature for Stamm, who also solos here along with the composer's discordant trombone. Both soloists reappear on the soul-influenced "Waltz of the Prophets," which runs far too long for its limited inspiration. Carl Saunders reflects my own opinion when he says, "I didn't like Barton's charts on either 'Turtle Talk' or 'Waltz of the Prophets' too well. It was kind of trite, repetitive stuff, and I got tired of them real quick."

By the time the *Adventures* albums were recorded in December, Sam Donahue had left to front the Tommy Dorsey orchestra, but Sam came back to reprise his solos on *Adventures in Jazz*. "Body and Soul" was Sam's feature, and his own orchestration, but at times Donahue feels constrained to hit the high notes that no law-abiding tenor sax should be able to reach, and his solo lacks the taste and inventiveness of past masters Cooper and Perkins.

Ray Starling's feature is "Misty," a lovely ballad, well-arranged by Gene Roland. Carl Saunders again takes up the story: "Gene wrote the chart for 'Misty' on the bus, and I remember he didn't write a score, he just wrote out the first trumpet part and passed it on to Dalton, and then he sat and copied out the second trumpet part and passed it to Bob Rolfe, and so on. It was kind of unbelievable, he just copied out the parts for the whole band out of his head, though of course if you really listen to 'Misty' it's not that complicated. But Ray played a great solo on it, and some of his solos out on the road were even better than the studio recording."[15]

As Gabe tells it, Stan approached Baltazar's feature in traditional Kenton fashion: "In 1961 Stan said to me, 'Gabe, I want to showcase you on a song that'll be your signature, like Charlie Mariano had 'Stella by Starlight' and Lee Konitz had 'Lover Man' and so forth.' I didn't have anything in mind, so Stan suggested 'Stairway to the Stars' which I knew was a nice tune, and when I got Bill Holman's arrangement I loved it very much. It was well written, and it involved the mellophoniums, so it became my signature tune, and I still play it today." Even so, reactions among his peers were mixed. In Ray Florian's view, "Gabe Baltazar was an exceptional musician and an outstanding soloist, as well as a great lead player." But Carl Saunders would opine, "Baltazar was a good, energetic lead alto, but I didn't hear too much substance in his solos."[16] Unanimity is a rare commodity in jazz appreciation!

Of course, the piece de resistance, the "rabble rouser" as Dwight Carver called it, was "Malaguena." If ever Stan loved a chart it was Willis's dynamic interpretation of Lecuona's Latin extravaganza, and the band played it as a concert-climax until the end. "One of the best arrangements ever written," said Carl Saunders[17] (who wasn't always easily pleased!). I asked a more pragmatic Holman how he approached writing a score which ten years earlier would have been anathema to him: "When Stan asked me to write 'Malaguena' he had the mellopho-niums, so that added one theatrical layer, and the tune itself is kind of theatrical, so I just took my cue from that and said, 'Well this is what the chart has to be, it can't be a swing chart, this is something different.' And I was newly in love at the time, and I just poured all my emotions into it."

"That chart lay just perfect," related Jerry McKenzie. "It was an absolute crowd-pleaser. There's that wonderful moment two-thirds of the way through, when it suddenly goes into 4/4 time, and the way that swings after the fast Latin provides a phenomenal sense of release. And then it goes back, starts soft, and builds up to the climax, it's absolutely fantastic. Probably the most spectacular, heavy-duty crowd-pleaser of them all!"[18]

"Malaguena" was indeed a concert bobby-dazzler that never failed to provoke enthusiastic audience reaction, but it serves less well on repeated live recordings because of the absence of improvisation. The entire album is something of a mixed bag, with little that is truly radical, and the very title *Adventures in Jazz* is debatable when compared with the truly controversial nature of Kenton's Progressive Jazz or Innovations in Modern Music. I find it is not an album to which I can return with unreserved enthusiasm.

The music of Gene Roland's *Adventures in Blues* was exactly what it said on the can. A haunting, poignant quality distinguished the slow pieces—"Dragonwyck," "Aphrodisia," "Blue Ghost"—but Carl Saunders pointed out to me during two separate interviews that "Roland wrote a whole slew of arrangements. There were a few good ones, but a lot of duds. He would take simple themes and make something out of them, and every now and again he got lucky. 80% of his output was kind of blandioso." Three of the compositions were sufficiently catchy to become popular items—"The Blues Story," "Reuben's Blues," "A Night at the Gold Nugget"—and somewhat paradoxically, "Stan used to say how these charts that we played a lot made the Kenton band swing like Basie," said Joel Kaye.[19] And Dwight Carver agrees: "Roland had as a good Basie-ish feel to his arrangements in the *Blues* album as anyone could wish for, especially with such an unwieldy big-band instrumentation."[20]

A lot of the album's character comes from Gene's own improvisations, though Marvin Stamm is also extensively featured. Gene could solo with authority on a whole range of instruments, and on *Blues* he switches between mellophonium and soprano sax, which Stan related caused Roland problems, because the instruments are in different keys, "And Roland had kind of a short memory span anyway."[21] "Basically he played in a blues style," reflected Baltazar. "He was not a fast, technical player, but he used a lot of blue notes, and he flowed easily, not like a bebop player. He was like a Lester Young of the mellophonium."

Comprehensive as Capitol's coverage was in 1961, many jewels would have passed unremarked were it not for Wally Heider's live recordings. "Polka Dots and Moonbeams" is a lovely tune to start with, but in an inspired move Lennie Niehaus has invented a stately counter-melody of his own that frames the five-minute arrangement to perfection. Other highlights are Sam Donahue's altoish tenor solo, followed by mellophoniums riding high with the melody over the top of the orchestral melee. Equally gorgeous is Wayne Dunstan's classical approach to the war-time standard "I Remember You," featured originally by Jimmy Dorsey in the Betty Hutton musical *The Fleet's In*. By coincidence, both recordings are on Tantara's *Horns of Plenty Vol. 1*, as is Gene Roland's ten-minute sliver of an arrangement of "Stompin' at the Savoy," which doesn't try to compete with the Holman classic, but is simply an excuse to link together improvisations by the band's leading soloists: a jam session in all but name.

But the writer who got the rawest deal on records was Ray Starling. Many of the arrangements on Capitol's *Adventures* series swing, but they swing Kenton-style. With "Four of a Kind" and "Mellophobia," Starling moved the band swing-style, and there is a difference. Fortunately, both charts were recorded (and subsequently CD-issued several times) for the U.S. Air Force Reserve *Sound '62* transcriptions. On both charts everyone in the mellophonium section solos in turn, quasi-Herman's "Four Brothers," and seemingly that raised the same old bogey, for according to Noel Wedder, "Stan thought that Starling's arrangements sounded like material for Woody Herman. Nothing any of us said could sway Stan's attitude. It was only later that Stan admitted Ray added a much-needed dimension of fire and enthusiasm to the band, and that he was indeed a great composer as well as a gifted mellophonium player."[22]

As the orchestra disbanded for a Christmas recess, Kenton had good reason to feel satisfied. The mellophonium band hadn't broken any sales records, but it was turning a profit, and 1961 had been the most creative period musically since the mid-Fifties. Stan took the time to rest, reflect, and write. All of his recent albums had enjoyed moderate sales but none had hit the big-time in terms of monetary returns relative to the huge investment involved. Now Lee Gillette suggested an album that would team Stan with one of Capitol's biggest money-makers. The results would be controversial, but bring few plaudits to either of the parties involved.

# 21.

## Adventures in Time

### (1962–1963)

**Tex Ritter was Capitol's foremost** C&W singer, Stan Kenton the label's leader of experimental jazz. Any chance of a musical alliance seemed remote, yet Lee Gillette was enthusiastic, and Kenton quickly became equally convinced. Only Ritter remained deeply skeptical. Stan was an enigma. His heart belonged to jazz, but his head (his own talent and ability) was often elsewhere. Writing in the jazz idiom did not come easily, and for every "Harlem Holiday" or "Opus for Tympani" he could produce a dozen accompaniments backing Gene Howard, or dance-band ballads featuring his inimitable orchestral sound, but which lacked a clear jazz content.

In this instance, Kenton's reasoning was deeply flawed: "I wanted to make the album with Tex to prove a point, that a jazz band can be compatible with other kinds of music, in this case C&W. I believe that if there's character and sincerity and dimension to a performer, it should fit into anything."[1] Which may be a thesis for debate, but using jazz musicians in itself does not make the music jazz. Stan wrote inventive arrangements for brass and rhythm which expertly conjure up visions of the old West while preserving something of the Kenton sound, but the jazz content is zero, and the music could equally well have been played by a bunch of competent studio musicians. Ritter was not expected to modify his style or repertoire, so almost all the concessions came from the Kenton camp.

Noel Wedder was present on the dates: "Tex was very nervous during the recording sessions. He couldn't read music, and was afraid he'd be embarrassed because he'd get lost in the charts. Initially he had a difficult time knowing when to come in, but this was solved by Alvino Rey sending him hand cues. Alvino was there on guitar to provide him with a bridge to country-western. In other words, he was a familiar face and helped Tex feel a bit more comfortable in front of Kenton's rather formidable brass section. Tex was also afraid his fans would be alienated by his decision to make an album with Stan Kenton, and he was right."[2]

Instead of a double demand from admirers of two popular artists, sales were minimal because Ritter fans found the unfamiliar accompaniment totally out of character, and Stan's devotees shunned the album, appalled by Ritter's booming voice and exaggerated accents and songs like "Home on the Range" and "The Last Round Up." As for the musicians, Carl Saunders opined, "They were Stan's charts, all bland stuff, and we just went in and did it. We were just there, we made the sessions and got our checks and left. Everybody on the Tex Ritter sessions just wanted to get it over with."[3] Even Stan became a bit blase about the whole exercise: "When the album came out, people thought we were crazy. Jazz fans thought I'd gone off the deep end, and when C&W fans asked Tex, 'What did you do that for?' Tex would say, 'Oh, Stan made me do it!'"

There were two important newcomers when the band reassembled in 1962. Jean Turner was Stan's last full-time vocalist, a skilled, jazz-tinged 26-year-old—and black, which led to some troublesome occasions during a time of social upheaval difficult to imagine in the 21st century. Visually stunning, multi-lingual and quietly spoken to the point of reticence, Jean radiated a charm and charisma that captivated the guys in the band. Kenton's own respect for his new singer is well illustrated by my own remembrance of Stan seated at the piano, a look of total satisfaction on his face, quietly digging Jean's performance.

Bass player Val Kolar recalled one unpleasant racial incident: "We were booked into an exclusive private club in Baton Rouge, Louisiana, and as we embarked from the bus the manager asked, 'Who's the black girl?' Practically in unison the band responded, 'She's our vocalist!' The man said, 'Oh no, she isn't singing here tonight.' With that, all our spirits dropped to zero. I believe the band that night sounded the worst we ever played. Jean had to spend the entire evening on the bus, and often in the South she had to stay at separate hotels from the rest of the band. It's really tragic that experiences like that could happen to such a deserving artist, within the USA and such a short time ago."[4] And before anyone seeks to criticize Kenton for not taking a firmer stand, pulling out of the Baton Rouge engagement altogether wasn't an option. The band could have survived the loss of one night's revenue, but Stan would also have left himself wide open to potential ruin by being sued for willfully refusing to honor his contractual obligations, with the consequent full-time break-up of the band.

The other notable new face was returnee Charlie Mariano, but on tenor sax rather than his more familiar alto. "Charlie sounded just fine," commented Gabe Baltazar, "but I could tell he wasn't comfortable at first. If you're an alto player and you switch to tenor, it takes some getting used to, because it has a very different feel. You hear different sound, different timbre, and the response is altogether different." But to non-saxophonist Carl Saunders, Mariano's magic was as passionate as ever: "When Charlie came on the band he played the 'Stella by Starlight' chart that Bill Holman wrote for him on alto in '55, but now he played it on tenor, and he just made you cry when he soloed. Now there's a guy with substance—he had soul! I learned a lot from Charlie, he was so full of emotion and warmth and depth and beauty. He could send a chill down your spine when he played, which is very rare—he's just exceptional."[5]

Some of the musicians were unhappy with the rhythm section. The main target was "the trio drummer from Minneapolis" (Bill Blakkestad), but at the same time Ray Starling was lobbying for his buddy Bucky Calabrese to come in on bass. So changes were already on the cards when Kolar relates that "one night we were playing a country club dance near Boston, when during an intermission our drummer disappeared. In other words, he didn't show up for the next set. He was out somewhere digging the sky. Anyhow, Dee Barton volunteered to cover for Bill, and we roared through that next set like never before. Barton's knowledge of the trombone book helped him kick the band, but it really surprised a lot of us to hear him play that chair so well."[6]

After that, things moved swiftly, and by June 1962 Bucky Calabrese was in on bass, and Dee Barton had moved permanently from trombone to drums, a position he would retain until the end of 1963. If Calabrese made little impression one way or the other, Barton more than compensated by the way he took command from his driving seat on percussion. Dee was never going to play with the finesse of a Shelly Manne, but what he lacked in refinement he made up for in raw talent and enthusiasm. Not everyone liked Dee personally ("Barton played real well for the obnoxious drunk he was at times," opined Dwight Carver[7]), but there is near-unanimity that Dee's drumming kick-started that Kenton band:

Gabe Baltazar: "To play drums in the Kenton band you have to be a strong-minded *gorilla*! And Dee Barton was one. At first he didn't really have the chops, but he had the gumption, and the courage, and the incentive, and the bull-headedness, and that's what you need, and he went on and just chopped away. And as the weeks went by he became stronger and stronger, he got his chops together, and it was amazing. Dee really kicked that band."

John Worster: "Dee Barton played drums with such spirit! Dee's unorthodox, uninhibited, clumsy style—his brute strength and *total* concentration—was a great influence on me. Dee gave 100% every single song: every bar he played, he played as well as he could, like it was the last thing he was ever going to play. He didn't have any chops as a drummer, no technique at all, but he never let up, and for someone who wasn't a good drummer, he played pretty goddamn good."[8]

Jerry L. McKenzie: "Being originally a trombone player, Dee knew how to phrase things, and he carried that over to his drums. He didn't have strong technique in his hands and wrists, but on Stan's band you didn't need to be able to play Buddy Rich drum solos, the main thing was to keep the time, to play the right Latin patterns, and keep the band moving, and Dee certainly did all that."[9]

Among such praise for the more prominent alumni, it's easy to overlook the less conspicuous but equally diligent musicians. One such was Joel Kaye (though he is featured playing piccolo on the novelty number "Little Boy Blew" by Ray Starling, issued on Dynaflow), and it takes Mike Suter to point out that "Joel Kaye is an absolute master of the bass saxophone, to the point that the orchestra didn't sound as clean or precise without him. Stan used to say that the string bass was the 'cop' that kept the band moving forward. Well if that's true, then Joel was the Chief of Police!"[10]

I believe the two foremost multi-CD sets of Kenton's music are Mosaic's *Capitol Studio Recording 1943–47* and Tantara's *Revelations*. The latter contains two very different titles from an August 1962 Clinic at Michigan State University, united by their excellent audio, and recorded by a band on fire. Gene Roland's seven-and-a-half minute "Saga of the Blues" is a fun chart designed to allow the band's soloists to let rip. Opening with a mock-Dixie beat, the chart soon develops into a real swinger, and though seemingly spontaneous is actually soundly structured, with undisguised quotes from "Ol' Man River" and Duke's "Rockin' in Rhythm." Stan liked to let his hair down occasionally, and the guys certainly sound like they're having a ball.

The second piece is a very different proposition, a highly organized and serious work by Johnny Richards that has gone largely unremarked because it was never officially recorded. "Festival—Toccata and Fugue" was a difficult composition that required considerable preparation ahead of its commissioned premiere at the Midwest Jazz Festival (August 17–19). "Festival" is an audacious and spirited work, an exercise in energy combining classical and jazz elements into a creative whole, while leaving room for solo contributions from Allan Beutler (baritone sax), Gabe Baltazar, Ray Starling, and Marvin Stamm. It is a significant addition to Richards' repertoire.

Noel Wedder was the band's publicist during the Sixties and is as well-positioned as any to point out the problems Stan faced during the mellophonium years: "Money was very tight. Good, well-paying dates were hard to come by. I saw most of the contracts and was appalled that Associated Booking would sign us into $850 and $1200 engagements. Because money didn't flow as fast as it should have done, more than a few of the sidemen were getting by on coolie wages of $125 per week, the lead players and 'name' soloists maybe around $300. Often it was a scramble to get good players to go out on the road, especially if they were married with children. Consequently, although he tried valiantly to fill the chairs, Amlotte came up with a few less than satisfactory players. Some had an abysmal time sight-reading. Some had a difficult time melding themselves into the section they were assigned to. Some had massive personal problems. And some didn't give a damn and were just along for the ride. But when the band was up, and everything fell into place, it was time to watch The Machine roar through one outstanding chart after another. You always knew when Stan was excited by what he heard because that big smile never left his face."[11]

There was a lot to smile about when, after six months of hard labor, Johnny Richards presented Stan with *Adventures in Time*, the third album of his Kenton trilogy. It had been Stan's idea to apply to his big band the principles that had brought such acclaim to certain small groups, in particular Dave Brubeck with "Take Five" and similar tunes. Kenton told me, "Jazz had been trapped too long in 4/4 and 2/4 times, and it was strangling us. I wanted to get into changing time signatures as fast as we could, and I wanted John to write the music. I told him to take as long as he needed, but I wanted it to be a great album."[12]

Stan knew that of all the contemporary writers, Johnny Richards came the closest to his own ideals of how the music should sound, well-described by Gabe Baltazar as "A form of swing, with a symphonic sound." Richards often took a theme from mythology or different cultures as inspiration for his more serious compositions, and with his "Concerto for Orchestra" it was numerology and the planets of our galaxy. Nor was this an affectation. He was able to lecture the band at length on the subject, until he felt the men were ready to play his music the way he wanted. For his part, Kenton was determined that *Adventures in Time* should be one of the orchestra's seminal recordings and poured unlimited resources into the project. The earliest rehearsals took place a full six months before he and Johnny decided they were ready to record.

As Stan remembered it, "Sometimes it can be very hard to adapt to new rhythms, and the final rehearsals were very difficult. I thought the band was going to break up, we got into such fights. We would rehearse a bit, and then we'd take the sections into separate rooms to rehearse by themselves, and then we'd come back and try to put it all together again. The one we had the most trouble with was the 7/4 'Septuor from Antares.' We just couldn't get started on that, it was a very, very difficult thing." (In fact, one section of "Septuor" finally had to be cut out altogether because the band simply couldn't play it.)

Joel Kaye confirmed the problems with "Septuor," but claimed that "'Apercu' had a passage at the beginning that was impossible for me to play. I asked John if I could play it on the baritone sax instead of the bass saxophone. I was sure I could get through it then, but John said, 'NO! I want that struggle. It's like the viola part in that Wagner opera, nobody can play that either, and that's what I want.'"[13]

*Adventures in Time* is perhaps the last mind-bending album of Stan's recording career. It took six three-hour sessions to complete the recordings to everyone's satisfaction, and as the music business continued to slide downhill, it became increasingly unprofitable to pour that sort of money into a single album, especially on music that was difficult to feature in live performance. One title that was played at concerts was the only movement in 4/4 time, the majestic ballad "Artemis and Apollo," which, Ray Florian noted, "Swells to a tremendous climax and features Ray Starling in the most beautiful mellophonium solo ever recorded."[14] Another was "$3 \times 3 \times 2 \times 2 \times 2 = 72$," which has the catchiest melody and exciting Don Menza tenor, the musical equivalent of "El Congo Valiente" from *Cuban Fire*. (The significance of that title is that $3 \times 3 = 9$, and $2 \times 2 \times 2 = 8$, and the number features a 9/8 time signature.) Stan was immensely proud of the completed album, which proved to be the final collaboration between the Kenton orchestra and perhaps the greatest of jazz composers. Richards died from cancer in 1968 at the all-too-early age of 56.

In a quid pro quo with Capitol Records, and wearing his "pop artist" hat, Kenton recorded the narration for a sentimental piece of schmaltz called "Mama Sang a Song," with backing group and choir assembled by Ralph Carmichael. Stan reasoned that if it made money to help support the band, it was worth the effort. (The single reached No. 47 in Billboard's Top 100 on November 3, 1962.) I recall a quick meal in 1972 with Kenton and some Decca Records executives, one of whom was rash enough to mention "Mama" in semi-mocking tone. The "Don't fuck with me!" glare he got from Stan was sufficient to freeze his tongue for the rest of the meal. Sure, Stan was one of the good guys, but he wasn't a man to mess with. You were either for him, all the way, all the time, or you were against him. There was no half-way house.

As Band Manager, Jim Amlotte exercised the power behind the throne, particularly as he did all the hiring of new players. However, Stan remained responsible for firing, and next to incur the Kenton wrath was Lou Gasca, leaving a hole in the mellophonium section to be filled by Tony Scodwell, recommended to Amlotte by Herb Pomeroy. "Playing the mellophonium for the first time was quite an experience," commented Scodwell, "because it truly was a bastard instrument, and I thought, 'Man this is a real drag, this horn does *not* want to play in tune,' and all of that." But encouraged by his fellow players, Tony persevered, and to his surprise early in 1963 found himself section leader.

It happened purely by chance. With Starling having left, Dwight Carver was due to reassume the position, but was very late for a record-ing session (due to a flat tire on the Pasadena Highway), a cardinal sin in Stan's eyes. "So Stan looks at me," continues Scodwell, "and says, 'You're the new lead player,' which I didn't really mind, because I was used to playing lead trumpet, and by then I felt comfortable on the mellophonium."

The session was one of the *Artistry in Bossa Nova* dates, Kenton's belated attempt to cash in on the new dance craze. Stan's close affinity with Latin music is indisputable, but always with the hard-hitting, high-volume Afro-Cuban rhythms, the diametric opposite of the calm, ethe-real "cool samba" from Brazil, already exploited so well by Stan Getz and the Bud Shank/Laurindo Almeida partnership. The basic flaw to the project was that there could be no satisfactory synthesis—Stan Kenton and Bossa Nova were incompatible.

To make matters worse, Stan rejected the standard Bossa Nova reper-toire in favor of grafting the rhythm onto his own classics from the past (the "Eager Beavers" and "Painted Rhythms"), which was like adding chalk to cheese. Three indifferent new Kenton originals and the absence of solos of any consequence only compounded the problem.

Of course, no one could have told Stan to his face, but the musi-cians knew what was wrong. "The Bossa Nova album was strictly a com-mercial venture," volunteered Ray Florian. "It was never intended as a jazz LP. It was just an attempt to jump on the Bossa Nova bandwagon, which was the hot idiom at the time. I thought the charts were a cut or two below Stan's usual standards; maybe if there'd been some solos the album might not have been quite so dull."[15] Or as Gabe Baltazar put it,

"Bossa Nova was supposed to be light and easy, but Stan's album came out kind of heavy and clumsy, not smooth like a light samba should be."

The irony is, the orchestra plays so beautifully one has to admire the glorious Kenton Sound, especially the high trumpet work of Bud Brisbois (not Dalton Smith as the liner notes wrongly claim. Capitol wrote Bud a letter apologizing for the error!). Quite noticeable compared with Stan's previous writing is the absence of any emphasis on the mellophonium section, and there were suggestions that Capitol's engineers had deliberately toned down their volume in order to avoid complications at the mixing stage when they played out of tune.

After a month of touring, Dalton Smith up and quit the band, and he was missed, as Jiggs Whigham recalled: "Dalton was a big bear of a guy, strong, and an excellent lead trumpet. After he left we had a couple of guys come in and try to play the first trumpet and they didn't have the stamina. You really had to have the strength of a horse to make it go. And then somebody got the idea to bring in Tom Porrello, and this little guy comes in, kind of skinny, and we thought, 'OK, here we go again, fun and games time!' And he pulls this trumpet out, and it sounded fine, it was wonderful. And the big test was 'Yesterdays,' because if you're going to crumble that's the one, but if you get that one nailed, you're OK. And the sound that came out of that trumpet, and the energy, and the high G was clear as a bell, strong and loud. And Stan's face lit up, and we all lit up, and it was simple as that. He got the gig, and Tommy was beautiful, one of the best lead trumpeters ever."

The only person who had any reason to feel miffed was Tony Scodwell, who would have loved the position himself. In fact, Stan had told Tony the first trumpet was his, if he could persuade Ray Starling to come back on mellophonium. But Ray had settled in New York and was unmovable, and Tony was too valuable to Stan on mellophonium to be allowed the change-over. Not only that, but Scodwell also found himself having to take the mellophonium solos, which wasn't his forte at all: "I didn't want to do it, but there was truly no one else. On 'Peanut Vendor' and 'Misty' I managed to put some licks together, where I don't think it was too embarrassing, but when I had to stand there and play 'Artemis and Apollo' and those heavy things, it was getting a little shaky, and I tended to gravitate to the upper register a lot, because that's where I felt most comfortable. But I was never at ease playing the jazz, and solowise I don't think the mellophonium ever really found its own voice. It made the greatest impact as a section."

Marvin Stamm was much missed in the 1963 line-up. Jazz trumpet for much of the year was Buzzy Mills, who didn't really match Marvin's talent. But then few players straight out of college did, though Jiggs Whigham was another exception to the rule. "I got Jiggs on the band," related John Worster. "He was only 19 at the time and didn't come in as the lead player, they hadn't settled on the lead, but after one half of one concert, Jiggs was the new lead. A marvellous trombone man!"[16]

Worster himself was one of the band's major assets: "Joining Kenton was the greatest musical experience of my life. I couldn't help but feel myself grow and expand. I'd never been exposed to such a variety of music in one orchestra, or a band that could get that soft and sensitive, as well as ROAR and play that strong."[17] Bob Curnow, new on trombone, confirmed: "John Worster was a driving force. A good bass player will change the character of a band completely, and John did that just by keeping time as beautifully as he did. And Dee Barton was one of the best in terms of time, and the way John and Dee interacted you never had to think about it. It was always there."

Any band that has worked so hard to pull itself up by its boot-strings looks for two things: fresh charts that will become identified with that band, and recordings that will provide permanent evidence for future generations; and on both counts this band was short-changed. True, Stan cut two Capitol LPs in September, but both were vocal albums with the orchestra confined to a purely accompanying role. Possibly Kenton felt there was sufficient mileage left in the current book, or there was insufficient money available to pay for additional scores.

Instead of presenting the band in a jazz setting, Stan indulged himself with another album of Kenton "classics" mainly from the Forties, this time with lyrics added by Milt Raskin, and sung by an 18-voice mixed choir accompanied by trombones and rhythm. *Artistry in Voices and Brass* was in reality a Pete Rugolo album. Pete arranged the music, conducted on the sessions, and was named as leader on the AFM contracts. It is a high-class product, but the lyrics are pretty meaningless, and some solo voices with a jazz edge instead of the incessant chanting by the highly professional but somewhat bland chorus, could only have improved the rather vapid end product. Any appeal would be only to Stan's hard-core supporters, and I very much doubt the album resulted in anything other than red ink in Capitol's ledgers.

At least the full orchestra accompanied Jean Turner on her only feature album, but without any opportunity to strut their stuff, and that was the result of a policy decision. In Christy's day the orchestra and voice were partners in well-planned productions—think of Roland's "Four Months Blues," or Rugolo's "Willow Weep for Me." Most of Turner's tunes are over far too soon, the arrangements are minimal, and the accompaniment might be anybody's band. There is no attempt to project Jean's performances into an integrated totality of voice and orchestra that could be considered distinctively "Stan Kenton."

Lennie Niehaus wrote the majority of Turner's charts, and explains: "Jean picked the songs for her Capitol album, and she sounded great with Stan's band. But her style was different from the earlier vocalists, and I decided with her arrangements to cut straight to the chase, and not clutter up the scores with long intros or a bunch of solos, but just to highlight her voice."[18] (Bill Holman followed suit: his "It's a Big, Wide Wonderful World" lasts exactly 1:38 minutes!)

Jiggs Whigham perceptively realized what was amiss: "Jean Turner had a small, sweet voice, she had a good sense of time, and was a good singer, but she never really caught on. I don't think she fitted the band in the traditional sense. Maybe the packaging was wrong. Niehaus and Holman wrote good scores, but they weren't really feature showcases for the band, and any singer could have come out and sung the same arrangements; the stamp of Jean Turner wasn't on them." Perhaps because they were less lightweight, Jean did best on the ballads. "I think 'Day Dream' was very nice on that record," offered Jiggs, "but of course, that's Duke, which gives it a head start." And Lennie picked out "Someone to Watch Over Me," "Which featured the trombones backing Jean, and some nice, improvised little fills by Joel Kaye on alto flute."

Capitol had recorded three Kenton albums during 1963, not one of which was jazz-oriented, and it's *Concert in England* on Astral Jazz, recorded live on November 23, that showcases this band as it really sounded. From the opening bars of "I'm Glad There Is You" it is evident this is a class act. From this ballad beginning, the band goes straight into an intriguing Ray Starling swinger called "Patterns" (written in 1961), an insinuating theme that reinforces the view Starling was a grossly overlooked composer of real merit.

This is the finest performance of "Granada" I have heard, the vibrant recording quality emphasizing the grandeur of this example from Holman's "Spanish period." Scodwell's thematic solo opens tentatively, but grows in confidence as the tempo accelerates. Tension builds through dramatic orchestral passages and Baltazar's red-hot alto, and only the drums finale seems slightly down-beat, ending with four somewhat clichéd dissonant chords, which nevertheless, Noel Wedder points out, allowed Stan to conduct in histrionic style, "With arms outstretched while turning slowly to face the audience, casually dropping his left hand as the last chord rang out like a runaway locomotive. Great writing. Great theatre. Great way to emotionally drain an audience."[19]

Jean Turner performs from her usual repertoire, including the inevitable "Day Dream" and "Sleepy Lagoon," but gains added luster from the fact she is so well miked she could be standing inside the listener's loudspeakers. The concert climax is not the standard "Malaguena," but the "Cuban Fire Medley," combining "Fuego Cubano," "Recuerdos," and "El Congo Valiente," performed without a pause and reduced to 11 1/2 minutes playing time. It seems apparent over 50 years on that *Cuban Fire* has become Richards' definitive masterpiece, his magnum opus, at least in terms of popular appeal, unmatched for combining fevered excitement with immaculate musicality. Bob Curnow's "Congo Valiente" trombone solo is a gem, disorganized and all over the place, but strong and confident, and totally in keeping with the context.

"We had flown out of New York," Curnow recalled, "and Stan and I were sitting together, and someone asked Stan if he'd made arrangements to play 'God Save the Queen,' which was obligatory at the end of every theatre performance in Britain at that time. Stan hadn't thought about that, so he asked me to do the orchestration. I wrote it on the airplane, and when we arrived in England we played it at sight on the first gig—very poorly I might add. The guys really scuffled with the key, but once we got used to playing it everything was fine." The practice would soon be abandoned, because cinema audiences made a mad stampede for the exits as soon as the closing credits started to roll in order to avoid standing silently while the anthem was played. But instead of the usual resigned irritation, audiences were transfixed by Kenton's unique performance, especially at the end as the trumpets rose majestically out of the ensemble, only to be surpassed by a closing chord from the mellophoniums.

And the band that came to England in November 1963 definitely was the *mellophonium* band. "We could play louder than the whole brass section together," boasted Tony Scodwell. "We were stuck right out in front, we were showcased, and we were loud. Everybody who came to hear that band heard us and remembered us."

The trouble was, not enough people did come to hear them, as I can testify, and John Worster vividly relates: "Stan really wanted to go back to England. He hadn't been there since 1956, and he expected to do very well, based on that previous experience. The band went over in high spirits, we were just a bunch of young kids, glad as hell to get the opportunity. The band was good, we'd been together for seven or eight months, and we were playing really well. We didn't have any of the big jazz stars that there'd been in the past, no big names, but as an ensemble band we were certainly ready to compare to any band that had been heard in Britain.

"So we went over there, and it was one of the biggest disappointments of Kenton's life. The 1963 UK tour really hurt him—he's never forgotten it. You mention the '63 tour to him and you'll see that little hurt in his eyes. The band had been a success in the States, but it was costing an awful lot of money, and not really happening quite like it should. And then he comes to England, and it's just *nothing*, where he used to be a big seller, and people don't even know about him any more, and that really hurt his ego. People had tried to warn him, but he kept saying, 'Bullshit, the band is big over there.' Then he got to England and saw it wasn't, and he couldn't believe it. But Stan doesn't believe a lot of things that he sees, and then all of a sudden it's like total perception, he sees it very stark. The people that did show up were really responsive. They seemed to enjoy the music, and to feel they'd heard a good band, but there just wasn't enough of them. And during the time we were in England President Kennedy was assassinated, and that had a terrible effect on all of us."[20]

In the States the orchestra had survived by its reputation as a dance band. In Britain, Kenton's status was based on his jazz credentials, which had suffered as he sought to widen his appeal. UK critics almost to a man were united in their disapproval of anything Kentonian, EMI had belatedly issued only a selection of Stan's latest albums, and a new generation of youngsters had grown up more attracted to the Beatles than the beat. On Kenton's arrival in London, a reporter asked his opinion of the Beatles. "I've never heard of them," replied Stan.[21] (When he did discover the Fab Four's influence on popular music, Kenton reportedly declared, "You know what this means don't you? We're fucked!")

Stan wasn't far wrong. Despite excellent local and national reviews, halls in England were rarely more than half-full, many first and second houses were merged into a single show, and the final London appearance was cancelled before the tour even started, due to poor advance ticket sales. Kenton's observation as he prepared to go on-stage was, "Let's meet the enemy!" —the foe being the rows of empty seats. "It was planned to disband at the end of the UK tour anyway," observed Worster, "but it took so much out of Stan the band was off the road for over a year, he got so depressed."[22] Even when things were going well, the dark side of the "glamorous" road band life, carefully hidden from public gaze, was literally slowly but surely killing Kenton. "You never saw Stan out of control at a performance," said Tony Scodwell, "but after the gig the vodka would flow freely. He needed that release, and when Stan drank, he did it hard and fast. The whole idea was to get out of it as quickly as possible, and then he'd crash and sleep until morning."

Two alumni summed up the state of play in 1963 better than any other I have ever seen. "The mellophonium orchestra," observed Jiggs Whigham, "was one of Stan's last bands that really did it—a precision band that had a real identity. The Neophonic did what it did, but when Stan went out on the road again, there was a difference. Those later bands didn't have the same *sound.*"

The reason was pinpointed precisely by North Texas State University (now University of North Texas) alumnus and bass trombonist in the 1960 band, Bobby Knight: "It's my feeling that there came a point in time, maybe '63, '64, '65, when it became an ex-college band instead of a professional band. When Dalton was on the band, and Jay Saunders and Dee Barton, guys like that, it really, really *roared.* But when you've got a *whole band* of youngsters, they play great, but they're not gonna move along like we were able to. What can you learn, being on a band where everyone has the same background?"[23]

Stan returned to California, demoralized but vowing to honor a court order that stipulated he should remain at home if he were to retain custody of his children by Ann Richards, Lance and Dana. His "new voice," a costly addition to the Kenton Sound never fully accepted by the musicians, had now been rejected by an apathetic public, albeit in a foreign land. Stan would return to music, but never again use even a single mellophonium in his orchestra. The great experiment was over, to the regret of many—including this writer—who had found the instruments added an exceptional luster and richness to an already illustrious orchestral voice.

# Adventure in Emotion:
# The LA Neophonic

## (1964–1968)

**For much of 1964 Kenton was turned off** from music alto-gether, in what may have seemed like over-reaction to a mere two weeks' poor reception overseas, but which Stan explained in a long letter to Joe Coccia dated September 7, 1964. This is just a short extract: "I haven't been any place other than at home with the children, they need me so much to be with them. I've been through a period of adjustment, from wanting to give up music for something else, or retiring completely on a low budget. I've had terrible depressions and hardly any creative drive. I'm delighted to tell you, however, that I'm about to come out of it, and I realize I've had these dry periods before, but that doesn't seem to make it any less painful while they're taking place."

John Worster also explains how Stan's psyche could easily put things out of perspective: "Stan Kenton is a man who's immense in everything he does. When he trips, he doesn't just stumble, he falls flat on his face. Everything he does is done exaggerated, and all his emotions are exag-gerated. When he's happy, he *is happy*; you and I aren't ever that happy! And you and I are never as sad as he is. He's a very emotional, exag-gerated person, and if you hurt him you hurt him deeply, or you don't scratch the surface at all. If you get through to him, you *get through* to him, and he'll never forget it. If you do him a wrong he'll never forget it; and if you really please him he'll never forget that either."[1]

Most bandleaders (think Glenn Miller, Les Brown, Count Basie) found their niche and stuck with it. Often buffeted by market forces, Kenton was never quite sure whether his was a dance band, a jazz band, or a semi-symphonic concert orchestra. The latter was his prefer-ence, but audiences for such music were thin on the ground, and even in the "good old days" had been too few to support a national tour. So since he was confined to LA anyway by his children, in conjunction with his new managers George Greif and Sid Garris, Stan conceived a plan to front a resident concert orchestra of the finest Hollywood-based musicians, playing only avant-garde music, and limited to around four concerts a year.

The prospect was enough to shake Stan out of his doldrums, and restore his creative drive. He started writing for an instrumentation similar to the "New Era" orchestra, but with five French horns replacing the unpredictable mellophoniums. Possibly sensing a certain kudos to be gained from their participation, Capitol was initially enthusiastic, and gave Lee Gillette the green light to suggest an album of Wagnerian themes recast in Kentonian terms. At first Stan rejected the idea, but as he related, once he became interested, "It took about three months to write all that music. What I had to do was take the guts, the important things, out of those Wagnerian scores, because a lot of those things last for ever. So it was the editing that was crucial. But outside of trying to figure out how they were orchestrated, there wasn't really any great problem."[2]

Clinton Roemer did all the copying of Kenton's scores, and he agreed: "The album was pretty much a literal transcription for a different-sized orchestra of what Wagner wrote. If you compare the Kenton charts with the originals, you'll see that the 'advanced' writing was Wagner's, not Kenton's."[3] Interestingly, Bill Russo (who knew his classical music) made much the same point when reviewing "Prelude to Act III of *Lohengrin*" during a Blindfold Test: "I thought perhaps Stan hadn't made the work enough his own, hadn't sufficiently taken the material and made it into his own personality, that he had simply reset it rather than remade it."[4]

It is hard to envision precisely the audience *Kenton-Wagner* was intended to satisfy. Certainly not the classicists, who would to a man reject any tampering with the original compositions. Certainly not the jazz fans, for whom this totally "traditional" approach would hold nil appeal. Nor even the average Kenton-lover who revelled in the likes of "Painted Rhythm" and "Peanut Vendor." The tiny minority left was unlikely to cover even the cost of the impressive art-work. The whole album was a top-drawer product from start to finish, brilliantly played by the cream of Hollywood's studio/jazz musicians, but the listener's appreciation will be qualified by his attitude to the use of classical music in this way, as Jiggs Whigham explained, "I didn't like the Wagner album. I'm a purist in that I don't like to hear any jazzed-up Bach, even though Wagner's music lends itself to the Kenton style. Somewhere in Stan was the reincarnation of a very Germanic spirit!"

Bill Perkins remembered the whole experience with some horror: "Stan was a competent arranger, but a terrible conductor, in the sense that this was very precise, legit music. I just couldn't understand how Lennie Niehaus leading the saxes could follow Stan at all. That's a shortcoming on

my part, but I remember the whole album as being kind of an ordeal."
Classical music requires conducting of a very different kind than the
more casual jazz or dance, and Jim Amlotte confirms it was not Kenton's
forte: "Stan liked that kind of bombastic, heavy music, and I thought he
transcribed those compositions very well. We played some of the Wagner
music in concert, and the 'Pilgrims' Chorus from *Tannhaeuser*' went well
enough, but when we reached 'Prelude to Act III of *Lohengrin*,' we got
into big trouble. It was a train wreck! The way I saw it, Stan was reading
the score, and he forgot to look up and cue us. So the trombones didn't
come in at the right spot, and it was a disaster. But Stan was very proud
of the album, even though it sold very little." Just how little Capitol had
yet to discover, but when they did it was enough to turn them off the
whole project altogether. The Neophonic movement would receive scant
backing from Capitol Records. The Wagner album has never been reis-
sued on CD, and in 1998 the CD of the Neophonic Orchestra itself was in
and out of the Capitol catalog so fast, if you blinked, you missed it!

Stan cast his net wide, and solicited scores from composers in all
schools of jazz. Most wrote in the Kenton idiom, despite his name not
being directly attached to the orchestra, which he insisted should be
called the Los Angeles Neophonic, a coined word meaning New Sounds.
But Stan paid the bills. Only the writers contributed their charts for
free, glad of the opportunity to hear their most ambitious works played
before an appreciative audience. But the AFM insisted the musicians
be paid full Union rates, copyist Clinton Roemer could not afford to
work for nothing, and the prestigious Dorothy Chandler Pavilion in Los
Angeles' imposing Music Center did not come cheap. (It almost didn't
come at all, because Mrs. Chandler had stipulated the hall should feature only classical music. It was only after much persuasion the Center's committee relented, and then Kenton was relegated to Monday
nights, when the hall was normally "dark.")

Such were the costs, it was later calculated that even if there'd been
full houses at every concert (which was far from the case), it would have
been difficult for the Neophonic to turn a profit. Not that such consid-
erations would have even entered Kenton's head as he prepared for the
premiere concert of the 1965 season. His only concern was to prove once
and for all that there was a place in American society for an art form
that raised jazz music to the same level as that of the renowned European classical composers of earlier times. Whether or not he succeeded
artistically, commercially the venture was soon in deep trouble.

Accurately described as a "Non-Profit Organization," the Neophonic
was never financially successful. Even before the echoes of the opening

concert had died away, *Variety* was reporting the orchestra to be in "financial troubles,"[5] and this final attempt by Kenton to present a new American art music proved as doomed as his previous endeavors. Despite inflated attendance figures released to the press, rarely were more than 2,000 seats of the 3,250-capacity Pavilion filled by paying ticket-holders, a pathetic number in relation to the population of metropolitan LA and its environs.

The Neophonic stumbled on through three seasons, performing a total of just 11 concerts:

1965—concerts 1–4

1966—concerts 5–8

1967—no concerts

1968—concerts 9–11

Rehearsal time was at a premium, because all had to be paid for. The first anyone saw of the scores was immediately prior to their performance, so an evaluation had to be made on the spot. As Kenton said, "Even though they were all important composers with good reputations, you never knew what the quality of the writing would be like. Some wrote very bad music, and some of them wrote great music."[6] Obviously, the musicians had to be skilled sight-readers, and manager Jim Amlotte signed up the best available, men like Conte Candoli, Milt Bernhart, Bud Shank, and Shelly Manne, who were conversant with the Kenton style. But the difficulties inherent in even assembling around 26 top studio musicians at a time that didn't clash with their regular assignments are readily apparent.

Perhaps because it was not "officially" the Stan Kenton Orchestra, or because so much of the music was ephemeral, played the once and never heard again, the Neophonic has never made such a lasting impression on Kenton fans as many of Stan's bands. As Bud Shank put it, "We saw the music for the first time in the morning, rehearsed it and played it at the concert that night, and it was gone, finished with."[7]

Nevertheless, a representative number, though by no means a majority, of the most important compositions did get onto records, albeit often played by college bands or the composer's own recordings, as well as the single LP reluctantly put out by Capitol. The Music Center recorded everything played there, but reportedly most tapes were destroyed in 2001, though two concerts (numbers 1 and 3 from the 1965 season) were "rescued by a sound engineer," and subsequently saw several CD releases, most notably on Tantara's two-volume *New Horizons*.

The supposed highlight of the premiere concert on January 4, 1965, was Czech pianist Friedrich Gulda playing his own near half-hour-long composition "Music for Piano and Band." The rousing finale was certainly received enthusiastically (and reprised as an encore), but Milt Bernhart was less than impressed: "Gulda displayed virtuoso technique to burn, but not a crumb of jazz in sight. His music didn't thrill me. It was 'third stream' I suppose. Maybe fourth! But mostly it was just plain hard."[8]

Milt was leading the errant trombone section on Wagner, and right after that first concert he resigned: "After that first night I said, 'Stan, I can't do this any more, it's impossible.' That first concert was a nightmare. Stan didn't think so, he was having a great time! But composers like Marty Paich, Bill Holman, and Lalo Schifrin, everyone, wrote as much as they could possibly write, and there wasn't the money to pay for more than something like a three-hour rehearsal beforehand, so we were really sight-reading everything, and it was miracle-time. Then when the curtain went up I saw all the royal family of music in the front three rows—Ella Fitzgerald, Norman Granz, Count Basie, Dizzy Gillespie, George Shearing—and I thought to myself, 'I can think of better ways to get in big trouble!' Even Stan lost his place while he was conducting his own orchestration, so he looked up at Shelly and whispered, 'Where are we?' And Shelly looked surprised and said, 'Are you crazy Stan? We're at the Music Center!' It was the trial of the century!"[9]

But John Worster remembered the whole endeavor very differently, and offers the best description I have seen from his first-hand experience: "I made 15 albums with the Kenton association, but the best music I've ever played, or possibly ever will play, was the Neophonic album. Those concerts weren't just another gig to anyone; all the musicians took it very seriously. They treated the music with respect, and after rehearsals nobody was running to leave, everyone was looking over parts and checking phrasings and asking questions. I've never been part of a more healthy attitude in regard to anything. I remember Shelly coming in an hour early to talk over tempos with Stan. And Bill Perkins sent his check back to the organizers. He didn't want the money, he was doing it because he believed in what it was—a clearinghouse for original, new, needed music. And Stan of course held it all together. This was his dream come true.

"The LA Pavilion is beautiful. Everything about it has a feeling of class and seriousness. I love the huge, gorgeous chandeliers, but it's not a gaudy display at all, and you sense in that hall a dedication to more than just entertainment. The first concert was formal, black ties, tuxedos, everything. On the opening piece 'Fanfare for the New,' the string bass is tacit, so I was just standing there looking out at the people in this magnificent concert hall. It was the first jazz presented there, and the people were jammed in and so expectant, waiting for us to play good, new music, and not asking us to play nostalgia or bullshit. And the band was marvellous! Bud Shank, Bill Perkins, Frank Rosolino, everybody was on the bandstand. In fact, by the time they got through with the piece, I was so nervous looking around at all these musicians I'd respected for so long, I was scared to death to play!

"The composers wrote whatever they wanted. Everybody wrote like it was the last thing they were ever going to write, and it was an awful lot to subject an orchestra to. We played long concerts, nearly all new music, and all of it hard. I remember during rehearsals something came up for the French horns, and we had Vince DeRosa and his whole section, the best in LA, and Vince doesn't make mistakes. But he kept clamming this one, they kept missing it, and finally Stan had to say, 'Vince, is it poorly copied, or poorly written, or too high, or just too hard?' And Vince says, 'Stan, it's impossible, but you'll have it tonight.' And he had it that night! All the music was hard, because all the shackles were taken off, and the composers could finally just write. So much excellent music came out of that!"[10]

When it came to recording his concert orchestras, Stan took no prisoners. As with Innovations and the ill-fated *City of Glass*, for Capitol's only Neophonic album Kenton chose to fill almost half the LP with Russ Garcia's "Adventure in Emotion," an abstract and enigmatic five-movement work described by Bill Perkins as "Quite something! That was the first time I'd heard the word 'disbigliando,' which I guess is a legit term for organized chaos in music!" But the fans preferred Jim Knight's "Music for an Unwritten Play," and charts like Marty Paich's exciting "Neophonic Impressions," or Stan's own "Opus for Tympani" would surely have made for increased sales and enhanced the Neophonic's reputation and longevity.

"Opus for Tympani" is a revelation, a catchy theme (but none the worse for that!) variously explored in three distinct movements. One can only speculate why Kenton chose not to include it on the LP, when he did record so many of his own far less memorable compositions. There's one miraculous moment during the middle, slow section, when the saxes swoop in and feature one of those switchback soli Stan was famous for, but the brass writing is no less spectacular. In the company of the most skilled writers on the scene, with "Opus For Tympani" Stan could hold his head high.

And those writers included the cream, men like Shorty Rogers, Ralph Carmichael, and Bill Holman, though Stan did not limit himself to "the usual suspects," and extended invitations to such non-Kenton-ites as Gil Melle, Don Ellis, and Oliver Nelson. The Neophonic really was an orchestra for everyone, and a few of the later concerts were even conducted by others, including Bill Russo and Michel LeGrand, but then audience figures fell even more.

Broadly speaking, the more new music was presented, the more the people stayed away, and guest stars like Dizzy Gillespie and Gerry Mulligan were hired to lure the jazz fans in. The biggest draw of all was Mel Torme's "California Suite," which had first been recorded by Capitol as far back as 1949. Doubtless to Kenton's chagrin, Torme drew the first season's only SRO crowd, which at least helped the Neophonic survive for a second year.

Today, we can evaluate only that small part of the Neophonic music that has survived, including the recordings by the Collegiate Neophonic and the University of North Texas Neophonic Orchestra, both featured on Tantara's *Horns of Plenty* CDs. A complete book could be written on the Neophonic alone, but to pick two compositions of distinction, "Phrygia," a work in three movements by Jack Wheaton, is bound to provoke comparison with Gil Evans and *Sketches of Spain*, but these "pictures of the Spanish Mediterranean" (as the composition was announced in concert) are actually much wider in scope, and for me more emotionally involving, with lovely guitar by Tom Morell (Collegiate Neophonic). Van Alexander's "Three Bs for Percussion" are also programmatic. Part 1, "Bangkok," paints a typical Far Eastern portrait, all fluttering woodwinds and shimmering finger cymbals. Part 2, "Brazil," is an attractive samba (not the pop song), and definitely not as Xavier Cugat would have played it. The final "Bora-Bora" is literally an explosion in sound that I'm sure brought a beam to guest-conductor Kenton's face, and satisfaction to the North Texas percussionists. (Both compositions were also played in concert by the LA Orchestra, but like so many other works have never surfaced from that source.)

However masterly the music, audiences didn't pick up, Capitol refused further support, and the LA Neophonic finally folded in April 1968 after just 11 brief but brilliant public performances. After the final concert on April 15, even the often abrasive Leonard Feather was moved to write, "The orchestra has again shown that it fills a vacuum in Los Angeles' musical life. Every effort should be made not merely to keep it alive, but to expand its activities and stimulate public interest in this brave and unique venture."[11]

But Feather's conversion was too little, too late to make any difference. By then the die was cast, the decision made. As is only right, Stanley has the last word: "The Los Angeles Neophonic Orchestra was very important to the minority group that supported us. It was a very difficult project, and it was rough getting the concerts organized in the circumstances we had to do them in. You have no idea of the thought and the worry that went into that thing—that's what gave me a lot of white hair!"[12]

# 23.

## Marking Time

### (1965–1966)

Kenton had hoped that the Neophonic movement would grow and spread to other cities, but when it became apparent that even the Los Angeles Orchestra was doomed without hefty subsidies from his own pocket, a new source of revenue became urgent. In 1965 Dana was eight (nine on September 10), and Lance (born January 16, 1958) only seven. Stan loved both dearly, to the extent he had forsaken his own career to be with them, though he probably was not strict enough in enforcing his own rules during their childhood. Whatever, children are a constant expense, and now Stan needed income. For the first time ever he seriously considered following the lead of so many of his alumni and becoming a studio musician/composer. Through his manager George Greif, Kenton made contact with TV producer James Komack (himself a big fan of the band), and was signed to write the theme song and background music for the pilot of a new NBC comedy series *Mister Roberts*.

But even if he came up with a suitable theme, writing film music involved a strict set of rules and criteria for which his experiences left him totally unprepared, even after consulting Pete Rugolo for advice. The music had to be completely subservient to the on-screen action, and timing to a split-second was essential. Film editor (and Astral Jazz producer) John Loeffler was himself working at Warner Brothers, and caught sight of Stan recording his music on the studio sound-stage with the help of the supervising music editor. John was not able to hear the music itself, but observed how uncomfortable Kenton appeared, and that he was clearly out of his depth. In the diplomatic words of producer Komack, "We put the music into the pilot and junked it. It was too strong. It wasn't Stan's fault, he wrote beautiful cues, a beautiful theme. It was just too soon in 1965 to lay down Stan Kenton music with a half-hour TV series."[1] Another luminary amongst jazz composers, Johnny Mandel, was hired instead.

The only alternative was to form a part-time band to play local gigs in the LA area, combined with short tours that didn't deprive the children of their father for too long. There was no incentive or money to pay for new charts, so the mellophonium book was dusted off, with Stan playing the horn parts on piano. "I loved the mellophoniums," said Stan, "but I had to cut down somewhere because money was awfully short at that time."[2] Since in addition most of the musicians were young and inexperienced (i.e. inexpensive), it is clear that these bands were never going to be vintage Kenton.

When baritone saxist Gene Siegel couldn't make one of the rehearsal dates in June 1965 Larry Dougherty subbed: "Stan was late showing up, arrived in his 1963 Porsche coupe looking hung over, lit a Camel, took a high-back chair and turned it around with his arms draped over the back, and called for 'Reuben's Blues.' He didn't play any piano, and showed little or no emotion the entire rehearsal, but just listened intently."[3]

Apart from the brass leads (Dalton Smith and Bob Fitzpatrick) there were few familiar faces. Ray Reed was a latent talent leading the saxophones, and another newcomer on baritone sax was Bill Fritz, who relates: "I had no desire to go on the road, as I was getting a fair amount of studio calls, but I *did* want to play with Stan Kenton, so I called a number of the ex-Kenton men with whom I had worked and asked them to recommend me to Jim Amlotte. The group was quite weak at the beginning, only 4 or 5 of the men had been with Kenton before, but by the time we played San Francisco in August things had come together more. Stan was constantly talking about 'a new direction' and 'burning the book,' but the only 'new' idea he came up with was using the less-usual time signatures, which eventually led him to depend so heavily on Hank Levy."[4]

In other words, Stan was coasting, marking time. "The guys liked Kenton and wanted to play in his band," observed John Worster. "They wanted the reputation of having played with Stan, but not quite as much as in 1963. It takes a while to really build up a band, and these bands were part-timeish. They lacked the 'family feeling' of a full-time orchestra."[5]

It was during one-nighters in November that a young trombone player, whom Worster described as "The perfect sound for a Kenton band" and who would soon become section lead, and eventually band manager, assistant conductor, and Stanley's personal friend, first joined. Dick Shearer knew all the Kenton records, and was familiar with the sounds of Winding, Bernhart, Burgess, and Fitzpatrick, so he knew just what Stan required. "I knew Jim Amlotte well," Shearer told me. "We'd worked around LA together a lot, and I'd always wanted to get on the

Kenton band. Of course, in 1965 it was basically a part-time job, but I was still thrilled very much."

Stan had re-signed his contract with Capitol only after they had agreed to record the Neophonic orchestra. Capitol's beautifully packaged Neophonic album had been issued with a flourish, and promptly sank without a trace. Now it was pay-back time, with the Company demanding some albums that might stand a chance of turning a profit. And with Stan some $30,000 in the red by the end of the Neophonic's 1966 season, Kenton had to agree. The only thing missing was the music!

The 1966 road tour lasted two months (June and July), and to quote Bill Fritz, was preceded by "An experimental rehearsal at Valentine's studio, trying various instrumentations and different time signatures. We tried out some new things Stan had written ['Five before Four,' 'Taboo Montuna'], a cute piece by Bob Cooper that was never heard of again ['The Toy Factory'], several fragments by Dee Barton in odd time meters, and my own 'Soon It's Gonna Rain.' During my stay with the band I contributed around a dozen charts to the book which were used a great deal at dance jobs, as they were all pop tunes, though 'Shadow of Your Smile' and 'Aquarius' also found their way into show usage."[6] (Fritz' more intellectual composition "Sinfonia," subtitled "A Symphony in Miniature," had been premiered at the Neophonic concert on April 4, 1966, but was never heard again.)

Kenton enthusiast Doug Hughes caught this band fairly early in the tour at the Starlight Ballroom in St. Louis on June 14, and sent this report to Kentonia: "The band really wasn't sounding very good. Almost every tune was a potential train wreck. The rhythm section [John Worster(b) and Ed Soph(d)] was holding them together—just barely. Half the dates the prior week had been dances at ballrooms, so the band should have had the dance book under their fingers. They didn't!"[7]

Faced with the necessity to find the formula for a commercially successful record, and without any ideas himself, Stan did what he always did, and turned to Gene Roland. Gene came out to the coast to travel with the band that summer and conceive something new. Rock 'n' roll was hot with the kids who bought records, so Roland's plan was to fashion an album using pseudo-rock rhythms matched with the excitement of the Kenton band sound—an idea that would happen in the near future. Gene wrote both originals and standards in the R&R idiom (eg. "Monkeyshines," "The Kook"/"Bill Bailey," "The Saints"). According to Roland, when it came to the crunch, in 1966 Stan couldn't bring himself to become associated with rock, and scrapped the whole thing, despite Gene's belief that such an album would sell well.

Bill Fritz remembered the circumstances rather differently, and told Steven Harris: "We spent all summer waiting for Gene to write something. The band would have a rehearsal and he'd bring only half an arrangement, and you could tell Stan was getting steamed."[8] Gene desperately tried to please Stan with a last batch of compositions with intriguing titles (eg. "Thing for Alto and Brass," "Opus in Plaid"), but Fritz says these were pretty bad: "A rehearsal at Shelly's Manne-Hole on September 25 was when Roland brought in his final bombs and was dismissed. Gene was sent back to New York after being with us the whole summer and having been able to put nothing in the book."[9]

In a perverse sort of way, Roland's failure to produce may have gratified Kenton, insofar as it confirmed Stan's own indispensability—he had to write the Capitol album himself. Whether the results, issued as *Stan Kenton Plays for Today*, were any better than Roland's efforts we'll never know, but Gene's could hardly have been much worse. Herb Alpert's Tijuana Brass was hot at the time, and it may have been coincidence that Stan's writing was also for trumpets and Latin rhythm. Whatever, when I less than diplomatically suggested to Kenton there might be a connection, I was subjected to THE LOOK, and frostily informed by Stan that he "Didn't copy anyone!"

However, Stan went on to admit that *Plays for Today* (recorded by a studio band, not the regular orchestra personnel) was a bad LP. "Most every album that I designed for Sixties radio play was a bomb! The only one that came out pretty good was *The World We Know*, with 'Girl Talk' and 'Sunny.' That trumpet album was a terrible failure commercially, and musically it was contrived. I was trying too hard for different things. Whenever you start creating anything new, there's a great risk of destroying it by being contrived."[10]

The only "different" aspect of Stan's approach to such mediocre melodies as "Spanish Eyes," "Never on Sunday," and "Somewhere My Love," is the application of Latin percussion, which adds to the rhythmic appeal but is never intrusive. Otherwise, the emasculated trumpets carry the arrangements, never even remotely capturing the fiery, vibrant Kenton sound, while remaining tied to the melody without diversity or variation. Stan's piano, devoid of any passion or personality, is the only solo instrument. Because they are harmonically more interesting, the Sinatra-associated "Strangers in the Night" and "It Was a Very Good Year" come off better than most, and surprisingly, "The Sound of Music" is the most intriguing chart, at least as compared with the unimaginative scoring heard elsewhere. *Plays for Today* may be explained as a calculated attempt to gain radio-play and public acceptance, but musically it remains the most anonymous, pedestrian album ever to carry the Kenton name. Those of us who revere all that "Stan Kenton" stands for would do well to avoid it at all cost. When I asked John Worster his opinion, he dismissed it as briefly as possible: "We couldn't take it seriously. We didn't know much about it before it happened, and we never played the music again afterwards. It was just a one-time shot, we went in and tried to make an album and played as well as we could, and that was about it."[11]

In retrospect, 1966 was perhaps the most disappointing year of Kenton's career (Neophonic concerts apart). Even nostalgia took a knock when the Rendezvous Ballroom at Balboa, almost Stan's alma mater, was burned to the ground on Sunday, August 7. When this had happened before, the ballroom had always been rebuilt, but not this time. It marked the end for the famous dance-spot, once the home of the big bands and an institution in itself, but most recently home to a motley collection of rockers. Appropriately, the name of the last group to play the Rendezvous was The Cindermen. The one bright note was that things could only get better in 1967!

# 24.

## Delights and Disappointments

### (1967–1969)

**With the children growing up fast,** Kenton felt able to leave home in 1967 for two three-month tours, which combined with all the local gigs made the band feel less part-timeish. A number of sidemen had made it their priority to stick with Stan in preference to other jobs, including Jay Saunders (tp), Ray Reed (as), Bill Fritz (bs), and John Worster (b), as well as a near-complete trombone section of Dick Shearer, Tom Whittaker, Jim Amlotte, and Graham Ellis, bringing a much-needed sense of stability. And now two newcomers, the powerful trumpet of Jay Daversa and the dynamic returnee Dee Barton on drums invigorated and revitalized the organization. The band was in better shape than for a number of years.

Tantara's *Road Band '67* proves this was a Kenton orchestra worthy of the name, sparked by the exuberant Barton drums, and aided by the superb bass of John Worster. This remarkable rhythm section both cushioned and drove the orchestra at the same time, providing a strong foundation for the rest of the band to build upon, while in Daversa and Reed, Kenton had soloists of world-class dimension. "Jay grew up in the LA area, and was always a very original player," observed Dick Shearer. "He often had a boppish style, but whatever was called for Jay had it down, a fantastic reader with excellent technique and range." "Daversa played quite conservatively when he first joined the band," added Bill Fritz, "but as time went by his solos became farther out and more angry."[1] Whichever, Jay was good enough to have Miles Davis ask Stan his name when the band played the Village Gate in New York, an accolade more worthy than any poll award!

"Ray Reed," said Shearer, "was a very serious guy, very thoughtful about what he did, a very academic player. He practiced all the time. Whenever we'd get to the hotel, he'd go to his room and practice. Ray had a willowy appearance, but his physique was all right, he just looked that way." Essentially a melodic player, Reed's personal signature was one of Bill Fritz' best arrangements, the classic Kurt Weill-Ira Gershwin ballad "My Ship," which Stan never saw fit to Capitol-record. Ray never played the piece the same way twice, but always inspirational ideas cascade from his horn in a waterfall of notes that leave the listener—if not Reed—breathless. Over the tour Reed was influenced by Daversa, and his playing became more far-out when they soloed together on the pieces now being introduced into the band by Dee Barton.

Barton was a prolific writer, though by no means was all of his work accepted by Stan. When Dee wrote well he took the music into a new dimension, but according to Fritz, "Barton brought in several nice pieces, but the vast majority of his work was utterly tasteless. Dee wrote something for the Neophonic called 'Passion Suite,' and after the rehearsal one of the horn-players commented, 'If that is his idea of love, I'd hate to be his wife!'" On the other hand, Dee's striking arrangement of "Here's That Rainy Day" really appealed to Stan, and its ultra-slow, funereal tempo set the style for ballad-writing well into the next decade. But instead of recording this and some of Fritz' charts on his next Capitol album, Kenton preferred to play only his own arrangements, presumably for commercial reasons, because they were not always the best.

*The World We Know* was a mix of newer ballads, as always, alas, sans solos, and some brighter numbers, though the two clichéd originals "Interchange" (a reworking of "Five Before Four") and "Changing Times" indicated only that Stan should leave the writing of unusual time signatures to those more conversant with the art. Commercially, "Girl Talk" hit the button, as did the up-tempo "Sunny," a happy, snappy tune by Bobby Hebb that is unashamedly entertaining, but in jazz terms far inferior to the "Southern Scandal" and "Painted Rhythm" of 20 years earlier.

Fortunately, the album also features Stan's last recorded concert orchestration. "Gloomy Sunday" contains all the elements of surprise and adventure one looks for in Kenton: an impressive combination of exciting counterpoint with dramatic shifts in tempo, a good sense of symmetry, some fine lead trombone work by Dick Shearer, and an awesomely ferocious solo from Jay Daversa. At least *The World We Know* is a vast improvement over *Plays for Today*, and this time Stan allowed his regular band to make the recording, with only a couple of studio men replacing transient players. (And on just $175 a week, out of which they paid for their own food and hotel rooms, the guys could do with the extra cash.)

Kenton's divorce from Ann Richards had been finalized in 1962, and now between tours he found time to marry for the third time. Stan had first met Jo Ann Hill the previous year while she was working as a production assistant at KABC-TV, and felt a strong attraction. Despite repeated warnings from those close to Stan that he was being too hasty and should cool it for a while, the couple were married in Las Vegas on July 6, 1967. The honeymoon was even shorter than that with Ms Richards. Relations between the pair soon became strained, and though there is no suggestion Jo Ann was using Stan in the way Ann had done, they separated in 1969, with divorce following in 1970. I wouldn't agree with those alumni who asserted that Kenton's marriages "ruined" his musical career, but at the same time they certainly did it few favors.

All year the band had been playing the innovative new Dee Barton charts, so they were really ready to record in December. Barton was a diverse arranger, equally able to write in many different styles and situations, and by now he was well tuned-in to what turned Kenton on. "Dee was a very strong-willed guy with a lot of anger and frustration that he put to good use," said tenor-man Kim Richmond. "He was rebelling against the commonly accepted way of writing music, especially harmonically, and he hit upon a completely individual and powerful style that really fit with Stan's psyche."[2] And Jim Amlotte confirmed, "Dee's writing was very different from what anyone else had done, and in Daversa and Reed he found soloists who were also quite far out. Jay's melodic structure and his creative lines were new, and Ray was a real nice guy and very quiet, didn't say much, but you had to respect his playing."

Stan's idea had been to call the album *Modern Man*, but he and Barton often disagreed over titles (deja vu!), and it finally came out as *Stan Kenton Plays the Jazz Compositions of Dee Barton*, a really catchy handle (not!), though it did have in Capitol's eyes the merits of including Stan's name. It was the first "jazz" album since 1962, so Stan expected it to do well, and when it failed at the box office he blamed Capitol for a lack of promotion. But equally likely, with its unconventional time signatures and discordant solos, it was too far off-center and in 1967 too radical a departure from the Kenton mainstream to become widely accepted.

Dick Shearer had especially fond memories of this band: "I think that's one of the finest jazz albums I've ever played in my life. We've tried to play some of that music since, and we could never quite achieve what we did with that orchestra. It was a very academic band, with a very schooled, methodical, thought-out way of playing. We were there from the very beginning—we knew exactly what Dee wanted. We went into the studio and cut the album in two sessions, whereas it normally takes three or four. That's a deep album, a hard one, and some of the greatest things like 'Three Thoughts' and 'The Singing Oyster' are the only takes. That's how good the band was at that time, very schooled and disciplined. It might not have been what you'd call a down-home, swinging band, but it swings on that album. It was very well planned, and everyone knew exactly what they were doing."

Because it is different from the Kenton-style jazz they are used to hearing, some will find the Barton album not to their immediate taste. But those who listen intimately and with an open mind will find intriguing tone colors and attractive themes interacting with typical Kentonian sounds and dissonance. If anything, it's the sometimes savage solos of Daversa and Reed on such pieces as "Dilemma" that are often as "advanced" as anything in Barton's inventive writing. And as Amlotte said, "This was what Stan wanted. He didn't want a copy-cat of what had gone before. Stan didn't like to look back—he was always moving forward to the next thing."

The upturn was not to last. An ill-defined project partnered between Kenton and Barton called *Personal Sounds* was intended as a *Prologue*-type album with narration, but featuring sections of the orchestra rather than individual men (who kept changing with the speed of a rocket). Stan rather vaguely described the concept as "A thing Dee and I worked on together to dramatize big band jazz music."[3] Capitol humored Kenton and recorded Barton's interesting snippets in four expensive sessions, and cannot have been best pleased when Stan abandoned the whole idea as unworkable.

Stan reverted to searching for something that might sell, and when Lee Gillette suggested an LP of tunes from the popular musical *Finian's Rainbow*, Kenton agreed to write the charts. The memory of that album was still painful to Stan in 1975, though he blamed the songs rather than his own lackluster writing (aided and abetted by Dee Barton who fared no better). "*Finian's Rainbow* was bad," Stan told me. "That was a bad album. Warners were making the motion picture, and I didn't realize the music was so weak. *Finian's Rainbow* was a famous show, and it's got a couple of lovely melodies in it, but after I got into the rest of the score I told Gillette, 'This is the worst crap I've ever tried to write in my whole life, and I think we'd better change the whole direction of the album and throw in some motion picture themes to try and save it.' The aim was to try for an album that would sell and get some radio play, rather than produce anything of artistic value. But it died!"[4]

An imaginative arranger can transcend "crap" and turn it into something else, but Stan was very dependent on the quality of his material because he never strays very far from the original melody. He awards "Old Devil Moon" a nice treatment, with good fugal effects spoilt by a clanging guitar, but one expects so much more from Kenton than "nice." The nadir is perhaps the gimmicky "Glocca Morra," with Dee Barton vocally declaring his own arrangement will MAKE it—and what follows would be bettered by Billy May on a bad day. With the exception of the pleasantly voiced, Latin-tinged "People," the movie themes are so dire as to preclude comment.

The knowledgeable Kenton authority Terry Vosbein was equally outspoken: "The *Finian's Rainbow* album is mostly generic instrumental arrangements that get loud somewhere along the way with a few over-used Kentonesque voicings. Far too much silly repetition, and when they start whistling the cowboy-like tune on 'Villa Rides' . . . talk about a BAD arrangement! The performances on this album are particularly uninspired. Sounds more like an anonymous studio session."[5]

Even commercial writing should have a sense of purpose, of character, of integrity. With *Finian's Rainbow* Kenton finally came to realize that neither the fans nor the wider public were buying what he was selling, and put away his pencils for good. Stan had written important music in earlier years, and frequently pointed the direction for other, more skilled arrangers to follow, but those days were past. To Bill Fritz, "It seemed obvious by the haste in writing and the lack of quality in the arrangements, that Stan was simply fulfilling his contract with Capitol. There was the feeling that Kenton was only there 'for old times' sake,' and everyone knew that Capitol wouldn't push this particular product."[6]

Kenton had long harbored the idea for a documentary film of the band, showing the hardship the men endured during a lengthy road tour, and it happened during the spring tour of 1968. Photographer Baldwin Baker and sound engineer Harold Etherington followed the guys around and traveled on the band bus, constantly filming as they went. Dee Barton wrote tantalizing musical cues linking the sequences, and slowly the whole thing came together. Kenton kept strict editorial control, until he was satisfied his movie portrayed a typical tour, with all the satisfactions and frustrations of the one-night grind: the boredom of long hours imprisoned on the bus and the grey streets of hick cities, to the artistic high of a well-played concert before an appreciative audience. The very essence and reality of the life of a touring orchestra, 1968.

Stan called his hour-long movie *Bound to Be Heard*, which proved to be anything but the case. What he hadn't realized was that a long-ish film of bored-looking musicians on the move, was going to prove equally boring for most members of the public to watch. Even fans were frustrated by the brevity of the musical interludes, which were invariably quickly faded in favor of off-screen dialogue from Kenton or narrator Bill Marlowe. Probably Stan did not want to culminate with a "grand concert" like the *Benny Goodman Story* movie, but at least for music-lovers it would have provided a satisfying climax after all the foreplay. The result was that after all Stan's hard work and his expense of an estimated $75,000, when it was all finished no one in the television industry wanted to know! It simply did not make for arresting TV viewing.

This time Stan blamed jazz rather than the possibility he had not made the film sufficiently compulsive: "Nobody wanted to show it, because they felt like there wasn't enough interest in jazz music. I first believed that NBC-TV would buy it, and it was designed with them in mind, but the Vice-President told me, 'We can't use it. There's just not enough interest in jazz.' So then it was taken to a syndicated company, and they refused it too. So after that I just said, 'To hell with it, I'm not going to embarrass myself any more hawking it around.'"[7]

Eventually *Bound to Be Heard* (retitled *A Crusade for Jazz* in 1970) was shown in truncated form on KTLA (an independent Los Angeles station), as Fritz put it: "I think mainly as a favor to Stan, because even with editing to 46 minutes the networks found it too uncommercial."[8] In Dick Shearer's view, "It wasn't commercial because many people thought it was too realistic. We depicted things like they really are, rather than making it all rosy and having a ball. We showed some of the hard times. We thought it was very successful, but the TV men said the audiences wouldn't buy it. It was shown one time locally in LA to good reviews, and we showed it for a while at the Clinics, but it's dated now. The guys have all got short hair, and it looks like it was done about 1920. The kids don't relate to it any more."

Any Kenton fan will obtain pleasure from *Bound to Be Heard*, with more than a hint of nostalgia when Stan speaks directly into the camera while standing on the vacant lot that was once the site of Balboa's Rendezvous Ballroom, then jumps into his Corvette and speeds away to the strains of "Artistry in Rhythm." But the overall impression is that the film was perhaps as much fun to make as it is to watch, and that the series of short, separate montages lack a strong, central storyline with which the viewer can readily identify.

Oddly enough Leonard Feather, often considered Stan's critical bete noir, emerges as the film's champion: "Never has the flavor of the very private, very special world of a touring big band been captured more acutely than in *Bound to Be Heard*, a study of Stan Kenton and his Orchestra on the road. On and off camera the band plays a series of darkly attractive works by Dee Barton, while Kenton emerges as a man of tremendous conviction, a Goliath of a conductor, and a leader with an unquenchable sense of commitment. *Bound to Be Heard* ought to be seen."[9]

There had been a tacit understanding with Dee Barton that if his first album was successful it would be followed by a second, and during February 1969 Clinton Roemer copied a group of Barton compositions with booth parts for recording purposes. But when it came to the test, Stan rejected all eight charts, thereby effectively ending his relationship with the irascible Dee. I've never heard the music, but titles like "Fun City" and "The Third Millennium" sound promising, though I have more trouble imagining Stan announcing "Posie" or "The Spanish Ant Army March"!

Barton's writing had always been erratic, from the joys of "The Singing Oyster" to the horror of "How Are Things in Glocca Morra," but in recent years he had exercised the only fresh, creative influence on the band, and his departure deprived Stan of his head arranger with no obvious candidate to fill the void. In the past there had usually been budding writers within the organization (think of Bills Russo and Holman), but those days had passed. In an apparently desperate attempt to "modernize" his music, Stan commissioned Bill Fritz and Cerritos College student Steve Spiegl to arrange some current pop tunes in rock style. Fritz responded with a hard-rock version of "Aquarius" which lacked any of the subtlety of Ralph Carmichael's upcoming concoction. According to Spiegl, Stan offered him the post of chief arranger, and suggested "Hey Jude" and "Do You Know the Way to San Jose" to score as his first assignment.

Ray Reed and Bill Fritz left the band at the start of the spring 1969 tour. Jay Daversa had also quit, so there were no major soloists in the new line-up. "I left the band," said Fritz, "partly from boredom, but mostly disappointment at the poor quality of compositions being performed, and because of the immaturity and lack of grace of a large part of the band."[10] The guys were juvenile because almost all were kids straight out of school, with few older hands to call the shots; and hey—they were playing with Stan Kenton and His Orchestra!

In fact, only six men remained from the previous year, so the ensemble was bound to sound rough until Stan had whipped the new guys into shape. "Stan was going for young bands," explained Fritz, "because he believed in the kids, and it didn't hurt that they were cheap. The spring 1969 band just had too many inexperienced players at the same time."[11] Dick Shearer, who had become band manager when Jim Amlotte left in 1967, was now one of the "old hands," and already an indispensable aide to Kenton's Svengali.

"Dick really impressed me with his stamina," said new jazz trumpet player Dave Hayward. "What chops Dick had! Used to arrive for a gig and with help from maybe one other cat would set up the bandstand, dress, and play maybe three or four arpeggios on his horn, then proceed to lead and solo trombone all night faultlessly. Set such an example for 20 guys who at times were bone-weary and brain-boggled with the need for a day off and release from the 'iron lung' (the band-bus!)

"Stan is a trouper! I remember him scrunched up, all 6' 5" (or whatever) of him, in the bus seat day after grueling day, and never complaining. I always dug Stan's piano, with shades of Tatum and many others. The music helped make up for all those hours on the bus, with the all-night parties and the inevitable vomiting by the ones who weren't used to drinking! The better the band played, the slower Stan wanted the ballads to be. This lent a symphonic air to the tunes, which made them even more moving, and I found it very inspiring to play solos with that powerful brass choir behind me.

"Musically I thought the band a bit heavy. Fred Petry was a good drummer, but he lacked the strength or the experience to kick such a heavy band—have to give him 'A' for effort though."[12] Perhaps Stan was already regretting Barton's loss, because it had been clear from day one that Petry was not practiced enough to function as drummer in a Kenton band, but Stan kept him on because there was no immediate alternative, and it was only a short tour anyway.

Stan had finally succumbed to the inevitable and brought in the Fender bass guitar to spice up the authenticity of the rock charts and keep the kids at the Clinics on-side. Barton's "MacArthur Park" had been recorded as a single for Capitol without much impact (teenagers no longer bought Kenton records), but became quite a hit in live performances, with the guys providing comic visual effects during the band-vocal, and then stunning the kids with the impact of the up-tempo central section. However, it was the execrable but popular "Hey Jude" that really hit "rock" bottom. As arranged by Spiegl, this Beatles hit of limited melodic worth clashed with the Kenton brass to produce a hybrid that built into an undeniably clamorous experience, and introduced a veneer of contemporaneity into the repertoire. It thrilled the kids, but I found it impossible to play all the way through, and fortunately, unlike other leaders such as Miles Davis and Woody Herman, Kenton declined to go any farther down this route than was essential to maintain his finances.

Perhaps aware of Stan's easier attitude towards rock, and following the success on stage of the hippie rock-musical *Hair*, Capitol decided they wanted to put out a pop-jazz version of the music as a means of fulfilling their contract with Kenton—as long as Stan himself had as little to do with it as possible. In all fairness, *Hair* was by no means the first Kenton album with little Kenton input (think of the Rugolo strings LPs, or *Artistry in Voices and Brass*), but it was the only album from which Stan's exclusion was not of his own choosing.

According to Stan, "One day Gillette phoned while we were out on tour and asked if I'd mind if he got Ralph Carmichael to record *Hair*, because he said if we're going to make any money out of it the album should be on the market right away, and we'd never get it done otherwise. So I said, 'OK. If you want to do it, do it.' I did get home just in time to play a couple of solos. I was in the studio throughout the recording, but it was Ralph's and Lee's project, so most of the time I stayed out of the road. Once in a while they'd ask me what I thought and I'd tell them, but I didn't have much to do with the album.

"Jack Sheldon played the solo on 'Sodomy,' and that was a masterpiece. And Lennie Niehaus had a hand in the music, because I saw the scores and recognized his handwriting. Lennie did a lot of ghost-writing for Ralph. Carmichael is like a lot of us, he waits till the last minute to get anything done, and then he'll write day and night without stopping. On the last day that *Hair* was recorded I thought he was going to drop dead on us, because he hadn't slept, up all night writing. Billy May is another one like that, puts things off till the last minute."[13]

Niehaus' involvement was confirmed by Carmichael: "The logic for making *Hair* was to introduce Stan to a younger audience. In other words, take kids' tunes and give them a Kentonish treatment. Lee Gillette asked me to arrange the album, but I was so busy I wasn't able to complete all the writing in time. Lennie Niehaus is a great friend and a fine arranger. He's fast and he's good. So when the midnight before a session rolls around and you still have three charts to write . . . call Lennie!"[14]

On Broadway, *Hair* defied convention and achieved notoriety with its defiant use of bad language and full-frontal nudity. But musically it was actually quite melodic and far from the excesses of full-blown rock, while its profound anti-war message was skillfully conveyed through song and story. *Hair* was jazz-tinged theatre far better than its infamous reputation allowed, and Carmichael was exactly the right person to give the music a stylish interpretation. Using every rhythm instrument at his command, he brought a light touch and deftness to these songs that superseded their rock-based origins.

The results could certainly have been improved. "Hare Krishna," "Frank Mills," and "Let the Sunshine In" are little more than vehicles for the chorus to chant the lyrics, but as sheer entertainment *Kenton's Hair* has many merits. In the hands of soloist Jack Sheldon, "Sodomy" emerges with a spiritual flavor. Several charts—"Hair," "Aquarius," "Walking in Space"—contain interludes in which the soloists (Sheldon, Shank, Perkins) and the ensemble interact with flair and ingenuity. Woodwinds are frequently used to good effect, while the brass is lively and loud, and often takes off into the stratosphere in true Kenton style: there's wonderful contrast between Stan's melodic piano figures and Bud Brisbois flaunting his technique above the hard-hitting brass on "Easy to Be Hard." And the enlarged eight-piece rhythm section uses contemporary devices with skill and subtlety, while never degenerating into the generic heavy drums/electric bass beat that tarnished some of the Levy music of the Seventies.

I speak as a minority. Few fans will admit to liking *Hair*, and with a playing time of only 32 minutes, why Capitol omitted the well-constructed title-track "Hair" is beyond comprehension. It's also unlikely Stan approved of the new recording techniques, which inevitably resulted in a pre-ordained inflexibility, and was the antithesis of cooking jazz, where the men work together and inspire each other, as Dick Shearer explains: "When the horns came to record, the rhythm tracks had already been laid down. There were only a few things that we did together with the rhythm men in the studio. Otherwise it was head-sets and all that crap, so we did our part of it, and then they put the singers on top of that." John Worster had no doubts about the results: "The music from *Hair* should never have been recorded. No one ever talks about that. It was terrible. Stan was forced into it by Capitol—one of the many reasons why Stan chose to start his own company."[15]

But by no means has all high-profile opinion been so negative. In John Harner's view: "The *Hair* album wasn't awful. It was different. Some of the most incredible playing I have heard, with Bud Brisbois screaming Gs above double C. The chorus had some of the best singers in LA. Maybe it didn't fit the usual Kenton genre, but once again Stan was trying to be the innovator."[16] Jiggs Whigham concurred: "The *Hair* record for me was really exciting. Ralph Carmichael is a terrific writer, and the alumni band took that music and made it sound a lot better than the original." And Mike Vax confirmed: "I like many of the cuts from Kenton's *Hair*, AND SO DID STAN. We were playing a few of those arrangements well into the Seventies."[17]

I suspect these positive views reflect Stan's own opinion of the music. Had he strongly disapproved he had the right and the ability to refuse its release under his name. The fact Ralph Carmichael was the creative force behind *Hair* is inconsequential. The Christmas album in 1961 had largely turned into a Carmichael vehicle in all but name. In any case, all bandleaders relied heavily on their arrangers. Billy Strayhorn was Duke's alter ego, and the 1945 Herd owed as much to Burns and Hefti as it did to Herman. Being a successful bandleader was a profession in itself, and few even tried to combine the achievement with writing the music. What I fancy did hurt and humiliate Stan was not the final product, but the way it had been planned and implemented in his absence, so that he was presented with a fait accompli, and was almost surplus to requirements.

Whatever, *Hair* was a one-off studio creation, and in no way projected a future course for the orchestra on Capitol. In that respect, Worster was right. Kenton wanted to play forward-looking, big-band jazz, and Capitol's interest in such music had sunk to zilch. Recording a 20-piece band playing music that no one bought was very expensive, when a four-boy group with a couple of guitars sold a million copies and rising. Increasingly the band leader and the record label were coming to the same conclusion: as the 1970s loomed, Kenton and Capitol were incompatible. Something had to give. Meanwhile for all its assets, *Hair* proved once again that Kenton and commerciality were uneasy bedfellows. As Stan himself commented with a wry chuckle, "As far as sales went, that was another one that was a failure."[18]

Stan re-formed the band in July, with a 10-day booking at San Francisco's Basin Street West, preceded by five days' rehearsal. Larry Dougherty was present as an observer: "My friends Don Rader, Mike Morris and Mike Vacarro were on the band. Stan had an open rehearsal for any fledgling arranger to bring their arrangements in for him to audition and possibly buy. Many writers brought along their charts, and I remember Stan being the perfect gentleman and using great patience to offer encouragement and constructive criticism to each one. I don't think he bought any of the arrangements however!"[19] Perhaps Stan was saving his pennies for his divorce settlement from Jo Ann, which dragged on until September 1970, with "Kenton ordered to pay $34,000 alimony over a 30-month period, and 50% profit from two movies he has made."[20] The latter bequest, relating to *Bound to Be Heard* and a short educational film *The Substance of Jazz*, must have brought an ironic smile to Stan's face, since both cost far more to make than was ever recouped from sales!

"The September band," opined Bill Fritz, "is a good deal more sound than the spring group. One of the biggest improvements is Ray Price, formerly of England, on drums."[21] But the most significant newcomer, because of his experience and writing ability as well as his baritone sax, was 41-year-old Willie Maiden, a veteran of the Maynard Ferguson band. Willie (scruffy, ill-kempt, and plain spoken) and Stanley ("an impeccable dresser with an enormous wardrobe," said Larry Dougherty[22]) were never ordained to be best buddies, but each had respect for the other's musical expertise. On September 1, 1969, Maiden introduced his first arrangement into the band, a happy swinger punned "A Little Minor Booze," which probably didn't especially float Kenton's boat, but which would become a highly influential chart in the next decade, and against which all other similar swinging charts would be measured.

No one could pretend that Kenton's 1960s post-mellophonium bands were the creative equal of the great orchestras of the past, but despite their transient nature and lack of fresh, distinguished scores, these bands were in fact far better than one would ever imagine from the often sterile Capitol albums of the period. The few good-quality live recordings attest to the sharp playing and skillful execution, and this despite the constantly changing personnel which rendered many of the musicians "names without faces." The year 1969 alone had begun with Dave Hayward on jazz trumpet. In the summer it was Don Rader, and by the time of the autumn tour Tom Harrell held down the chair. By contrast, Chico Alvarez had remained associated with the band (save for war service) for some 11 years. Small wonder Stan would declare, "I really believe that over the last number of years it's the overall Kenton sound that has become the identifying feature of the band, rather than individual musicians."[23]

The autumn band was recorded October 26, 1969, at the Golden Lion in Dayton, Ohio, with Don Piestrup's new-to-the-book "Dance" issued on Tantara's *Revelations*. A superior concert-chart, "Dance" features a distinctive, majestic theme backed by complex rhythms, indicative of the way Kenton was advancing with the times while retaining his individuality. The score affords a rare opportunity to sample the muscular tenor of Mike Morris and the lyrical trumpet of a very young Tom Harrell (who would play with Stan only for this brief tour).

As the decade came to a close it was clear the status quo between leader and record label was no longer tenable. By common consent Kenton and Capitol decided to call it quits, and their contract (which actually ran until May 26, 1970) was quietly revoked. There was no bad feeling on either side, proven by Stan's unique arrangement with Capitol whereby he was able to lease his deleted recordings from the company to sell by mail-order LPs on his own Creative World label, a name derived from his long-time slogan, "The Creative World of Stan Kenton." The first seven-album release, ranging from *City of Glass* to *Kenton's Christmas*, was announced in *Down Beat* dated September 18, 1969.

For Kenton, losing the backing of the record company that had supported, protected, and promoted him for 25 years was rather like detaching the umbilical cord. Most artists flit from label to label with abandon, but Capitol had been Stan's home, his rock for most of his recording career, and to lose that shelter at 58, and be cast adrift in a world growing ever more hostile to everything he represented in music and the arts, was shattering. But Kenton had always thrived on new adventures, and the success of his own record label was a challenge to strive for. After several years of virtual stagnation, Stan's Creative World would grow in future years, and together with a revitalized, permanent orchestra, would catapult Kenton into the Seventies, and see him regain his place as the leading trendsetter in the advancement of big-band jazz.

# The Creative World of Stan Kenton
## (1970)

**Several prominent jazzmen had dabbled** briefly with their own record labels in the past: Gillespie with Dee Gee, Herman on Mars, Mingus and Debut. All had quickly found it unprofitable, and had sold out to an established company. Even Sinatra and Reprise had finally succumbed. Kenton had the advantage of access to his entire back catalog, on lease from Capitol and Decca Records, plus a highly loyal if relatively small fan-base on which to build. Even so, Kenton LPs were not prone to fly off the shelves, and Stan knew that more than anything else it was personal appearances that stimulated record sales. The time had come to form a new orchestra!

"The band was really just thrown together, you know,"[1] commented drummer John Von Ohlen. But how it was thrown! Stan was no longer able to afford high-profile names, but with Dick Shearer's help he assembled a band of largely untried youngsters whose technical skills and reading ability were the equal of more experienced musicians, and whose ensemble playing was more accurate and energetic than any other permanent, touring orchestra of the period.

At the same time, the band assumed a rougher, less polished "edge" than that associated with earlier orchestras. In better times, musicians had risen through the ranks of lesser groups until they were good enough to join the big-name bands. Youngsters with special promise learning on the job, like Bob Cooper or Bill Holman or Marvin Stamm, had been surrounded by older, accomplished veterans from whom they could learn and take advice. Now, the training grounds provided by second-grade bands no longer existed, and the men moved straight from music school into one of the few touring bands that still remained, such as Stan Kenton, Woody Herman, or Buddy Rich. They were often highly proficient players, but lacked maturity and experience, especially essential to play meaningful solos with style and substance.

Kenton (himself approaching the age when many retire altogether) explained the solo dilemma best of all: "The problem is these guys are often young and immature, and haven't had the opportunity to grow. They fail to develop continuity, and they play something out of context that could fit into any tune. They know their chords, they're very well schooled, but they lack the taste that comes with experience. Playing solos should be like telling a story, it's got to have a beginning, and it has to develop and serve a purpose, and then it has to die. Players like Zoot Sims and Lee Konitz and Charlie Parker, when they played 'Body and Soul,' they played 'Body and Soul,' they didn't just play a lot of jibber-jabber."[2] Nor was the position improved by the fact most arrangements coming into the new book were concert-length, extending far beyond the old three-minute playing time encouraged by Capitol, permitting the soloists to stretch out at lengths rarely allowed in the past.

But the problems extended beyond the solos, though few went as far as tenor sax alumnus Kim Richmond, who comments, "The bands [during the Seventies] used almost all college students, and the intonation suffered tremendously. I stopped buying the recordings of the band because I was so disappointed in that."[3] Jiggs Whigham had his own explanation: "The bands of the Seventies didn't have the same *sound*. It may have had something to do with the changing times, something the Germans call 'Zeitgeist.' Sociologically there had been a breakdown in respect for authority, and this is reflected in the changing styles of music. You cannot separate music from the time in which it is created. The mores of the time color society and its culture, and the Seventies were not as disciplined as earlier times."

Whatever, most fans simply welcomed the fact that Stan had returned to music with a concert-jazz orchestra. Dances were consigned to a side-line category, something made possible only because of the increasing number of college bookings, usually combined with an afternoon clinic. The downside was this youthful audience would inevitably be reflected in the band's repertoire and style. Every artist is attracted by the nectar of applause, and wants to be loved by their audiences, and Kenton was no exception. Stan knew he had to engage the youngsters attracted to currently popular rock rhythms, and had to incorporate this in his music, while retaining enough of his traditional trademarks not to alienate his older fans. It was a difficult tightrope to walk, and he probably succeeded in satisfying many listeners only part of the time. So, dependent upon your age and inclination, there were many pros and cons associated with the new band, but overall the outlook was brighter than for many years. As John Worster put it, "The band was now a full-time thing in Stan's mind. The musicians knew it, and it was infectious. It was a more totally serious venture on everyone's part."[4]

Musicians from the Seventies often feel like the underdogs, because they know they played good music well, yet in general it is the earlier bands that are most often feted and remembered. In moments of honesty, however, many will admit they understand and endorse this comprehension. The truth is, none of the few remaining touring bands of the Seventies, whose leaders roamed the land like the sole remaining dinosaurs of an almost-extinct species, were quite the same as they had been in their younger days. Conditions were so totally different the decline was inevitable, especially as age and illness took its toll. But it is also true, many talented musicians worked for Kenton in the Seventies, and a lot of significant music was played. The listener who ignores this last decade will be the loser.

At least Mike Vax will endorse the last couple of sentences above, even if some other comments leave him seething! Of all the alumni, Vax remains one of the staunchest Kenton supporters, commenting, "The day that Stan gave me the encouragement to want to play lead trumpet in his band, at the 1960 summer clinic, changed my life forever." Mike achieved his goal in 1970, leading the high-powered trumpet section of Jim Kartchner, Dennis Noday, Warren Gale, and Joe Ellis. Of his team, Vax claimed Warren Gale to be the most significant soloist in the band: "If ever there was a fiery jazz trumpet player that was perfect for the Kenton band it was Warren. I don't know that Dennis Noday is a great lead player in terms of consistency and swing, but he's certainly the loudest trumpet player I've ever played with. If he wanted to he could bury me, and I'm pretty loud. But he never did—I had him to rest on.

"Dick Shearer was the most important person on the band. I think that Stan felt about him like a son. Dick was a good soloist, even though he didn't play any jazz. Very rarely did he ever improvise much. Most of 'Bon Homme Richard' was written, and he would play it pretty much the same every night, which really contradicted what Stan liked from his soloists. But the thing is, the way Dick played trombone, that was the Kenton sound. Dick's trombone was derivative of all the great Kenton lead players, going all the way back to Kai Winding. But sometimes the person who's the end of a legacy, becomes the culmination of the legacy, so I think Dick was the greatest lead trombone player of them all."[5]

Shearer himself spoke well of both saxophone soloists, Quin Davis on alto and Richard Torres tenor, telling me, "Torres was always very concerned about his health, he'd walk out with a sweater and top-coat even when it was 100 degrees, but he was a great saxophone player, with a really big sound. Listen to the recording on London/Decca of 'Yesterdays,' and what a marvellous solo that is. Richard became more daring as he got older. The longer he stayed with the band, the less inhibited he became, and his solos were farther out. He took more chances, and that's how you develop. You've got to take chances." However well both saxes could play, it's also true that when Torres and Davis were reduced to honking and squealing, as on "Hey Jude" or "Keep on Truckin'," I remembered the more musical times of Perkins and Mariano, who would never descend to such tactics, with renewed affection!

Perhaps the biggest impact of all, the spark that ignited this band and made it roar, came from the fresh young drummer John Von Ohlen, affectionately nicknamed by Stan "The Baron," "Because he looks like one." I well remember Stan's beaming smile, and the picture of total admiration on his face, as he watched John beating the hell out of "Artistry in Percussion" during the band's 1972 UK tour. At the same time, as a youthful player nurtured during the ascendancy of rock in popular music, Von Ohlen's influences were inevitably colored by the current rock drummers as well as the swing giants, and even the traditional Afro-Cuban rhythms of "The Peanut Vendor" assumed rockish vibes under John's tutelage. Inevitably, some of the precision associated with past Kenton orchestras was sacrificed in favor of energy and spirit.

Stan had always plowed his own musical furrows, but the orchestra had always been influenced by current trends in jazz. Though Stan didn't personally care for bebop, in 1948 bop had certainly found its way into the repertoire. So, via the likes of Bob Cooper and Art Pepper, had the cool saxophone sounds ushered in by Stan Getz, even though Stan's preference was for the deeper tones of an earlier generation. Similarly, Stan would have preferred to ignore the rock idiom, but while Stan never, ever, led a "rock" band, if only for financial reasons he recognized the need to acknowledge the new direction, telling me, "Rock has changed the rhythms of jazz, there's no doubt about it,"[6] and Von Ohlen was the perfect player for this purpose.

Seen in the flesh, rather than hidden by the anonymity of records, John was very much more than just the drummer. His physical presence seemed to fill the stage; he charged the band with his personality and set every section blazing, yet without any showmanship or dramatics. On stage he followed hawk-eyed Kenton's every movement with a devotion that suggested if Stan asked for his life-blood he would give it, unstintingly. And Kenton in turn clearly felt a strong rapport, and was himself inspired by the eagerness, the enthusiasm, the spirit of his protégé. Von Ohlen resembled an even more dynamic Dee Barton but with more contemporary technique, and had similarly started out on trombone, only switching to the percussion on which he was entirely self-taught at age 17, after hearing the inspirational Mel Lewis with the Stan Kenton orchestra.

Musicians in the band were themselves quick to recognize John's qualities:

> Mike Vax: "John Von Ohlen was just perfect for Stan Kenton. John could swing, but he loved doing the more way-out things as well. The Levy time-charts were nothing to John—real easy."

> Dick Shearer: "John never had a dull moment, he was always extremely bright. The minute we got on the stand, no matter how he felt, or how long we'd traveled, he got right in there. He would lift the band up all the time—he had such spirit. A very musical drummer, and a very strong player."

> John Worster: "John to me was just amazing. Music is everything in the world to John. Music is 100%. It's a religion with him. He's eliminated a majority of other things from his thinking: he quit drinking, and almost has excluded women from his life. Everything just to make more room for music. It's really amazing—his ability to devote himself that completely. That's why he was so easy to play with." (To author, October 4, 1976)

> John Von Ohlen: "We take the money for riding the bus. The music we play for free!" (*Crescendo*, November 1971)

A new start and a new band required a new book. The mellophonium library of a decade earlier didn't make it in the 1970s, and Mike Vax put it as succinctly as anyone: "There were three principal writers when I was on the band (1970–72): Willie Maiden, Ken Hanna and Hank Levy. We were playing such a diverse kind of music, it wasn't like the earlier bands where there was a direction that became the focus of a single writer. Willie kept us swinging, Ken kept us romantic, and Hank Levy kept us befuddled!"

Always looking for change, Kenton saw unusual time signatures as the only viable direction, and turned to the arranger who had already become prominent in that movement with the Don Ellis orchestra. Hank Levy was amenable, but there were immediate problems. Whereas Ellis concentrated almost exclusively on that single style, so that his men were geared up 100% to tackle whatever time changes were thrown at them, Kenton had a much wider repertoire, and required his musicians to switch from swing to Afro-Cuban to slow ballads to different time signatures in succession, and that was an almost impossible task for young and inexperienced musicians to cope with. Levy had to temper his charts to make them easier to play than some of the things he had written for Ellis, at once making them less far-out, or "progressive."

Mike Vax remembered well how it all began: "At the first rehearsal of 'Chiapas'—and I'll tell you, it was in the attic of the Hotel Bradford in Boston—Stan enthused, 'This guy's been writing for Don Ellis, and I want to do some of that, I really like it!' So Hank came in and he brought 'Chiapas,' and the only person in the band who could figure out how to make it sort of semi-swing in five was John Von Ohlen. The rest of us were fumbling, and we were trying to get through this thing, and it was just not happening. And I can remember Stan sitting at the piano, and he's going like, 'Oh God, this is terrible, what am I doing!' 'Cos he wanted to feature this music, but none of us were used to playing it, and in the beginning it was a real chore. Later on it became easier, but we still had to concentrate more on Hank Levy's stuff."

For Stan, Levy's charts provided a double-edged bonus. They offered a new direction in the vanguard of modern big-band innovation, and they also allowed him to introduce the rock beat—so necessary to keep the kids on-side—into the band's regular vocabulary under the guise of advanced jazz. It wasn't necessary to use rock rhythms in conjunction with exotic time signatures (Pete Rugolo certainly hadn't in 1947, nor Johnny Richards in 1962), but in keeping with the times, almost all of Levy's charts include a heavy rock beat as an integral part of the arrangement, which from my point of view often renders the music unpalatable. Worst "offenders" are the more basic pieces like "Hank's Opener" and "Blues Between and Betwixt," while the scores with stronger thematic foundations, such as "Chiapas" and "Ambivalence" work better for me, because the rock elements may be more constrained. Some Levy lovers no doubt will hold diametrically opposite and equally valid views to my own.

Hank himself told me, "My charts are a new concept in jazz that at present is controversial. At first the guys used to cringe when they saw me coming, because they knew my scores meant more rehearsals and confusion, but in general the acceptance by Stan and the band has been gratifying. As a writer I try to leave room in a chart for the personality of the band to come through. I believe that after some playing, a chart begins to settle, and the band will make some subtle changes, and I am very much in favor of this. Most of the time the final results are a great improvement over the original—the music comes alive, and it is more realistic. I must also say how much I respect Stan for even attempting a totally new concept at this point in his career. Not many leaders would make such a radical change, but Stan is an innovator. He respects new ideas, and if he believes in them he doesn't mind sticking his neck out. I owe a great debt of gratitude to the 'Old Man.'"

But Mike Vax's thoughtful insight into Levy's music indicates that though certainly different in the one respect, the Emperor's new clothes if not actually invisible, were in reality pretty threadbare: "Stan really believed that Hank's music was a good direction [to move in]. But once you got past the time signatures, Levy's charts weren't nearly so involved musically as the Holman things, or even Ken's and Willie's, because basically it was a theme that was set up, and then there were interludes and backgrounds and solos. Hank's music wasn't something that built in a classical manner, say like a Russo piece. There wasn't a theme that was built upon and changed around and things done with, like in classical music. It was basically like a bebop band. OK, let's play the head, now we're going to have a bunch of solos, we'll have some backgrounds, and then we'll replay the head or go out on a shout chorus. So I guess that's why some people thought Hank's music wasn't as meaningful as that of earlier bands, because it didn't build in the same way compositionally, and that's also the reason a lot of Hank's pieces sound rather alike. Holman's the master at compositional building. How many counter-melodies and different things go on in a Holman chart! That's almost classical composition, and of course, Bill Russo also. And Pete Rugolo—boy, is his stuff challenging! Levy's things were sort of fun, but I don't think I'd have been happy if that had become the focus of the book."

If Mike was ever-so-slightly circumspect in expressing his views, Willie Maiden had no such qualms. At 42, Maiden was set in his ways, a swinger very opposed to Levy's difficult scores. Many regard Willie as the more innovational writer of the two, including Kenton researcher Terry Vosbein: "Willie Maiden was by far the most experimental, creative composer from the '70s era. His arrangements frequently were the hardest swinging pieces in the book, as well as the most innovative."[7]

Noel Wedder concurred: "Willie Maiden made major contributions to the 1970s library, and thanks to his writing those bands roared. Willie wrote within the frame-work of the Kenton sound, yet artfully manipulated phrases so as to place his own personal signature on his charts. Granted Willie wasn't the snappiest dresser on the scene—his insistence on wearing argyle socks with his band uniform drove Stan into a tizzy—but none of us could ever figure out why Stan picked on him so much.

Maiden stretched the boundaries with his cleverly designed constructions, and although Stan sometimes felt the need to 'beat him up,' he had the utmost respect for Willie's compositional and soloing skills."[8]

As a final testimonial, Mike Vax played alongside Maiden and gave me his opinion: "Willie Maiden was a curmudgeon! Willie Maiden was great! I don't know if I ever saw him sober, but I never saw him drunk, and I certainly never saw him when he couldn't take care of things. The band probably liked his charts better than Stan, because they were more like Willie wrote for Maynard, in swing style. The definitive 1970s swing chart is 'A Little Minor Booze'—maybe one of the best swing charts ever written for the band, and that includes Holman and Niehaus. Willie did all his writing on the bus, and I asked him once how he wrote so fast. And he said, 'I don't write fast. When I put it down on score paper, the arrangement's done, I'm just transcribing what's in my head.' And there was never a mistake. If there ever was a mistake in a Willie Maiden chart, it was due to the copyist."

The third figure in the triumvirate was the writer I personally admired the most. "Ken Hanna," said Stan, "has been very important to the band. He's one of the greatest romantic writers ever, and a very talented composer. Ken went through a lot of difficult challenges. He wanted to sail round the world—he's quite a skipper—but got caught in a storm somewhere off the coast of Mexico, and the boat got beached. So Ken was in trouble in Mexico for quite a while around 1969, and became very depressed.

"So when Ken came by the office to say hello, I asked him what he was going to do, and he said he didn't know, and I told him, 'I know what you're going to do. You're going to start writing your butt off. There's manuscript paper in the back, and I want music brought in here as fast as you possibly can.' Ken was reluctant at first, but after a couple of weeks around the band he became very enthusiastic, and Ken is writing now better than he's ever written in his life. Some of the new things he's written for the band —'Tiare,' 'Lonely Windrose,' 'Bogota,' 'Fragments of a Portrait' —are just thrilling."[9]

A soft-spoken, kindly man, rather uncertain of his own abilities, Ken Hanna was the most gifted melodically of all the arrangers, and his writing closest to the Kenton tradition of changing tempos and varied tonal colors. "I enjoyed playing Hanna," said Mike Vax, "his music was so beautiful. But it could be a real endurance test for the trumpets, because he'd write these slow backgrounds, and we'd be playing long notes up high in harmon mutes. But I thought Ken's writing was fresh and modern, it didn't sound like what the band had played in the '40s and '50s. To me his writing was almost like romantic-period classical music. There was so much emotion in songs like 'Tiare' and 'What Are You Doing the Rest of Your Life.'"

As the time drew near for the first original Creative World recordings by the new band, Stan was still uncertain whether leaving the security of Capitol's womb had been a wise move. All his career he'd simply had to lead his men into the studio and be paid to concentrate on the music, with (generally) Lee Gillette on hand to offer advice. Then he simply waited until a 12-inch vinyl LP housed in a pretty cardboard cover emerged at the other end. Now the choice of music was his alone, but so was the responsibility of recording, mixing, mastering, packaging, promotion, and distribution, all of which had to be paid for out of his own pocket. Freedom came with a heavy price tag!

The cost and accountability weighed heavily, and Kenton became over-anxious that the first album under his own aegis should be successful. "Stan was pretty scared about leaving Capitol," Mike Vax explained, "and not too long before our first recording for Creative World, Stan became an ogre. Stan became a Buddy Rich! We all understood the reason, but we were scared to death. He was threatening to bring in Joe Romano for lead alto, and Buddy Childers or Al Porcino for lead trumpet, and Conte and Rosolino for the jazz, 'cos he was afraid that without any big names, the record wouldn't sell.

"And it was Willie Maiden, rest his soul, who pulled Stan over to one side, and said, 'Stan, if you bring in one ringer, you can't record any of my music. You've got a band with some of the best young kids in the country right here, and they've been playing for you every night on the road, and this band is swinging, you don't need any ringers. This will sell!' And that sort of knocked Stan back into reality. He wanted so much for this first Creative World album to really do something, and the funny thing is, of all the stuff issued, and all the years of Creative World, the biggest selling album is *Redlands*."

Stan chose to record during the August Clinic at Redlands University to avoid expensive studio costs, and being "live," as much music as needed could be recorded for free, with musicians paid recording fees only for those titles actually selected for release. As engineer, Stan chose Wally Heider, who had privately taped the band so often under similar conditions. And as Mike Vax says, "Redlands was just magic! We recorded over several evenings, with an audience mainly of students at the camp. We'd be dead tired, because we'd been teaching and rehearsing the students all day, but boy, the band would just come up for it every night."

Kenton played it safe, with only around half the music on the double-LP *Redlands* set being brand new. In fact, the earliest titles are from the Forties, with Stan's "Artistry in Rhythm" (1941) and "Peanut Vendor" (1947). Two rearranged "mellophonium" charts (played without the horns) are Bill Holman's vigorous ideas on "Tico Tico" and "Granada," while Dee Barton is represented by "MacArthur Park" and the iconic 1967 ballad "Here's That Rainy Day," which features mournful trombones at dirge-like tempo alternating with blistering trumpet crescendos. "Even the '70s ballads," noted Mike Vax, "had an even-eighth note sort of rock feel to them. They weren't like the older-time dance-band ballads, because we played them so slow. We used to open every night with 'Rainy Day,' and the funny thing was, the more we played it, the slower it became. Stan loved ballads, and when he found something like 'Rainy Day' he really milked it. By the time we recorded the song at Redlands, Jim Kartchner had started having 'chop' problems and was afraid of messing up at the concerts, which is why I took over the lead two days before we began recording the album. Kartchner was a great guy and a real mentor to me, and it was only later that we found out Jim had been suffering from a brain tumor that eventually killed him."

The most striking role on "Rainy Day" fell to the trombones, which played the authoritative opening voicings, and according to trombone alumnus Mike Suter, it is Dick Shearer who deserves most credit: "He's sometimes maligned as a caricature of all who preceded him, but that's a very unfair assessment. Dick changed the concept of how the trombones played as a section, *by playing softer*. The concentration needed to pull off the choir sound on 'Rainy Day' was enormous, and Dick wanted us all to play these things at the same volume—almost inaudibly, with no voice dominant. By changing the dynamic balance in this way, for much of the time the trombones functioned as the foundation upon which the rest of the band played, allowing for more varied and challenging voicings in the other instruments. And by 1974 the opening trombone soli on 'Rainy Day' was played at a true classical pianissimo (as soft as possible), so that the fortissimo climax (still no louder than it had ever been) was perceived by the audience as pure and utter thunder."[10]

Ken Hanna's "Tiare" had been played by the Neophonic in 1968, and it was Kenton who suggested Ken rescore it for the jazz band, without French horns, but still in concert format. "That's what Stan liked so much in later years," Hanna said, "the idea of making almost every tune a concert piece."[11] Ken's other Redlands chart was "Bon Homme Richard," a sophisticated showcase for the trombone solo styling of Dick Shearer. Hanna's titles were sometimes based on his love of the sea and sailing. "Bon Homme Richard" was the name of one of America's first eighteenth-century warships, though the musicians facetiously inter-preted the title as "Go Home, Richard"!

The verve, vivacity, and excitement of the unrestrained *Redlands* band blowing up a storm hit the moribund big-band jazz world in 1970 like a whirlwind of fresh air, earning a justified five-star *Down Beat* review. Exceptional virtues of the album were its variety and musicality—with a couple of exceptions. The Joe Ellis vocal tribute to Clark Terry's "Mum-bles" called "Terry Talk" was just a piece of fun, but the Beatles' "Hey Jude" was agonizingly awful. "Stan would often play a lighter piece of music that he hoped would have a broad appeal," noted Dennis Noday. "Maynard did the same. Both leaders were concerned with finances, and had to play pop tunes that attracted a younger audience. It's nothing new—bands have been doing it since bands began."[12] "'Hey Jude' was like a comedy show," opined Mike Vax. "Willie Maiden wound up con-ducting the piece, so to me this was just time to have some fun, and forget about anything serious. The problem was, we were doing it every single show, and a lot of the guys became real bored with it. It certainly wasn't my favorite."

Enthusiast Neal Finn was a 16-year-old student at Redlands in 1970, and attended all the concerts: "It was an interesting week. The band played several of the charts every night, including 'Hey Jude'—we were getting sick of it by Wednesday! One night they brought in Don Menza and Joe Romano to solo with the band. Menza blew on 'Jude' and we loved it, but it pissed off many of the guys in the band, and the takes were never used. The one that gave the most trouble was 'Chiapas.' Hank Levy conducted on it, but they just couldn't get a decent take. Hank had to stop them a couple of times. Later that night we heard the strains of the band emanating from the concert hall after midnight. Stan had called a rehearsal, and the band was hard at work on 'Chiapas.' The next night they got a usable take.

"The band recorded at Redlands in the 'V' formation, with mikes on every chair and two solo mikes in front of the band, which the soloists used only occasionally. Most of the solos were taken from within the section."[13] The "spread" formation Neal mentions was as controversial as the audio on the *Redlands* album, which underwent several mutations before its final digital transfer to CD in 1986. The musicians preferred the traditional stack or "three-tier" system, with sections on risers behind each other, because the wide spread (derisively termed "The Flying V" and "B-25") meant the end players were 20 yards or more apart, mak-ing it much more difficult for the guys to hear each other. "Very hard to play like that," commented Bobby Knight. "It looks great. Looked like the band was taking off. Stan was a great one for the dramatics."[14] And John Harner confirmed, "Most of the guys did NOT like it. The distance between everyone made it really hard for the band to swing. We lived for the small jazz clubs where we had to sit in a stack set-up. And when we did, we swung our ever-lovin' butts off!"[15] But Stan preferred the spread, because not only was it more exciting visually, it allowed the rhythm section to be brought down front, and he could lead from his seat at the piano. Originally the set-up as viewed by the audience looked thus:

| SAXES | TRUMPETS | | TROMBONES |
|---|---|---|---|
| PIANO | BASS | DRUMS | LATIN |

Despite the opposition from the band, Stan maintained this spread formation to the end, though in 1973 saxes and trombones switched sides, because the trombones were better equipped to play over the piano than the saxophones.

To a large (some might say disproportionate) extent, public perception of a band's ability has always been governed by its phonograph recordings, which can give a very distorted picture of its actual accomplishments. By contrast, the *Redlands* album was an accurate representation of a rejuvenated orchestra with a new fire in its belly, playing modern, meaningful jazz music. At the same time, it is necessary to keep things in perspective. The new writers could not sustain the mega-achievements of past composers like Rugolo, Russo, and Richards. Nor could the soloists match the unsurpassable skills of the likes of Conte, Konitz, and Kai. But this was 1970, with the desert that was now the landscape of popular music firmly established. For many it was achievement enough that a revitalized Kenton was back playing an uncompromising brand of concert-jazz, and had opened Creative World with a "hit" album that did much to restore Stan's position and prestige among both his devotees and the wider jazz fraternity.

# 26.

## Macumba!

(1971)

**"Without Stan the band couldn't exist** very long. Well, it's his music. You can play Stan Kenton music, but you can't really get that sound unless you've got him there. I mean, the arrangement will do it, but a great leader gives it that added dimension," said John Von Ohlen.[1]

The leader *makes* a band.

It is his name, his reputation that draws the people.

It is his presence that is a guarantee of quality.

It is his skill and personality that sells his music to the audience.

He is the focal point for public respect and admiration.

He is the *star*!

No one knew this better than Stan Kenton, who over the years had attracted more dedicated fans than any other leader in the business, and no one knew better than Stan the likely consequences if ill-health forced him off the road for any length of time. In 1947 the band had collapsed the same day he did, with consequential lost bookings and cancellation fees, and in 1971 with a burgeoning record company to take care of, the results would be even more catastrophic.

Clinton Roemer had been Stan's friend and confidante since he collected tickets as a youth at the Rendezvous in 1941. After war service, Clinton had become the band's chief copyist, and in 1970 he had relinquished a thriving music-copying business in order to become part of Stan's big adventure by taking charge of Creative World Records. Clint knew Kenton as well as anyone, and was aware that far from being a hypochondriac, Stan firmly believed in the power of "mind over matter," and that doctors should only be consulted as a last resort.

That time came after Kenton had experienced quite severe stomach pains for some months, which he originally believed would cure themselves, but in fact worsened to the extent that he finally consented to medical tests in March 1971. The results were inconclusive, but through-out March the "abdominal discomfort" continued, the fear being cancer, which only exploratory surgery could determine. An "extremely thor-ough" operation took place at UCLA Medical Center on April 7, and to everyone's relief proved entirely negative, but did nothing to solve the cause of Stan's distress. Kenton was quickly discharged, and after a brief convalescence returned to the band before the month was out.

That should have been the end of the matter, but in fact Stan's des-tiny was determined by that episode, insofar as it marked the beginning of a slow deterioration in his health that meant he would never be quite the same again, and resulted in his death before the end of the decade. For the immediate future, far from being cured, it was clear within days that Stan was seriously ill. After a hasty return flight to LA, Kenton was met off the plane by Roemer and rushed to UCLA, where an emergency operation was performed next day (May 5), "To correct bad drainage which was causing all sorts of side effects after the first operation."[2]

It remains unclear whether medics had bungled the original op, or if Stan's body had finally rebelled against a conspicuously unhealthy life-style. Or possibly a bit of both. This time Stan remained in the hospital three weeks, and was not released into his mother's care until May 26, with the warning that recovery was bound to be long and difficult, if only because of his very weakened state. His body weight was down some 28 pounds, and to top it all infection of the wound persisted, causing a feverish condition that seemed like it would never end. The irony was that this had all resulted from elective surgery that had proved unnecessary in the first place. The fever persisted for the best part of a month, and after that it was a slow haul until on July 17 Roemer could report: "Stan is looking good, feels good, and has picked up most of the weight he had lost. Looks definite he'll be rejoining the band on July 23."[3]

The miracle was that there was any band to return to! Between them, Shearer and Vax had kept the orchestra on the road for the best part of four months. While the Creative World publicity machine had consis-tently underplayed both the gravity of Stan's condition and the problems resulting from the leader's absence, the reality was far different. Disap-pointed audiences arrived expecting Kenton to be present, and had to be won over every night. And many promoters (some of the venues mob-controlled) often demanded a substantial reduction in the band's fee once they discovered Stan was absent. Mike Vax, the more abrasive of the two substitute leaders, was particularly good at convincing these sometimes unpleasant characters to pay what was owed!

In addition, even Kenton sometimes had problems maintaining discipline on long tours with 18 disparate, headstrong, road-weary young men fuelled by high levels of testosterone, and whose fractious behavior was bound to increase without Stan's authoritative presence. Both Vax and Shearer spoke to me at some length about this difficult period, and it is clear there was even some rivalry between the pair, insofar as both believed they were the one who had held the band together.

"I was doing all the announcing and taking care of business matters, and I was the one who had to confront the promoters and convince them to pay us what we were due," said Vax. "I ran myself ragged, lost a lot of sleep, and did everything I could to keep the band together during a very difficult time. Stan told me several times later on, he really appreciated what I must have gone through. I even had to threaten to fire guys on the band. I remember one time screaming at Mike Jamieson (who was one of my best friends) 'cos he said, 'You're just having too much fun with this, you're becoming an ass-hole because you're the leader.' But I knew if I let the guys do what they wanted we'd be late for the gig, and I'd say, 'This is what we're doing, and if you don't like it get off the bus—you're fired!' I went ape, and I did make decisions that weren't always popular. But in the years since, I'd say at least 10 guys who were on the '71 band have come up to me and said, 'Back then we thought your ego just went off the deep end, and you were enjoying being the big shot, but we've come to realize that if you hadn't acted the way you did the band would have folded.'"

Dick Shearer was equally emphatic: "I filled in for Stan, in that I took over and kept the band together. Contrary to some of the things that have been written, it was my responsibility to keep the band from falling apart, and it *was* hard. I think our biggest problems were with the promoters. Stan wasn't present and they wanted to cancel, but we had to convince them to go ahead, because we had to stay on the road. So we'd play a tune first, before telling the people Stan wasn't there. We'd do a happy number like 'Stompin' at the Savoy,' and then we'd make the announcement—and nobody left! One time we did a huge concert, there must have been 3,000 people, and we found two people had quit. And it was always that way. We had to keep on our toes, the band was under a tremendous amount of pressure, and we had to play night after night knowing people were going to be disappointed at Stan's absence, and try to get them to like us in spite of that."

The truth is, the short-fused Vax and the more conciliatory Shearer probably complemented each other without even realizing it, and together made an admirable team representing both sides of Kenton's own character. The pair remained close right up to the time of Shearer's death in 1997, Vax telling me, "Dick and I were like brothers, one of the nicest people I've ever known, a great trombonist and a great friend. Everybody liked Dick." Occasionally a nominal leader was hired so the band would have a "name" standing out front. Attempts to engage Maynard Ferguson didn't work out, and Charlie Barnet (May 28–30) proved to be neither use nor ornament. Don Ellis (June 19–26) did play one or two trumpet solos nightly, but overall the band was better off without hired "mercenaries." Several pianists were brought in as subs, principally Claude Sifferlen and Dan Haerle. No one could replace Stan, but they could certainly help the band "swing." John Von Ohlen relates: "While Stan was away we still had his sound. But I must say, the band was much different then. It was almost like a Woody Herman band some nights, or maybe we'd get into a Willie Maiden rehearsal band style thing. Then when Stan came back—boy, there we were blowing like crazy again. We'd forgotten what it was like to blow, until he starts waving his hands to signify that he wants more. We thought we were giving everything we had, but Stan likes to hear or feel that energy when we're giving our all and a little bit more as well."[4]

As Von Ohlen indicates, Kenton returned to the band in good spirits, convinced he would soon bounce back to his old self. But age and life-style were against him. Whether Stan made more than a token effort to follow his doctors' directions to eliminate smoking and drinking in favor of a healthy diet is doubtful. Certainly he did nothing to reduce his hectic routine on the road as also ordered. His immediate purpose was to bolster Creative World with a new recording, and *Redlands* had been so well received there seemed every reason to repeat the formula of that album.

Within three weeks of his return, Stan was set to record at Brigham Young University on August 13. The two-LP set was co-produced by Ken Hanna and sound engineer Bill Putnam, and featured new music by Levy, Hanna, and Maiden, with a couple of older arrangements by the perennial Bill Holman. "Malaga" was written in Bill's bravura Latin style which Stan liked so much, and Holman told me it "has a connection with 'Malaguena,' but it's not musical. Roger Schuller who was the band director at Millikin College in Illinois, called me one day in the Sixties and said he was in love with 'Malaguena,' and could I write a chart for his band that was somewhat like it. I found the town called Malaga on a map of Spain, so I got the title like that. Stan went to a concert that Schuller's band put on where he played 'Malaga,' and Stan liked it so much he got a copy from Roger, so it came to the Kenton band through the back way." "Malaga" certainly received greater recognition with Kenton than it would otherwise have gained, and Stan played it frequently until 1974, but even so Holman's original composition never achieved quite the iconic status of the even more spirited and instantly recognizable "Malaguena."

Bill's other chart, "Rhapsody in Blue," is a workmanlike but unremarkable arrangement for baritone sax (in this case Chuck Carter), originally written in 1965 for the first LA Neophonic concert. Unlike most solo features by Holman, Bill's strict adherence to the classical construction of the Gershwin composition allows for a virtuoso performance, but affords little opportunity for personal expression. (For a radically different approach to "Rhapsody," try Johnny Richards's 1949 arrangement for Charlie Barnet on Ajaz LP 225.)

Levy's pair of charts are farthest from the Kenton tradition. "Hank's Opener" in 7/4 features rock rhythms throughout, while "A Step Beyond" offers more variety with an almost menacing theme and a far-out Maiden baritone solo, before Gary Pack plays strong jazz trumpet over a heavy rock beat. Maiden's own contributions are pleasant enough without being especially memorable. "Love Story" is set to a gentle Latin rhythm and features an effective Davis/Maiden duet. It's hard to get a handle on the restless, choppy "Kaleidoscope," with its intricately interweaving patterns which never settle into a groove, while "April Fool" is an attractive ballad announced by Shearer's trombone, and originally written for the Maynard Ferguson sextet in 1955. It's Ken Hanna who is the real star of the *Brigham Young* album.

Beautiful as his ballads were, to typecast Hanna as only a romantic writer is to do him a disservice. In the words of arranger-leader Mark Masters, "A talented man, Ken's creativity was boundless, with a gift for writing music of great depth and perception."[5] Stan liked to open concerts with a standard ballad that people would recognize, and now Hanna's compelling "What Are You Doing the Rest of Your Life" joined Barton's "Here's That Rainy Day" and Maiden's "(We Almost Made It This Time) Didn't We" among that select group. But Ken's other contributions to *Brigham Young* are from an entirely different bag. This concert rendition of "Bogota" is unrecognizable from the version recorded by Hanna's dance band for Capitol's "Kenton Presents Jazz" label in 1955. Extended percussion solos owe as much to visual appeal as aural, but Ken's spirited vision of the Colombian capital is a joyous affair, by no means limited to Ramon Lopez's conga drums. "Bogota" remains the Seventies' most exciting addition to the Latin repertoire, and was featured by every edition of the band between 1970 and 1978.

Hanna's magnum opus was the 15-minute "Macumba Suite," inspired by a TV documentary depicting life in the Brazilian favelas (slums). The practice of Macumba (a form of black magic with religious overtones) is prevalent among the slum-dwellers as a release from the deprivations of their everyday lives. "Macumba" made a deep impression among the musicians, who were perhaps intuitively aware that much of the current music though pleasant enough, was less meaningful than the band's experimental music of previous decades.

Both Richard Torres and Dennis Noday expressed the opinion that "Macumba" was "important music," but it's Mike Vax who elaborates the point most lucidly: "'Macumba Suite' for us was almost like going back in time, because it was like we got to play something that was almost close to Graettinger. It was very hard to play and maybe even weirder than Graettinger, in that we were doing all these sound effects, like buzzing on mouthpieces, and we were supposed to be the shrieks and devils, and at one point I'm the virgin that gets sacrificed! When Ken first brought it in we were all very excited, because we felt like we were getting to play experimental music of the sort that Stan's been known for over the years. Because if you think about it, 'Macumba' was the only really extended work that we played during my time on the band. It was my link with the music I'd always associated with Stan Kenton."

While Mike relates the music with Graettinger, most comparisons are with Johnny Richards. Hanna himself confided in conversation that he believed Kenton considered "Macumba" inferior to John's writing, and had recorded it only as a favor to his chief arranger. In addition, whether subconsciously or as a deliberate tribute to Richards I didn't care to ask, the central movement "Omulu" is very similar both thematically and in title to "Oluo Anu" from Johnny's *Rites of Diablo*. Whatever, Hanna's work as recorded was at a distinct disadvantage as compared to Richards' studio albums. *Cuban Fire* had taken five sessions (up to 15 hours) to perfect, and *Adventures in Time* even longer, over six sessions. The complete "Macumba Suite" was recorded live during a single concert at the same time as some 14 other titles, with next to no opportunity for alternate takes or second chances, and without the bonus of extra percussion players. And instead of being issued on a single Ken Hanna "Macumba Suite" LP, it was buried inside a very mixed double-set *Brigham Young* album.

"Macumba" was premiered at the Newport Jazz Festival on July 2, 1971 (Jasmine Jasbox 1-3), according to Vax: "Because Stan especially wanted it to be played. The audience reaction was very good, though it was just too heavy to be played very often in public." In Stan's absence,

Mike introduced Hanna to conduct the orchestra, adding, "Because Ken writes charts which are so hard, the band has nicknamed the piece 'Bloody Massacre'!" Duke Ellington was congratulatory afterwards, commenting, "It's not right for you people to play that African music and do it so well."[6] But Dan Morgenstern in *Down Beat* was far less enthusiastic: "'Macumba Suite,' apparently intended to be the piece de resistance, was a stale rehash of all the worst 'progressive jazz' clichés of yore."[7] So much depends on one's own perspective and point of view!

I very much doubt whether anyone can genuinely evaluate the complexities of "Macumba" after just one hearing, and it certainly took me a while to get to grips with the piece. Unlike Richards' Suites, each part of which has a separate identity, and can be played on its own without loss, Hanna's less flexible Afro-Cuban work is descriptive, programmatic music, each segment dependent on the preceding part, and is played without interruption as a single composition. The plaintive "Twilight in the Favelas" depicts a melancholy picture of the pitiable inhabitants, while suspense mounts during "Procession to the Terreiro" where the ceremony of Macumba will take place. The most controversial section is the lengthy "Omulu," depicting the trance-like behavior of the frenzied participants during the sacrificial ritual. While Richards would typically develop his theme with statement, solos, and variations (in that order), Hanna substitutes clamor and commotion for compositional development, with far-out, atonal solo voices, particularly Torres (tenor sax) and Jamieson (trombone), and it is during this disorder that some listeners find "Macumba" less lyrically satisfying than the more clearly structured Richards' writing.

"Macumba" is a deep, intense creation, not really comparable with either Graettinger or Richards. The writing is indelibly Hanna, and the work probably the most meaningful, exploratory composition played during this final decade. Vax echoes my own belief when he says, "I thought 'Macumba Suite' was a very interesting, program-type piece, what with the sound effects and the thematic idea of black magic in South America. It may not be right up there with *Cuban Fire*, but I think it was a very worthwhile thing to record."[8]

Jay Saunders had joined the band for his longest assignment (after two short stints in the Sixties) in July 1971. Kenton was impressed by Jay's progress, and by November had decided he wanted him as lead trumpet, a decision seemingly endorsed by Stan's sounding-board Dick Shearer, who told me, "Jay not only had great technique, but that rare ability to bring the band to life. Jay's personality truly matched his musicianship. He was always fun to be around." The ticklish problem lay in convincing Mike Vax, who had held the position for over a year, that the change was in everyone's best interests including his own, because everyone knew that lead trumpet was "top gun" position in the band, and a move to the high trumpet chair was hardly promotion. That the switch was effected without rancor does credit to Kenton's powers of tact and diplomacy. "Stan talked to me and suggested it might be good to have Jay play the lead, and me do more of what Maynard did when he was on the band," said Mike, "and that is what happened. I wasn't sure about it at first, but I was really burning myself out trying to play lead and the high note chair as well as being road manager. So it worked out for the best, as did most decisions that Stan made."[9]

The difficulty of the Kenton book had always meant separation of the lead and high trumpet roles, and Vax enjoyed his position of road manager, with its sense of authority and proximity to Kenton: "On the Kenton band the road manager was a lot more important and influential than on most bands, because Stan didn't want to be involved in the business matters. He had Harold Plant in LA taking care of all his real finances, and all Stan wanted to do was the music, so the road manager became in a lot of ways like the assistant leader. I had to attend receptions, and I was Stan's 'out.' He'd give me 'the look' when he'd had enough, and then I would remind him he had an interview coming up, and we had to leave—I was the guy who would get him out of there." At the same time, whoever was band manager at the time, I'm sure Shearer also regarded himself as "assistant leader," and it's certainly true Dick remained close to Stan long after Mike had departed the scene. My impression was that Shearer operated subtly, with a low-key outward profile, but with great leverage in a quiet way behind the scenes.

In the same section as Vax, Ray Brown had succeeded Gary Pack as jazz trumpet during September, but truth to tell I doubt many fans recognized the difference. Solo competence had replaced individuality as the overriding factor, and it was the overall sound of the ensemble that determined the excellence of this Kenton orchestra. Despite all the problems with his health during 1971, Stan was slowly honing this band—his "instrument"—into one that would rival the great orchestras of the past, and which despite renewed health setbacks would reach its peak during the coming 18 months.

# 27.

# Height of Ecstasy

(1972–1973)

With the traumas of 1963 still clear in his mind, it must have been with some apprehension that Stan embarked in January 1972 on his first European tour of the decade. If so, he need not have worried. Stan's newly deserved jazz status had preceded him, and only in Germany were some poorly advertised dates ill-attended. In the UK in particular the band received a rapturous welcome, with appreciative applause extended to all the music, and with Kenton himself surrounded by a genuine, tangible warmth. Stan was now the elder statesman of Progressive Jazz, his place in history assured, yet still pressing ahead with a prestigious orchestra playing new, original music.

Reviews were generally ecstatic, reflecting the enthusiasm of the audiences, and commenting on the excitement the orchestra generated. Yet occasionally, doubts were raised that have persisted to this day about the soloists and the scores of the Seventies. "The soloists of yesteryear had distinctive styles resulting in uniqueness of sound, a feature sadly lacking today," observed Christopher Moreby in *Melody Maker*.[1] *Crescendo*'s Dave Doubble was equally outspoken: "Whilst the Kenton material of the late Forties and Fifties struck with its sheer daring, and generated years of controversy, the impact of a Kenton score and band now is only a legend. It is debatable whether this is because we have become accustomed to the dazzling sounds of the best American orchestras, or whether the music is, as I suspect, just the 'safe' side of the line."[2] In other words, the music was not adventurous enough.

Doubble's suggestion may be tested by a study of the double-LP set recorded by Decca (UK) at Croydon's Fairfield Hall in February 1972. The initial proposal to hold studio sessions had come from Decca, but this was subsequently changed to live recordings on the grounds of cost. Perhaps Kenton was not displeased by Decca's parsimony. Studio dates implied detailed planning using fresh material, and Stan undoubtedly preferred to retain his newer music for his own label. There is a big difference between the Decca/London album and those from 1970–72 on Creative World. CW's albums were in reality carefully organized recording sessions taped before invited audiences in an auditorium instead of a studio. Decca's album was made at a regular, public concert which just happened to be recorded, with no changes to the current, all-purpose repertoire.

Doubble's perception was that three decades on, the newer charts were no more innovational than those retained in the book from the 1940s, like "Opus in Pastels," "Interlude," and "Artistry in Percussion." True or not, practically every piece on the Decca album can be heard in superior performances on other recordings, and that is in no small part due to the controversial nature of the audio. Having rejected the Hammersmith Odeon as the recording venue because of its notoriously poor acoustics, Decca's engineers now found the Croydon hall no better. After the first house the play-back tapes sounded way off, partly due to poor initial mixing (16-track quadraphonic was being used), but also because Von Ohlen's drums swamped the orchestra. For the second concert a high baffle wall was built around John, in an effort to contain his sound.

By now "recording nerves" were prevalent, and while Kenton retained his affability, the guys knew he was in reality willing them to succeed. Particularly on newer pieces like "Ambivalence," mistakes were made, causing Stan to stop the band and start again. In addition, some of the featured soloists out front had played away from the recording mike, like Fred Carter's largely inaudible trombone on "23°N-82°W." Thanks to the good offices of Ken Hanna, Pete Venudor and myself were invited to attend the Decca studios next day to hear the first run-through of the tapes, and in those ideal conditions in quadraphonic sound, the band sounded well.

Hanna's job was to protect Stan's interests and assist Decca producer Ray Few to select the best cuts and ensure a well-rounded program. Not surprisingly, Few wanted to open with a fast-paced Kenton blockbuster, but Hanna pointed out that these days Stan preferred to start with something softer. Few was not easily convinced, but Hanna's quiet insistence won the day. Pencilled in to open the album was Ken's own ballad chart "What Are You Doing the Rest of Your Life."

I long ago learned that audio is a very subjective matter on which few agree. Drummer Elvin Jones was played "Artistry in Percussion" on a Blindfold Test and opined, "Tremendous arranging, and the quality of engineering on this one was beautiful. You can hear everything, the separation was beautiful, and the whole aspect of that recording was good: absolutely excellent. I liked it—6 stars out of 5!"[3]

Creative World's Clinton Roemer was of a different mind. On hearing the preview tapes, Roemer was distinctly unimpressed: "Frankly, I was appalled, the balance was terrible, and my recommendation to Stanley was that the whole project should be junked."[4] But Stan demurred, believing it would be unfair to Decca, and that the promotional aspect of having a new Kenton record on sale in the shops would benefit sales of all the band's recordings. Clint of course may have feared the opposite, and that the cut-price shop-sold album would cut into sales of the mail-order Creative World product for which, as general manager, he was ultimately responsible. So when, more likely through default than design, Decca reneged on its contractual promise to promote Creative World on the LP liner of the initial UK release, Roemer hit the roof. Never strong on diplomacy, he sent Few the strongest-worded wire he could devise. Stickers bearing the Creative World address were hastily applied, and in the States an entire column of the LP cover was devoted to publicizing the Creative World message. So perhaps in the end honor was salvaged all round!

Demand for quadraphonic recordings being zilch, Decca converted the tapes to stereo for public release, the final results being listenable but far from spectacular. It is an enigma that using the "primitive" equipment of the Forties, Capitol's technicians regularly captured the band in outstanding audio, whereas in the technologically "advanced" Seventies, recording engineers frequently struggled to reproduce the Kenton sound in acceptable quality. "The London album was very poor engineering and a poor recording," commented Ken Hanna. "We had to fight to get the sound as big as it should be, and we still didn't get anywhere close."[5]

Mike Vax agreed: "The main technical trouble was to do with Von Ohlen's bass drum. It sounded like it was in a wind-tunnel, a very boomy sound, and there's a lot of echo from the back of the hall. The sound is nowhere as good as the sound on some of the other live records, but the spirit of the band, and the rapport between the band and the audience is just phenomenal, and in that sense it's one of my favorite albums that I recorded with Stan. One of the titles we played that couldn't be released was 'Vax.' Ken Hanna and Hank Levy wrote that together to feature my trumpet, but it was a very hard thing to play, and not a great piece of music. I think they were trying to recreate Graettinger, because it was really far-out, and somehow just never seemed to work. I still have the chart, but it would need a lot of rewriting before it could be used."

An unusual hazard throughout that 1972 UK tour were power cuts resulting from low stocks of fuel caused by a coal-miners' strike. Blackouts would hit without warning at any time, though most larger venues had their own generators, and would quickly restore lighting. Less fortunate was Ronnie Scott's jazz club in Soho, London. As the band rocked into "Chiapas" the whole place was plunged into darkness, but to quote Kenton devotee Roy Holmes, "The band didn't miss a note. It was a case of Kenton by candlelight."[6]

It was bassist John Worster that Dick Shearer recalled in this context: "John is so strong he doesn't need an amp. When all the lights went out at Ronnie Scott's, John's bass went on without a change, he just sounded like he always did. John enjoyed his music very much, he lifted the band, and when he and Von Ohlen, both those guys, got roaring, they had nowhere to go. I don't care how tired you were, they made you feel great, and you had to play—they *made* you play!"

During this tour, plans were finalized to form a European division of Creative World in Holland. Instead of granting a franchise to an established firm, Stan preferred to enter into an agreement with Jan Levering, a Dutch businessman and fan of the music. For legal reasons, Capitol albums leased by Kenton still had to be imported from America, but to save on excise charges, Stan's own post-Capitol LPs were pressed in Holland from masters imported from the States. Running an office in Amsterdam (managed by Pete Venudor and his partner Ann), plus production of a regular European version of the Creative World booklet was high maintenance, and Levering soon found monies pouring out were far in excess of revenue coming in from LP sales. Unlike Kenton, Levering had no income from an orchestra to off-set his losses, and after a disastrous investment in a poorly attended German tour the following year, Creative World (Europe) collapsed in chaos, amid threats of legal action and much incrimination. No doubt, both Levering and Kenton suffered heavily financially from a project which, viewed in retrospect, might be seen as doomed from the start.

As soon as the band returned Stateside in mid-February 1972, John Von Ohlen quit. Stan opted for a drummer he considered a safe pair of hands, and Jerry (Lestock) McKenzie came in for his third major stint. Jerry's playing had not noticeably changed since 1961, but the music had, and whereas Von Ohlen had led the charge into different time signatures, McKenzie found them less comfortable to play. Jerry was a more conventional drummer, without the demonic intensity the more flamboyant Von Ohlen had displayed. Worster interpreted the difference as lack of commitment, and he resented the change.

McKenzie was a good drummer, but there is a common consent among the alumni that he found it difficult to adapt to the band's more contemporary stylings, something Jerry implied to me: "I really should tell you, I felt that a lot of the band did not enjoy playing the odd time-signatures, but wouldn't say anything about it. Those charts were interesting, and a challenge to play, but musically a lot of the time it wasn't really happening."[7] Things came to a head between Worster and McKenzie the day of the band's next recording at Butler University (June 22, 1972), as Worster relates: "Jerry McKenzie and I had a scene, and Jerry gave Stan his notice the same day. I think it had an effect, there's not a total positiveness about the rhythm section's playing on that album. I don't think Jerry knew for sure whether he wanted to return to drums full time, or go back home to be with his family as a policeman, or what. And all this indecision just kinda came to a head at that time."[8]

The double-LP recorded at Butler was the final act of the trilogy of Creative World live albums, and was made against Roemer's advice. Clinton had warned Stan that each two-LP set was selling only around half the copies of its immediate predecessor, and urged for a more musically selective single LP, but Stan still believed he could repeat the success of *Redlands*, and went ahead anyway. Actually, he increased the load by recording a double set with the Four Freshmen at the same time.

The Freshmen album was not a success. Of the 17 songs released, only seven were band arrangements (all but "Girl Talk" by Willie Maiden), the remainder being the quartet on their own. But the group was in far from top form that day, and re-recorded their solo performances at United Studios in Hollywood at a later date (and presumably at their own expense). Costs prohibited a similar exercise with the Kenton band, and the original recordings had to stand. The Pastels' song "After You" has a certain nostalgic glow, but the most unusual track, jocularly introduced as "Stan's favorite song," is the gag version of "She'll Be Coming Around the Mountain," complete with bizarre "progressive" orchestral introduction and out-of-tune piano effects from Kenton, not entirely incompatible with the Freshmen's own performance on this occasion!

Regarding the *Butler* album itself, Mike Vax told me: "Of the recordings I played on, musically I thought *Butler* was the weakest. There wasn't a lot of memorable music on that album." Had *Butler* been the first of the university recordings rather than the last, I feel the reaction would have been a lot more enthusiastic. Stan again featured charts from Hanna, Levy, and Maiden very similar to their previous work: good music, but without that special aura of challenge and innovation associated with Kenton at his best. There is perhaps a sense of déjà vu, and the soloists do not play with sufficient emotion or individualism to compensate.

Hanna's ballads are distinguished by their melodic themes, though even these all follow a similar pattern, with an introduction by Stan's impressionistic piano, a faster central section, and a subdued conclusion. "Fragments of a Portrait" was originally distinguished by a highly complex, orchestral opening, but this was soon discarded in favor of a simple but less effective piano statement. "Lonely Windrose" has no floral connection, but stems from Ken's love affair with boats, a windrose being a navigational instrument used at sea. As always, Hanna inspires his writing with a majestic quality befitting the Kenton persona, and makes effective use of the band's soloists, especially Shearer's distinctive trombone and Ray Brown's flugelhorn (probably the most inventive of the current soloists). In contrast to his mood pieces, Ken's "Beeline East" is more typical of Maiden's writing than Hanna's, a difficult "swing" chart that has nothing to do with the Orient, but was Ken's way of expressing the band's appreciation that they were heading towards New York.

Maiden's own weirdly exciting "Height of Ecstasy" at times resembles parts of Hanna's "Macumba" extravaganza, a far-out composition originally named the more explicit "Orgasm," a title Stan apparently found too outrageous (though he would quite happily announce the playing of "Sodomy" from *Hair*!). If "Ecstasy" is Maiden at his most explosive—sorry, expressive—everyone has their off-days, and Willie's came with his version of "Tenderly," written to feature bass trombone. Mike Wallace was a really nice guy, but Kenny Shroyer he was not, and this performance is really quite alarming. I remember colleague Pete Venudor and myself wondering whether it was actually meant to be humorous, and almost plucking up the courage to ask. Fortunately, caution won the day! Mike Suter later picked up the chart, and told me, "Wallace didn't like playing solos. It did distress him. He'd even shake a little, and he had to sit on a chair when they recorded 'Tenderly.' I took it over before Wallace left the band, and I'm sure Mike was relieved to be free of it."[9]

"St. James Infirmary," on the other hand, was intentionally comic, and had been really funny back in 1948 (and earlier) with the band heckling Stan as he attempted to sing the lyrics. But in 1972 the spontaneity is lacking, and it seems forced and contrived. The most amusing part is John Worster's "gay" sequence, regrettably brief on this take. (A much superior version is to be found on the Wally Heider-recorded *Magic CD 87*, from February 1973.) Nevertheless, while my own personal preference (put it down to age and ignorance if you're a fan!) would be to lose the Levy rock influences, *Butler* remains an impressive performance by a magnificent band at the peak of its powers. Probably room wasn't found for Al Davis' "The Duchess" because he wasn't one of the regular writers. This outstanding chart, a mood piece of great depth and intensity, builds to a soaring climax during which the orchestra seems about to implode upon itself. Granted that a major improviser like Shank or Mariano would have brought more empathy than Quin Davis was able to achieve, "The Duchess" (found in good audio on Tantara's *Revelations*) remains a model of unpredictability in an era of uniformity.

Jerry McKenzie worked out his notice until July 10, "And when Jerry left," said John Worster, "is when Peter Erskine came on the band."[10] Peter was a highly intelligent, articulate musician, who hid behind a straggly black beard in an attempt to disguise his youthful 18 years. Though Peter never quite achieved the same physical dominance as the Baron, his style was similar to that of Von Ohlen, and perfectly suited the current Kenton orchestra. He even warranted the Worster seal of approval!

Erskine had grown up enjoying the sounds of jazz, but "A couple of years before joining Stan, I began listening more and more to bands like Weather Report, Miles Davis, the Mahavishnu Orchestra and Herbie Hancock. So by the time I joined Stan I was fresh out of fusion school more than anything else; it was the electricity in the musical air of the times. Still, I had the Kenton Sound in my ears and in my blood. Stan always encouraged us to play our hearts out, and the tradition and the music of the band demanded as much. Whatever I lacked in finesse or subtlety, I probably made up for in enthusiasm and energy. Which might well define the musical current of the early 1970s.

"Hank's music was some of the most fun for me to play because of its rhythmic challenges and its backbeat-oriented nature, and I respected the work of Ken Hanna. The band LOVED to play the Lennie Niehaus and Bill Holman swingers whenever we could get away with it, and I also enjoyed playing any of the Johnny Richards and Dee Barton music. There was an excitement and a nobility to it. Believe it or not, I enjoyed this music much more than the 'contemporary' or 'fusion' stuff." Perhaps without realizing it, Erskine was confirming what a lot of others believed: the older scores were the better scores!

Within a month of joining, Erskine found himself in the recording studios for a two-LP set that certainly involved no "fusion." *National Anthems of the World* was one of those quirky projects that appealed to Stan's quixotic nature, but which was based on the entirely false premise that because UK fans had reacted so positively to the mellophonium arrangement of "God Save the Queen" (as opposed to the insipid versions they normally endured), they would similarly appreciate the Kenton interpretations of the anthems of some 37 other countries. Believe me, they would not! To the average Kentonite, "Lift High the Flag of Ghana" and "We Shall Love Burma Evermore" had all the appeal of a vacation in Outer Mongolia.

Since it was Bob Curnow who had scored the British anthem in 1963, Stan asked Bob to write the arrangements for this extended project. "The *National Anthems* album was a very curious thing for me, psychologically if you will," Curnow commented. "I had doubts about the validity of it at first, but as I worked on it during the spring and summer of 1972, I really began to believe that the concept made very good sense, and I enjoyed doing it."[11] Bob wrote the charts in batches, and delivered them to the band on the road, so that the musicians might become acquainted with at least some of the music before the recording dates in August.

Mike Vax remembered those sessions as "Very hard! We'd record all afternoon at Western Recorders in Hollywood, and then blow for five hours every night at Disneyland. Plus, the nature of that music was very different from anything else we played. Curnow had to stick to the formal tradition of the anthems, yet score them with a Kenton flavor, and the writing was phenomenal. A lot of the music we'd never seen before, so we'd play it down and talk it over with Bob, and then we'd make the recording. It's too bad the final album didn't sell well."

"That was a great band," Curnow reminisced, "and in the beginning the men went into the studio pretty much hating the project. But I had patterned the writing on the band's ballad tradition, with saxophone soli and so forth, and the guys gave me everything they had on those dates. We really worked at it together, and today many of them think it's their favorite album with me. It's always been Dick Shearer's and Jay Saunders' favorite, and Peter loved it. They just think the band never sounded better, which is kind of freaky, isn't it!"

The downside was that Kenton was already succumbing to illness during these sessions, which were really captained by conductor Curnow. Bob explains, "It was apparent that Stan was having a lot of difficulties. He was struggling physically. I don't think he even knew what was going on. He didn't play his solos well, so I had to go back into the studio and re-do a lot of his piano tracks." [12]

Many may agree that so much talent, enthusiasm, and money would have been better spent on more promising jazz material than national anthems. Kenton no doubt hoped the unusual project (for a jazz band) would generate prestige and international acclaim, and to this end albums were sent to the embassies of all the countries involved. Many sent gracious replies, but some were hostile, including Communist China who bitterly resented their anthem being featured on the same record as that of their arch-enemy Taiwan. Others, probably bewildered by the whole exercise, did not respond at all. Jazz fans naturally steered well clear, and sales, in Clinton Roemer's words, were "Very disappointing," to the extent that the music has never been even part-released in CD format. Stan himself made the final valediction when he commented, "The *National Anthems* album Bob wrote was great, though commercially it died—it was a terrible failure."[13]

Following the anthems experience, an amusing anecdote, possibly apocryphal, is that Willie Maiden was in danger of being lynched by his peers, when he playfully threatened to suggest to Kenton the idea for an album of nursery rhymes as the orchestra's next assignment. Apparently some of the guys were afraid Stan might actually approve of the concept!

On a much more serious note, following Kenton's incapacity at the *Anthems* sessions, disaster struck the very next day, September 1, 1972, when Stan was laid low with his second major illness in as many years, and which this time would keep him away from the band for the rest of the year. "Stan suffered an aneurism in the aorta," reported Clinton Roemer. "An aneurism occurs when pressure causes a balloon-like swelling in a blood vessel leading from the heart to the kidneys, and eventually to the legs. Without immediate medical attention the result is fatal, and we were fortunate Stanley was in the office at the time and we were able (against his most strenuous arguments) to call an ambulance. Had he been by himself, or out on the road, with his 'mind over matter' philosophy the outcome would have been quite different. As it was, another 15 minutes and we would have lost him here.

"We really thought we could keep this quiet, in order that the problems in keeping the band moving could be kept to a minimum. But the issue was compounded by June Christy, who happened to be in the office at the time waiting for an appointment with Stanley. Although she never did see him, and we managed to get her out before the ambulance arrived, there was no way to hide from her the fact that something was drastically wrong. June rushed home, got on the phone, and began calling all those whom she was sure Stanley would want to know. By the next day we were getting calls galore, the stories ranging from heart attack, through open heart surgery, stroke, incurable cancer, etc. etc. You name it, we got it.

"Once the blood vessel was repaired, the initial estimate was for two weeks in hospital and another two weeks at home for recovery, but as in 1971, complications set in. A tracheotomy had to be performed, periodically his lungs had to be pumped out, and he damn near got pneumonia. After all that, Stanley slowly began to regain his strength, but as the doctors kept explaining to him, this wasn't just major surgery, but major-major surgery." Finally, Roemer was able to pick Stan up from the hospital on October 7, for protracted convalescence at his mother's home in Torrance, but it wasn't until mid-November Clint was able to report that "Stanley has been coming into the office these past few days. He is still quite weak and tires rapidly, but is improving daily. He is impatient to rejoin the band, but of course, this depends on future progress."[14] In actual fact, Stan remained out until after the Christmas vacation, rejoining December 29, 1972.

Meanwhile, once again the band kept going for the full four months. This time there was no friction between Vax and the guys, because Mike had already given his notice, which he did not rescind, and left on September 4. Some maintain Vax was "eased out" by Stan, but Mike himself is adamant he quit of his own choosing, and he should know. As well as promoting the Kenton style of music with his own band, no one has shown more unswerving loyalty to Stan's memory over the years than Mike Vax. In 1972 the trumpet section was weakened by his loss, especially as Jay Saunders had also left a couple of days previously. But otherwise the personnel remained remarkably stable, with Dennis Noday taking over as trumpet lead.

The Monterey Jazz Festival on September 15 was the occasion on which promoter Jim Lyons wanted a star name to appear with the band in Kenton's absence, and got Buddy Rich to sit in on a couple of numbers, including "A Little Minor Booze" (Dynaflow 2006-1). Harvey Siders wrote, "Was Stan missed? Does Duke Ellington love us madly? The band is a good one: tight, well-disciplined, alert, and dedicated to swinging. The section work is clean, the solo work good but not spectacular, and the charts are typically Kentonian . . . I missed Kenton, but Buddy Rich's musical personality helped to compensate—Buddy's solo on 'Intermission Riff' was brilliant."[15]

Dick Shearer was officially the band's assistant leader, but as in 1971 he assumed a backstage position, and it was Ken Hanna who became principal conductor and emcee. "I don't know why Dick did not take on more of an interactive role with the audience," Peter Erskine told me, adding interpretively, "Maybe he was shy." According to Dick himself, "Ken Hanna acted as front man, but I called the tunes, and the hard things like 'Malaga' and 'Malaguena' I always conducted. Very few dates were cancelled by the promoters, and the guys didn't get undisciplined at all. I had to holler now and then, but mainly everybody just took care of business. We stretched out sometimes on numbers like 'The

Blues Story' and 'Reuben's Blues,' and we were lucky to have Nat Pierce on piano. I told him what had to be done, and he did it."

Others saw the Pierce influence very differently. With his strong Herman connections, Nat was a highly controversial choice, and as well as bringing in some of his own charts, he changed the character of the swing numbers completely. The band swung in a very non-Kenton way, and the guys loved it. Mike Vax tells the story of how in 1971 he had called Stan in the hospital, to be greeted with the words, "Don't think I don't know what you and Shearer are trying to do with my band! I know how you're starting concerts with 'Stompin' at the Savoy,' trying to turn my band into a swing band."[16] But Stan had appreciated the reasoning behind this program change, and after a pregnant pause had laughed, never mentioning the matter again.

This time was different. Seemingly with Shearer's approval, Pierce was turning the band into a clone of the Herman Herd. It was Stan's biggest nightmare that the critics would actually prefer a swinging, Kenton-less orchestra to the restraints imposed on the band when he was present. When he heard tapes of current concerts, Stan blew his top. Nat Pierce was summarily dismissed, and while "Savoy" was permitted to remain concert-opener in order to catch people's attention in a happy way, otherwise the 1972 programs stayed very similar to the norm.

In Worster's words, "Sure, with Pierce the band got a little too loose at times. So then we called in Alan Pasqua, a marvellous pianist, but great as he was, Alan played a little bit further out than the band did, so that too was kind of awkward. The band will never sound the same without the Old Man out front!"[17] In Peter Erskine's recall, "That was not a good time. Piano players changed, and I remember a general mood of angst and a lot of chaos, with changed bookings and many people working very hard both in the office as well as the 'front of the bus' to ensure that the band would be able to continue to work."

Clinton Roemer's task at the office was actually now considerably less stressful since the appointment of Audree Coke (nee Audrey Willsey) as publicity manager. "Some months back," wrote Roemer, "I thought of Audree for a PR role, discussed it with Stan, and we both agreed she was the right person for the job. I have known her for over 35 years, we were at school together in Santa Ana, and Stanley has known her since 1941 when she showed up at Balboa as Jim Lyons' date—they were later married and quite naturally, later divorced. Audree has been in public relations all her life, working in LA, New York, and Hawaii. Stanley and I both talked with her, she got an immediate grasp and understanding of the situation, and her initial presentation was very imaginative. We wound up hiring her to work full time for Creative World."[18]

Creative World personnel in general came and went, sometimes seemingly as if caught in a revolving door, but Audree was there to stay. She would eventually take over the running of the entire Creative World organization, as well as assuming a personal role in Stan's affections. Stylish, sharp, and Hollywood-smart, Audree was always very helpful to me, though her eventual position of power would generate considerable criticisms from some of the alumni. The normally outspoken John Worster chose his words carefully in January 1976 when he opined, "Audree Coke set out to make herself indispensable to Kenton, and she succeeded."

Inevitably the band had been marking time during Stan's absence. As he returned at year's end, everyone hoped this latest misfortune would see an end to his ill-health, but that was not to be. At the comparatively early age of 60, but with his body weakened by two major operations in as many years, from now on Stanley would experience increasing fatigue and medical complications, aggravated by the constant rigors of life on the road. More than ever, he would find it increasingly difficult to fight the trend towards fusion that was threatening to engulf jazz music, as well as to summon the energy and stamina necessary to turn a good band into a great one: though with his present organization still intact, that was not an immediate problem.

Wally Heider came to Britain in February 1973, bringing with him all the bulky equipment required to record the band during its upcoming UK tour. Just why Wally chose to record in England rather than his native America is unclear, unless it was to utilize the resources of two willing English assistants, Arnie Chadwick and Reg Wing. Chadwick in particular poured all his prodigious energies into the project, rushing around each night like a headless chicken, fixing here, repairing there, ensuring Heider the maximum potential to record the band in the best possible circumstances. The technically spectacular results would prove to be Wally's last live recordings of the band, fortunately caught in depth at the peak of its power over 16 nights of non-stop concerts.

The orchestra itself brought with it one of the few truly great soloists of the decade. To quote Ken Hanna, "I think this band is playing even better, and I'm particularly proud of John Park. He was my choice and recommendation. I'm totally in love with his playing, and I know Stan is also."[19] Park had joined the band on January 5, 1973, and came from the Springfield, Missouri, area of the Ozark Mountains, where he'd been playing tenor saxophone with a local trio while doubling as a car

salesman. Kenton's was his first job with a band of international reputation, and as Park often said, "I'm a jazz tenor player making his living
as a lead altoist."[20]

An extended version of Kenton's original 1951 arrangement of
"Street of Dreams" was built around John's lyrical ballad style, and
most nights not only the audience but the band would applaud at
the close—a rare tribute to Park's skill and good taste. Dick Shearer
agreed: "I think John's one of the most fantastic alto players I've ever
heard. He was always so inventive, a very melodic player. No matter
how far out John would go he'd always resolve. Everyone respected
John, he was an older player, very involved in his music—he wanted
perfection every time." At the same time, while not disputing for one
moment that Park was a very talented improviser, and a fluent, creative player, it is also fair comment to point out that John stood out in
an age of solo anonymity. In direct competition with some of the other
alto greats who had passed through the band—the likes of Bud Shank,
Lee Konitz and Charlie Mariano—John might well have found himself
spoken of in slightly less deferential tones.

While Park rightly garnered the solo glory, Bob Winiker and Paul
Adamson were both under-rated, extrovert trumpet players; Shearer,
Harvey Coonin, and Lloyd Spoon were all capable of cutting the trombone spots; Torres and Maiden remained in the sax section; and Worster, Erskine, and Lopez combined to achieve a stimulating, integrated
rhythm foundation. In short, this band was as good as the Seventies
were going to get, as illustrated by the several "unofficial" CDs culled
from the Heider tapes, and the Creative World LP titled *Birthday in Britain*
(so-called because Stan's official birthday had occurred at Nottingham
on February 19).

However, apart from the opening bars of "Happy Birthday to You,"
all eight tracks on the LP (itself highlighted by the colorful cover design
of the Union Jack flag and a cartoonish Guardsman in full uniform)
were recorded the last night of the tour (February 23) at Croydon's Fairfield Hall, where Heider achieved a sound far superior to that obtained
by Decca's engineers a year earlier. To celebrate Stan's sixty-first, Wally
had commissioned Bill Holman to devise a full-length concert arrangement of the traditional "Happy Birthday" song, which the band had
allegedly rehearsed in Kenton's absence in order to surprise him on the
night. Willis achieved the near-impossible with a swinging orchestration
that extended the piece far beyond the simplicity of the original tune,
during which Bob Winiker shoots in with a crackling solo all the better
for its brevity and relevance, with Harvey Coonin not far short of the

same standard. Always conducted by Dick Shearer, "Happy Birthday" remained in the book for four years, well into 1976.

Holman's other contribution is "The Daily Dance," so-named, Bill said, because of the performance he and Stan went through every time he submitted a new score. It's an exciting work, with a substantial, memorable theme, though with a seven-minute playing time too much extended repetition. In the opinion of future drummer Gary Hobbs, "'Daily Dance' was the fastest of all the charts we played during my years on the band. It was very hard to play the time and make the figures at that tempo, but the band played the doodoo out of it."[21]

Two of the album's most rewarding charts are from the inventive pen of Willie Maiden, in John Worster's opinion "A master writer, one of the greats!" Worster was featured on the string bass specialty "For Better and for Worster," during which playful reed figures punctuate John's expressive skills to good effect. "Willie and I talked about the kind of score I'd like," said John, "and I told him a happy, light, fun chart. Willie always tried to make feature charts what the player wanted, but after that I didn't get to see it in progress, only when it was ready."[22] "No Harmful Slide Effects" doesn't feature trombones particularly, but is one of those well-structured, swinging pieces the band loved to play, with authoritative Torres tenor. Stan even allowed Maiden to retain his pun-ridden titles, probably because he couldn't suggest anything better!

Hank Levy's "Ambivalence" was previously recorded at Croydon for Decca, but this is the definitive version, with the band polished and assured, and the featured John Park in peak form. The title refers to the two conflicting moods, the mysterious, brooding introduction contrasting with the free-style, up-tempo alto improvisations that follow in lieu of compositional development. There is symmetry in the short finale, and a pleasing lack of rock rhythms, which cannot be said for Hank's "Blues, Between and Betwixt"; what this facile crowd-pleaser lacks in good taste, it makes up for with standard, elementary clichés.

Of the several "unauthorized" CDs from this tour, the best is surely the two-CD Status set recorded in the Grand Ballroom of London's swish Park Lane Hilton Hotel on February 21. The occasion was a private party open only to the guests of Wally Heider, and the band responded to the convivial mood with an evening of relaxed, confident music. Stan was in eloquent form, giving as good as he got in friendly banter with the likes of Marion Ryan (a popular English singer, and the wife of promoter Harold Davison). No one could have guessed from Stan's demeanor that (as he confided) he actually disliked these private occasions, and much preferred public concerts open to his regular fans. The concert benefits from several dance titles flown over at Wally's special request, including Bill Fritz' "Shadow of Your Smile" and Willie Maiden's bossa nova take on "Watch What Happens." (Unfortunately for Wally, who had hoped to announce his engagement that evening, nothing did happen, as his proposal was rejected.)

Stan had so often repeated his mantra that his present band was his best, he may even have come to believe it himself. Guys in the band knew better, and there was general consent among a group when (in Kenton's absence!) Mike Wallace opined that the current band couldn't begin to compare with some of the earlier orchestras. Mike considered the '52–'53 band the best ever, and in his view none of the present members would have been good enough, or disciplined enough, to have earned a place in that band.

This opinion extended to the writers. Bill Fritz told me, "A majority opinion of the band on current arrangers as of August 1973 would be: 'Ken Hanna is an old, lost cause. Hank Levy is a pain in the ass—after the time signatures there is little of musical value. Stan doesn't play enough Willie Maiden or Ray Brown.' But remember—the '53 band probably said they played too much Russo and not enough Holman, so time must be the judge."[23] (Ray Brown, jazz trumpet for a year in 1971 to 1972, contributed a number of charts, including "Mi Burrito" and "Neverbird," but seemingly Stan didn't fancy his work because none was ever commercially recorded.)

Off-stage while on tour, Kenton lived in a closeted world where music seemed almost the only topic of conversation. Stan was a STAR, and generally people he met treated him with the respect befitting a celebrity. (Outsiders who failed to conform experienced an unforgettable, icy glare and the big freeze.) I recall one surreal group meeting with Stan in someone's hotel room, lasting perhaps a couple of hours (I think Ib Glindemann was present), during which plans were discussed to release recordings by the Danish Radio Big Band on Creative World. Amongst the growing excitement and enthusiasm, no one cared to come down to earth sufficiently to raise such mundane matters as the fact the recordings belonged to Danish Radio, not to conductor Glindemann, or that none of the musicians involved had been paid recording fees. Perhaps it was assumed Kenton would foot all the bills, when in fact he could barely afford to record his own orchestra. Whatever, everyone seemed to believe it was a done deal, and went away contented—after which the matter was presumably promptly forgotten. Certainly, Creative World never issued any recordings by the Danish Radio Big Band.

A trivial anecdote illustrates the deference to which Kenton was accustomed. After one concert, a group close to Stan gathered for a late-night drink, and addressing Kenton, Pete Venudor made the mistake of beginning a sentence, "Back in 1948 when you were big . . . " The unanimous gasps of disbelief as all eyes turned on Pete with horror at this implication Stan was no longer "big," caused Venudor (who had to think in Dutch but speak in English) to pause, as he struggled to realize his error and redeem himself. In fact, of course, Pete was correct. In '48 Kenton had been top of the big bands and a huge money-spinner, whereas in 1973 he was an anachronism, struggling to survive in a hostile world. Fortunately Stan was fond of Venudor, and smilingly rescued him with words of reassurance, and everyone relaxed.

Though within the confines of the bus Mike Suter assures me debate was far more open and controversial, my impression as an "outsider" (albeit a lucky one) was that most people around Stan told him what they believed he wanted to hear. There was a blinkered acceptance that every piece of music played was a masterwork, and anyone who failed to appreciate "Stan Kenton" simply lacked the necessary perception and sophistication. Certainly a more generous, honest and sensitive man than many of his peers, Kenton still required his ego massaged. Often surrounded by sycophants, Stan was to an extent cocooned from the inhospitable world outside, and when that happens over many years even the smallest negativity becomes magnified. Most influential of all the voices in Kenton's ear was Stan's long-time employee and drinking partner Dick Shearer.

Shearer himself was something of an enigma. Excessively deferential in Kenton's company whenever I was around, Dick was also desperately shy in public: while he was leading the band during Stan's illnesses, he had gotten Vax or Hanna to announce at concerts. At the same time, Shearer had definite views, and was the guiding force in leading the politics that went on incessantly among the insiders who bent Kenton's ear. In 1973, the prime target was Creative World's Clinton Roemer.

Strong-willed, plain-spoken and stubborn, Roemer differed from most Kenton employees and was nobody's yes-man. He had guided Stan's record label with skill and determination since its inception in 1970, and had consistently sought to place the business on a firm financial footing. Kenton himself being a likewise strong-minded man (and Clinton's boss!) it was probably inevitable that the pair would eventually clash.

Kenton thrived on taking chances, whereas Roemer was strongly opposed to what he saw as over-expansion of a record label still far from turning a profit. To some, Roemer seemed timid and over-cautious, and a handicap to rapid growth. Those around Kenton were urging him to make a change, and while in my presence Stan simply smiled and said nothing, events proved he was persuaded. As soon as the band arrived back in the States on March 25, Roemer was summarily sacked. As Clinton told it, "I met Stan at the LA airport, and over one drink at the bar, our entire association came to an end. The only reason I was given was that I didn't get along with people—partially true I'll admit, if you include all the 'ass-kissers' that Stanley is inclined to hire."[24]

It was one of the most disastrous decisions Kenton ever made, and would have an immediate and deleterious impact on the band's music. Without Roemer's guiding hand, Creative World's already precarious financial position plunged into disaster mode. The label was left rudderless, and neither of Clinton's short-lived immediate successors, Chuck Anderson and Dennis Justice (both ex band-bus drivers) were able to steady the tiller. By the summer of 1973 the label was in crisis, until Stan enlisted the support of Bob Curnow to offer fresh hope, and most definitely a new direction for the band's music. Bob was charged to guide Creative World Records back on an even keel, and to head the orchestra's arranging staff, not that there was a lot left to head. Willie Maiden had already quit the band in May, and Hanna was going through a dry spell. Levy's writing was probably more to Curnow's taste, but Hank's main job had always been teaching at Towson State College (now Towson University), with writing for Stan an enjoyable side-line.

Major changes in the band's style in the past had often come after a break (as between the Artistry and Progressive Jazz bands), with a change in name-tags, or with new instrumentation (the Innovations' strings, or the Mellophonium Orchestra). In 1973 the switch was unannounced and therefore less distinct, but still very real. The "Curnow band" was a very different proposition, really a new start, causing Mike Vax to opine, "What really gets me is that a lot of people just consider the Seventies' bands as a single entity, so that the emphasis on rock music which came later becomes lumped in with the early '70s band. I wasn't a big fan of the rock influence. I understood why Stan did it, but it's not my favorite music, which is why it's so frustrating to me when the earlier band gets associated with that."

# 28.

## Kenton Goes Rock

### (1973–1974)

Bob Curnow was 31 when he joined the Kenton organization, ten years older than his first stint with the mellophonium orchestra in 1963, but still a young man. He was certainly young enough to have been influenced by the fusion music that had actually worked both ways, with a few of the rock bands like Chicago and Blood, Sweat and Tears injecting a little from the jazz idiom into their arrangements. Much as Bob might have preferred to get straight into writing for the band himself, his first, full-time task was to ensure the survival of Creative World Records.

At the same time, Bob's impossible instructions from Stan were to expand the label by recording other artists, so that CW was not dependent solely upon the Kenton orchestra. But Curnow had neither the experience, nor (more importantly) the finances to groom the better pop artists who helped subsidize the jazz and classical catalogs of the major companies; and popular jazz stars were not only expensive, but generally contracted to other labels. Curnow had little option but to feature new jazz talent, but if anything sells slower than established jazz groups it is little-known names, and after some few releases by such as Les Hooper and John Von Ohlen, this part of the project was abandoned, leaving Bob free to concentrate on obtaining a "hit" record by Kenton himself.

In consultation with Curnow, Stan was persuaded this could best be achieved through "fusion," a combination of jazz that he hoped would retain the regular fans, and rock to involve the younger generation. In other words, the music was to be dumbed down. Stan had little choice if Creative World was to remain operational, but at the same time his musical instincts resisted the change, so that he was never 100% committed. To live in two musical worlds at the same time is a precarious existence, but some artists had achieved the near-impossible, Miles Davis being the prime example.

Over the summer of 1973 the character of the band changed considerably. As Stan looked to implement his new policy, he commissioned Gene Roland to come up with a rock-oriented album while retaining the Kenton sound, seemingly overlooking (or possibly forgetting) Gene's previous failure at the same task. Although he traveled with the band for three months, Roland's glory days were long behind him, and he was no more successful in 1973 than he had been in 1966. Most of Gene's output was unceremoniously dumped, and only two titles made it onto the new album now coming together. "Those Roland compositions were not up to his earlier standard," observed Bob Curnow, "and that's why you don't hear them any more." But whether "Blue Gene" and "Country Cousin" were any worse than the other titles on *7.5 on the Richter Scale* is a matter of opinion. Hank Levy hit "rock" bottom with "Down and Dirty," and even Hanna's band vocal version of "It's Not Easy Bein' Green" is embarrassingly bad. The two big "hits" were both melodically dire film themes: Curnow's "Live and Let Die" and Dale Devoe's adaption of "2001" retitled "2002—Zarathustrevisited" for copyright reasons.

*7.5 on the Richter Scale* was produced by Bob Curnow and largely conducted by Hank Levy, with seemingly minimum Kenton participation. "The album was done in a very hurried fashion in one of Wally Heider's small studios," commented Curnow. "It was a low-budget deal, and a lot of the music had never been played before the session, and that band was not at its strongest sight-reading. The change in style arose out of the Company's poor financial state—we were looking for something that would sell."

And set amongst all this dross was a single jewel that shone like a gem, an oasis in a desert wasteland. Marty Paich's vision of "Body and Soul" was orchestrated in the same classical style as his previous "My Old Flame," an almost cruel reminder in this setting of how fine the music of Stan Kenton could sound. "A beautifully crafted work of art," opined Mike Suter. "When 100 years down the road Kenton is rediscovered, 'Body and Soul' will be the representative of the last decade. It's fitting!"[1]

There's a wicked irony in the fact Stan had set up Creative World in order to enjoy the freedom to record the music he wanted, and now economics were forcing him to compromise just as he had at Capitol. Although Stan's lack of judgment (the sacking of Clinton Roemer in the States, and the floundering Dutch subsidary in which he held a 51% stake) was partly to blame, the band was now very dependent on university and college bookings. Every artist likes to bask in audience approval, and the rock charts created more enthusiasm from the kids than "Body and Soul" ever did. As final proof (if any were needed) that junk always sells better than serious music, Audree Coke confirmed: "*7.5 on the Richter Scale* was an attempt to appeal to a younger audience, and is turning out to be the biggest seller we have ever had."[2]

Like most of us, Stan Kenton frequently changed his mind. In 1948 he had told *Down Beat* that strings produced a thrilling sound, but were definitely not for his band. In 1950 he had fronted the Innovations Orchestra, featuring a full 16-piece string section. The following quotes to me are also set two years apart:

> Stan Kenton, February 22, 1973: "I've always felt that jazz is jazz and rock is rock, and I never felt that we should get into playing rock music."
>
> Stan Kenton, February 6, 1975: "Rock rhythms are more exciting than the old-fashioned jazz rhythms. Rock rhythms have become fused with jazz, they're part of today's music, and there's no going back now."

But again like most of us, Kenton sometimes said things that were expedient rather than what he really believed. So was it a case that Stan had genuinely changed his mind, or more that he was making the best of a bad job? Lillian Arganian asked Hank Levy, who had already done more than anyone to introduce rock into the band, for his opinion. "He didn't believe in it that much," said Hank.[3]

Trombone player Howard Hedges also told the story that whenever Levy submitted a chart that had "rock feel" written on it, Stan would rehearse the music and say he liked it, but would subsequently pass. Hank discovered that if he retitled the SAME CHART and inserted "Latin feel" instead, the music would make it into the book.[4]

Some of the young musicians naturally liked the rock influence more than others. In Peter Erskine's view, "A good number of Hank's charts did employ 'backbeats.' Hank specified 'Jazz/Rock' and we played it as such, for better or worse—but the man's writing should not be indicted. Hank Levy was a lovely gentleman, and I know that Stan cherished their musical association."[5]

A different view of Levy's music (and much closer to my own) was offered by Mike Suter: "Hank was a wonderful man. I loved him dearly—and loved is the word I have chosen after careful consideration. He was totally committed to jazz and jazz education. But he was NOT a good composer or arranger. His gimmick was time charts. For Kenton he stuck pretty much with 5/4 and 7/4 time signatures, probably at Kenton's request. But I've played many of his more 'adventurous' pieces, and they all share the same deficiencies as those he wrote for Kenton: they're predictable, forced, harmonically weak, and unimaginative. I hate to say all this because he was such a great guy. So incredibly supportive. But he was a college-level writer at best. That Kenton recorded so much of his music reflects just how far the band had declined in those last years."

At best, Stan's commitment to rock was half-hearted. "For one thing," observes Suter, "rock is a rhythm-based music led by the guitar, and the Kenton band had only three full-time rhythm players—drums, bass, and Latin percussion—but no guitar and only an occasional piano. Therefore any true rock was impossible. Both Stan and Hank were from an older generation, and neither had any real understanding of rock. In my opinion, Bob Curnow proved best at melding rock and Kenton."[6]

The prospect of Stan Kenton playing rock piano was as preposterous as Benny Goodman trying to switch from swing to bop 25 years earlier, so Hank Levy and Dick Shearer tried to convince Stan to hire a younger pianist who would add the textures of electronic keyboards to the band. As Mike Suter recalls, "Stan was playing less and less, so many of the jazz players were looking for more support, and Hank had a kid he was high on who played synthesizer. Hank and Dick hatched the idea that this kid should join the band and play keyboard parts—synthesized piano on traditional tunes and more modern sounds on our version of rock—when Stan chose not to play.

"According to Dick, Stan wouldn't entertain the idea. Dismissed it out of hand. The fans would never accept another piano player. Stan simply said 'No,' and that was it. Hank kept on to Stan, but Dick dropped out after the first time Stan said 'no.' Dick recognized the tone and stopped. He knew it was pointless —and maybe even dangerous—to continue. In my view and Dick's, the idea had merit. Synthesized sounds would have helped the inadequacies of what Hank wrote and called rock, but would have aided Curnow's music the most, because Bob was the best at reshaping music from the rock idiom to fit Stan's style. I don't remember Dick mentioning whether Curnow played any part in the effort to add a keyboard player. Personally, I'd bet Bob stayed out of it—no evidence, just a gut feeling."[7]

Curnow confirmed he had no knowledge of the move at all, adding, "I never felt the necessity for a second pianist, and even if I had felt the need for electronic keys of some kind, I would NEVER have mentioned it to Stan. One didn't 'discuss' things with Stan very often. You made your (hopefully) well-thought-out suggestion, and then waited for his decision."[8]

So (thankfully in my opinion—and that's phrasing it mildly!), the Kenton band never became a rock band, though it went far enough to alienate some older fans, but not far enough to really enthuse the rock generation. At concerts, the contemporary music like "2002" and "Live and Let Die" was interspersed with more traditional Kenton music, resulting in the very real danger that in trying to please everyone, you end up fully pleasing no one. Stan returned for an extensive tour of Europe in September 1973, its relative failure (especially in Germany) being attributed to "over-exposure"—this was the second visit to England in the same year—rather than a failure to connect with its core audience.

As often happened after an overseas tour, personnel changes took place once the band returned Stateside, among them John Park, who was forced to leave following a heart attack on October 10, soon followed by saxists Kim Park (John's step-son) and Mary Fettig, who had formed a relationship that allegedly resulted in pregnancy. Also given notice was Dale Devoe (trombone), whom Stan appreciated more for his writing than his playing. "2002" had been a sizeable hit for the band, though it was the bossa nova-ish "Love Theme from *The Godfather*" that was the more musically attractive. Dale was a youngster just getting started, and probably wasn't best pleased that Stan had considerably simplified his arrangement when recording the *7.5* album, so that it emerges as effective but over-bland. Much more cutting-edge Kenton was Dale's "El Cordobes" (named after the Spanish bull-fighter) which Stan never saw fit to record. But Dale's biggest hit was "Roy's Blues" for Roy Reynolds, which remained in the book to the end. From Devoe's own account in Steven Harris' invaluable book *The Kenton Kronicles*, Dale's stay in the band was short but not always sweet, and he perhaps fits Bill Fritz' comment as well as any, that "The tragedy lies in the minds of those who join the band with great expectations, and end up dwelling on what might have been."[9]

From producing one of CW's top sellers, Bob Curnow moved to one of its weakest: *Solo—Stan Kenton without His Orchestra*. Even the ever-prudent Audree Coke admitted, "The *Solo* album is selling rather slowly."[10] The truth was, the fans had always adored Stan despite, rather than because of, his instrumental abilities, because as a jazz pianist Kenton didn't even reach the starting gate. There were literally hundreds of piano players in the business with more jazz feeling and rhythmic sense than Kenton brought to the keyboard.

By the Seventies, as his fingers stiffened, Stan was featuring his "concerto" piano style most extensively. Arrangers found their charts were more likely to be accepted if they included a piano solo, often as an introduction to the piece. Audiences appreciated this "hors d'oeuvre," an appetizer, knowing that the orchestra would soon come roaring in, and

Kenton basked in this warm glow of affection. But remove the "main course"—the band—and an audience would soon have grown restless. Stan Kenton and his orchestra could fill New York's Carnegie or London's Festival halls. But be honest, how many "bums on seats" would a Stan Kenton Piano Recital have filled?

There had been suggestions for a Kenton piano album for many years, but Stan had always deferred, perhaps sensing it wasn't his greatest strength, and also because he invariably tensed up and became very apprehensive when recording solos. By all accounts Kenton suffered agonies during the sessions, and a hilarious compilation of out-takes that includes Stan's many expletives is a mind-boggling prize among serious collectors. Bob Curnow relates: "I remember when we first went to record at United and Western, the studio was in darkness, but a light from the control room was focused on this nine-foot grand—this big, black, Baldwin piano—and as Stan saw it he said, 'I feel like El Cordobes walking into the ring, and that's the bull!' And it was quite an experience, a real eye-opener. Some things Stan played beautifully, and some things he played terribly. A lot of times he didn't even remember his own compositions, and I had to go out and find the sheet music for things like 'Theme to the West.'"

For Kenton to record an entire album without even rhythm support was certainly a brave—some might say foolhardy—venture on his part. There's very little "jazz" on the completed album, and even then you are by no means hearing the music as Stan played it, as Curnow explains: "It was very hard. We recorded something like 11 hours of music, and then I took the tapes and edited those 11 hours down to 42 minutes. Every note on the album is Stan's, but it's a real patchwork quilt of many takes over many days on quite a few of the cuts. My memory tells me there were well over 150 intercuts and edits in the final album. I worked on it for an entire month before going back into the studio to put together the master. What a labor of love, with an emphasis on the LABOR part!"[11]

The best summary of *Solo* that I have seen comes from Ed Bride on Kentonia: "To me, the Kenton solo album is more of a personal statement than great jazz piano-playing. You hear melodies of compositions that were played by the big band, and you get to think about what might be going on in his mind. He's talking to us. It's more personal than musical, at least to me."[12]

The next musician to cause the greatest stir after John Park was also an alto sax player. Tony Campise joined in March 1974, the most "avant-garde" soloist the band had ever featured (and that includes Jay Daversa), giving rise to strong pro and anti opinions both inside and outside the orchestra. Kenton allowed Campise complete freedom of expression, and featured him at concerts on such disparate titles as "Inner Crisis" and "Street of Dreams" (from rock to ballad). I asked Stan how he found Tony compared with Park: "Campise's an exhibitionist and Park isn't. Campise has such tremendous technique he can't help but use it, and sometimes he plays too much. He'd take a lot of wild chances and scare guys to death, the things he'd get going on that horn. But he didn't play with the taste that Park played with."[13]

Dick Shearer continues, "Campise probably knew more about saxophone than anyone I've ever heard in my life. Technically he knew how to do everything, and he could change styles: if he wanted to sound like Johnny Hodges or Lee Konitz or whoever, he could do that very easily. There were times when he'd be playing he'd do something like that just for the fun of it. Every time he played you didn't know what was going to happen. Tony had no inhibitions, whatever he felt, whatever he wanted to do, he did it. His lead playing was always fine, but I'm less sure whether his solos always fitted the style of the band.

"Tony was popular with the public, and sometimes he'd get these ethnic-type things going, where he'd talk like a Japanese, or he'd do his Mexican imitation. And he could literally talk backwards. He could speak what sounded like nonsense into a tape recorder, and when you played it the other way it came out as, 'Yes, my name is Tony Campise.' Tony's the type of person who could hear a language once or twice, and have the pronunciation down, whether or not he understood what was said."

Despite Campise's strong personality, Mike Suter insists this was the "John Harner band." John played lead trumpet through 1974–75, and according to Suter: "Brought phrasing and dynamics back to Stan's music. John willed the band to excellence and personally burnished the rough edges. I wish I knew *how* he did what he did, but I don't have a clue. He would decide to make a change, and somehow through his sound we were aware that a change was coming, and be ready. I'm afraid Stan's ambiguity towards John prevented him from recognizing his talent until it was too late. Great lead players only come along a few times, and Stanley blew it."[14]

Following a successful if less than overwhelming tour of Japan in April, the band plunged into a brace of new scores written by Bob Curnow, a very diverse talent whose skills ranged from the traditional *Anthems* music to the fusion charts he saw as the best way for Stan to make contact with the younger generation. Bob's original concept had been an album featuring the music of Chicago, and another from

Blood, Sweat and Tears, but Stan was never fully convinced. While he could endorse translating classical composers like Wagner into the Kenton idiom with composure, rock groups carried a certain stigma that he found impossible to overcome. Kenton ended up advising Bob to use some music by both groups on a single LP, and even that should be filled out with some original Curnow compositions. One senses Stan's lack of conviction from his comment (displaying more optimism than realism), "We used music made popular by Chicago because we felt it would call attention to the band and gain a lot of the younger listeners—and we've begun to believe now that we didn't have to do it, because the kids are coming to us in droves anyway."[15]

Even post-Kenton with his interest in Pat Metheny's music, Curnow never wrote pure rock; at most his music might be described as "fusion," and the centerpiece of the *Chicago* album ("Chicago Suite III") veers towards jazz. As Mike Suter phrased it, "Bob was the best at melding rock and Kenton. He squeezed the music into the Kenton mold, writing great arrangements, let's say 85% Kenton and 15% rock, that worked. At the same time, the music itself, regardless of the arrangements, doesn't have the 'drama' that a Kenton piece should have." While I might quarrel slightly with Mike's percentages, he is right that the music isn't really strong enough to support Bob's imaginative arrangements, so that a sense of total fulfillment is lacking. Music from rock groups might be a workable basis to sell records, but it was never going to replicate the great Kenton achievements of the past. And the Chicago music had the disadvantage of seldom being played in public, according to Curnow because, " 'Chicago III Suite' was a very complicated piece of music. They played it for just a few months after the recording, and then stopped because Stan would get lost, and it'd get all screwed up. Stan was aware he wasn't as sharp any longer, and he couldn't do it justice. And that's why in the Seventies he allowed the arrangers to conduct their own things on the recording sessions whenever possible."

Kenton's deterioration since his operations was highlighted by Mike Suter: "The Stan Kenton I knew in 1974 was very different from the man I knew in 1963. His health problems had taken a huge toll. He still loved being a bandleader, standing in front of his brainchild. He still loved the Clinics, which to him wasn't just a way to rake in a few extra bucks—his belief and leadership in jazz education was for real. He even still loved the road. But he no longer had the drive, the energy, to be the front-running innovator he once was. He no longer drove the band as in earlier years; now the band drove him."[16]

More to the taste of Kenton traditionalists (and possibly Stan himself) were the two Curnow original compositions, which showed no trace of rock influences. "First Child" is a sombre, sololess work, dedicated, Bob said, to his first-born son, replete with all the majesty one associates with Kenton music. "Rise and Fall of a Short Fugue" is more experimental, with weird Campise flute, written, Bob said, because "Stan wanted something which he could play every night and conduct differently. Originally the piece was constructed in such a way that there were different directions to work through, so that Stan could change tempos, appoint different soloists, and bring out the backgrounds behind the soloists at his bidding. That piece could comfortably go ten or twelve minutes, and be pretty interesting." But this recording is over all too quickly in just four, and the basic concept worked no better than it had with Russo's "Improvisation," resulting in the title soon being dropped from the repertoire.

Much was clearly expected from Curnow, as illustrated by these quotes to me:

Stan Kenton: "Bob Curnow is basically a brilliant composer and conductor, and he shouldn't be wasted running Creative World—he's got too much to say." (February 6, 1975)

Dick Shearer: "He's my brother! I think Bob is the new Johnny Richards—he's marvelous!" (February 18, 1975)

Audree Coke: "Bob is remarkable. He is talented, intelligent and totally creative, and he writes specifically and correctly for the Kenton band. Bob is the logical successor to Pete Rugolo." (February 19, 1975)

I asked Curnow why it didn't happen, and his simple explanation was that Stan eventually found him most indispensable running Creative World successfully, and there was no time to write as well, so the *Chicago* album was Bob's swan-song. (Two further titles were recorded in 1975, but left on the shelf.) Stan returned to relying on his two reliables Levy and Hanna (especially Hank) and a sprinkling of other writers, but never found anyone to replace Maiden. Fusion was lost in the shuffle, but Stan had no great ideas to replace it with, so that the band lacked a clear direction. It's a real potpourri on *Fire, Fury and Fun*, a pretty meaningless album title itself, and since Curnow's idea was to fashion an LP featuring the band's soloists, something drawing attention to that concept might have been more explanatory.

Stan's thematic piano is prominent (though not really a headlined soloist) on Levy's "Quiet Friday" (not so hushed during its rockier moments) and Hanna's "Montage." I appreciate Hanna's ballads are not universally regarded with the same admiration I have for them, but "Montage" is one of Ken's finest achievements, a dark, brooding work with a powerful theme that builds to a dramatic orchestral climax. Conducted by Curnow in Hanna's absence, the initial arrangement has been considerably simplified for recording purposes, yet still presented problems on the date. The recording log shows it took 14 takes to perfect "Montage," and Stan became tetchy, afraid the session would run into overtime he couldn't afford. During a break, Shearer gave Suter the nod to switch from tuba to bass trombone, because (said Mike), "The tuba part was just impossible, but in the end we never played 'Montage' again as good as we got it on the record."[17] And they never went back to playing the original, superior orchestration again either!

The remaining pieces are more legitimately solo features, the "fun" presumably intended to come from Tony Campise's voice and flute on "Hogfat Blues," if you find pig-like noises masquerading as music amusing. A much more musical score comes from veteran arranger Chico O'Farrill for the conga drums of Ramon Lopez. Ramon told me he chose Chico based on his previous writing for Stan and Machito, and that he specified the congas should melt in and out of the music, rather than just being percussive. Chico slows the tempo mid-piece for a short piano spot which cleverly leads into the closing section, and as Lopez notes, "We made only two takes, and the band played so great we left it at that. Stan didn't like the original title 'Hit and Rum' [Ramon's favorite tipple], and elected to put my name on it instead."

The album's big hit was "Roy's Blues," which according to composer Dale Devoe experienced changes to its structure along the way. A basic blues chart of no great melodic worth, it was one of the few Seventies titles to really take the public fancy. Reynolds started out on baritone sax as heard here, the tone of which I preferred to the tenor he adopted in January 1975. Both Reynolds and the band soon grew tired with the monotony of the piece, and Suter relates, "We tried Roy on a lot of other charts, but none were as effective. Roy played 'Yesterdays' a few times, and it was beautiful. But the audiences didn't want to be touched, they wanted to be thrilled. The band was still playing it in '78, and the crowds still ate it up. It got one of the biggest reactions every night."[18]

Peter Erskine certainly displays a deal of "fire" on "Pete Is a Four-Letter Word." The piece is orchestrally structured, and is certainly not an endless drum solo, though whether Levy's score is better musically than Rugolo's for Shelly Manne almost 30 years earlier is a matter of opinion. "I think the feature was Stan's idea," said Erskine, "but I had no input into the chart's design or form, and it wasn't an easy tune to play—a bit 'left-handed' rhythmically. Typical procedure for the band at that time was to play a piece a couple of times (at most) in concert before the recording session, then go into the studio and scramble like crazy to get a decent take for the album, and then begin playing it nightly until the album came out."

Under these conditions, considering the inexperience of most of the band and Stan's loss of vigor since his illnesses, it's not surprising producer Bob Curnow worked under pressure. In a comment that showed how much Stan's attitude had changed since earlier times, Bob explained: "The Creative World albums were hard, especially in the post-production stage, because I had to go in and mix-out all the clams, and some of the solos were troublesome. More time should have been put into the recordings, and *Fire, Fury and Fun* was done in just two days: the band was in and out of the studio because they left Chicago after that real fast. Stan really left everything in my hands. He rarely expressed any interest in anything like the art-work or liner notes. On the sessions he rarely interfered or said anything. He'd leave it to me to decide whether we needed another take, and I always pushed for one more. I wanted that extra something that wasn't there yet, and that nearly always turned out for the best."

# 29.

# The Road to "No Where"

## (1975–1976)

Stan's physical deterioration when he next returned to Britain in January 1975 was all the more marked after an absence of 16 months. Overweight and stooped, and in near-constant back pain, Kenton moved with difficulty, and appeared 10 years older than his 64 years. Happily, Stan remained mentally alert, though his physical ailments meant he often led the band by hand signals from his seat at the piano, circumstances which precluded any unfamiliar, difficult music that required vigorous conducting.

I'd been warned in advance by a friend in America who caught the band a few nights before they left for the UK: "I hope Stan doesn't drop dead over there, as he looks the worst I've ever seen him—he must be in agony. He really plops down the last few inches to his piano bench—and such an effort to move! Also, his body fluid capacity must be enormous, as he appears very bloated. Piano solos were impaired as he could barely move around at all, and I'm sure his fingers and wrists were giving him pain. But this is one hell of a blowing band, and the bass and drummer are superb—just kids too. [Mike Ross and Peter Erskine] The brass screams as always—everything fff as usual. It was a superb evening, and the band was absolutely wonderful—a real treat."[1]

The fact was, despite Kenton's own limitations, this was a band on the rise, and the UK tour was a well-deserved success, with near-full houses at most venues, and Stan receiving an incredibly warm personal welcome at each and every concert. The band lacked a really outstanding soloist (one story was that Stan had tried to lure Lee Konitz back for the trip but was turned down), though Roy Reynolds scored well, and Dave Keim was never less than excellent, especially in the brisk trombone duet with Shearer on "Mother" from "Chicago III Suite."

Then things got even better, as personnel changes took place. Mike Suter tends to shoot from the hip, and has suffered a lot of ill-health, but also speaks a lot of sense. His opinions always deserve consideration:

"Gary Hobbs replaced Peter on drums in Rochester [March 31, 1975]. The band was immediately transformed, though I'm not sure how. It wasn't better. It wasn't worse. It was just different. If I had to choose between the two . . . I'd pick both. They're so different, but both were so right for the Kenton band. At the time, Peter was the more well-rounded drummer, but you just knew that Gary was gonna be a killer. He was gonna master any style he chose."[2]

My impression was that Hobbs was a more "traditional," swing-styled drummer, at least on the numbers that didn't require a rock feel to them—though Gary was perfectly capable of traveling that route when necessary. Concurrently, Tim Hagans moved into the jazz trumpet chair, and Dave Keim to the jazz trombone, and (to continue Suter's dialogue): "Steve Wilkerson joined on alto, eliminating our last weak spot. I'd say without reservation that those seven months from the time Steve joined until he quit in October [1975] was one of the top three bands Stan Kenton ever had. The primary soloists (Tim Hagans, Dave Keim, Steve Wilkerson) were superb. The band's ensemble work was as good as any Kenton band—before or after. And Stan was out of his doldrums.

"In those last years he never played much piano backing solos, and when the bands weren't very good he'd just sort of sit there and stare at the keyboard. But when the band was HOT he never took his eyes off the band or the soloists. During this period he watched the band a lot. And smiled. I wish I could remember where, but one night after we'd played 'Daily Dance' and (inexplicably) 'All the Things You Are' leading up to the intermission, Stan told the audience this was the best band he'd ever had. He never did that at a concert. It wasn't like him. I remember it because I looked at Dick, and he was crying. I've never been more proud to be on any stage.

"But by the time they recorded *Kenton '76* the spark was gone. Wilkerson was gone. The two other new saxes were not up to par. Greg Sorcsek [bass trombone] and I (ego aside) were gone. I wish we could have recorded around the time of Stan's amazing compliment. Then the folks that sell the '70s era bands short would have to eat their words. But they'd love it because they'd know there was greatness left near the end."

The centerpiece of *Kenton '76* (recorded in December 1975) was a new seven-and-a-half-minute work commissioned by Bob Curnow from Bill Holman. "Tiburon" was named after the town in California, and says Bob, "Turned out to be a disappointment to me. It was a good piece, though I think Willis has written better music, but it didn't seem to hang together. I don't think we did well with it. Stan at that time wasn't so quick to come to grips musically with what was happening.

I was in the booth and he was conducting, and it was a real struggle." Holman has composed a gripping, haunting theme, but instead of logical development, this slow, poignant melody suddenly and disjointedly switches to up-tempo trumpet improvisations, which seem to belong to another piece. Curnow is right; as a composition it doesn't "hang together" well, although the climax, with eye-watering high-pitched notes squeezed from Steve Campos' trumpet leading into the final theme statement, is impressive.

Dave Barduhn's "My Funny Valentine" had been in the book 18 months before the recording, a direct throw-back to Barton's "Rainy Day" dirge-like ballad style, and frequently used as a concert-opener, until it was superseded by the even more iconic "Send in the Clowns." According to Noel Wedder, Stan initially rejected "Clowns," and in Mike Suter's memory the chart had to be "corrected" before it was accepted, something Dave refutes. Curnow declined to comment about Barduhn at all, so the history remains obscure; but what really matters is the music, with its emotional piano figures and stirring climax, during which John Harner leads the trumpets from a deceptively quiet beginning into a majestic crescendo that contrasts so well with the deep, lustrous textures of the full band within the same piece.

Both of the band's final arrangers are now on the scene. Alan Yankee had joined on baritone sax in March 1975, and his "Theme from *Jaws*" was recorded but not issued. (A live take of this "fun" chart is on Tantara's *Revelations*.) Mark Taylor never played with Stan, but his baptismal score "Samba De Haps" skillfully blends the band's traditional regard for Latin music with more contemporary rhythms. The term "haps" was band-code for "sex," hence the innocent sounding, "Did you get any haps last night?" It's certainly played with gusto, and according to Suter, "One day Mark was running by some phrases with us to see if they worked, and a couple of days later he turned up with this wonderful chart. It just stunned us, it was so good."[3] In fact, the band liked the piece so much they clapped Mark after the first run-through, while on the recording date Stan congratulated Tim Hagans on his five-star solo. Taylor himself recalls, "At the time there were a lot of sambas going on in jazz, and I felt the rhythm would fit the band perfectly, and luckily it did. I'm sorry Steve Wilkerson was no longer with the band when we did the record, because I wrote it with him in mind some six months earlier. When first played it was a lot slower, but the tempo crept up, and it ended up being recorded far too fast!" Hank Levy has three charts on the LP, my preference being "Decoupage," with its rock-free rhythms, compelling theme, and what Curnow described as a "strong sense of swing and pretty changes."

Around this time, Stan had tried to cut down on the booze, with periods of abstinence followed by lapses which had sometimes found him under the influence on stage, a development which was new and very disturbing to those around him. Stan had always made it a strict rule NEVER to drink before a performance—afterwards was quite another matter. Now he was concerned and frustrated by his continued health problems. On October 7 Kenton had flown to Buffalo on a free day for the removal of a small growth on one eye. After staying the night at his doctor's home, he had rejoined the band the very next day, even refusing to wear an eye patch as directed until the stitches could be removed.

An extra-long Christmas vacation was now scheduled, in order that Stan might undergo an operation on his stomach muscles to reduce his weight, which had been troublesome for years, and which would require a short period of convalescence. With time on his hands, there was an opportunity to catch up on some quality music, and one night he was listening to Duke's last album. Stan just sat there looking at the cover, until he threw it down and exclaimed, "Goddamn it, I'm *not* going to die. I'm just going to go on and on!"[4] And then he gave that familiar laugh of his, which made you almost believe it could be so.

But nothing seemed to go well during these last years. The orchestra vacationed until January 19, 1976, while Stan recuperated, and then played a mere six days before disaster struck in Beaumont, Texas. Stanley woke on January 25 and (as he said afterwards) thought his hour had come. He was rushed to a hospital in Houston, and operated on twice to remove infection from the wounds, which had healed on the outside, but not on the stomach's inside walls, the same sort of problem he had experienced after previous surgeries. The setback was impossible to conceal from the fans, and Audree Coke reported, "There were the usual crop of rumors, that Stanley had suffered a heart attack, or was incurably ill from cancer, which was all nonsense and completely untrue. I think he's recovered now, though he does get very tired, and he doesn't like to walk much anymore, or be very active."[5] The operation had not only been unsuccessful in itself, but had actually exacerbated the very problems it had been designed to alleviate.

This time Kenton decided to cancel the tour and not try to carry on in his absence. Yet even as once more the bus marked "No Where" was halted in its tracks, throughout his hospitalization (which lasted until there was no fear of his pulling stitches or suffering a haemorrhage), instead of planning his retirement and an easier life, Stan was preparing his return to the bandstand. Meanwhile, in a mutually agreed-upon move, Bob Curnow resigned from his post at Creative World in order to return to teaching. "I really didn't like the record business," Bob told me, "it's a dirty game, working with the big players and all the crap that goes on there." Though not naming names, Bob's main business would have been with Capitol, who had not always been as helpful as they might have been with Roemer either. When Clinton had wanted to use the original LP cover designs for his CW reissues, he was informed (either from ignorance or deliberate obstruction) the plates no longer existed, although they were found fast enough when Capitol wanted them for their own use.

Curnow explained further: "When I took over Creative World I had never been in business before, and didn't know an invoice from a shipping slip. So it was a terrifying time for me, to be working for my idol in a million or two million-dollar company—I don't know what it was. But I was responsible, and it was very difficult, and that's one of the reasons I left—I was just burned out. And working for Stan in a business capacity was terribly frustrating, because Stan didn't want anything to do with it. I couldn't get him to respond or give an opinion to a lot of things I felt we should do. Stan showed tremendous courage to start the company, but after that to work with it on a day to day basis was of no interest to him.

"Interestingly enough, [Curnow warmed up] Chuck Anderson was fired before me for making what I think was a good business decision. Chuck decided to take this massive mailing of the CW bulletin we'd been sending at first class rates, which was a ton of money, and mail it at bulk rate for a third of the cost. The down-side of that is, you never know when it's going to be delivered. Chuck's mistake was that details of the itinerary in one part of a tour didn't reach the fans until a week after the band had played there. And Stan fired him because of that one mistake.

"Stan was really isolated on the road, and he loved that isolation. From 1970 when the band went back out, Stan never wanted to come home. He didn't even have a home for a few years. When he was in LA he stayed at a hotel, and he liked it that way. He didn't want to be hooked up, because his kids were going through all that crap, and he didn't want anything to do with that. He just didn't want to be reminded of the 'daily dance,' and that made it very hard from my perspective."

Bob told Tony Agostinelli another reason for his departure: "I had set up deals with Sony Japan and about six other large companies worldwide to market the Creative World label. Things were going very well with some lucrative deals for Stan and CW, when Stan suddenly got cold feet and decided he didn't want to sign the contracts. I never really knew why. I was very disappointed, and ultimately I felt there was little reason to try to expand the company at that time. Not long after that I returned to teaching. but we parted ways amicably, and Stan graciously supported me and my family until my teaching gig started a few months later. What a guy!"[6]

There was some consideration of manager Scott Cameron assuming Bob's role, but in the end the job of running the office actually fell to Audree Coke. However, Curnow did return in August 1976 to produce what proved to be the last album for Creative World. The band itself was not in the best shape, though John Worster was back on bass, a dedicated Kenton man whose playing Stan enjoyed, and whose experience and professionalism were needed in a band with so many untutored youngsters. The sax section was in particular trouble, centered around controversial lead altoist Terry Layne, whose playing had aroused conflict within his section. Especially critical were Greg Smith and Danny Salmasian, who wanted a change of lead, and confronted Kenton on the matter. Like Jim Amlotte before him, Dick Shearer did the hiring (and sometimes made poor choices), but Kenton did the firing, and pushed into a "him or us" situation, Stan chose to back Layne. Smith (baritone) and Salmasian (tenor) worked their notice, and trombonist Dave Keim left at the same time. "Dave couldn't accept what was going on, he couldn't live with it at all," says Worster, who believes Stan made an error of judgment by keeping Layne: "Stan hates to admit he's made a mistake, but he must know the section was weakened."[7]

The new LP was described by Dave Dexter in *Billboard* as "cerebral,"[8] though compared with many of Kenton's past endeavors, that isn't the word I'd choose. Even the album title *Journey into Capricorn* (named after one of Levy's scores) smacks of the meaningless jargon of contemporary pop groups, and there is too much pseudo-rock for my taste. The traditional choral section sounds that identify "Stan Kenton" are missing, and it's essentially the fiery brass that announces this as Stan's band. Nor is the music representative of the orchestra's well-rounded repertoire, and two distinguished ballad arrangements of Yankee's "Lush Life" and Hanna's "Sensitivo" were recorded but left untouched.

Two charts stand out, neither original compositions. Closest to the conventional Kenton legacy, and opening with a sensitive piano statement by Stan, is Mark Taylor's orchestration of Stevie Wonder's "Too Shy to Say." "This is a great song that I was into at the time," says Mark. "I tried to write a concert ballad in the style of Marty Paich. I was surprised that Stan liked it, because there is some free improvisation and some weird chords here and there, but the band played it beautifully." The other is Alan Yankee's 12-minute, multi-textured interpretation of Chick

Corea's "Celebration Suite," in three distinct movements, which Curnow wryly observed was not dissimilar in concept to his own Chicago music. It's exciting, bold and adventurous in a contemporary kind of way, though with perhaps a little too much pomp and not enough circumstance. Or as John Worster phrased it, "Alan did a good job of orchestrating a piece that should probably have been left to a small group. His writing is imaginative, and has some good colors, but I don't think it totally comes off in a big band situation. This is not a funk band, and it can't play funk charts. It plays 'MacArthur Park' and a couple of the Chicago things effectively, but that's about all in that idiom. That was Curnow's direction, he wanted to get the band more widely accepted, and he would have compromised more than Stan was willing to I think. Much more than I'm willing to! Stan's only got a few years left, and I hope he goes out like he's been for 35 years, with modern jazz. It's too late to try and make a fast buck now!"

It seemed like Worster was to have his way. Noel Wedder had intimated Kenton had experienced a "fall-out" with Hank Levy, suggesting as the reason that Hank was dusting off old material and presenting it to Stan as newly written. In any case, however intriguing, I won't report important factual items without corroboration, and that comes from the eminent Canadian author and Kenton champion Peter Newman, who while praising Levy's writing to Stan was cut-off in mid-stream. In Peter's words, "Stan shut me up by shooting back, 'Naw, that's crap. We got to move on to something new.'"[9] While Hank's music remained in the book, during the upcoming European tour, far from plugging his *Capricorn* album (which had been 50% Levy titles), rarely was more than a single Levy chart played per concert, often the unrecorded non-rock ballad "A Time for Love," and more frequently no Levy piece was played at all.

For many months reports had filtered through of Stan's growing fatigue, caused by his age, illnesses, and life on the road, which is rough enough within America, but compounded ten-fold with all the hassles of the extended European tour that began in August 1976 in Copenhagen. The trip had opened badly with only four saxophones when Dave Sova couldn't bring himself to fly, and dropped out at the last minute. In Denmark they picked up Teddy Andersen out of the Tivoli Gardens band, "A marvellous tenor player," said Worster, "and a beautiful guy. It took him only a day or so to figure the whole band out, and he's made the entire trip with us. I wish he could have stayed longer."

Then for two whole weeks they traversed Sweden on a sponsored tour which was far too long for so remote a land. Audiences were enthusiastic but small, Worster related: "Certainly no one was beating down the door to get tickets! There were often long mileages and double concerts, and the band was worn out. To make matters worse, Stan contracted a bladder infection. He was very ill, and lost control of his bowels for two days, even on-stage. He looked terrible, I thought he was going to have a stroke or something, he was shaking and was just awful. The doctors told him he had to rest, but he wouldn't, he didn't even cut a tune or anything. I thought he was going to die on us, it really crossed my mind."

Warsaw (Poland) came next, then under Soviet rule, and while Stan and Audree received the royal treatment, the band was housed in a run-down hotel about 40 miles out of town, in tiny rooms with just a bunk, a chair, and a sink. Even worse, the place was filthy and spider-ridden, with vermin literally falling off the ceiling onto the guys, many of whom stayed up all night rather than try and sleep in such conditions.

After that things could only improve, and Worster continues: "Our concert in Cologne was good, and so was Holland: well, Veghel wasn't, it was a jazz festival in a tiny village, and no one showed up. I think we had 120 people, it was just embarrassing, and that was the night Decca recorded us. They're going to dub applause onto the album. But despite the fact it was a strange hall, and very few people, I thought the band played with a lot of fire. The feeling is good, even if there are occasional clams—the spirit more than makes up for it."

Decca had planned to record the band in England as in 1972, but when the still-blinkered British Musicians Union refused permission, Decca simply took their equipment to Holland instead. The resulting *Live in Europe* was Stan's last official recording, made exactly one month after *Journey into Capricorn*, but as different as chalk from cheese—a mixture of older favorites and new music from Alan Yankee, with not a hint of rock or "fusion" throughout. Strayhorn's famous "Lush Life" opens with Stan's opulent piano and seems about to follow the standard ballad line, but instead is full of twists and turns, switching tempo and temper at will, a worthy addition to the Kenton lexicon. Stan often announced "Fire and Ice" as "dedicated to Maurice Ravel," because the work was inspired by his famous "Bolero"—though it's unlikely Ravel would have realized the resemblance. "Tattooed Lady" is an up-tempo swinger, so-called, Yankee said, because he wrote it in the Lydian mode (ask a musician!), and Groucho Marx used to sing a song called "Lydia, the Tattooed Lady."

John Worster described Yankee's writing as "a little inconsistent—some very good charts and some less so. I think 'Lush Life' is very effective, and there's a nice saxophone soli at the start of 'Tattooed Lady'—I'm glad Alan is bringing that back, it adds color and makes it much more effective when the whole band comes in." The album concludes with the band's "Theme," and it seems appropriate that Stan's long recording career should end in much the same way it started—to the strains of his famous "Artistry in Rhythm."

The band did well in the UK's large cities, but less so in some of the smaller towns. At Southend, Stan publicly criticized the promoter for organizing two houses, each only half full, when a single concert would have sufficed. Of course, the promoter might have responded that Kenton was equally to blame for not drawing the sell-out crowds he'd hoped for! In truth, this was a good band, but not the equal of some of the great Kenton orchestras, as John Worster acknowledged: "The saxes are the weakest section, because we don't have a lead alto. Terry Layne's an inexperienced, rock-oriented player who hasn't got his instrument down. His solos are inconsistent, he's not careful about changes, and his pitch varies—he hasn't really learned to control the instrument, and that's not the proper chair for someone to learn to play on. This band has too long a history of good lead alto players, and the section cannot sound well without a good lead.

"Stan has mellowed. He lets things go by that he never used to—phrasing, carelessness in playing, attitudes. He hardly ever yells at the band any more, he takes out all his built-up inner tensions by getting juiced, but sometimes things get so bad he just has to yell at us, and it's amazing what a couple of words from him will do to pick up the band. He's still involved with the music, but I don't get that total, 100% involvement he used to have. He gets tired more easily, and is having to save his energy. To me, Stan's greatest talent of all is the ability to bring things out of you, and it's still there, but not like it once was. It used to be that if you had 13 inside of you, he got 13 out of you, instead of just 12 or maybe 11. Once in a while I get the feeling we're just putting time in, and that really bugs me."

The band's last date before flying home was an all-day session at the BBC Television Studios in Ealing, London, for the prestigious "Omnibus" series, which looked in depth at major exponents of the arts. This was not a videotaped concert before an audience, but a legit film featuring the band's music, to be interspersed with interviews by some of the orchestra's icons filmed in Hollywood, including Bud Shank, Bob Cooper, and Shelly Manne. Resplendent in their current "country and western" outfits of brown shirts and blue denim suits, the band worked from 11 a.m. to 5:15 p.m., and as usual on a film set, there were lengthy breaks and delays to adjust lighting, sound, and camera angles. Though he stuck at it like the professional he was, Kenton was clearly exhausted by the process, spending most of the time between takes slumped in his piano seat, occasionally improvising pop tunes, but generally lost in reverie. His attitude was as sharply defined as a "Don't bother me!" notice, and nobody did, instructions by producer Alan Benson being relayed by intercom from the control booth high above the set.

Towards the end of the day, Stan's daughter Leslie and two grand-children slipped into the studio and stood watching at the side. By the time "Body and Soul" was reached around 5 p.m., the whole band was fatigued after so long under the lights, but immediately the final OK was given, Stan's whole demeanor suddenly changed. He jumped to his feet with an animation hitherto well hidden, strode across the floor without a word of goodbye or glance at anyone, and with his arms around the children swept out of the studio. It's said music was the most important thing in Stan's life, but on that day at least, his actions indicated family ran music a very close race.

Probably on the strength of the *Anthems* album, Stan had been commissioned by the Masons to record an album of music written for or identified with the Masonic movement, and had allocated the writing to Ken Hanna, who spent many hours laboring over straight music neither he nor the band were very enamored about. Sections had been rehearsed and privately recorded during the summer "Jazz Orchestra in Residence" courses ("Finlandia" is on Tantara's *Revelations*), and a December recording date was already set, when the whole project had to be abandoned because the Masons suddenly changed their minds and withdrew financial support. While frustrating to everyone at the time, I don't think Kenton's fans suffered any great lasting loss from the debacle!

Audree Coke told me she believed Stan's greatest legacy might prove to be his work and involvement in jazz education, and Worster agreed it was a major interest, while also pointing out the band probably owed its continued existence to college bookings: "It's gotten to the point where the educational situation is much to our advantage. Musically and financially the schools are the mainstay of a tour, it's sort of booked around that. Schools are not allowed to book you as an attraction, but they can buy you from an educational standpoint. They haven't always got a big budget, maybe only enough for the Clinic, but then they add a concert for a total fee of $4000 or $5000 to try and make the money back, so that's the way they work it. It has turned out to be a very lucrative thing."

On November 8, during a day off in Philadelphia, Kenton had a full medical check-up, because of his exhaustion and high blood pressure.

The doctor put him on medication, a diet to lose 20 pounds, and once again Stan was told to lay off the alcohol. Having already allegedly given up smoking, Stan would try to keep off the bottle as advised, but when the pressures grew and tensions mounted, drink was the only release left to him. When the band broke up for Christmas, Kenton traveled to Tulsa to see "Doc" Walt Kempe, who placed him in the hospital for a couple of weeks, mainly to ensure Stan obtained rest and the correct medication. But already the date was set for the band's return on January 16, 1977, and Stan would once again be ready for the off.

# 30.

# Accident!

## (1977)

When the band reconvened in January 1977, Terry Layne was gone, his place taken by Michael Bard, a fluent soloist and an excellent lead who transformed the sax section and somehow lifted the morale of the whole orchestra, so that John Worster was able to report, "You won't believe how much better this band is than last year's. So much more life, more musical, and all the new guys are very fine players. A MUCH BETTER BAND!"[1] Dick Shearer agreed the orchestra had taken on a new spirit, and fresh charts were coming in from Alan Yankee, Dave Barduhn, and Ken Hanna for a new ballad album scheduled for spring recording.

The best example of the band's resurgence is Tantara's *Artistry in Symphonic Jazz*, a slightly pretentious title perhaps, but descriptive of the music, and a CD in every respect the equal of any official album of the period. The repertoire covers all eras, from a spirited reading by the revitalized saxophones of "Opus in Pastels," through a solo-driven "Intermission Riff" and a beautiful Michael Bard solo on Niehaus' "But Beautiful," to newer charts like John Harner's "Satin Doll" and Hanna's "This Is All I Ask." I don't know how well this band was received by younger guys, the closest it comes to contemporary rhythms being Mark Taylor's "Granada Smoothie" (named after a particularly potent Mexican drink), though probably more Levy music was played at college gigs.

Only the same old bogey of fatigue seemed to haunt Stan, a condition which time seemed unlikely to alleviate, and his spirits will not have been raised by the death of his mother aged 87 in March. However tiring, Kenton actually enjoyed life on the road, and all it entailed: frequent all-night traveling, snatched meals in greasy spoons, living out of a suitcase; a life-style youngsters less than a third his age often found intolerable. But as compensation he required the soothing effect of alcohol, and consumption had grown over the years until he regularly experienced what Suter called "zone-outs," which enabled him to sleep at night. Unfortunately, when drinking earlier in the day, in later years these sometimes occurred at less opportune moments, and several musicians (including Rugolo) have described how Stan occasionally even passed out as a result.

What is certain about the awful events of May 22, 1977, is that the band had traveled all day to the Abraham Lincoln Motor Inn in Reading, Pennsylvania, arriving at about 6 p.m. with a night off, and that around two hours later Kenton was found lying unconscious with severe head injuries, the consensus being on the concrete floor of the motel parking lot, several floors distant from the location of his room. More than that veers on speculation, because newspaper reports are contradictory, and Noel Wedder's postings on Kentonia uncorroborated.

The suspicion of course was that Stan had been drinking, there was no suggestion of foul play, and with no performance that night he had no reason to abstain. As Roy Reynolds put it, "Everyone likes a travel day with a night off, the guys have a kind of party on the bus, drinking, and that kind of stuff. By the time we arrived at Reading everyone was pretty tired, and what really happened is still kind of vague. A reporter happened to be checking into the hotel when the ambulance was called, so in no time at all the news was all over the networks. Even so there were many conflicting stories, some reports said he'd had a stroke, and others that he was drunk and fell and hit his head."

Hospital tests the next day disclosed that Kenton (suffering convulsions and partial paralysis) had sustained a five-inch skull fracture, complicated by blood clots placing pressure on the brain. On May 24 two blood clots were removed during emergency brain surgery lasting two and a half hours, the Reading hospital reporting the operation as "successful," though Stan's condition was variously described as "serious" and "poor." According to Stan's personal manager Scott Cameron, "Kenton came out of surgery conscious, and yelling that he wanted to get back to his musicians."[2] Placed in intensive care, Stan recognized Cameron and his son Lance when they visited him May 25, and was suffering no paralysis of speech or limb; asked by Cameron if he knew who he was, Stan replied, "You're god-damn right I know who you are, you're Scott."[3]

Ten days later, back in the regular nursing unit and on solid foods, the memory was unfortunately not in such good shape. Stan had to be reminded he was a bandleader, and he often did not recognize people close to him, or remember names and events, though the medics assured him this was normal after such extensive brain surgery, and should correct itself automatically given time. Throughout June, Stan remained in the Reading hospital, gaining strength as the fracture healed, while the band continued under Dick Shearer's leadership, mainly in order that the summer Clinics might proceed as planned.

By July 7, Kenton was well enough to leave the hospital and return to LA, where he moved in with Audree, who would care for him during a recuperation that was bound to be difficult and lengthy. To fill his time, Stan tried to revive his writing skills without tangible success, and as always when he became bored, reportedly reverted to the bottle, a big no-no in his present condition. Alleged complicating factors in his health included hardening of the arteries and emphysema (the abnormal presence of air in tissues or cavities of the body). Nevertheless, after a couple of months in California, Stan was looking better, but still experienced great difficulty remembering names; he visited his own band at Costa Mesa in August, but the only player whose name he could recall was Dick Shearer—for the other guys he invented nick-names to get by.

The orchestra went on for three months without Stan, but with Shearer becoming increasingly confident in his position as leader. With neither Vax nor Hanna to fall back on, Dick was by default forced to overcome his diffidence, and assume the leader's role, both conducting and announcing effectively in public despite the ever-present fear of rejection on the part of the promoters. "Dick did a tremendous job at short notice," said Roy Reynolds, "and he certainly did the best he could to keep the band going. It was very difficult, because once they knew Stan wasn't with the band, a lot of promoters would cancel the engagement. One week we were booked for seven nights and five of them got cancelled, so there was this terrible feeling of uncertainty as to whether we could keep going or not."

As had happened on previous occasions when Kenton was absent, the band rapidly assumed a very different dimension, a change caused by the fact Shearer and the band liked to "swing," while Stan didn't—at least not all the way. Mike Suter explains, "Stan's vision was straight eighth notes in the ensemble parts in order to create a dichotomy between the band and the rhythm section and soloists. I don't think we ever played 'Stompin' at the Savoy' without him growling 'straight eights' just before counting it off. (After a while it seemed like this threat was part of the title.) And of course, we never played it exactly that way. But his admonition was sufficient to 'take it off the boil' just enough to create the dichotomy he wanted. The band could swing ferociously when given its head, and when Stan was gone and Dick had it alone, it did."[4]

Roy Reynolds confirms: "I must say the style of the band did change with Dick in charge. We played a lot more swing charts, and at times we sounded more like Woody Herman or Thad Jones/Mel Lewis than the Kenton band. We played a lot of arrangements that I don't think Stan would have played himself. A lot of people commented on it, saying that it didn't sound like Stan's band very much, though we did play a lot of the older charts as well, like 'Intermission Riff,' 'Street of Dreams,' 'Peanut Vendor' and so on that Stan was famous for."

A couple of those new "swing" charts, both long pieces allowing the soloists plenty of freedom, were "The Buzz" by Mark Taylor, and Curnow's "Writer's Cramp," which Bob had not written for Kenton at all but which Dick wanted the band to play. Considerable emphasis was also placed on Stan's replacement, the technically gifted pianist Fred Simon, who was even allowed to feature on one of his own compositions at most concerts, usually "Morning Song" or "Night Traveler." "Nobody could fill Stan's boots as regards playing the piano within the orchestra," commented Reynolds, "but Fred did try, and he did play very well."

To add a "name" attraction, Buddy De Franco fronted the band at times, a seemingly odd choice in view of Stan's well-known indifference to the clarinet. "Buddy came in as guest soloist," Reynolds confirmed, "and we worked that by playing Kenton arrangements, but leaving a part open with just rhythm so that Buddy could improvise on things like 'Intermission Riff' and 'Body and Soul.' Buddy also brought in two or three of his own arrangements, big band charts featuring clarinet solos. And the audience thought it was great, and Buddy's such a nice guy and such a fine player, he did a tremendous job. I think our agent, Willard Alexander, figured there was a much better chance of keeping the band working if there was a 'name' in front of the band, and another time we had Herb Pomeroy with us a couple of nights in Boston as featured trumpet soloist to help sell the band to the promoters."

Each time the "boss" had been away, the character of the band had changed to a more overtly swinging outfit, partly as a means of containing the guys in the absence of the "old man." If this time the trend was even more noticeable, and the music more truly the Dick Shearer Orchestra than that of Kenton, it was also true that many of the warhorses remained true to the Kenton spirit, and Michael Bard on alto was a stunning soloist, especially on the old Holman chart of "Stella by Starlight," partially rearranged to accommodate Bard's almost freeform style.

Also very effective was a new version of "Artistry in Rhythm," without piano. Worster opens with a slow rhythm, then Hobbs joins in, followed by Lopez; then each trumpet begins to play a Latin instrument one at a time, all the while there being no indication that they are playing the "Theme." After this long intro, the saxes at last stand up and begin to play the melody, followed by the usual trombone and trumpet pieces, and finally back to the rhythm while Dick introduces each guy and thanks the audience on their behalf and his, and "especially Mr. Stan Kenton," and then the big trumpet climax. After that the audience is on its feet applauding—a very, very effective ending.

Something of a tussle went on that summer behind the scenes. Willard Alexander, whose agency booked the band, was willing to back the orchestra if it continued under Dick Shearer, until Stan was (hopefully) able to return. And Wally Heider (with Dick's approval) was keen to record the band under the title *Carrying On! The Stan Kenton Orchestra Without Their Leader,* using the new direct-to-disc recording technique. After joint consultations with Stan and Audree, Scott Cameron turned down both suggestions. With no likelihood of his quick return to the podium, Stan was unlikely to want the band to continue without him indefinitely, his objection to a Kenton "ghost" orchestra being well known. And there was a very real threat that the critics might well prefer this newly swinging band to the original, and even that Fred Simon might be compared favorably to Kenton's own piano prowess.

Audree Coke had no doubts: "It would have been a mistake to record the band without Stanley there. The band did not sound the same, and some of the things Dick chose to play were not what Stanley would have played. Dick had them play things that were a lot of fun for an audience, but it was not the Kenton sound. Dick did a beautiful job, he worked very hard, but he changed things to his own liking, and the band itself did not sound like the Kenton band. Dick had the same personnel, the same people, but he could not get the same thing from the players that Stanley got. They would work for Stanley; they'd do anything in the world Stanley wanted, even if it meant holding a note until they expired, they would try. But they wouldn't do it for Dick, so he didn't have the same cooperation Stanley always had."[5]

Shearer was naturally disappointed at what he saw as a lost opportunity to keep the orchestra together, and the chance for a new recording under his direction, commenting that they had enough new charts to record two albums if need be. Whatever, the opposition was inflexible, and the orchestra disbanded on August 21, 1977, and the guys scattered across America, taking other jobs, or returning to their studies. Jay Sollenberger and Dave Kennedy from the trumpets went to Woody Herman, Gary Hobbs got married, and Steve Campos went into teaching. Both Dick Shearer and John Worster turned down offers to join Count Basie, Dick preferring to teach at Wittenberg College as well as playing in Detroit, while John enrolled at North Texas and began working on his ultimate goal of a Master's degree.

Throughout the autumn Stan continued slowly to improve. With the advantage of regular meals and stable living conditions, physically he looked better than for some while, and as the weeks passed his memory seemed to be improving. By November tentative bookings were being taken for mid-January 1978, though the doctors had not given their consent for Stan to travel by that date. There was also some opposition from the promoters. Many would book the band only if a positive guarantee could be given that Kenton would be present, something no one could say with certainty after Stan's recent track record. One suggestion was for short tours only, so that if Kenton had to drop out for any reason fewer bookings would be lost, and in addition the pace would be easier for Stan with less extensive touring. The drawback was that such a band lacked momentum and continuity, and by mid-December, bored by the inactivity, Stan was as intent as ever on returning full-time, and with his doctor's reluctant permission, began contacting his musicians for rehearsals in Buffalo starting January 11, 1978.

Meanwhile Scott Cameron resigned as personal manager, and two who declined invitations were John Worster and Gary Hobbs. Also absent from the roster would be Stan's right-hand man Dick Shearer, the trombone sound of the Seventies who hadn't missed a tour since first joining the band in 1965. Shearer's absence was a blow to the band, and it's impossible to square the circle, given the varying accounts for the reasons surrounding his departure. What seems indisputable is that Dick was very concerned about Kenton's health problems, and told Stan he didn't believe this was the right time to go back on the road, advice which probably didn't sit well with a stubborn Kenton intent on getting his own way.

Audree told me there was no friction between Stan and Dick, and Shearer was offered his old job back, but he turned it down; and Dick himself told Tony Agostinelli he was tired of "Carrying the 'Old Man' on his back,"[6] though it should be noted the term "old man" was one of endearment frequently used to refer to the leader, and not a literal description. "Dick thought about it," to quote Audree, "and decided he didn't want to do it. So he settled down, first in Dayton where he had personal ties, and then in Detroit."[7]

In the latter city, however, Dick lived with alumnus Mike Suter and his wife for over a year, and Suter tells it very differently, saying Dick wanted desperately to be on the band, but "out of the blue Audree called and told Dick his services wouldn't be needed, intimating that it was Stan's decision."[8] Suter is supported by Mike Vax, who also believed Stan was badly advised, and who told me, "Basically, Dick was just let go, and they left with Roger Homefield instead. And I think the fact Dick wasn't asked to play on the last tour is what started his over-indulgence with food and drink, so that he ended up weighing 500 lb." (A condition that led to a fatal heart attack one day shy of Dick's 58th birthday on September 20, 1997.)

Whatever the circumstances or the politics going on behind the scenes, and whoever's decision it finally was, it is sad that the man who more than any other apart from Stan himself had brought luster and professionalism to every one of the Seventies' bands, should have missed out on the final tour. Shearer's expertise and experience were going to be sorely missed by a leader who truly shouldn't have been out on the road at all. But Kenton was a proud and determined man who needed his nightly fix of music and the oxygen of public acclaim. Unfortunately events would quickly prove Shearer's assessment of Stan's situation correct, and the wonder now, in retrospect, is not that this last, sad tour was to fail, but that anyone ever really thought it might succeed.

# 31.

## Wounded Warrior

(1978)

The musicians assembled in Buffalo, New York, that cold January day quickly realized it was going to be a bumpy ride. Stan Kenton was more obviously candidate for a convalescent home than the rigors of life on the road, particularly in the East Coast's severe mid-winter weather conditions. Those first few days were especially rough, as Stanley struggled to adapt himself to what he had come to call "My tragedy."

Kenton was clearly a sick man, mentally and physically fatigued after six days riding the bus clear across the continent from California, Audree Coke accompanying. In her view, Stan was far from ready for the road: "Stanley's health during that last tour was not good at all. He should have stayed home for a longer period. He had only seven months between the brain surgery and going out again in January '78. No, I don't think he was ready, he was pushing himself, he was forcing himself. He was still having trouble with his memory, and his word patterns were sometimes disarranged. He was not ready to go back at all, but I couldn't hold him at home any longer, he was going to go, and that was it. Stanley was a very stubborn man. So against everyone's better judgment, out he went, with the band."[1]

Roy Reynolds was one of the old faithfuls (Ramon Lopez was another) who stuck out the entire tour: "When Stan reformed the band, we rehearsed for about three days in the Statler Hilton Hotel, and it was obvious that Stan wasn't himself. It wasn't the old Stan. But he still gave a little talk to the guys, and he was determined he was going to get better. He definitely wanted to get that band going again, if it was the last thing he ever did. He kept saying, 'I know I'm not really well yet, but I'm going to get well, and if you guys will bear with me if I forget a few things now and then, we'll be OK.' And he did forget things. For instance, he would call out 'Street of Dreams' and start playing the introduction to a different tune, like 'Body and Soul.' And little things like that would happen, especially in those first few weeks. And he really had a hard time remembering the names of the guys in the band, he even forgot my name, and Ramon's. Bob Flanigan, one of the Four Freshmen, called in to see Stan in Ohio, and Stan didn't recognize him at all at first. So, it was a very sad thing when these things happened."

With that, the fans were in agreement:

David Hoffman: "I saw a concert on that tour, and was just about in tears by the middle of the first set. Stan was extremely ill, the band was discouraged, and the whole evening was just awful." (Kentonia, May 12, 2006)

Bill Jadlos: "Baltimore, February 19, 1978. Stan was there, but he wasn't really participating—he couldn't identify the band members and couldn't say what they had just played or what they were about to play. Only when he was at the piano did he appear to be 'into it.' One of the saddest things I have ever seen." (Kentonia, May 12, 2006)

Peter Newman: "Toronto, May 26, 1978. Stan and I had dinner just before the concert, and he sat there, listless, obviously in pain, tuning in and out of our conversation and his surroundings like a short-wave radio. But what really shook me was that when the concert started, nothing changed. Though he still played beautifully, watching him slumped over his piano that sad evening, I realized it was all over, and I cried." (Kentonia, July 7, 2002)

"The nurse who had looked after Stan in the Reading hospital came to visit him some months later," said Roy Reynolds, "and she said that after such an operation a small amount of fluid usually builds up around the brain, which causes a little pressure and affects the memory. It's the normal healing process, and as time went by his memory would improve. Which I think it did, though towards the end of the tour he was very tired, and his health seemed to be going downhill in other areas." What the nurse's general prognosis did not take into account was the fact that Kenton's memory loss and general fatigue had begun long before his accident, and the brain surgery had simply aggravated an already existing situation, which must have made the probability of a real recovery more doubtful.

Reynolds continues: "Stan was supposed to take medication each night, and one of us would make sure he got to his room, because Stan still liked to have his drink after the job. But he was very independent and he always liked to go on his own, so we'd follow discreetly so he didn't know we were there. There was one time he got a little too far gone, and we had to take him, and I noticed all these pill bottles on his dressing-table, and I asked him if he was taking his pills OK, and he said, 'No, I'm not. I hate to admit it, but I can't get the goddamn tops open.' So I called Audree, and she came out and stayed with Stan for a couple of weeks, and she made sure he took his pills, and also kept him off the booze for a while. While Audree was around, Stan was great, he'd do all the things he was supposed to do, but as soon as she'd left, he went back to having his little drink at night, and you know Stan, he liked his vodka, and no matter what we said he was going to have it, and that was *it*. But one of us stayed with him all the time, even when he went to eat, so we looked after him that way.

"Stan had problems getting around, and didn't care to move from his piano seat during concerts. So because Michael Bard sat in the middle of the saxophone section where everyone could see him, we agreed that Michael would stand up and cut the band off at the end of numbers. A lot of people got the wrong impression that Bard had taken over as kind of co-director, but that wasn't true at all. If anything it was Alan Yankee who took Dick Shearer's place when it came to rehearsing the band. Dick's replacement in the section was Roger Homefield, a great lead trombone player in the Bernhart/Fitzpatrick tradition, and a Kenton fan from way back. There was a fine arrangement that Alan Yankee did of 'Chelsea Bridge' that kicked off with a trombone solo, and Roger played it beautifully every time." (Dynaflow: *Artistry in Omega*)

"Every time" is right, because the band played the same tunes with little variation at every concert. Roy Reynolds explains: "Stan had a program sorted out in his head, and we played the same numbers night after night after night. And some of the guys got really bugged about this, because they wanted to play different things, but they didn't understand, these were the songs Stan knew, and he didn't have to worry about what to play next, because he had the list in front of him on the piano."

At dances they had to vary the repertoire, and then Stan got into real trouble. At the recorded Sunnybrook Ballroom dance-date in Pottstown on February 17, he forgets the title of "Chelsea Bridge" while announcing, lays out on his piano feature "Sunny," forgets the chords on "My Funny Valentine" and "Begin the Beguine," and packs up altogether on the under-rehearsed "My Way." Sometimes audiences failed to realize the extent of Stan's recall problems, and laughed when he mispronounced names, not *at* him but *with* him, in the mistaken belief he was joshing with them. At other times, audience members would call out to help him with names he was struggling with. The strain on Kenton must have been enormous. At another recorded date in Baltimore on February 19, in his opening remarks Stan comments that Johnny Richards composed "Body and Soul," says "feet your hurlings" when he intends "hurt your feelings," refers to Hank Levy as "Hanky Lovey," and is generally unsure of titles, yet chats about Dee Barton faultlessly. It is indeed painful for those who knew the younger Kenton to listen as Stan stumbles along, waiting for the mistakes to occur, yet hearing in that resonant voice the same love for his music and his men that was always the heart and soul of Stan Kenton.

At another concert attended by Randy Taylor (Mark's father), Randy relates: "The tunes played were the same as they've been playing, opening with 'Body and Soul,' then 'Minor Booze.' He bungled on the third one, starting to play 'Body and Soul' again. Ramon kept telling him to switch, and he finally got the message and slipped into 'All the Things You Are.' He has a lot of problems with his speech and memory. It just breaks your heart when you recall how sharp he was. He stayed at the piano the whole evening, even during the breaks.

"The next night Stan was 100% better. He was in one of his funny moods, had the band singing 'Let Me Call You Sweetheart.' From one day to the next there was such a change. I think it was because we got him talking, and that in turn got him thinking, instead of sleeping on the bus, or just looking out of the window. Stan and I had some conversation by ourselves. He said, 'You know, I really messed up last night. I couldn't remember the titles, and I goofed by starting to play "Body and Soul" after we'd already played it. That bugs the hell out of me. I can't introduce the new guys because I can't remember their names. The doctor said it was going to take 18 months before I'm completely cured. It's been about a year now. I'm going to get better. There's so much I've got to do, and first I have to get these guys recorded.'"[2]

Among the new titles was a Cuban "Afro-Minor Summit" by Mark Taylor, "Terracotta" from a suite by Hank Levy, and Alan Yankee's "Warm Up the Bus." But Stan didn't really want to record, knowing he couldn't cope with unfamiliar music, and would be little more than a spectator at his own sessions. "The band was ready to record," says Roy Reynolds, "we all wanted to do it, and we had enough new material. We all thought if we did an album now, it could very well be the last one the band ever made. But Stan wouldn't commit himself, so I guess he just didn't feel like he wanted to record at that time." In the absence of an official recording by the last band, the best representation of a typical concert comes once again from Bill Lichtenauer's Tantara label, called *A Time for Love—The Final Chapter*, recorded on April 21, 1978.

Despite all the leader's problems, this is still a Stan Kenton band, and that awesome Kenton Sound remains intact. The trombones under Roger Homefield attain a dark resonance, the saxes led by Michael Bard are full-bodied and rich, and Tom Baker's lusty trumpets crown that wall of sound. But to call this one of Kenton's best bands would be to overstate the case. With Stan below par and Shearer absent, there was no clear catalyst among the lead players for the band to follow, and the men play carefully, more anxious to avoid mistakes than to create music, especially on the notoriously difficult funereal ballads, which despite the tempo need a certain levitation to attain balance. It's Michael Bard's alto that time and again provides that extra life that lights the fire, splendid on his feature "Stella by Starlight," and outstanding on "Minor Booze," a meaningful solo that grows and builds in intensity, with avant-garde inferences along the way. The whole band plays more confidently on the up-tempo numbers, Roy Reynolds is authoritative on his short spots, and "Malaguena" attains a fiery brilliance. And by the time "Artistry in Rhythm" is reached, sentiment kicks in and one is grateful that the Kenton Sound shines as illustriously as ever. If Stan *had* to go, he was leaving with that Sound ringing in his ears.

The first of the important sidemen to leave had been Alan Yankee in February. Kenton had hired Alan's wife Melanie, a young girl fresh out of college, to take Shearer's place as band manager, a job for which she was totally inexperienced and unsuitable. So when the pay-roll got messed up, and the band arrived at hotels and found no rooms reserved for them, Stan was irked, and fired Melanie, leaving Alan with little choice but to leave with her.

Then Michael Bard was fired in May, losing the band its most exciting and original soloist, according to Reynolds because "he kept bugging Stan to rehearse the band and play some different tunes instead of the same numbers each night. It was one of those dumb things that happened sometimes, but I think Bard had done a couple of arrangements himself, and he wanted the band to play them, but Stan wanted to stay with the things he knew." Tom Baker quit at the same time, explaining, "Stan liked to hold his arm out on the last chord [of a tune], and when he heard the lead trumpet fold, THEN he would cut off the band. He thought that was funny. I didn't."[3]

In retrospect, for his own welfare it should have been Kenton who resigned. The road is a hard taskmaster even on the young and fit, but for someone of Stan's age and in his state of health, it was suicidal. Smoking and drinking too much, while not eating enough, he complained of constant tiredness. Once always immaculately turned out, he would now appear on-stage unshaven and dishevelled, sometimes sleeping in his clothes. "No one can get him to change his suit," commented Randy Taylor. "We tried to encourage him to wear some of his other suits, but he said he couldn't lift his suit-case, though when one of the guys offers to help he always refuses."[4] Possibly Dick would have known how to deal with the situation, but even in his weakened state, no one cared to argue with the boss.

The question everyone was asking, "Why is Stan pushing himself like this?" has one easy answer. Quite simply, Stan lived for his music, and without it he didn't exist. Bass trombonists towards the end of the tour were Howard Hedges and Mike Suter, and on this point both were agreed. In the opinion of Hedges, "I feel that the 1978 band brought Stan another year of life. Everyone on that band had Stan's best interest in mind at all times. Many people have told me that last orchestra was the best he had had in years. The spirit was strong because we played every night as though it was the last—which it very well could have been."

Mike Suter concurred: "By rights, Stan should not have been on the road. He had good days and bad days, but much of the time he was not aware of his surroundings. He could not take care of even his most basic personal needs. But he was doing exactly what he wanted with his life. He wanted—he needed—to be leading his own band. Without that, he'd have no reason to live. Life without his band would be purgatory. In retrospect, I can only applaud his actions, and hope that I'm as fortunate at the end of my life."

But regarding the quality of the band, it was Suter who had the more Kenton experience, and who was probably the more objective. In Mike's opinion, "There were a few duds, but individually most of the members of the last band were good to adequate players, but they never jelled into a cohesive unit that played the MUSIC instead of just the notes. The hallmark of every Kenton band had been that they played better than any other band. We phrased together. We breathed together. We thought together. The last band was too ragged, too undisciplined, to warrant my respect. For example, even though we played much the same program at every concert, the band couldn't manage even some of those 'every night' tunes. They had the same train wreck at the same place on 'Turtle Talk' every night. Right in the middle of the chart there'd be five or six seconds of anarchy as they sorted things out. It never got fixed. I can't imagine how they handled dances—we didn't play one while I was on the band. It's true some people say it was a great group, but those are mostly the same people who believe that everything about Kentonia was great. It's a reflection of Stan's impact on people and music, but not necessarily accurate."[5]

Kenton aficionado Peter Young caught the band at a shopping mall concert in Paramus, New Jersey, on July 11, 1978, and wrote a devastatingly graphic account of the experience to discographer Jack Hartley, of which this is but a short extract: "The guys were behind the bandstand, doing what musicians always do before they get it on. They were running their scales, clearing their mouthpieces, adjusting, tightening, loosening up. Except that unlike any other group of young jazzmen I had ever seen, these guys indulged in absolutely no horseplay, no clowning around. Indeed, they hardly said a mumbling word. There was a small three-step platform going up to the stand, and I stood next to it, observing the very strange behavior of these young dudes. Strange, that is, by comparison with all the other backstage moments I have ever known.

"The band's road manager, a veritable ox of a young man, suddenly emerged and shouted at the guys: 'I'm bringing Stan out! Everybody on stage!' So help me, all those young musicians stopped in mid-air (or musical phrase) and marched up those steps, looking for all the world like a Marine platoon leaving the relative security of Firebase Charlie for a recon mission in the jungle. This band doesn't just play gigs; it goes to war every night. As they marched up those steps, their very bodies seemed to say: 'Look pal, tomorrow night we may all be back in Omaha pumping gas. But *tonight* we're the best, we're the Stan Kenton band, so just get out of our way!'

"Now I spotted the roadie bringing Stan through the crowd, heavily supporting him under the left shoulder as they waded through. They got to the three-step platform, and there the roadie *lifted* the clinging Kenton—all 6' 4" of him—up those three steps and onto the stand.

"Stanley, thus transported to the stand, indeed, perhaps transported by *being* on the stand, waved his arm to the crowd in acknowledgment of their applause. He walked slowly over to the piano, sat down on the bench, and spoke softly into the microphone: 'Thank you . . . We're going to play . . . some jazz tonight. I . . . won't . . . bother announcing . . . the numbers . . . until we've played . . . several.'

"With that, Stan draped himself over the keys and began plinking out several choruses of 'Body and Soul' that were almost dream-like in their oddly affecting quality. The brass section suddenly stood up as one man, and I wondered how Stan was going to stand for his usual enthusiastic conducting chores. Answer: he doesn't. He continued to sit on the bench, gave the brass the most subtle kind of 'come on' cue with his left hand, and then sat back, baby, just sat back, his face wreathed in that old Kenton smile, as the brass wham! came on strong enough to blow that North Arcade away. Hallelujah, pal, yes, yes, yes! The sound we've chased so long *is* still there!

"This same week as the Paramus concert, young jazz critic Gary Giddins of the *Village Voice* was out in print in praise for the band, tempered with the observation that 'Kenton looked and sounded too ill to be on a bandstand.' Young Mr. Giddins is perfectly correct in this observation, but what he doesn't understand—how could he?—is that if Stan doesn't get that nightly shot of *sound*, like a big jolt of mainlined B vitamins, he is purely *through*.

"The program continued through perhaps an hour or so of their old war-horses. Stan didn't do much if any bantering with the crowd. He introduced very few numbers, stood not at all except at the very end, and the one time he tried to credit a soloist—the brilliant tenor sax star Roy Reynolds—it came out as 'Roy, er . . . Rizzuto.'

"The technical name for this problem with words is 'aphasia.' Whether the brain damage comes from a stroke or a bullet or a blow really doesn't make much difference. Aphasia is what you get, or rather, what you're left with. Sometimes, and often to a surprising extent, it's reversible. Brother, has Stanley some reversing to do!"[6]

Peter's account is at once emotional yet accurate, tender yet truthful. The circumstances make it unlikely great music is going to be produced, and in a sense Stan is doing what he disliked most, living in a past nostalgia-land. But that is all he could give, and the fans wanted it, cherished it, demanded it. Stan hung on until he had completed that summer's Jazz Orchestra in Residence educational seminars, the most important dates in the calendar to him, and which at least offered brief respites from travel. Several studios were vying to record the band, and at Towson in July a number of newish charts by Hanna, Levy, and Taylor were rehearsed in case it went ahead, but in his heart Stan knew it wasn't going to happen. It should have. Stan's piano may be hesitant and faltering on Hanna's "What's New" and Taylor's "Lonely Tears" (both on Tantara's *Revelations*) but the sections are strong, and Jim Farrelly (alto) on "New" and Bob Doll (trumpet) on "Tears" are both effective soloists. "I do wish we could have recorded 'Lonely Tears,'" says Taylor. "It was originally a tenor feature I wrote for the Army Blues band, but I changed it for Bob Doll, I'm not sure for the better." Whichever, this lovely ballad further demonstrates an ability which could have propelled Mark to great achievements in modern jazz, had he not lost his public platform when Stan retired.

The orchestra played evening concerts at Towson, mainly the usual tunes Stan felt confident with, but Suter's presence must have struck a chord in Kenton's mind that revived memories of Mike's old bass trombone feature. "One night at Towson," Suter recalled, "Stan stared at me for a long time between tunes, turned to the piano and started 'Tenderly.' After I played it and took my bow, he stared for a long time again before turning slowly to the audience and telling them: 'I can't remember the name of the tune or this guy's name, but . . . here he is.' And that," Suter added poignantly, "is the best intro I ever got."[7]

It couldn't go on indefinitely, and by August Stan was ready to admit that he was just too tired to continue. August 20, 1978, was a Sunday. The orchestra played an afternoon concert at the Sigmund Stern Grove in San Francisco. As Audree Coke recalls, "It was a beautiful afternoon in a lovely setting—an outdoor ampitheatre with many trees. The band was very unhappy that we were breaking up, lots of tears and lots of vodka flowing; it was not a celebration, it was a wake."[8] As the final strains of "Artistry in Rhythm" died away, the band broke up. It was the last time the "Theme" would ever be played by Stan in public, the last concert ever to be played by a Kenton orchestra.

Roy Reynolds relates: "We all said at the time, Stan's doing the right thing, he'll take two or three months off, and then we'll all get back together again. It's what we all thought, but it wasn't to be. The band played so well at that last concert, and it was a fantastic audience. And then we all got on the bus and drove to the airport, Stan had paid everybody's fares to wherever they wanted to go. And that was the last time I ever saw him."

Stan went home with Audree and vehemently asserted to *Billboard* that he and his musicians were simply "taking a long vacation. It appears I went back on the road too soon. By next January, all will be normal again."[9] For a while it even seemed it might happen. In December Audree wrote that "Stanley intends to reconvene the band in the spring. We have committed ourselves to doing five summer Clinics, beginning the last part of June, so the band will certainly have to be working before that time. Stan's health at the moment is the best it has been since the accident. He is quite anxious to return to work he is feeling so well."[10]

Also in December 1978, Stan and Audree attended a concert by the California State University Jazz Band, at which Stan failed to recognize even Bob Curnow, and clearly remained a far from fit man, his condition doubtless aggravated by his distress at charges of attempted murder brought at this time against his son Lance. Privately, Audree admitted Stan was having some good days on which he felt quite sharp, but often there were bad days, on which he felt very tired, and frustrated by his lack of progress. It was now well over the time limit set by the doctors for his health to return, and as the weeks went by it seemed increasingly likely that *this* time Stanley was fighting the final battle that he was destined not to win.

# 32.

## The End of an Era

### (1979)

An indication of the severity of Kenton's plight is that almost overnight he switched from parading his problems in public to secluding himself in his own home. Word on the grapevine in early 1979 included several reports concerning a new tour to begin in April, suggesting Stan remained as keen as ever to re-form the band, with only his health acting as a deterrent. Then in March came the bombshell that all bets were off, with even the summer Clinics cancelled. There would be no new band until 1980, because according to the Willard Alexander office, "Stan didn't feel up to it, and whenever he comes back he wants to do it first class."[1]

It was at this point that Audree Coke emerged as a major player. Undoubtedly the most important person to Stanley during the last years of his life, she had re-entered Stan's world at a time when he increasingly needed a woman's support, and now she alone took on the responsibility of caring for him at his time of greatest need. Without Audree's business acumen the Creative World organization would have long since foundered, but at the same time she also became a center of contention that lasts to this day. Certainly true is the fact that Audree was as strong-minded and determined as Stanley himself, and in turn provoked strong reactions. (I use the past tense, because she is now an elderly lady who has largely retired from an active role in public affairs.)

Initial criticism was that Audree was preventing Stan from seeing his friends and intimates, and certainly it seemed to many that she shielded Kenton from the public gaze like a she-tiger protecting her cubs. Even close associates like Pete Rugolo and Jim Amlotte were denied access, as was *Down Beat* writer John McDonough, who nevertheless penned an article that appeared in print June 7, 1979, though John's prognosis that Kenton was "about 98% recovered" was wildly optimistic. Audree admits, "Many people thought I was being over-protective towards Stanley. It was terrible. People said I was hiding him, which couldn't have been further from the truth. He was living in his own home, in the way he had chosen. I wasn't protecting him. People would call at the office and they would want to see Stanley, and I would say, 'I'll tell him.' But when I'd get home and told Stanley so-and-so would like to see him, Stanley would say, 'No!' It was his choice, it wasn't mine—but the woman always gets the blame in a case like this. They felt I was running his life, and I had hidden him away somewhere up there in the hills, and they couldn't get to him—which is exactly the way Stanley wanted it!"

Stan was most certainly not a prisoner, and the "old" Kenton would have made damn sure he got about, met people, talked music. Though of a totally different kind than the affection he felt for Audree, Stan's love of his musicians and his music was equally valid and real for a major part of his life. A proud man who did not seek sympathy or consolation, it must have been Stan's own decision to shut himself away, and that must have been caused by his deteriorating health, an awareness that he lacked the same grasp and mastery as hitherto, and the fear he would fail to recognize even close acquaintances.

Audree resumes: "When the band broke up in August '78 we'd intended to take a break. Stanley was very tired, and he realized he wasn't functioning as well as he should. Stanley and I had lived together for many years. We were quite discreet about this, and it was not generally known, but we had bought a lovely house together in 1975, situated on a high hill in Hollywood, and that was where we were going to settle down.

"There was no sudden deterioration in Stanley's health that caused him to call off the tour that we started to set up in '79. He simply changed his mind. He decided it wasn't a good idea, and he wasn't ready to do that. Stanley himself was extremely tired, and he had finally admitted to himself that he didn't feel as well as he should. We had talked a lot about retiring, and that's what we had planned to do in 1982, and he was ready for that. He might have gone out for brief periods, two or three months, and do a series of concerts, but he had pretty much made up his mind it was time to get off the road.

"We never did marry, we probably should have, it would have been easier, and the children, Lord knows, kept pushing us all the time—all four of them. [Stan had three children, Leslie, Dana, and Lance, and Audree had one daughter, Cynthia.] But we never thought that was necessary, somehow. We'd both been married three times, and we were afraid of it. We never did it, though we made plans. Finally we were going to get married in August [1979]. It was the week Stanley was in the hospital, when we had engaged a minister to come up to the house. We were going to be married at home, and the two girls [Dana and Cynthia] were going to stand up with me, and Lance was going to stand up with Stanley. It was going to be a little family thing, but that couldn't happen."

Audree did not believe the bizarre business with Lance had any long-term effect on Stan's health or decisions. Charged with another defendant with the attempted murder of Los Angeles attorney Paul Morantz, Stan's son had allegedly placed a rattlesnake in Morantz' mailbox, because of the attorney's legal battles with the Synanon Foundation, of which Lance was a dedicated member. A long, drawn-out court case resulted in November 1980 in a guilty verdict and a year's jail sentence. "Stanley's health wasn't up to it, so I was the one who engaged attorneys and got Lance bail and so on," said Audree. "Stanley was certainly upset and disappointed, but whatever Lance did he's paid for and that's over. But no, I don't think the affair affected Stanley's health. Stanley was a strong man, he'd been through many, many things in his life and this was just one more thing, that's all."

Full realization that the band really had played its last bars left dedicated fans like myself shell-shocked. While Stan was active, there was always the hope of new ideas, new music, and that seemed finally dashed on May 4, 1979, when in an emotional move, the band bus, Stan's "home" on the road for so many years, was sold. More than any other, the action signified that Kenton's touring days were past.

The final blow came at 3 a.m. on Friday, August 17, 1979, when Stanley suffered a stroke at home, described by Audree as "quite sudden, a very abrupt thing. Part of Stanley's pattern at night was to get out of bed, go out to the kitchen, and have a glass of milk, smoke a cigarette, have a glass of wine, something like that. I was so used to him, he'd do this two or three times a night, because he was rested; he'd sleep during the day while I was working at the office.

"And I sort of had him tuned out, because he'd go out to the kitchen, and I was tired. This particular night, it was 3 o'clock in the morning, coming back to the bedroom, he fell, very heavily—that was the stroke. I called the paramedics, who were very good; they came immediately, and took him to an emergency hospital. At about 5 o'clock in the morning they ran him through the initial tests, and decided that's what had happened, he'd had a stroke. But he was still conscious, he was still talking to me, and he was still very much aware of what was happening. It's not true one side was paralyzed, it never was, though a stroke will always affect one side of the body, left or right, depending on where the stroke is.

"About 6 o'clock I got to talk to his doctor, and we moved him to the Midway Hospital we both preferred, where the nursing is excellent, and Stanley was put into intensive care. But his condition simply deteriorated, and the week he spent in intensive care was all downhill. There was no hope for him at all, and on Friday, August 24, the doctors told me he had, at the most, 48 hours to live. Stanley's children, Dana and Lance, and I were on hand almost all the time, and the end came when Stanley died at 5:40 p.m. on Saturday, August 25th."

To those of us who had loved the man and been deeply touched by his music, the news was, if not unexpected, unbelievable. Stan Kenton, who had always seemed so strong, so firm, so indestructible, was dead. No more the strains of "Artistry in Rhythm" to echo through the concert hall; no more the Kenton Sound to thrill the senses and excite the mind; no more the booming laugh, the beaming smile. Stan Kenton was at rest. The band-bus heading "Nowhere" had reached its final destination.

Stanley Newcomb Kenton was cremated in accordance with his wishes, and on Wednesday, August 29, his ashes were committed in the rose garden at Westwood Village Mortuary, a small sanctuary located where Wilshire Boulevard intersects with Westwood. Present were Audree Coke and her daughter Cynthia, and Stan's children Lance and Dana. The urn was buried, and a rose bush planted with a small marker bearing Stanley's name and (false) birth-date. The Village is a select resting place for the entertainment aristocracy, including Nelson Riddle, Mel Torme, Buddy Rich, and Marilyn Monroe. Stan is in good company!

To quote Audree again, "As Stanley had requested, there was no funeral, and no memorial service of any kind. Stanley and I had made all the arrangements many years ago, as we were always concerned that something might happen to him while he was out on the road. Many friends and particularly fans were offended because there was no memorial service, but that was exactly what Stanley had wanted to avoid."

Stan's Will was a complicated document, and it was over two years before the legalities were finally settled. The Estate, valued in the press at around $500,000 (though that figure could be speculative) was divided among Stan's three children, one-third going to Leslie, and the remainder placed in a Trust, the income to be divided equally between Dana and Lance. Stan's personal effects, and control of the eight companies making up the Creative World organization, were left to Audree. Though many dozens of scores were lost over the years, the existing music library was donated to the University of North Texas, where it remains, an invaluable source of information to both musicians and scholars, and recatalogued in great detail in 2008 by researcher Terry Vosbein. In 1983 the Creative World music tapes were sold to Gene Norman, and most of the albums have enjoyed a welcome restoration in CD format as a division of Gene's Crescendo Records.

Though Harold Plant, Stan's business manager for 27 years, and Stan's attorney Jim Roosevelt were co-executors of the Estate along with Audree, the day-to-day management was securely in Audree's hands, the children seemingly having no desire to play any active role in conducting their father's affairs. The court decided the Kenton Archives belonged to Audree under the terms of the Will, and she in turn donated the collection to California State University at Los Angeles. "Several prestigious Universities were interested in the material," Audree noted, "but I felt that I would rather keep the Archives in Los Angeles, because LA is Stanley's home town, and I felt they belonged here.

"According to the Will, the orchestra is to be disbanded, and specifically there is to be no Stan Kenton ghost band. Stanley despised these things, he considered them travesties and found them very offensive. He couldn't speak nicely about the Glenn Miller, Tommy Dorsey and similar ghost bands, and he was determined this was not going to happen with his music. So that was the end of a touring orchestra using his name. The Will says specifically, no musical group may use his name."[2]

Few artists in the world of entertainment, and possibly none in the jazz arena, ever built a more loyal, dedicated, and enthusiastic following than Stan Kenton. What they lacked in numbers (relative to the population of America), these devotees more than made up for in passion and commitment. And that fervor was not something that could be switched off overnight—it continues long after Stanley's death. So when the Estate interpreted that last clause very literally, denying approval for tribute concerts and recordings, musical conventions, or use of the Kenton name, the fans and musicians (already denied any sort of public gathering as a means of expressing their collective grief) became resentful and frustrated. And the target for that resentment was most often focused upon Audree Coke.

Audree, I am sure, sincerely believed she was following Stan's wishes, and for a time she enjoyed some success. But what neither Stan nor Audree had seemingly foreseen is that public distress at the passing of someone they cared about so passionately must have an outlet. If it is bottled up and denied expression it will eventually burst forth of its own accord, like flood waters breaching a dam. As more and more Kenton-inspired activities took place, both in America and the UK, it became clear that legal measures to prevent recordings like Paul Cacia's *Alumni Tribute to Stan Kenton* (Happy Hour Music) and the Murray Patterson/John Healey-organized conventions "Rendezvous in

Britain," would be both expensive to implement and unlikely to succeed. The best of projects like these were respectful acknowledgments of Stanley's legacy, and provided an outlet for people to honor their champion and commemorate his music. As Mort Sahl wrote in his liner note to the Paul Cacia CD, "The music was like a tidal wave, defiant, relentless," and I defy any true Kenton devotee to listen to the spoken tributes on "Kenton in Portrait" and still have a dry eye by the time the concluding "Auld Lang Syne" is played.

Some of the fans and alumni were virulent in their criticism of the Estate's disapproval of Kenton-associated events, Mike Vax being one of the more moderate commentators: "I think when he was alive, Audree was Stan's true friend and lover, but I think she's misguided in the way she believes she's somehow protecting what Stan put in his Will. Dick and I talked with Stan about the 'no ghost band' clause when he made the stipulation, and at no time did Stan imply no one should trade on their Kenton association. My main claim to fame is my stint with Stan, and I am proud of that." (Mike leads his own part-time orchestra billed as The Mike Vax Big Band featuring Alumni of the Stan Kenton Orchestra, playing a mix of original charts and numbers from the Kenton library.)

While I didn't always understand Audree's priorities, she holds my respect for her loyalty and devotion to Stan (probably not a model patient!), and also my gratitude for the support and kindness she has always shown to me. Audree maintained a valued correspondence until 2003, granted me several interviews (without which this chapter would be very incomplete), and on my single visit to LA in 1981 met me at the then-functioning CW office on S. Robertson Boulevard and spent the entire day chatting, taking me out to lunch and showing me places of interest connected to Kenton in the area. It was an act of pure altruism—I was no more than a mere fan, albeit one slightly known to Stan from my discographical research with Pete Venudor, with no business connections or even accredited writing association with a national journal. She afforded similar hospitality to Arnie Chadwick, another UK fan on his visit to the City of the Angels. (For the record, Audree, Stan's widow in all but legal paperwork, changed her name twice in later years, first to Audree Coke Kenton around 1988, and finally to a simple Audree Kenton by 1994.)

What irked the Estate probably more than anything else was that which fans desired the most—fresh music from the Kenton Orchestra itself. And that could only come from past recordings in the form of "bootleg" or "unofficial" issues, about which Stan had always been unequivocal in his condemnation, even though in his lifetime he had been powerless to prevent LP labels springing up. With the CD revolution, that dribble became a flood. "Bootlegs" come from many sources, but principally private recordings like the Wally Heider archives, network broadcasts recorded over the years, and transcriptions such as AFRS and C.P. MacGregor. Kenton had no objection to fans acquiring such recordings by private trading, but was implacably opposed to commercial labels selling his music for personal profit, with no compensation being paid to himself or his musicians.

But Stan was also a pragmatist, and whether he would have maintained this stance into the future can only be speculation. Because of course bootlegs are not confined to Kenton, but include prolific issues by every band imaginable, the number being contingent on the artist's popularity. Even though they rarely received royalties, many bandleaders welcomed the attention, believing their reputation was enhanced and would likely lead to increased demand for their legitimate recordings.

Legal opposition to big-band bootlegs is negligible, and they are sold through every possible outlet, nestling side by side in record stores with big label product. I know of no instance where a prosecution has been brought, or even of successful action to suppress release. (Music owned by legitimate record labels and protected by copyright laws is quite another matter.) Of course, "unauthorized" Kenton producers seek pecuniary gain, some entirely so, while others like Bill Lichtenauer (Tantara) and the regrettably retired John Loeffler (Astral Jazz) have genuine interest in the music, and plough any profits back into more adventurous future productions. What is certain is that Stan's fans would have a very narrow and incomplete understanding of the music if they were dependent solely on Capitol product for their recordings during the orchestra's most creative years, with regards both to the repertoire and the band's often freer, more flexible feeling on live dates.

Stan Kenton was a visionary who literally lived his music. His ideas and orchestras expanded the frontiers of jazz for nearly forty years, and every listener will discover new sounds and secrets whenever replaying even well-known pieces, keeping the music forever fresh and stimulating. But those who knew Stan will be equally grateful for his integrity, his warm humanity, and his friendly personality. The man has perished but his music has survived. Its influence endures.

# Postlude

## Stan Kenton

### (1911–1979)

*"To my way of thinking, Stan is the giant of jazz in our time. And even more important—he's a marvellous human being."*

—Hank Levy to author, April 9, 1972.

Over 30 years after his life ended, one thing is beyond question: Stan Kenton is assured of his place in the pantheon of jazz. He is an heroic figure, a musical crusader. He experienced more triumphant achievements and suffered more humiliating failures than most people would encounter in half a dozen lifetimes. Stan Kenton is as strong as his music. To his fans he is immortal.

At the same time, even Stanley's enormous reserves of enthusiasm and energy were insufficient to enable him to achieve his greatest goal, and fairly early in his career he realized that his quest to establish a new American concert music that filled the void between jazz and the European classics was doomed to failure. There was simply insufficient demand for such music as represented by Innovations and the Neophonic, so instead Stan settled for advancing the music of jazz within the finest orchestras he could muster. For Stan Kenton was of necessity a realist. He could compromise his art to a far greater extent than an idealist like Bob Graettinger, or his contemporaries Bill Russo and Johnny Richards were called upon to do. The big difference was that none of these men was responsible for leading a permanent, unsponsored, full-time touring orchestra whose members required payment, week in, week out. The Orchestra was in reality both an extension of Stan Kenton and his greatest achievement, just as was the trumpet to Dizzy Gillespie or the saxophone to Charlie Parker; it was Stanley's instrument far more than the piano or pen, and without the band he was incomplete.

Stan treated his musicians with far more respect than was common among bandleaders, and earned their loyalty in return. Milt Bernhart got it right when he wrote, "After leaving Kenton in 1948 I joined the Benny Goodman bebop band, but Benny is hardly the compassionate man that Stan is, and I had been spoiled."[1] But Kenton was certainly not soft. His great strength was his capacity for leadership, which meant exercising authority and discipline. (Who can forget Fred Carter's famous quote, "If you ain't been screamed on by Stan Kenton, you ain't been screamed on at all!"[2]) Stan worked his musicians hard but fairly, and his ability to draw the best out of his men by virtue of sheer will-power and charisma is legendary. Few have expressed it better than Bill Mathieu from his fourth trumpet chair: "Stan could make you play for him better than you thought you ever could. His lanky conducting drew it out of you. Even in the Elks Club of an anonymous town we rode the magic energy of his long arms. Kazam! The trombones. Abracadabra! The saxophones. Shazam! The rolling cymbals. Then a cry of sexual passion and the trumpets like lightning brighten the sphere. You are potent air, part of a stream that blows into the man facing you, and out through him into the body of the crowd."[3]

Stan could also be an enigma to those who knew him. One of his quirks puzzled Bill Fritz: "To speculate over why Stan would prefer the work of one composer over that of another (obviously more gifted) composer, or why Stan would retain a bad musician while ignoring a good one, is entirely moot. It has been going on for years, and that is Stan Kenton."[4] The apparent incongruity must be due partly to personal taste, but another factor is inter-active "chemistry." Stan felt both good and bad vibes very strongly, and if a personality attracted him, he would overlook many failings. Surely his long friendship with Gene Roland, whose drug habit was contrary to all Stan's professional instincts, was based on more than the occasional hit record Gene provided?

Deep within the Kenton psyche was his identification with jazz. The music attracted Stan strongly, yet all his life he fought to remain outside the jazz mainstream, not only because of his perennial fascination with other types of music, but because of his refusal generally to allow his band to freely "swing." Stan himself was not a "natural" jazzman. Neither his piano-playing nor his writing would ever have made any major impact in the jazz world without the thrill of the orchestra as back-up. And Stan was the force that made that orchestra and all the music it played communicate in Kentonian terms. As Noel Wedder points out, "Invariably he altered the tempo and dynamics [of a chart]. He had a superb way of enhancing little nuances within a score that the arranger either was not aware of or didn't have the same flair as Stan to pull forth. Professional as they were, the men just weren't comfortable with anyone else telling them how to play. Every ship needs a captain, and Stanley was theirs."[5]

Bill Russo phrased Stan's influence most eloquently: "Stan Kenton, leader of one of the most successful jazz bands of our generation, is neither a great musician nor a great composer. Kenton plays piano well, but he will never be remembered as a great jazz pianist. He writes arrangements for the band, but the works of the Kenton orchestra that have won the most critical acclaim were not his. It is his leadership and the ability to extract the most from each individual who works with him, that will assure Stan Kenton an important place in the history of American jazz. When he directs, Kenton 'plays' the band like one gigantic instrument, creating the sounds and the dynamics he wants. Whenever possible, he hires musicians who reflect his thinking, and his band thus becomes a projection of himself, even though his writing and playing are not dominant in it."[6]

Kenton commenced his career as piano player in 1930s dance bands, and remained set with the jazz styling established during these most impressionable years. Placing objectivity above fanaticism, he would never have become a cult figure on account of his jazz piano alone. Stan himself said as much: "I myself am no great piano player, but play exactly as I like to hear it in a band, to provide color sounds and embellishments. A piano has no place in a rhythm section, it slows it up and makes it logy [dull, lethargic]. I very rarely play straight rhythm, only accents."[7]

Since the piano has long played a major role in most rhythm sections (remember the brouhaha over Gerry Mulligan's piano-less quartet!), it might seem that Kenton was adopting a theory to accommodate his own deficiencies. Because whatever special qualities Stan's playing did possess, rhythmic piano was not one of them. Lennie Niehaus amplifies: "Stan was greatly influenced by Earl Hines, and some nights he would sit down and really surprise the band. But after we got into bebop and all that, he was not comfortable comping behind the soloists. He would leave it to the bass and drums (and guitar when we had one), and Stan wouldn't play, because his style of playing was not the style or the way the soloists were playing as the years progressed."[8]

Many alumni confirm this opinion:

Max Bennett: "When he was in the rhythm section, he didn't know what to do! Stan was not a rhythm-oriented swing player, you could say." (*The Kenton Kronicles* by Steven Harris, 151)

Buddy Childers: "He always wanted to play jazz, and when he started clonking away, he was kind of hung up with an early Thirties rhythm style, and he never got beyond that." (To Steve Voce, *Jazz Journal*, November 1997)

The laconic Lee Konitz was well aware that less can be more. When asked by Mack McShaffrey if the band members ever had jam sessions while on the road, Lee answered, "No, not really. You see, we don't have a piano player." (From liner note to Astral Jazz JCD-101, *Concert in Weisbaden.*)

With post-bop players like Candoli, Konitz, Holman, and Rosolino, Stan felt increasingly out of place, and stayed out of their way. (And if he didn't, someone like Konitz would soon wise him up!) Noel Wedder commented that "the reason Stan gave was that he didn't consider himself a very competent player, and didn't wish to be compared to such masters as Oscar Peterson, Brubeck, Ahmad Jamal, Tatum, Bill Evans et al."[9] Don Reed agreed but added his own perceptive comment: "Stan's old Fatha Hines type of stride piano did not fit the band at all, but at the same time I think his playing made the band more interesting. If he'd played more in the style of the band I don't think it would have been so interesting, for some reason or another."[10]

Stan's most popular piano style with the general public was the "one-finger melody" syndrome that came to the fore in the later Fifties, partly at the suggestion of Lee Gillette, and mainly for commercial reasons. It was certainly not new and stretched back to earlier days—it was the same Gillette who excised a pedestrian piano introduction to Anita O'Day's "I Want a Grown-Up Man" when this January 1945 title was first issued in 1962 (though this was restored on the 1995 boxed Mosaic release). Because these simple piano exercises on the melody sold records, Stan and Capitol collaborated to continue the practice, often on Kenton-arranged ballad LPs, for some twelve years (1957–1968). It was less evident on live dates, where these arrangements were scattered amongst the work of other writers, and Stan often surrendered his solos to horn players instead.

Occasionally downright corny (try "Some Enchanted Evening"!) but usually pleasant enough if entirely predictable, this picking out the melody did nothing to enhance Kenton's reputation as a jazz artist, since it required scant technique and there was little scope for improvisation or even embellishment. The closest comparison is that of Claude Thornhill during the previous decade, a leader whose ballad style Stan admitted was an influence on his own work. On one of the Wally Heider-recorded dance dates a band member jokingly calls out "Blue Barron" (the name of one of the dance band era's particularly undistinguished commercial pianist-leaders) as a comment on Stan's own playing. I don't know how long that unidentified player retained his job, but it is an indication of how the band often regarded Stan's one-finger solo-work.

Fortunately Stan had another string to his bow, a very personal way of playing "concerto-style" that had little to do with jazz, but which impregnated the orchestra with character, substance, and sophistication—an integral part of the Kenton Sound. "He could really mash a piano," opined Buddy Childers, "but when he played beautiful things and stretched out, like he'd do on his theme song 'Artistry in Rhythm,' that was gorgeous. On some of his piano solos, like the introduction to 'Collaboration,' he was marvelous. The left hand playing the arpeggios underneath the melody, that was a very specific style of his. That was when he was at his best."[11]

Other players confirm this belief. In Conte Candoli's view, "Stan's piano-playing was unique. I've heard other people try to play the overture to his theme song, and it just didn't sound right. The a cappella [unaccompanied] solos that he played were just perfect for that band." But perhaps the most significant and accurate observation of all was made by long-term Kenton savant Bob Curnow: "I don't know that Stan was a great improvisational pianist, but the way Stan played within the texture of the band was certainly unique, and that's greatness in its own way."

Stan's writing for the band was as varied as his playing. His most meaningful composing was nearly all accomplished during the early years, but every fresh work took a great deal of effort and energy, both at a premium in the Forties as he struggled to establish his orchestra. The "Opus in Pastels" syndrome was ever-influential, but titles like the foundation-building "Eager Beaver" and "Southern Scandal" were little more than riffs—it was the band's revolutionary interpretation that made them so much more. Eddie Bert frequently played these early titles: "Stan's own arrangements were pretty basic. They were chromatic, like they would go chromatically up or down, and make a riff and repeat it in a different key. That was basically Stan's style. He wasn't a very complex writer, he wrote simple things."[12]

Bob Curnow might have been describing arguably Stan's most iconic composition "Concerto to End All Concertos" when he told Bill Lee: "Stan's talents as a composer-arranger were significant. I don't think he was an exceptionally gifted or clever writer, but what he did was so stylish and so much him. No one else ever wrote that way, so it became a force, very special."[13] Certainly no other composition demonstrated with such clarity the singular sounds of the brass and reed choirs as "Concerto," which actually dates from 1942, not the 1946 recording. (Likewise, "Fantasy" was more than a gleam in Stan's eye long before the association with Capitol.)

Stan strove for more, and as late as 1959 would write to his sister Beulah, "I know that I have talent and can conceive and create, but what a lack of technique! This I must gain and will . . . "[14] To this end he studied harmony and advanced counterpoint with teachers Dave Robertson and Dr. Paul Held for many years, but with some few exceptions composing remained an elusive art. Stan was always far more prolific as arranger of other's tunes, and when I tentatively suggested his own writing veered towards the commercial, Stan agreed: "It's true! Many of my arrangements have been designed to appeal to a wider public than much of the band's music. We needed music that was more generally appealing, and I couldn't get anybody else to do it!"[15]

At the same time, Stan frequently pointed the route for other, more adroit writers to explore. "The direction of the band has always had to come from me in some way," Kenton told me. "In other words, after I had written a couple of arrangements, the other guys would see what I was talking about and start writing." A good example followed the introduction of the mellophoniums in 1960, a brand new instrument that no one was sure how to apply. Kenton lit the path with his voicing of unison mellophoniums on "Midnight Tales," and his 1961 ballad albums. And can anyone doubt that Barton's "Here's That Rainy Day" and Barduhn's "Send in the Clowns" were extensions of a style Stan started with "September Song" and "Street of Dreams"? A number of musicians were perceptive enough to identify Stan's role:

Joel Kaye: "Kenton tended to write things to give the other arrangers kind of a direction, a way in which he wanted the band to function; how to utilize the sections, and the kind of things he liked." (To author, January 1998)

Conte Candoli: "Stan was one of my favorite writers. He wrote so well for the saxophones, and the voicings he used on five trombones were unique. Rugolo, Russo, Holman—they all learned from Stan." (To author, May 3, 1998)

Joe Coccia: "Stan was the first and foremost of all the writers. He showed the way, he set the pattern—true characteristics of leadership." (To author, October 6, 1992)

Certainly any writer who hoped to see his inventions enter the book was wise to adhere to the innovative Kenton Sound that Kenton himself had done so much to help create.

Stan's arranging could be very erratic, and he had his share of duds, but the many positive examples will endure long after the trivia is consigned to history. Almost all the post-Forties alumni interviewed seized on Stan's ballad writing as his finest personal achievement, and with good reason. The standards of the great American song-writers provided a fertile breeding ground for Stan's style of orchestrating. "I'm Glad There Is You" opened many a concert, and achieved iconic status for that reason. "Stan was a competent arranger," opined Bill Perkins, avoiding any hyperbole. "He was very good with ballads—I don't think he ever considered himself a swing arranger. He would get nervous if the band swung too much. He liked heavy music, that was what he loved."

Ray Florian played tenor in the 1962–63 mellophonium band and expressed his admiration with rare insight: "Stan was a master at ballad writing. Most of his charts contained some beautiful figures and harmonies for the sax section—I especially enjoyed 'Opus in Pastels.' All of Stan's ballad arrangements followed basically the same formula. The band would start softly, gradually building a crescendo to a powerful climax, and then come down again to finish quietly. Two of Stan's charts I loved playing were 'Street of Dreams' and 'All the Things You Are.' They're simply gorgeous! Some nights it was difficult to play some of those charts because they were so beautiful and full of emotion. They brought tears to your eyes while you were playing them!"

Despite the caveats, what can be said with certainty is that it would have been a very different orchestra without Kenton's personal input. His creative juices were the band's life-blood, and his authority was stamped on everything the orchestra played. In the words of Audree Kenton: "Stan certainly set a lot of fires. Some of them burned out, some didn't. But he tried. He was always in there doing things!"[16]

# Notes

Quotations by Stan Kenton and alumni are an essential feature of this work: they speak from first-hand knowledge that the author could never possess. At the same time, memories can be tainted and facts misrepresented. For this reason, some quotes have been slightly adjusted to ensure accuracy and clarity, without ever changing the speaker's intent. Occasionally, two quotations by a musician on the same subject have been amalgamated, in which case the primary source is given in the notes.

Note that though not continually repeated below, Pete Venudor co-conducted with the author the Stan Kenton interview on February 22, 1973, and Tony Cox was present at many of the alumni interviews held during Murray Patterson's "Rendezvous in Britain" conventions held between 1992 and 2000.

Unless noted, direct quotations are from personal interviews or correspondence with the author as listed alphabetically below:

Jim Amlotte, personal interview with author, April 23, 2000, Savill Court Hotel, Egham, Surrey, England.

Chet Ball, letter to author, May 22, 1972.

Gabe Baltazar, personal interview with author, April 22, 2000, Savill Court Hotel, Egham, Surrey, England.

Dick Bank, phone conversation with author, June 3, 2002.

Bob Behrendt, letter to author, December 16, 1997.

Conte Candoli, personal interview with author, May 3, 1998, Savill Court Hotel, Egham, Surrey, England.

June Christy, letter to author, November 23, 1972.

Bob Curnow, personal interview with author, May 27, 1996, Daventry Hotel, Daventry, Northamptonshire, England.

Peter Erskine, letter to author, October 19, 2005.

Ray Florian, letter to author, May 9, 1997.

Howard Hedges, letter to author, March 7, 1981.

Bill Holman, personal interview with author, April 12, 1999, Savill Court Hotel, Egham, Surrey, England.

Lee Konitz, personal interview with author, May 26, 1996, Daventry Hotel, Daventry, Northamptonshire, England.

Dave Lambert, letter to author, September 4, 1967.

Kent Larsen, letter to author, June 1, 1973.

Hank Levy, letter to author, April 9, 1972.

Ramon Lopez, personal interview with author, February 6, 1975, London, England.

Mark Masters, letter to author, December 7, 1981.

Dick Meldonian, letter to author, July 10, 1972.

Bill Miller, letter to author, February 13, 1974.

Jack Ordean, letter to author, March 4, 1972.

Bill Perkins, personal interview with author, May 3, 1998, Savill Court Hotel, Egham, Surrey, England.

Roy Reynolds, letter to author, April 15, 1981.

Johnny Richards, letter to author, July 1964.

Pete Rugolo, letter to author, April 3, 1989.

Howard Rumsey, letter to author, April 3, 1972.

Bill Russo, personal interview with author, May 26, 1996, Daventry Hotel, Daventry, Northamptonshire, England.

Tony Scodwell, letter to author, November 1997.

Dick Shearer, personal interview with author, February 18, 1975, London, England.

Bob Snell, letter to author, August 19, 1966.

Mark Taylor, letter to author, September 12, 2002.

Bill Trujillo, personal interview with author, April 23, 2000, Savill Court Hotel, Egham, Surrey, England.

Mike Vax, personal interview with author, April 24, 2000, Savill Court Hotel, Egham, Surrey, England.

Bill Wagner, letter to author, May 18, 1997.

Jiggs Whigham, personal interview with author, May 26, 1996, Daventry Hotel, Daventry, Northamptonshire, England.

Tom Wirtel, letter to author, November 18, 1997.

## Prelude

1. Audree Coke, letter to Jack Hartley, August 26, 1980.
2. Stan Kenton, "Jazz at Its Best," Canadian Broadcasting Corporation (CBC) radio, recorded June 1969.
3. Stan Kenton, CBC radio, 1969.
4. George Avakian, *Down Beat*, October 15, 1939.
5. Buddy Hayes, undated letter to Pete Venudor.
6. Stan Kenton, CBC radio, 1969.
7. Buddy Hayes, undated letter to Pete Venudor.

## Chapter 1: Balboa Bandwagon

1. Clinton Roemer, letter to author, June 1982.
2. Audree Kenton, personal interview with author, February 1975, London, England.
3. Stan Kenton, CBC radio, 1969.
4. Stan Kenton, AFRS "Jazz Book," ca. late 1961.
5. Bob Gioga, letter to author, December 15, 1965.
6. Audree Kenton interview, February 1975.
7. Milt Bernhart to Steven Harris in *The Kenton Kronicles* (Pasadena, CA: Dynaflow Publications, 2000), 63.
8. Howard Rumsey to Tony Agostinelli, May 5, 1997.
9. Stan Kenton, *Band Leaders* magazine, January 1946.
10. Stan Kenton, personal interview with author, February 17, 1973, London, England.
11. Ralph Yaw, *Metronome*, April 1941.
12. Stan Kenton, CBC radio, 1969.
13. Stan Kenton, CBC radio.
14. Charles Emge, *Down Beat*, September 15, 1941.
15. Stan Kenton, CBC radio.
16. Milt Bernhart, personal interview with author, April 23, 2000, London, England.

## Chapter 2: Hollywood Highs and Big Apple Blues (1941–1942)

1. Audree Kenton to Bill Lee, *Stan Kenton: Artistry in Rhythm* (Los Angeles: Creative Press, 1980), 41.
2. Audree Kenton interview, February 1975.
3. Noel Wedder, email to Fred Augerman, March 30, 2001.
4. Tom Rockwell quote, *Down Beat*, September 15, 1941.
5. Clinton Roemer, letter to author, January 25, 1990.
6. Audree Kenton interview, February 1975.
7. Stan Kenton from *The Kenton Kronicles*, 254.
8. Audree Kenton interview, February 1975.
9. Count Basie story told by Ken Hanna to Pete Venudor, January 1972.
10. Charles Emge, *Down Beat*, September 15, 1941.
11. Howard Rumsey, letter to Tony Agostinelli, May 5, 1997.
12. Dave Dexter, *Jazz Magazine*, Fall 1979.
13. *Down Beat*, March 15, 1942.
14. Stan Kenton, *The Capitol* (Capitol Records magazine), December 1945.
15. Pete Rugolo, interview with Terry Vosbein, July 30, 2000.
16. Stan Kenton, CBC radio, 1969.

## Chapter 3: Hanging On (1942–1943)

1. Stan Kenton from *The Kenton Kronicles*, 50.

2. Stan Kenton, CBC radio, 1969.
3. Stan Kenton from *The Kenton Kronicles*, 233.
4. Charlie Shirley, letters to Pete Venudor, June 8 and July 7, 1966.
5. Buddy Childers, undated letter to author.
6. Bart Varsalona to Paul Bauer, *ITA Journal*, July 1982.
7. Stan Kenton from unidentified clipping in author's files.
8. Press report on Karl George from *Down Beat*, January 1944.
9. Stan Kenton, CBC radio, 1969.
10. Stan Kenton on "Eager Beaver" from Time-Life record liner, release number STBB-13.

## Chapter 4: Dance Band Days (1944–1945)

1. Buddy Childers from *The Kenton Kronicles*, 52.
2. Gene Howard from *Melody Maker*, 1953.
3. Milt Bernhart, personal interview with author, May 1, 1998, Egham, England.
4. Stan Kenton, CBC radio, 1969.
5. Al Anthony, letter to author, March 5, 1999.
6. "Anita jumped" from Chicago newspaper dated May 6, 1946.
7. Stan Kenton, personal interview with author, February 22, 1973, London, England.
8. Gene Howard from *Melody Maker*.
9. Stan Kenton, CBC radio.
10. Audree Kenton, untraced quote.
11. June Christy to George Simon, *Metronome*, July 1949.
12. Gene Roland to Stan Woolley, *Jazz Journal*, date untraced.
13. Stan Kenton, N.Y. *World-Telegram*, September 11, 1945.

## Chapter 5: A New Beginning (1945)

1. Stan Kenton, *Metronome*, January 1947.
2. Al Anthony to author, November 17, 1998, and January 20, 1999.
3. Milt Bernhart interview, May 1, 1998.
4. Buddy Childers to Steve Voce, 1997.
5. Noel Wedder email to Kentonia, May 15, 1997.
6. "Opus a Dollar Three Eighty," Pete Rugolo letter to author, April 1989.
7. Clinton Roemer, letter to author, September 2, 1989.
8. Pete Rugolo, *Metronome*, March 1955.
9. Stan Kenton, BBC radio, November 15, 1963.
10. Stan Kenton, from unidentified clipping in author's files.
11. Shelly Manne on "Jazz International" radio show, and letters to author, March 18 and April 24, 1972.
12. Al Anthony, letter to author, March 5, 1999.

## Chapter 6: The Arrival of Rugolo (1946)

1. Stan Kenton, personal interview with author, February 17, 1973, London, England.
2. Al Anthony, letter to author, January 29, 1999.
3. Milt Bernhart interview, April 23, 2000.
4. Buddy Childers to Steve Voce, *Jazz Journal*, November 1997.
5. Bob Gioga, letter to author, February 20, 1966.
6. Milt Bernhart interview, April 23, 2000.
7. Allyn Ferguson, Gene Lees Newsletter, November 2001.
8. Bill Russo to Steven Harris, *The Kenton Kronicles*, 92.
9. Pete Rugolo, personal interview with Terry Vosbein, July 30, 2000.
10. Pete Rugolo, Gene Lees Newsletter, November 2001.
11. Pete Rugolo interview with Terry Vosbein.
12. Bill Russo, *The Kenton Kronicles*, 92.
13. Pete Rugolo in Arganian, *Stan Kenton: The Man and His Music*, 44.
14. Stan Kenton to Pete Tynan, *Down Beat*, January 14, 1965.
15. Red Kelly, Gene Lees Newsletter, November 2001.
16. Milt Bernhart interview, May 1, 1998.
17. Pete Rugolo interview with Terry Vosbein.
18. Clinton Roemer, letter to author, June 20, 1989.
19. Clinton Roemer, letter to author, November 30, 1992.
20. Bill Russo, Interview broadcast on BBC Radio, 1963.

## Chapter 7: The Artistry Orchestra (1946)

1. Stan Kenton interview, February 17, 1973.
2. Milt Bernhart interview, April 23, 2000.
3. Phil Herring, *Crescendo*, March 1972.
4. Milt Bernhart, letter to author, June 2, 1972.
5. Bill Russo, interview on BBC Radio, 1963.
6. Kai Winding, Time-Life liner notes to STL-348.
7. Milt Bernhart, "Perfectly Frank," June 1993.
8. Milt Bernhart, personal interview with author, May 26, 1996, Daventry, England.
9. Kai Winding to Stan Woolley, *Jazz Journal*, April 1979.
10. Pete Rugolo interview with Terry Vosbein, July 30, 2000.
11. Milt Bernhart email to author via Tony Agostinelli, September 15, 1998.
12. Buddy Childers to Steve Voce, 1997.
13. Milt Bernhart interview, April 23, 2000.
14. Herb Jeffries to Steven Harris, *The Kenton Kronicles*, 40.
15. Milt Bernhart, personal interviews with author, May 26, 1996, and May 1, 1998, Daventry and Egham, England.
16. Stan Kenton radio interview, February 13, 1947.
17. Milt Bernhart to Steven Harris, *The Kenton Kronicles*, 66.

## Chapter 8: "Artistry off the Rails" (1947)

1. Stan Kenton, CBC radio.
2. *Down Beat*, April 23, 1947, p.1.
3. Stan Kenton to Brian Priestley, BBC Radio, March 1975.
4. Milt Bernhart interview, May 26, 1996.
5. Buddy Childers to Steven Harris, *The Kenton Kronicles*, 54.
6. Milt Bernhart interview, April 23, 2000.
7. Milt Bernhart interview, May 26, 1996.
8. Shelly Manne to Howard Lucraft, "Jazz International" radio show, 1957.
9. Stan Kenton, personal interview with author, February 22, 1973, London, England.

## Chapter 9: "Progressive Jazz" (1947)

1. Pete Rugolo interview with Terry Vosbein.
2. Roy Crimmins on Steve Voce radio program "Jazz Panorama," May 1998.
3. Pete Rugolo interview with Terry Vosbein.
4. Eddie Bert, personal interview with author, May 2, 1998, Egham, England.
5. Bob Cooper from his last interview, with Steven Harris, August 3, 1993.
6. June Christy in Arganian, *Stan Kenton: The Man and His Music,* 51.
7. Milt Bernhart interview, April 23, 2000.
8. Eddie Bert, personal interview with author, October 1, 2000, Bloomsbury Park Hotel, London, England.
9. Pete Rugolo interview with Terry Vosbein.
10. Audree Kenton quote in author's files, date untraced.
11. Milt Bernhart to Stan Woolley, *Jazz Journal*, April 2000.
12. Michael Levin, *Down Beat*, December 17, 1947.
13. Noel Wedder email to Kentonia, January 9, 2003.
14. Vic -?-, email to Kentonia, January 8, 2003.
15. Eddie Bert, personal interview with author, May 2, 1998, Egham, England.

## Chapter 10: "The Lost Years" (1948–1949)

1. Pete Rugolo interview with Terry Vosbein.
2. Milt Bernhart interview, May 1, 1998.
3. Robert Morgan, "The Music and Life of Robert Graettinger" (DMA dissert. University of Illinois, 1974), original in the Robert Graettinger Research Collection, University of North Texas Music Library, Denton, Texas.
4. Stan Kenton interview, February 22, 1973.
5. Eddie Bert, personal interview with author, October 1, 2000.
6. Art Pepper and Laurie Pepper, *Straight Life: The Story of Art Pepper* (New York: DaCapo, 1994), 73.
7. Eddie Bert interview, May 2, 1998.
8. Two quotations, Milt Bernhart interview, May 1, 1998.
9. Pete Rugolo interview with Terry Vosbein.

10. *Variety*, June 16, 1948.
11. Audree Kenton interview, February 1975.
12. Milt Bernhart, letter to author, June 1972.
13. Unidentified concert review, 1948.
14. Pete Rugolo interview with Terry Vosbein.
15. *Variety*, December 1, 1948.
16. Stan Kenton writing in *Picture Post*, March 31, 1956.

## Chapter 11: Innovations in Modern Music (1950–1951)

1. Stan Kenton, *Down Beat*, January 21, 1950.
2. Buddy Childers to Steven Harris, *The Kenton Kronicles*, 79.
3. Paul Weston, *International Musician* magazine, May 1950.
4. Bud Shank to Gordon Jack, July 1995.
5. Stan Kenton, CBC radio.
6. Ted Hallock, *Down Beat*, March 24, 1950 (abridged).
7. Stan Kenton to Max Harrison, BBC radio, broadcast December 6, 1997.
8. Buddy Childers to Steve Voce, *Jazz Journal,* November 1997 (abridged).
9. Milt Bernhart, letter to author, June 17, 1972.
10. Shorty Rogers to Steven Harris, *The Kenton Kronicles*, 88.
11. Shorty Rogers, *Jazz Journal*, October 1982.
12. Franklyn Marks, letter to author, August 30, 1967.
13. Ted Hallock, *Down Beat*, 1950.
14. Noel Wedder, email to Kentonia, June 2003.
15. Milt Bernhart interview, April 23, 2000.
16. Bud Shank to Steven Harris, *The Kenton Kronicles*, 90.
17. Bud Shank to Gordon Jack, July 1995.
18. Blaze and Cooper to Steven Harris, *The Kenton Kronicles*, 148, 57.
19. Milt Bernhart interview, May 1, 1998.
20. Stan Kenton interview, February 22, 1973.
21. Milt Bernhart interview, May 1, 1998.
22. Maynard Ferguson, *Melody Maker*, date unknown but late 1951–early 1952.
23. Eddie Bert interview, May 2, 1998.
24. Fred Augerman email to Kentonia, March 16, 2003.
25. Colin Goodall email to Kentonia, October 2, 1999.
26. Joel Kaye, letter to author, April 1998.
27. Bud Shank to Gordon Jack, July 1995.
28. Stan Kenton, CBC radio.

## Chapter 12: New Concepts of Artistry in Rhythm (1952)

1. Howard Lucraft, *Melody Maker*, early 1952.
2. Don Reed, letter to author, February 13, 1997.
3. Lennie Niehaus, letter to author, July 13, 1996.
4. Lennie Niehaus, personal interview with author, April 22, 2000, Egham, England.

5. Frank Capp to Steve Voce, 1980.
6. Frank Capp to Harvey Siders, *Down Beat*, March 21, 1968.
7. Lennie Niehaus interview, April 22, 2000.
8. Gerry Mulligan, *Down Beat*, May 19, 1954.
9. Noel Wedder email to Kentonia, November 22, 1996.
10. Bill Perkins, letter to author, June 24, 1978.
11. Phil Gilbert, letter to author, February 26, 2001.
12. Pete Rugolo interview with Terry Vosbein.
13. Bill Perkins, letter to author, June 24, 1978.
14. Stan Levey to Gordon Jack, *Jazz Journal*, September 1999.
15. Bob Burgess at "Viva Kenton" convention, Lees, Lancashire, England, April 30–May 3, 1987.
16. Sal Salvador to Tony Agostinelli, October 17, 1996.
17. Sal Salvador quoting Stan Kenton as told to Tony Agostinelli, October 17, 1996.

## Chapter 13: If It's Tuesday, It Must Be Belgium (1953)

1. Chris Connor to Tony Agostinelli, January 14, 2002.
2. Stan Kenton and Kai Winding, liner notes to Time-Life STL-348 by Robert Jones.
3. Chris Connor to Tony Agostinelli, January 14, 2002.
4. Stan Kenton interview, February 22, 1973.
5. Lennie Niehaus, "Rendezvous in Britain," April 22, 2000.
6. Bill Russo, phone conversation with author, December 14, 2000.
7. Joel Kaye, letter to author, January 1998.
8. Don Reed, letter to author, November 21, 1998.
9. Gerry Mulligan, *Melody Maker*, 1954.
10. Milt Bernhart, email to Kentonia, May 21, 1998.
11. Stan Kenton quoted by Audree Kenton to Lee, *Stan Kenton: Artistry in Rhythm* (Los Angeles: Creative Press, 1980), 172.
12. Bill Russo, "Rendezvous in Britain," May 1996.
13. Bill Holman, radio broadcast, 2000.
14. Don Reed, letter to author, March 1996.
15. Howard Lucraft, *Melody Maker*, 1953.
16. Gene Howard, *Theme* (magazine), January 1954.
17. Howard Lucraft, *Metronome,* March 1955.
18. Stan Kenton, *Theme*, January 1954.
19. Stan Levey, 1953.
20. John Loeffler phone conversation with author, 2004.
21. Stan Kenton to Barry Ulanov, *Metronome,* December 1953.
22. "Len," *Down Beat*, December 16, 1953.
23. Howard Lucraft, *Melody Maker*, December 26, 1953.
24. Bill Holman, liner notes to Mosaic MD4-136, 1990.
25. Bill Russo to Steven Harris, *The Kenton Kronicles*, 93.
26. Lee Konitz, liner notes to Mosaic MD4-136, 1990.

## Chapter 14: "Kenton Presents Jazz" (1954–1955)

1. Stan Kenton, personal interview with author, February 6, 1975.
2. Bill Holman to Will Friedwald, liner notes to Mosaic MD4-136.
3. Ralph Gleason, *Down Beat*, November 3, 1954.
4. Lennie Niehaus to author, April 22, 2000.
5. Stan Kenton, CBC radio.
6. Jack Tracy, *Down Beat*, March 9, 1955.
7. June Christy, *Down Beat*, October 31, 1956.
8. Noel Wedder email to Kentonia, November 8, 1994.

## Chapter 15: Stompin' at the Savoy (1955)

1. Information regarding Childers and Levey is from Dick Bank to author, June 3, 2002.
2. Three quotations, Max Bennett to author, September 1972.
3. Mel Lewis radio interview c. mid-80s, courtesy of producer Ted Daryll.
4. Two quotations from Lennie Niehaus to author, April 22, 2000.
5. Stan Kenton interview, February 22, 1973.
6. Mel Lewis radio interview.
7. Kim Richmond, email to Kentonia, October 30, 1998.
8. Lennie Niehaus to author, April 22, 2000.
9. Stan Kenton interview, February 22, 1973.
10. Mel Lewis radio interview.
11. Al Porcino, *Down Beat*, April 27, 1972.

## Chapter 16: Fuego Cubano! (1956)

1. Lennie Niehaus to author, April 22, 2000.
2. Don Reed, letter to author, December 7, 1998.
3. Don Reed regarding Fontana on "Intermission Riff," letter to author November 21, 1998.
4. Joe Coccia to author, November 11, 2000.
5. Phil Gilbert to author, April 17, 2001.
6. Lennie Niehaus to author, April 22, 2000.
7. Phil Gilbert to author, May 11, 1973.
8. Lennie Niehaus to author, April 22, 2000.
9. Don Rendell to Steve Voce, April 6, 1998.
10. Phil Gilbert to author, February 26, 2001.
11. Stan Kenton interview, February 22, 1973.
12. Mel Lewis radio interview, probably mid-1980s, courtesy of Ted Daryll.
13. Phil Gilbert to author, April 17, 2001.
14. Stan Kenton telegram in *Down Beat*, September 5, 1956.
15. Bill Russo email to Kentonia, March 23, 1998.
16. Mel Lewis, *Jazz Journal,* March 1990.
17. Mel Lewis radio interview.

## Chapter 17: Back to Balboa (1957–1958)

1. Howard Lucraft, *Melody Maker*, August 1957.
2. Don Reed to author, August 29, 1996.
3. Don Reed to Lee, *Artistry in Rhythm*, 223.
4. Phil Gilbert to author, March 6, 2001.
5. Don Reed to author, May 1996.
6. Archie LeCoque to author, December 1972.
7. Don Reed, personal interview with author, April 21, 2000, Egham, England.
8. Archie LeCoque quote told to author by Don Reed, September 19, 1996.
9. Noel Wedder email to Kentonia, November 1, 2000.
10. Archie LeCoque to Steven Harris, *The Kenton Kronicles*, 167.
11. Archie LeCoque to author, December 1972.
12. Don Reed, letter to author, December 7, 1998.
13. Stan Kenton, CBC radio.
14. Joe Coccia to author, May 26, 1973, and October 26, 1992.
15. Phil Gilbert to author, February 26, 2001.
16. Don Reed, radio broadcast, November 16, 1995.
17. Stan Kenton in Easton, *Straight Ahead*, 196.
18. Jerry McKenzie to author, May 10, 1972.
19. Archie LeCoque to author, December 1972.
20. Phil Gilbert to author, February 26, 2001, and April 17, 2001.
21. Phil Gilbert to author, February 26, 2001.
22. Don Reed to author, March 1996.
23. Phil Gilbert to author, March 6, 2001.
24. Stan Kenton interview, February 22, 1973.

## Chapter 18: Standards in Silhouette (1958–1959)

1. Clinton Roemer to author, April 14, 1972.
2. Phil Gilbert to author, March 27, 2001.
3. Milt Bernhart to author, May 26, 1996.
4. Noel Wedder email to Kentonia, July 5, 2003.
5. Archie Le Coque to author, June 21, 1997, and in Carol Easton, *Straight Ahead*, 202.
6. Lennie Niehaus to author, April 22, 2000.
7. Stan Kenton, *Metronome*, March 1959.
8. Bob Olson quote told to author by Jim Amlotte, April 23, 2000.
9. Lennie Niehaus to author, July 13, 1996.
10. Mike Vax email to Kentonia, August 12, 2003.
11. Bill Mathieu, "Counting the Ways," 1988, p. 12, copy in author's possession.
12. Archie LeCoque to author, November 9, 1972.
13. Jerry McKenzie (I) to author, April 28, 1972.
14. Noel Wedder email to Kentonia, December 12, 1993.

15. Bobby Knight email to Kentonia, March 1, 2002.
16. All Bill Mathieu quotes are from letters to author in 1997, and from Mathieu's unpublished reminiscences, "Counting the Ways," 1988.
17. Archie LeCoque to author, December 1972.
18. Bobby Knight email to Kentonia, March 1, 2002.
19. Ross Barbour and Bud Brisbois in Easton, *Straight Ahead*, 203.

## Chapter 19: The Restless Searcher (1960)

1. Stan Kenton, CBC Radio.
2. Stan Kenton, *Crescendo*, August 1962.
3. Stan Kenton, CBC Radio.
4. Dwight Carver to author, December 1, 1997.
5. Dwight Carver to author, January 8, 1998.
6. Noel Wedder email to Kentonia, September 3, 1999.
7. Keith LaMotte email to Kentonia, June 27, 2000.
8. Dwight Carver to author, December 1, 1997.
9. Joel Kaye to author, January 1998.
10. Noel Wedder on Bob Fitzpatrick in emails to Kentonia.

## Chapter 20: Four of a Kind: The Mellophonium Orchestra (1961)

1. Stan Kenton interview, February 6, 1975.
2. Ralph Carmichael to author, February 20, 2001, courtesy of Tony Agostinelli.
3. Jerry McKenzie to author, May 3, 1998.
4. Noel Wedder email to Kentonia, April 15, 2000.
5. Marvin Stamm email to Kentonia, April 15, 2001.
6. Marvin Stamm to Bill Lichtenauer, 2003.
7. Carl Saunders to author, November 1997.
8. Lennie Niehaus to author, July 13, 1996.
9. Joel Kaye to author, January 1998.
10. Dwight Carver to author, January 8, 1998.
11. Lennie Niehaus to author, April 22, 2000.
12. Stan Kenton interview, February 22, 1973.
13. This and the following two quotations from Saunders are from his interview with the author, April 12, 1999, Egham, England.
14. Joel Kaye to author, January 1998.
15. Carl Saunders to author, November 1997.
16. Carl Saunders interview, April 12, 1999.
17. Carl Saunders to author, November 1997.
18. Jerry McKenzie to author, May 3, 1998.
19. Joel Kaye email to Kentonia, May 9, 2003.
20. Dwight Carver to author, December 1, 1997.

21. Stan Kenton to Gerald Wilson, radio interview May 27, 1973, courtesy of John Loeffler.
22. Noel Wedder email to Kentonia, January 1, 1997.

## Chapter 21: Adventures in Time (1962–1963)

1. Stan Kenton interview, February 22, 1973.
2. Noel Wedder email to Kentonia, December 17, 1996.
3. Carl Saunders interview, April 12, 1999.
4. Val Kolar to author, January 14, 1974.
5. Carl Saunders interview, April 12, 1999.
6. Val Kolar to author, February 23, 1974.
7. Dwight Carver to author, January 8, 1998.
8. John Worster to author, January 1976.
9. Jerry L. McKenzie to author, May 3, 1998.
10. Mike Suter to author, October 3, 1999.
11. Noel Wedder email to Kentonia, July 10, 2003.
12. This and the following Kenton quotation are from Stan Kenton interview, February 6, 1975.
13. Joel Kaye email to Kentonia, March 2003.
14. Ray Florian to Tony Agostinelli, January 10, 1997.
15. Ray Florian to Tony Agostinelli and author, January 10 and May 9, 1997.
16. John Worster to author, January 1976.
17. John Worster to author, April 17, 1966.
18. This and the following quotation from Niehaus are from Lennie Niehaus to author, July 13, 1996.
19. Noel Wedder email to Kentonia, March 6, 2003.
20. John Worster to author, January 1976.
21. *London Evening News*, November 15, 1963.
22. John Worster to author, January 1976.
23. Bobby Knight in Arganian, *Stan Kenton: The Man and His Music*, 170.

## Chapter 22: Adventure in Emotion: The LA Neophonic (1964–1968)

1. John Worster to author, October 1976.
2. Stan Kenton interview, February 6, 1975.
3. Clinton Roemer to author, September 29, 1992.
4. Bill Russo to Leonard Feather, "Blindfold Test," *Down Beat*, August 25, 1966.
5. *Variety*, January 27, 1965.
6. Stan Kenton interview, February 6, 1975.
7. Bud Shank, "Viva Kenton" convention panel, Lees, Lancashire, England, April 30–May 3, 1987.
8. Milt Bernhart email to Kentonia, January 29, 2000.
9. Milt Bernhart to author, May 26, 1996.
10. John Worster to author, January 1976.

11. Leonard Feather, *Los Angeles Times*, April 17, 1968.
12. Stan Kenton interview, February 6, 1975.

## Chapter 23: Marking Time (1965–1966)

1. James Komack quoted by Noel Wedder, email to Kentonia, January 24, 2000.
2. Stan Kenton to author, February 6, 1975.
3. Larry Dougherty to author, January 28, 1996.
4. Bill Fritz to author, November 15, 1973.
5. John Worster to author, January 1976.
6. Bill Fritz to author, January 24, 1974.
7. Doug Hughes email to Kentonia, May 7, 2004.
8. Bill Fritz in Harris, *The Kenton Kronicles*, 247.
9. Bill Fritz to author, January 24, 1974.
10. Stan Kenton interview, February 6, 1975.
11. John Worster to author, January 1976.

## Chapter 24: Delights and Disappointments (1967–1969)

1. This and the following quotation from Fritz are from Bill Fritz to author, November 15, 1973.
2. Kim Richmond email to Kentonia, September 10, 1997.
3. Stan Kenton interview, February 22, 1973.
4. Stan Kenton interview, February 6, 1975.
5. Terry Vosbein to Kentonia, February 6, 2003.
6. Bill Fritz to author, January 24, 1974.
7. Stan Kenton interview, February 6, 1975.
8. Bill Fritz to author, January 24, 1974.
9. Leonard Feather, *Los Angeles Times*, July 31, 1969.
10. Bill Fritz to author, November 15, 1973.
11. Bill Fritz to author, January 24, 1974.
12. Dave Hayward to author, December 15, 1973, and January 31, 1974.
13. Stan Kenton interview, February 6, 1975.
14. Ralph Carmichael to author, February 20, 2001, courtesy of Tony Agostinelli.
15. John Worster to author, January 1976.
16. John Harner email to Kentonia, June 1, 2000.
17. Mike Vax email to Kentonia, April 18, 2002.
18. Stan Kenton interview, February 6, 1975.
19. Larry Dougherty to author, March 7, 1996.
20. Details of Stan's divorce settlement from *Toronto Star*, September 23, 1970.
21. Bill Fritz to author, September 13, 1969.
22. Larry Dougherty to author, March 7, 1996.
23. Stan Kenton recording for CBC Radio, July 22, 1971.

## Chapter 25: The Creative World of Stan Kenton (1970)

1. John Von Ohlen, *Crescendo*, March 1972.
2. Stan Kenton interview, February 6, 1975.
3. Kim Richmond email to Kentonia, September 10, 1997.
4. John Worster to author, January 1976.
5. Mike Vax email to Kentonia, 2000.
6. Stan Kenton interview, February 6, 1975.
7. Terry Vosbein email to Kentonia, July 26, 2000.
8. Noel Wedder email to Kentonia, January 1, 2003.
9. Stan Kenton interview, February 6, 1975.
10. Mike Suter emails to Kentonia, January 4, 2001, and April 14, 2003.
11. Ken Hanna in Arganian, *Stan Kenton: The Man and His Music*, 105.
12. Dennis Noday email to Kentonia, June 20, 1999.
13. Neal Finn email to Kentonia, October 17, 2000.
14. Bobby Knight in Arganian, *Stan Kenton: The Man and His Music*, 172.
15. John Harner email to Kentonia, March 29, 2000.

## Chapter 26: Macumba! (1971)

1. John Von Ohlen, *Crescendo*, March 1972.
2. Clinton Roemer to author, May 29, 1971.
3. Clinton Roemer to author, July 17, 1971.
4. John Von Ohlen, *Crescendo*, March 1972.
5. Mark Masters liner note to *Early Start* LP (Sea Breeze 2022).
6. Duke Ellington anecdote from Ken Hanna in conversation with Pete Venudor, January 1972.
7. Dan Morgenstern, *Down Beat*, September 16, 1971.
8. Mike Vax email to Kentonia, January 20, 1998.
9. Mike Vax email to Kentonia, December 16, 2001.

## Chapter 27: Height of Ecstasy (1972–1973)

1. Christopher Moreby, *Melody Maker*, February 26, 1972.
2. Dave Doubble, *Crescendo*, March 1972.
3. Elvin Jones, *Down Beat*, October 12, 1972.
4. Clinton Roemer to author, March 11, 1972.
5. Ken Hanna to Steven Harris, *Kenton Kronicles*, 258.
6. Roy Holmes, "Jazz at Ronnie Scott's" Newsletter, Number 150.
7. Jerry McKenzie to author, May 3, 1998.
8. John Worster to author, January 1976.
9. Mike Suter to author, May 11 and June 2, 2002.
10. John Worster to author, January 1976.
11. Bob Curnow, letter to author, March 19, 1994.
12. Bob Curnow in Harris, *The Kenton Kronicles*, 268.
13. Stan Kenton interview, February 6, 1975.

14. Clinton Roemer to author, October 4 and November 14, 1972.
15. Harvey Siders, *Down Beat*, November 23, 1972.
16. Mike Vax quoting Stan Kenton, email to Kentonia, September 25, 2004.
17. John Worster to author, January 1976 (two quotes).
18. Clinton Roemer to author, November 22, 1972.
19. Ken Hanna to author, March 11, 1973.
20. John Park from Jerry Atkins' liner notes to Jazz Mark LP 105, *If Winter Comes*.
21. Gary Hobbs email to Kentonia, March 11, 2003.
22. John Worster to author, October 4, 1976.
23. Bill Fritz to author, January 24, 1974.
24. Clinton Roemer to author, March 8 and May 4, 1973.

## Chapter 28: Kenton Goes Rock (1973–1974)

1. Mike Suter to author, November 20, 2002.
2. Audree Coke to author, February 13, 1974.
3. Hank Levy in Arganian, *Stan Kenton: The Man and His Music*, 180.
4. Howard Hedges story from email to Tony Agostinelli, May 25, 2005.
.5. Peter Erskine email to Tony Agostinelli, June 2, 2005.
6. Two quotations from Mike Suter are to author, September 7, 2005.
7. Mike Suter email to Tony Agostinelli, March 28, 2007.
8. Bob Curnow email to Tony Agostinelli, March 27, 2007.
9. Bill Fritz to author, November 15, 1973.
10. Audree Coke to author, May 6, 1974.
11. Bob Curnow to author, February 8, 1973, and May 27, 1976.
12. Ed Bride to Kentonia, October 24, 2006.
13. Stan Kenton interview, February 6, 1975.
14. Mike Suter email to Kentonia, April 3, 2000, and to author, September 5, 2002.
15. Stan Kenton, interview February 6, 1975.
16. Two quotations from Suter are from Mike Suter to author, September 7, 2005.
17. Mike Suter to author, May 11, 2002.
18. Mike Suter to author, June 3, 2002.

## Chapter 29: The Road to "No Where" (1975–1976)

1. Bob Smith to author, January 27, 1975.
2. Mike Suter to author, May 11 and September 21, 2002.
3. Mike Suter to author, November 20, 2002.
4. Stan Kenton quoted by Randy Taylor to author, January 14, 1976.
5. Audree Coke to author, September 30, 1976.
6. Bob Curnow to Tony Agostinelli, May 9, 2007.
7. All John Worster quotations in this chapter are from John Worster to author, October 4, 1976.
8. Dave Dexter, *Billboard*, January 13, 1977.
9. Peter Newman email to Kentonia, January 29, 2001.

### Chapter 30: Accident! (1977)

1. John Worster to author, March 7, 1977.
2. Scott Cameron, *Billboard,* June 25, 1977.
3. Scott Cameron from Randy Taylor to author, May 25, 1977.
4. Mike Suter to author, May 11, 2002.
5. Audree Coke to author, August 4, 1981.
6. Dick Shearer from Tony Agostinelli to author, December 29, 1989.
7. Audree Coke to author, August 4, 1981.
8. Mike Suter to author, April 2, 2002.

### Chapter 31: Wounded Warrior (1978)

1. Audree Coke to author, August 4, 1981.
2. Randy Taylor to author, June 13, 1978.
3. Tom Baker to Kentonia, April 8, 2003.
4. Randy Taylor to author, June 13, 1978.
5. Mike Suter to author, April 2, 2002.
6. Peter Young to Jack Hartley, July 1978.Quoted with permission.
7. Mike Suter email to Kentonia, July 16, 1999.
8. Audree Coke to author, August 4, 1981.
9. Stan Kenton, *Billboard*, September 9, 1978.
10. Audree Coke to author, December 18, 1978.

### Chapter 32: The End of an Era (1979)

1. Willard Alexander quote, *Billboard*, date not recorded.
2. All Audree Coke quotes in this chapter made to author, August 4, 1981.

### Postlude

1. Milt Bernhart to author, May 14, 1972.
2. Fred Carter in Easton, *Straight Ahead*, 28.
3. Bill Mathieu, "Counting the Ways," 15.
4. Bill Fritz to author, November 15, 1973.
5. Noel Wedder email to Kentonia, October 6, 2003.
6. Bill Russo, "Kenton: About the Man and His Music," *Playboy* 3, no. 2 (Feb. 1956): 43–47, 56, 66–67.
7. Stan Kenton to Michael Levin, *Down Beat*, January 14, 1948.
8. Lennie Niehaus to author, April 22, 2000.
9. Noel Wedder email to Kentonia, October 11, 2000.
10. Don Reed interview, April 21, 2000.
11. Buddy Childers to Steve Voce, *Jazz Journal*, November 1997.
12. Eddie Bert interview, May 2, 1998.
13. Bob Curnow to Lee, *Artistry in Rhythm*, 376.
14. Stan Kenton to Beulah Kenton, in Harris, *Kenton Kronicles*, 164.
15. Stan Kenton interview, February 22, 1973.
16. Audree Kenton to author, September 30, 1976.

# Bibliography

Many of the books about Stan Kenton are discographies. The following five are narratives, however.

Arganian, Lillian. *Stan Kenton: The Man and His Music.* East Lansing, MI: Artistry Press, 1989. Insightful interviews conducted by Arganian with leading alumni from the orchestra.

Easton, Carol. *Straight Ahead: The Story of Stan Kenton.* New York: William Morrow, 1973. A perceptive account of the band's history, and the only book to attempt a balanced view of Kenton himself, though Ms. Easton admits that "Kenton fans . . . may find a windfall of inexact minutiae" (xi).

Gabel, Edward F. *Stan Kenton: The Early Years, 1941–1947.* Lake Geneva, WI: Balboa Books, 1993. A very personal account by Stan's assistant and band-boy during this turbulent period.

Harris, Steven D. *The Kenton Kronicles.* Pasadena, CA: Dynaflow Publications, 2000. Consists largely of full-length accounts by alumni of their experiences in the orchestra, linked by occasional narrative from the author. The most detailed, factual history of the band on record.

Lee, William F. *Stan Kenton: Artistry in Rhythm.* Los Angeles: Creative Press, 1980. The authorized history of the band, edited by Audree Coke, with insights from alumni and many reprints of magazine and newspaper reviews.

# Index

Note that albums often had alternative titles, or differed in wording between the jacket and the label. In such cases, the most commonly used title is listed here.